Secrecy

Secrecy

Report of the Commission on protecting and reducing government secrecy

GOVERNMENT REPRINTS PRESS
Washington, D.C.

Printed in The United States of America
Ross & Perry, Inc. Publishers
717 Second St., N.E., Suite 200
Washington, D.C. 20002
Telephone (202) 675-8300
Facsimile (202) 675-8400
info@RossPerry.com

SAN 253-8555

Government Reprints Press Edition 2001

Government Reprints Press is an Imprint of Ross & Perry, Inc.

Library of Congress Control Number: 2001092399

http://www.GPOreprints.com

ISBN 1-931641-18-8

S. Doc. 105-2

REPORT

of the

COMMISSION ON PROTECTING AND REDUCING GOVERNMENT SECRECY

PURSUANT TO PUBLIC LAW 236
103RD CONGRESS

The Commission on Protecting and Reducing Government Secrecy

Daniel Patrick Moynihan, *New York, Chairman*
Larry Combest, *Texas, Vice Chairman*

John M. Deutch, *Massachusetts*   Jesse Helms, *North Carolina*

Martin C. Faga, *Virginia*   Ellen Hume, *District of Columbia*

Alison B. Fortier, *Maryland*   Samuel P. Huntington, *Massachusetts*

Richard K. Fox, *District of Columbia*   John D. Podesta, *District of Columbia*

Lee H. Hamilton, *Indiana*   Maurice Sonnenberg, *New York*

Staff

Eric R. Biel, Staff Director   Jacques A. Rondeau, Deputy Staff Director

Sheryl L. Walter, General Counsel   Michael D. Smith, Senior Professional Staff
Joan Vail Grimson, Counsel for Security Policy   Sally H. Wallace, Senior Professional Staff
Thomas L. Becherer, Research and Policy Director   Michael J. White, Senior Professional Staff
Carole J. Faulk, Administrative Officer   Paul A. Stratton, Administrative Officer (1995)
Cathy A. Bowers, Senior Professional Staff   Maureen Lenihan, Research Associate
Gary H. Gower, Senior Professional Staff   Terence P. Szuplat, Research Associate
John R. Hancock, Senior Professional Staff   Pauline M. Treviso, Research Associate

Appointments to the Commission

By the President of the United States

The Honorable John M. Deutch, Belmont, MA
Mr. John D. Podesta, Washington, DC
Ambassador Richard K. Fox, Jr., Washington, DC
Ms. Ellen Hume, Washington, DC

By the Majority Leader of the Senate

Senator Daniel Patrick Moynihan, Pindars Corners, NY
Professor Samuel P. Huntington, Boston, MA

By the Minority Leader of the Senate

Senator Jesse Helms, Raleigh, NC
Mrs. Alison B. Fortier, Chevy Chase, MD

By the Speaker of the House of Representatives

Representative Lee H. Hamilton, Nashville, IN
Mr. Maurice Sonnenberg, New York, NY

By the Minority Leader of the House of Representatives

Representative Larry Combest, Lubbock, TX
Mr. Martin C. Faga, Falls Church, VA

DANIEL PATRICK MOYNIHAN, CHAIRMAN
LARRY COMBEST, VICE CHAIRMAN

JOHN M. DEUTCH
MARTIN C. FAGA
ALISON B. FORTIER
RICHARD K. FOX, JR.
LEE H. HAMILTON
JESSE HELMS
ELLEN HUME
SAMUEL P. HUNTINGTON
JOHN D. PODESTA
MAURICE SONNENBERG

ERIC R. BIEL, STAFF DIRECTOR
JACQUES A. RONDEAU, DEPUTY STAFF DIRECTOR

COMMISSION
ON
PROTECTING AND REDUCING
GOVERNMENT SECRECY
WASHINGTON, D.C.
(202) 776-8727

March 3, 1997

Dear Mr. President:

We hereby transmit the report of the Commission on Protecting and Reducing Government Secrecy.

The Commission was created under Title IX of the Foreign Relations Authorization Act for Fiscal Years 1994 and 1995 (P.L. 103-236) to conduct "an investigation into all matters in any way related to any legislation, executive order, regulation, practice, or procedure relating to classified information or granting security clearances" and to submit a final report containing recommendations covering these areas. The Commission's investigation was the first authorized by statute to examine government secrecy in 40 years, and only the second ever.

The Commission's report is unanimous. It contains recommendations for actions by the Executive Branch and the Legislative Branch, with the object of protecting *and* reducing secrecy in an era when open sources make a plenitude of information available as never before in history.

Respectfully submitted,

Daniel Patrick Moynihan
Chairman

Larry Combest
Vice Chairman

The President
The White House
Washington, D.C. 20500

DANIEL PATRICK MOYNIHAN, CHAIRMAN
LARRY COMBEST, VICE CHAIRMAN

JOHN M. DEUTCH
MARTIN C. FAGA
ALISON B. FORTIER
RICHARD K. FOX, JR.
LEE H. HAMILTON
JESSE HELMS
ELLEN HUME
SAMUEL P. HUNTINGTON
JOHN D. PODESTA
MAURICE SONNENBERG

ERIC R. BIEL, STAFF DIRECTOR
JACQUES A. RONDEAU, DEPUTY STAFF DIRECTOR

**COMMISSION
ON
PROTECTING AND REDUCING
GOVERNMENT SECRECY**
WASHINGTON, D.C.
(202) 776-8727

March 3, 1997

Dear Mr. Speaker:

In accordance with Title IX of the Foreign Relations Authorization Act for Fiscal Years 1994 and 1995 (P.L. 103-236), we hereby transmit the report of the Commission on Protecting and Reducing Government Secrecy.

The Commission was created under Title IX of P.L. 103-236 to conduct "an investigation into all matters in any way related to any legislation, executive order, regulation, practice, or procedure relating to classified information or granting security clearances" and to submit a final report containing recommendations covering these areas. The Commission's investigation was the first authorized by statute to examine government secrecy in 40 years. and only the second ever.

The Commission's report is unanimous. It contains recommendations for actions by the Executive Branch and the Legislative Branch, with the object of protecting *and* reducing secrecy in an era when open sources make a plenitude of information available as never before in history.

Respectfully submitted,

Daniel Patrick Moynihan
Chairman

Larry Combest
Vice Chairman

The Honorable Newt Gingrich
Speaker of the House of Representatives
Washington, D.C. 20515

DANIEL PATRICK MOYNIHAN, CHAIRMAN
LARRY COMBEST, VICE CHAIRMAN

JOHN M. DEUTCH
MARTIN C. FAGA
ALISON B. FORTIER
RICHARD K. FOX, JR.
LEE H. HAMILTON
JESSE HELMS
ELLEN HUME
SAMUEL P. HUNTINGTON
JOHN D. PODESTA
MAURICE SONNENBERG

ERIC R. BIEL, STAFF DIRECTOR
JACQUES A. RONDEAU, DEPUTY STAFF DIRECTOR

March 3, 1997

Dear Mr. Leader:

In accordance with Title IX of the Foreign Relations Authorization Act for Fiscal Years 1994 and 1995 (P.L. 103-236), we hereby transmit the report of the Commission on Protecting and Reducing Government Secrecy.

The Commission was created under Title IX of P.L. 103-236 to conduct "an investigation into all matters in any way related to any legislation, executive order, regulation, practice, or procedure relating to classified information or granting security clearances" and to submit a final report containing recommendations covering these areas. The Commission's investigation was the first authorized by statute to examine government secrecy in 40 years, and only the second ever.

The Commission's report is unanimous. It contains recommendations for actions by the Executive Branch and the Legislative Branch, with the object of protecting *and* reducing secrecy in an era when open sources make a plenitude of information available as never before in history.

Respectfully submitted,

Daniel Patrick Moynihan
Chairman

Larry Combest
Vice Chairman

The Honorable Richard A. Gephardt
Minority Leader
U.S. House of Representatives
Washington, D.C. 20515

DANIEL PATRICK MOYNIHAN, CHAIRMAN
LARRY COMBEST, VICE CHAIRMAN

JOHN M. DEUTCH
MARTIN C. FAGA
ALISON B. FORTIER
RICHARD K. FOX, JR.
LEE H. HAMILTON
JESSE HELMS
ELLEN HUME
SAMUEL P. HUNTINGTON
JOHN D. PODESTA
MAURICE SONNENBERG

ERIC R. BIEL, STAFF DIRECTOR
JACQUES A. RONDEAU, DEPUTY STAFF DIRECTOR

**COMMISSION
ON
PROTECTING AND REDUCING
GOVERNMENT SECRECY**

WASHINGTON, D.C.

(202) 776-8727

March 3, 1997

Dear Mr. Leader:

In accordance with Title IX of the Foreign Relations Authorization Act for Fiscal Years 1994 and 1995 (P.L. 103-236), we hereby transmit the report of the Commission on Protecting and Reducing Government Secrecy.

The Commission was created under Title IX of P.L. 103-236 to conduct "an investigation into all matters in any way related to any legislation, executive order, regulation, practice, or procedure relating to classified information or granting security clearances" and to submit a final report containing recommendations covering these areas. The Commission's investigation was the first authorized by statute to examine government secrecy in 40 years, and only the second ever.

The Commission's report is unanimous. It contains recommendations for actions by the Executive Branch and the Legislative Branch, with the object of protecting *and* reducing secrecy in an era when open sources make a plenitude of information available as never before in history.

Respectfully submitted,

Daniel Patrick Moynihan
Chairman

Larry Combest
Vice Chairman

The Honorable Trent Lott
Majority Leader
United States Senate
Washington, D.C. 20510

DANIEL PATRICK MOYNIHAN, CHAIRMAN
LARRY COMBEST, VICE CHAIRMAN

JOHN M. DEUTCH
MARTIN C. FAGA
ALISON B. FORTIER
RICHARD K. FOX, JR.
LEE H. HAMILTON
JESSE HELMS
ELLEN HUME
SAMUEL P. HUNTINGTON
JOHN D. PODESTA
MAURICE SONNENBERG

ERIC R. BIEL, STAFF DIRECTOR
JACQUES A. RONDEAU, DEPUTY STAFF DIRECTOR

**COMMISSION
ON
PROTECTING AND REDUCING
GOVERNMENT SECRECY**
WASHINGTON, D.C.
(202) 776-8727

March 3, 1997

Dear Mr. Leader:

In accordance with Title IX of the Foreign Relations Authorization Act for Fiscal Years 1994 and 1995 (P.L. 103-236), we hereby transmit the report of the Commission on Protecting and Reducing Government Secrecy.

The Commission was created under Title IX of P.L. 103-236 to conduct "an investigation into all matters in any way related to any legislation, executive order, regulation, practice, or procedure relating to classified information or granting security clearances" and to submit a final report containing recommendations covering these areas. The Commission's investigation was the first authorized by statute to examine government secrecy in 40 years, and only the second ever.

The Commission's report is unanimous. It contains recommendations for actions by the Executive Branch and the Legislative Branch, with the object of protecting *and* reducing secrecy in an era when open sources make a plenitude of information available as never before in history.

Respectfully submitted,

Daniel Patrick Moynihan
Chairman

Larry Combest
Vice Chairman

The Honorable Thomas A. Daschle
Minority Leader
United States Senate
Washington, D.C. 20510

Table of Contents

Figures and Tables

Figures

Tables

Summary of Findings and Recommendations

It is time for a new way of thinking about secrecy.

Secrecy is a form of government regulation. Americans are familiar with the tendency to over-regulate in other areas. What is different with secrecy is that the public cannot know the extent or the content of the regulation.

Excessive secrecy has significant consequences for the national interest when, as a result, policymakers are not fully informed, government is not held accountable for its actions, and the public cannot engage in informed debate. This remains a dangerous world; some secrecy is vital to save lives, bring miscreants to justice, protect national security, and engage in effective diplomacy. Yet as Justice Potter Stewart noted in his opinion in the Pentagon Papers case, when everything is secret, nothing is secret. Even as billions of dollars are spent each year on government secrecy, the classification and personnel security systems have not always succeeded at their core task of protecting those secrets most critical to the national security. The classification system, for example, is used too often to deny the public an understanding of the policymaking process, rather than for the necessary protection of intelligence activities and other highly sensitive matters.

The classification and personnel security systems are no longer trusted by many inside and outside the Government. It is now almost routine for American officials of unquestioned loyalty to reveal classified information as part of ongoing policy disputes—with one camp "leaking" information in support of a particular view, or to the detriment of another—or in support of settled administration policy. In the process, this degrades public service by giving a huge advantage to the least scrupulous players.

The best way to ensure that secrecy is respected, and that the most important secrets *remain* secret, is for secrecy to be returned to its limited but necessary role. Secrets can be protected more effectively if secrecy is reduced overall.

Benefits can flow from moving information that no longer needs protection out of the classification system and, in appropriate cases, from not classifying at all. We live in an information-rich society, one in which more than ever before open sources—rather than covert means of collection—can provide the information necessary to permit well-informed decisions. Too often, our secrecy system proceeds as if this information revolution has not happened, imposing costs by compartmentalizing information and limiting access.

Greater openness permits more public understanding of the Government's actions and also makes it more possible for the Government to respond to criticism and justify those actions. It makes free exchange of scientific information possible and encourages discoveries that foster economic growth. In addition, by allowing for a fuller understanding of the past, it provides opportunities to learn lessons from what has gone before—making it easier to resolve issues concerning the Government's past actions and helping prepare for the future.

This does not mean that we believe the public should be privy to all government information. Certain types of information—for example, the identity of sources whose exposure would jeopardize human life, signals or imagery intelligence the loss of which would profoundly hinder the capability to collect critical data, or information that could aid terrorists—must be assiduously protected. There must be zero tolerance for permitting such information to be released through unauthorized means, including through deliberate or inadvertent leaks. But when the business of government requires secrecy, it should be employed in a manner that takes risks into account and attempts to control costs.

It is time to reexamine the long-standing tension between secrecy and openness, and develop a new way of thinking about government secrecy as we move into the next century. It is to that end that we direct our recommendations.

Ours is the first analysis authorized by statute of the workings of secrecy in the United States Government in 40 years, and only the second ever. We started our work with the knowledge that many commissions and reports on government secrecy have preceded us, with little impact on the problems we still see and on the new ones we have found.

In undertaking our mission to look at government secrecy, we have observed when the secrecy system works well, and when it does not. We have looked at the consequences of the lack of adequate protection. We have sought to diagnose the current system, and to identify what works and ways the system can work better. Above all, we have sought to understand how best to achieve both better protection and greater openness.

That the secrecy system that evolved and grew over the course of the 20th century would remain essentially unchanged and unexamined by the public was predictable. It is to be expected of a regulatory system essentially hidden from view. Some two million Federal officials, civil and military, and another one million persons in industry, have the ability to classify information. Categories of administrative markings also have proliferated over time, and the secrecy system has become ever more complex. The system will perpetuate itself absent outside intervention, and in doing so maintain not only its many positive features, but also those elements that are detrimental to both our democracy and our security.

It is time for legislation. There needs to be some check on the unrestrained discretion to create secrets. There needs to be an effective mode of declassification.

To improve the functioning of the secrecy system and the implementation of established rules, we recommend a statute that sets forth the principles for what may be declared secret.

Apart from aspects of nuclear energy subject to the Atomic Energy Act, secrets in the Federal Government are whatever anyone with a stamp decides to stamp secret. There is no statutory base and never has been; classification and declassification have been governed for nearly five decades by a series of executive orders, but none has created a stable and reliable system that ensures we protect well what needs protecting but nothing more. What has been consistently lacking is the discipline of a legal framework to clearly define and enforce the proper uses of secrecy. Such a system inevitably degrades.

We therefore propose the following as the framework for a statute that establishes the principles on which classification and declassification should be based:

Sec. 1   Information shall be classified only if there is a demonstrable need to protect the information in the interests of national security, with the goal of ensuring that classification is kept to an absolute minimum consistent with these interests.*

Sec. 2   The President shall, as needed, establish procedures and structures for classification of information. Procedures and structures shall be established and resources allocated for declassification as a parallel program to classification. Details of these programs and any revisions to them shall be published in the Federal Register and subject to notice and comment procedures.

Sec. 3   In establishing the standards and categories to apply in determining whether information should be or remain classified, such standards and categories shall include consideration of the benefit from public disclosure of the information and weigh it against the need for initial or continued protection under the classification system. If there is significant doubt whether information requires protection, it shall not be classified.

Sec. 4   Information shall remain classified for no longer than ten years, unless the agency specifically recertifies that the particular information requires continued protection based on current risk assessments. All information shall be declassified after 30 years, unless it is shown that demonstrable harm to an individual or to ongoing government activities will result from release. Systematic declassification schedules shall be established. Agencies shall submit annual reports on their classification and declassification programs to the Congress.

Sec. 5   This statute shall not be construed as authority to withhold information from the Congress.

Sec. 6   There shall be established a National Declassification Center to coordinate, implement, and oversee the declassification policies and practices of the Federal Government. The Center shall report annually to the Congress and the President on its activities and on the status of declassification practices by all Federal agencies that use, hold, or create classified information.

A statute will not change the current state of affairs overnight, but it will give officials grounds for saying No—and supervisors grounds for asking Why. Secrecy exists to protect national security, not government officials and agencies. There is not the least reason to think that our Government cannot make and then enforce this distinction.

---

* The term "national security" is used in the current classification order (Executive Order 12958, issued by President Clinton in April 1995 and effective in October 1995), as well as in previous classification orders. As Section 2 of the proposed statute makes clear, the President retains the authority and the discretion to determine which categories of information should be open to classification. Nevertheless, having considered this issue in detail, the Commission proposes several categories of information that it believes should be considered for classification. The list of those categories is set out in Chapter II of this report at pages 22-23.

A more stable foundation for the entire classification and declassification system, with more consistent application of established rules across all agencies that classify and less ability to "opt out" where there is disagreement with particular rules, is required. The tendency of individuals in a government agency to protect too much by erring on the side of secrecy will not change through mere exhortation, but only as a result of common principles that are grounded in statutory language. In short, a legislative basis for the classification system, establishing clear guiding principles while retaining broad authority within the Executive Branch to establish and administer the details of the system, offers a better and more predictable way to achieve meaningful changes.

To enhance the understanding of classification and declassification decisions, we suggest adopting the concept of a life cycle for secrets.

All information, classified and unclassified alike, has a life span in which decisions must be made with respect to its creation, management, and use. But the management of classified material should also involve the important consideration of whether the information should be classified at all, and if so, for how long. Some information needs to be kept secret for a day; some for a year; some for a generation or more.

Thinking about even highly sensitive information in terms of its life cycle can help resolve the inconsistencies between the protection that different information requires and the protection it actually receives during different points in its life cycle. The current classification system, however, is notable for the absence of clear standards to gauge the need for and type of protection.

Meanwhile, declassification procedures at the end of the life cycle often fail to distinguish between information that is still sensitive and that which no longer is—resulting in unnecessary protection. The public does have a right to know. A fair amount of information is eventually declassified, but too often—despite some recent examples of successful declassification of large sets of historical documents—only after years of expensive processing (and sometimes lawsuits) under the Freedom of Information Act. The costs of doing business this way are high: in 1992 (the last year for which such data are available), over $108 million dollars was spent simply to process FOIA requests, many of which yielded little or no material that actually was released.

This is hugely inefficient, but at the same time predictable. Government agencies will always feel (and probably *should* always feel) that they have better things to do than worry about and devote resources to declassifying information that may be a half-century old. There are few incentives for agencies to declassify, little accountability of the ways in which they do provide access, and a lack of coherent procedures to gain the release of what no longer requires protection. On the other hand, archivists and historians think there is nothing *more* interesting. And they are not wrong: understanding our past is absolutely crucial to negotiating our future.

To improve declassification procedures, we recommend establishing a national declassification center to coordinate how information that no longer needs to be secret will be made available to the public; among its roles would be to declassify information using guidance from the agencies that originate the information.

Declassification should be seen as a form of deregulation. Currently, there are over 1.5 billion pages of government records over 25 years old in government vaults that are unavailable to the public because they are still classified. Some of these are still highly sensitive and should remain secret, but others are at the end of their life cycle and should be moved out of the classification system.

The present regulatory system simply will not let go; it will not and cannot declassify enough material in a cost-effective way. The backlog of decades-old classified records exists in part because of the way the Federal Government is organized to provide access. Some systematic mode of deregulation needs to be established: declassification should not be a random procedure. However, because few agencies view this as a primary mission to which resources and expertise should be devoted, timely and cost-effective declassification of older government records of permanent historical value does not now occur.

Central coordination of declassification across the Government, taking into account the fact that the resources available for that activity are limited, is the best means to ensure that the current situation will change. Agency practices need to be identified and explored, not in an adversarial mode, but rather one of constructive oversight that coordinates declassification policy across the Government in a cost-effective way. The task should be given to an existing entity that understands, values, and rewards that activity. The entity that best meets this criterion is the National Archives and Records Administration.

The Declassification Center would perform a variety of services to streamline declassification, provide expertise, allocate resources, act as a clearinghouse for and establish pilot projects to develop new technologies to aid access, and avoid duplicative procurement and activities. Another important component of the Center would be an advisory panel to provide regular public input and advice on agency declassification priorities. The Center would not supersede agency control over substantive declassification decisions; indeed, agency heads may choose not to provide the Center with highly sensitive material. Rather, by promoting a partnership with agencies, enhancing cooperation across different agencies, and using agency-supplied guidance as appropriate, the Center would make declassification a more routine, efficient, and cost-effective process.

Investment in a Declassification Center would pay dividends over time in terms of savings in both financial and opportunity costs. At the same time, the Center would help build greater confidence in the Government's ability to distinguish between core secrets and information that may be made available at the end of its life cycle.

To promote greater accountability, we recommend establishing a single, independent Executive Branch office responsible for coordinating classification and declassification practice and enhancing incentives to improve such practice.

Any policy, including on classification and declassification, is only as good as its implementation. Accountability should be a hallmark of a well-functioning secrecy system. Those charged with creating and maintaining government secrets need to do it well, and they need to know that they will be expected to do so.

Unfortunately, the secrecy system has developed into one in which accountability barely exists. Confusion over the proper roles of existing oversight bodies in the Executive Branch, including the Information Security Oversight Office and the Security Policy Board, has hampered the development and oversight of sound classification policies and practices. The absence of adequate oversight across the Executive Branch and by the Congress has resulted in little accountability for decisions and little incentive to reduce the scope of government secrecy. We therefore recommend improving training and enhancing incentives so that classifying officials will consider more carefully the costs of secrecy and recognize that they will be accountable for their decisions.

The Commission recommends improving Executive Branch mechanisms by identifying a single office—independent of the agencies that classify and able to demand compliance—that would be responsible for coordinating oversight of classification and declassification practice. This office would make recommendations directly to the National Security Council for establishing classification and declassification policies. It also would ensure that classification and declassification are treated primarily as information management issues, not merely as extensions of security policy. The Commission also proposes improved oversight programs within individual agencies by enhancing positive incentives for officials to improve their handling of classified materials.

To ensure that classification is used more efficiently, we recommend improving the initial classification of information by requiring classifying officials to weigh the costs and benefits of secrecy and to consider additional factors in the decision to make or keep something secret.

The initial decision to classify is critical: it is the most important part of the life cycle of secrets, and the place where the entire regulatory process begins. The decision should be made sparingly, and then vigorously enforced.

Classification means that resources will be spent throughout the information's life cycle to protect, distribute, and limit access to it that would not be spent if the information were not classified. Classification means that those who need to use that information in the course of their work have to be investigated and the results of that investigation analyzed to determine whether access should be granted. Classification means that a document may have to be edited to remove certain sensitive details in order for the rest of the information to be more widely shared inside the Government. And classification means that some kind of review has to take place when the document containing that material is considered for declassification.

The initial decision to classify continues to be based solely on damage to the national security—to the exclusion of other important factors. This has implications both for the quality of protection and the reduction of secrecy overall. Given the importance of this decision, it is essential to develop a more thoughtful process for deciding whether information should be classified in the first place. It is imperative that officials weigh the costs and benefits of secrecy and consider additional factors—such as the vulnerability of the information, the threat of damage from its disclosure, the risk of its loss, its value to adversaries, and the cost of protecting it—in the decision to make or keep something secret.

We recommend that the national security question be weighed differently than heretofore. The issue for classifiers is not just to see if particular information can potentially fit within a category of material that is eligible for protection, but to analyze in the first instance whether information requires the protection afforded by the classification system. Absent a more thoughtful process for making initial decisions, we will continue to see classification by rote, without a careful analysis of whether there is a risk from release of the information that requires it to be protected through classification.

Although there has been progress in reducing the number of individuals authorized to create secrets, much information continues to be classified despite the lack of a national security reason to do so. There have been some serious efforts by agencies in recent years to improve classification management practices. The number of classification actions continues to decline—although in 1995 there were still an estimated 3.6 million new actions, just under 400 thousand of which were at the Top Secret level. Improving the means by which the initial classification decision is made can build on the achievements to date and instill a greater sense of confidence that important secrets will be protected and that other information will be more accessible to the public than at present.

To clarify the grounds for classifying intelligence information, we recommend that the Director of Central Intelligence issue a directive concerning the appropriate scope of sources and methods protection as a rationale for secrecy.

Underlying the rationale of "sources and methods" as the reason that information is kept secret is not the content of the information itself, but instead the way it was obtained. Yet the public and historians generally do not care how the information was collected; they want to know how it was used and what decisions it informed. Too often, there is a tendency to use the sources and methods language contained in the National Security Act of 1947 to automatically classify virtually anything that is collected by an intelligence agency—including information collected from open sources.

A more thoughtful approach is needed to identify and protect the highly sensitive material that needs protection but not overload the system with information that does not require the expenditure of limited resources to protect it. Clarification through issuance of a directive by the Director of Central Intelligence of the scope of and reasons for sources and methods protection would still ensure that sensitive information stays secret. At the same time, such a directive explaining the appropriate scope of that protection would help prevent the automatic withholding of all information that might relate in any manner, however indirectly, to an intelligence source or method.

To promote the use of personnel security resources in a manner that ensures more effective and efficient protection, we recommend standardizing security clearance procedures and reallocating resources to those parts of the personnel security system that have proven most effective in determining who should or should not have access to classified information.

Too often the personnel security system, used to decide whether an individual should have access to particular classified information, focuses resources on policies and programs that apply the wrong type and degree of protection. Today's personnel security system is still based on fear of subversion from Communist agents. This remains the case even though few people join the Government with the intent to commit espionage and, as experience repeatedly has shown, the main threat today comes from trusted "insiders" who already hold clearances and only later in their careers decide to commit espionage, typically motivated by some combination of personal difficulties and greed.

Currently, most resources are directed to the initial clearance process. This includes requiring investigative activities that provide little benefit in comparison to their cost, such as requiring in every instance interviews with neighbors who may barely know the individual under scrutiny.

Meanwhile, relatively less attention is placed on developing more effective procedures for assessing those who already have held security clearances for a number of years.

The Commission recommends directing resources where they are most likely to be of value in determining who should, and who should not, have access to classified information. This means, for example, that those parts of the process—such as neighborhood investigations— shown, both in studies and through experience, not to yield helpful information should no longer be required as a matter of course in every investigation.

The Commission also believes that in order to use resources more effectively, individuals with current clearances should be able to move from one agency or program that requires a particular level of clearance to another that requires a comparable level without replicating investigative and adjudicative procedures. Acceptance by agencies of security clearances granted by other agencies should become the norm, not simply an abstract goal commonly ignored in practice. This should be limited only by the need to take account of different agencies' divergent approaches to the polygraph. Achieving such "reciprocity" would expedite the clearance process and save precious personnel security resources so they may be applied where they can accomplish the most.

To reduce the redundancies and costs of special access programs, we recommend measures to standardize security practices in such programs.

During the course of the Commission's work, industrial contractors repeatedly expressed their concern with the redundancies and high costs of security practices in special access programs: those programs involving security controls that typically exceed what is normally required for access to classified information.

Special access programs can concern research, development, and acquisition activities; intelligence (including covert action); or military operations. Programs can range from rosters specifying who is to have access to the information to entire facilities being equipped with added physical security measures or elaborate and expensive concealment and operational security plans. Such measures often have been justified as the only way to provide the security necessary to protect information considered especially sensitive.

After examination of the oversight and accountability of these programs, the Commission concludes that despite efforts within the Defense and Intelligence Communities to address these problems, many aspects of the system are still in need of repair. Too often, the additional security costs imposed in these programs do not yield increased security benefits. In particular, the Commission believes that a pressing need remains for greater standardization of security practices in special access programs.

To promote more awareness of the threats to automated information systems, we recommend steps to focus greater attention and promote increased cooperation on means for protecting such systems.

This is an era of extraordinary change not only in information technology, but also in the very way that individuals communicate with each other. Information vital to the security and continued prosperity of the United States resides on a series of increasingly interconnected classified and unclassified systems. Those responsible for the protection of national security information face new and increasingly difficult challenges presented by the widespread use of computer networks linked by telephone lines, cable, direct broadcast service, and wireless communications, and by the proliferation of personal computers. New and rapidly changing electronic information systems, on which both secret and open information travels and is stored are threatened when their protection is not adequate to ensure the integrity of the content and meaning of that information.

This new environment requires a fundamental rethinking of traditional approaches to safeguarding national security information. Despite some recent efforts, however, there are no standards for protecting and managing automated information systems, nor is there any national forum designed to promote cooperation in this area. A more focused and directed approach to oversight of these issues on the part of both the Executive Branch and the Congress, and a reinvigorated and closer cooperation between government and industry, are key to developing and implementing effective and coordinated computer security measures.

In the future, better ways to disseminate threat information, improve public and government awareness of computer attacks and related incidents, and develop means for audit and intrusion detection all will be important to promoting greater awareness of the vulnerabilities to national information systems. The Commission sees it as vital that steps be taken in the near term to address these and other critical protection problems.

This report should be seen as a call for changes that may require years to accomplish and will not occur simply through new regulations or organizational restructuring. Many of the problems identified in the report developed and grew over generations and will not be fixed overnight. Key to ensuring that real change occurs will be the realization by senior government officials—whether career civil servants or political appointees—that it is in their own self-interest, as well as in the country's interest, to gain control over the secrecy system and, by so doing, to promote more effective protection of the information that should remain secret.

To do this properly will require a reevaluation of both how and why information is made secret and whether, how, and when it can later be made available. It will require individual agencies and departments to reexamine how they work together in a range of areas, from declassifying documents to permitting transfer of security clearances and identifying who can be trusted to have access to secrets. Finally, it will require new concepts of how materials can best be protected and, where appropriate, disseminated in an era rich in both information and new technologies.

The United States has successfully dealt with the dangers of the century now coming to a close. A new century awaits with its own dangers—some of which we can sense coming, some as yet untold. National security will continue to be the first of our national concerns, but we also need to develop methods for the treatment of government information that better serve, not undermine, this objective.

The proposals set forth in this report are intended to ensure both that our security endures and our democracy flourishes. Government secrecy is not an abstraction; it affects us all in ways large and small. These improvements are long overdue, and 1997, eight decades since enactment of the Espionage Act and a half century since the National Security Act, is the time to begin.

CHAIRMAN'S FOREWORD

The Honorable Daniel Patrick Moynihan
United States Senator from New York

It is a half century since the foreign intelligence system of the United States was established by the National Security Act of 1947. It is 80 years since the Espionage Act of 1917 established the present legal regime dealing with subversive activities within the United States itself. This has been a time of war and rumors of war without cease, global ideological conflict, and, with the onset of the atomic age, the possibility, at times even the prospect, that the human race might destroy itself in one climactic armagedonnic convulsion.

This age is in large measure past. Major conflict is no longer a prospect; ours is the only nation capable of waging a global war, and we have no such design. The ideological conflicts that arose in 19th century Europe are now largely spent; the totalitarian challenge is no more. (Totalitarian regimes persist, but make no ideological claim on the future.) Atomic peril has begun to recede, although the matter of stable controls in Russia is by no means resolved, and proto-nuclear powers proliferate. On the other hand, credible international regimes have begun to address matters such as chemical warfare. The world, if not at peace, nor likely to be, is even so not in imminent peril.

In this setting, it is reasonable and responsible to consider just how appropriate the security arrangements of that earlier age are to the one we have now entered. It is to be insisted that we *are* at the outset of a new era, for this fact is anything but plain. Wars used to end with homecoming parades and demobilization. Nothing so unambiguous happened after the Cold War, and so it requires an effort to think anew.

The 103rd Congress enacted legislation directing such an inquiry. Over the course of 80 years, notably in the later period, a vast system of secrecy developed within the American Government. So much that it has been termed a culture of secrecy. The system grew so vast, however, that it began to appear unavailing. Secrecy has been defined as "the compulsory withholding of information, reinforced by the prospect of sanctions for disclosure."[1] Almost everything was declared secret; not everything *remained* secret, and there were no sanctions for disclosure. In the course of 1996, the Select Committee on Intelligence of the United States Senate carried out a detailed inquiry into the decision by the President not to object to the shipment of arms to Bosnia by way of Croatia. A notable aspect of this decision was that it was never put in writing. The Deputy Secretary of State explained this to the Committee in these terms:

> Another reason that diplomatic transactions and internal deliberations do not end up on paper is because of the extreme sensitivity of the subject matter. What goes down on paper is more likely to come out in public, in inappropriate and harmful ways, harmful to the national interest.[2]

This, of course, is a privilege of the privileged within the system. For the grunts the rule is stamp, stamp, stamp. On the occasion, June 29, 1993, that the Subcommittee on International Organizations of the Senate Committee on Foreign Relations reported out the legislation creating the present Commission, Senator John F. Kerry of Massachusetts made this comment concerning classified documents that the Select Committee on POW/MIA Affairs had reviewed:

I do not think more than a hundred, or a couple of hundred, pages of the thousands of documents we looked at had any current classification importance, and more often than not they were documents that remained classified or were classified to hide negative political information, not secrets.[3]

It was just such anomalies that led to the Commission on Protecting and Reducing Government Secrecy (P.L. 103-236). This is to say, the judgment that unless secrecy is reduced, it cannot be protected.

In the course of the past 80 years, there has been only one other statutory inquiry into this subject. This was the Commission on Government Security, established in 1955 by the 84th Congress, known as the Wright Commission for its Chairman, Loyd Wright, past President of the American Bar Association. This was a distinguished bipartisan body, which included in its membership Senators John C. Stennis of Mississippi and Norris Cotton of New Hampshire, along with Representatives William M. McCulloch of Ohio and Francis E. Walter of Pennsylvania. President Dwight D. Eisenhower named as one his appointees James P. McGranery, Attorney General under Harry S Truman.

The Commission report, issued 40 years ago, is a document of careful balance and great detail. In proposing the Commission along with Senator Stennis, Senator Hubert H. Humphrey had asked, among other things, "What price are we willing to pay for security?" The Commission was especially attentive to this matter.

From 1917 forward, with only a slight lull in the 1920s, the issue of loyalty on the part of government servants had been one of acute concern. In 1931, the Civil Service Commission was provided with funds for fingerprinting Federal employees. In 1941, President Roosevelt ordered that this be done universally under FBI direction. That same year, the Attorney General, as the Commission stated, "advised the FBI that membership in the Communist Party, the German-American Bund, or in any of seven other organizations would constitute questionable loyalty within the intent of Congress." In 1944, the Civil Service Commission established a full-time Loyalty Rating Board to consider derogatory information. After World War II, just as after World War I, there was an extensive "Red Scare" which evoked an equal reaction by those who saw liberty threatened.

The Wright Commission was sensitive to all this and was sensible about it. It observed:

> The report which follows concludes the first complete and detailed study of the subject matter ever undertaken in the history of the Nation.

> In the firm knowledge that Americans are loyal and devoted to their country, the Commission has striven at every point to emphasize the protection and safeguarding of their rights and liberties equally with the need of protecting our national security from the disloyal few, even though it recognizes that the disloyal are dangerous and the Communist threat is both real and formidable.[4]

There are passages that deserve a place in the history of civil liberties:

> And at the very basis of the Commission's thinking lies the separation of the loyalty problem from that of suitability and security. All loyalty cases are security

cases, but the converse is not true. A man who talks too freely when in his cups, or a pervert [*sic*] who is vulnerable to blackmail, may both be security risks although both may be loyal Americans. The Commission recommends that as far as possible such cases be considered on a basis of suitability to safeguard the individual from an unjust stigma of disloyalty.[5]

This particular language reflects the social prejudices of that time, and would be unacceptable today. The more, then, might we admire the Commission's view that sexuality had nothing to do with loyalty, and that any such association would be an "unjust stigma."

The Commission was equally concerned with classification as a *cost*. Free inquiry, like free markets, is the most efficient way to get good results:

The report of the Commission stresses the dangers to national security that arise out of overclassification of information which retards scientific and technological progress, and thus tend to deprive the country of the lead time that results from the free exchange of ideas and information.[6]

The Commission set forth a great many proposals on topics ranging from Atomic Energy to Passport Security, but its legislative proposals were concise:

NEW LEGISLATION—Two new substantive laws are recommended.

The first would penalize unlawful disclosures of classified information with knowledge of their classified character by persons outside as well as within the Government. In the past, only disclosures by Government employees have been punishable.

The second recommended legislation would make admissible in a court of law evidence of subversion obtained by wiretapping by authorized Government investigative agencies. Wiretapping would be permissible only by specific authorization of the Attorney General, and only in investigations of particular crimes affecting the security of the Nation.[7]

e Commission was operating within the paradigm of a nation seriously threatened by aggression m abroad and subversion from within. A considerable national security system had been put in ice. It had become routine for government decisions to be classified. This, in turn, required that recy be protected. The Commission proposed to expand protection in ways which in retro-ct are out of character with the report itself. Its first recommendation amounted to prior traint of the press, in the sense that journalists and publishers would be subject to punishment for disclosing anything the Government had chosen to classify. The wiretapping proposal was more restrained, but it did constitute a further invasion of privacy. With time, there would be more wiretapping, but the First Amendment immunities of the press were left untouched.

In retrospect, the importance of the Wright Commission was not what it proposed, but that its proposals were never seriously considered. It had become clear to the nation, as David Wise and Thomas B. Ross would later write, "that even in a time of Cold War, the United States Government must rest, in the words of the Declaration of Independence, on 'the consent of the governed.' And there can be no meaningful consent where those who are governed do not know to what they are consenting."[8]

Indeed it could be fairly said that the temperament of the Commission *did* prevail. This was not an angry or accusatory group; rather the opposite. It proposed to expand the regime of national security as a regulatory mode. But it did so tentatively, and without conviction; certainly without any sense of urgency. There was even a touch of apprehension: had we already gone far enough, or even too far? Thus, the opening statement of the Summary of Recommendations:

> The Commission's recommendations, if put into effect, would enhance the
> protection afforded national security while substantially increasing the protection
> of the individual.[9]

A national security system was in place, and would thereafter be on the defensive more than otherwise. It became easy to argue that the *Government* was hiding something. Conspiracy theories emerged to explain misfortune or predict disaster. There is nothing novel in the appearance of conspiratorial fantasies, but it could be argued that it is something new for large portions of the American public to believe that agencies designed to protect them are, in fact, endangering them.

****

The Commission on Government Security was created at the height of the Cold War and of the near century-long crisis of the West that began in 1914. The present Commission was created after this era had, at long last, ended. The end, in the form of the collapse of the Soviet alliances in Eastern Europe and Asia, and the implosion and dissolution of the Soviet Union itself, came suddenly and, it could be said, without official notice. The Commission has no desire and no need to engage in any assessment of what went wrong with our estimates. (If indeed anything went wrong. What can there have been "wrong" in connection with the utter collapse of the Soviet Union!) Our concern is: What now?

Before turning to our own recommendations, it is appropriate to acknowledge the substantial work of the Commission on the Roles and Capabilities of the United States Intelligence Community, also established by the 103rd Congress (P.L. 103-359). The Commission was originally chaired by the Honorable Les Aspin, former Secretary of Defense, with the Honorable Warren B. Rudman as Vice Chairman. Following Secretary Aspin's death, former Secretary of Defense Harold Brown took his place and led the Commission to an incisive and hugely rewarding set of proposals for a now hugely complex system.

This was not the first inquiry into the *organization* of intelligence. To the contrary, these had proliferated in recent years as the public administration aspects of intelligence became more visible and, accordingly, open to the range of analysis now characteristic of contemporary public administration theory. Begin with the law of emulation. Organizations in conflict become like one another. Bureaucracies are inherently conflictual, competing for resources and position. (On preparing to leave his position as Director of the Central Intelligence Agency, the distinguished scientist and public servant John M. Deutch told the Senate Select Committee on Intelligence that the Director "has very little power" to influence what the dozen or so other intelligence agencies do.[10]) In an appendix to its report, the Aspin-Brown Commission produced an organization chart showing the relationship of some 21 departments, agencies, offices, or boards to the President.[11]

The Commission also listed recent administrative enquiries concerning this maze and the overall structure of the Intelligence Community:

> The ***Vice President's National Performance Review's*** report on the Intelligence Community, published in September 1993, had as its lead recommendation the enhancement of Intelligence Community integration. " . . . if it is to be a responsible player in government, the Community must find ways to share resources, be more efficient and effective, and reduce overhead. . ." "The goal is not to build big central bureaucracies. Rather, it is to create common frameworks in which the elements of the Intelligence Community can pursue their departmental and national intelligence roles." The Review also recommended that the Community develop integrated personnel and training systems, and the establishment of a common set of personnel standards and practices, one set of security policies and standards, community-wide language proficiency standards, a vigorous program of interagency rotational assignments, a consolidated training structure with the sharing of programs and facilities and the construction of a community-wide skills bank. *The Intelligence Community did not implement any of the NPR's recommendations.* [Italics added.]

> The ***Joint Security Commission*** issued a report in February 1994 recommending common standards for adjudications and a joint investigative service to standardize background investigations and thus take advantage of economics of scale, improvements in information systems security, a radical new classification system and a special permanent committee to replace the numerous existing fora that independently develop security policies. The classification recommendation was enacted in a Presidential Executive Order in April 1995, *some* aspects of personnel security were addressed by an Executive Order in July 1995 and a permanent Controlled Access Program Oversight Committee was established in August 1995. [Italics added.][12]

> The ***Intelligence Community Revolution Task Force*** (June 1995) strongly recommended the adoption of common management procedures and processes throughout the Community to facilitate movement of personnel and to cut infrastructure costs by creating a single personnel system, improving performance evaluations, consolidating recruitment and training, and creating common standards of security. *The Community leadership is still reviewing these recommendations.* [Italics added.]

> The ***Intelligence Community Task Force on Personnel Reform*** (July 1995 — also known as the Jehn study) identified four principal problem areas: a largely dysfunctional system of performance appraisal and management; a lack of systematic career planning and professional development across the Community; the variety and complexity of the various personnel systems; and the inadequate promotion of a sense of community among the agencies. This report was briefed to DCI Deutch in August 1995 and *the Community is reviewing its recommendations.* [Italics added.][13]

Note the language: "be more efficient and effective, and reduce overhead," "take advantage of economics of scale," "facilitate movement of personnel and to cut infrastructure costs," "largely dysfunctional system of performance appraisal and management." The 92 lines of the National Security Act establishing a "central intelligence agency" have bred a vast bureaucratic system, a source of constant worry, as are most such organizations. Note, also, the expense. The Commission produced a chart entitled: "Since 1980, Intelligence Spending has Grown Significantly More than Defense Spending." By mid-decade, Defense spending had risen 40 percent, but Intelligence 120 percent![14] Both spending curves have since declined, but Intelligence remains well above Cold War levels. This spending has come very much at the expense of the Department of State.

Our Commission has not been indifferent to organization theory. Our hearings began with an exposition of the writings of Max Weber, who first set forth, over eight decades ago, that secrecy was a normal mode by which bureaucracies conduct their business. These "bureaus" appeared everywhere in 19th century Europe, and were clearly a different mode of governance. Different from princely courts, or for that matter, parliaments. Rulemaking was the distinctive mode of bureaucracy. We came to call it regulation.

If the present report is to serve any large purpose, it is to introduce the public to the thought that *secrecy is a mode of regulation.* In truth, it is the ultimate mode, for the citizen does not even know that he or she is being regulated. Normal regulation concerns how citizens must behave, and so regulations are widely promulgated. Secrecy, by contrast, concerns what citizens may know; and the citizen is not told what may not be known.

With the arrival of the New Deal agencies in the 1930s, it became clear that *public* regulation needed to be made more accessible to the public. In 1935, for example, the *Federal Register* began publication. Thereafter, all public regulations were published and accessible. In 1946, the Administrative Procedure Act established procedures by which the citizen can question and even litigate regulation. In 1966, the Freedom of Information Act, technically an amendment to the original 1946 Act, provided citizens yet more access to government files.

The Administrative Procedure Act brought some order and accountability to the flood of government regulations that at times bids fare to overwhelm us. (It will be recalled that at the outset of his administration, President Jimmy Carter instructed his cabinet members that their departments were not to promulgate any regulation they had not personally read. One by one the cabinet officers came to the White House to confess that the task had proven impossible.)

Even so, "overregulation" is a continuing theme in American public life, as in most modern administrative states. *Secrecy would be such an issue, save that secrecy is secret.* Make no mistake, however. It is a parallel regulatory regime with a far greater potential for damage if it malfunctions.

This can take the form of espionage when, unknown to us, information presumed to be secret becomes known to adversaries. Given the danger of espionage, a secrecy system can become so constrictive that information is effectively withheld from those who need it. There seems to be no doubt, for example, that the Soviet Union deteriorated not least because the responsible actors rarely really knew what was going on. (If they had, very likely *we* would have!) Indeed, the study of economics provides the first principles here. Free markets provide the most information to economic players. As information becomes less free, markets become ever more imperfect, decisions less informed and, accordingly, less efficient.

We are not going to put an end to secrecy. It is at times legitimate and necessary. But it is possible to conceive that secrecy, a culture of secrecy, need not remain the only norm in American Government as regards national security. It is possible to conceive that a competing culture of openness might develop which could assert and demonstrate greater efficiency.

There is no way to make certain that this will happen. Yet, the competitive spirit *can* be put to work here. An example, on a subject that still troubles our foreign relations, is the abortive Bay of Pigs invasion of Cuba in April, 1961. Planned and carried out in secret, the object was to arouse a popular revolt against the regime of Fidel Castro, which had become unmistakably Communist in its orientation. No such uprising occurred, and the events were set in motion that arguably led to the Cuban Missile Crisis of 1962, the closest the United States and the Soviet Union came to a nuclear exchange during the Cold War.

It need not have happened. In the spring of 1960, Lloyd A. Free of the Institute for International Social Research at Princeton (no friend of the new regime, but a social scientist, withal) had carried out an extensive public opinion survey in Cuba. Polling techniques now common to American politics were already quite developed by scholars such as Free and his associate Hadley Cantril; in this case the technique was the "Self-Anchoring Striving Scale." One thousand Cubans were asked to rank their well-being at that time, five years previously, and five years hence. Cubans reported they were hugely optimistic about the future, and mostly dreaded the return of the previous dictator Fulgencio Batista. They would learn better, as peoples the world over would do as the earlier excitements of revolution gave way to Leninist terror and intimidation. *But they had not learned yet.* Free's report ended on an unambiguous note: Cubans "are unlikely to shift their present overwhelming allegiance to Fidel Castro."[15] Cantril later recalled:

> This study on Cuba showed unequivocally not only that the great majority of Cubans supported Castro, but that any hope of stimulating action against him or exploiting a powerful opposition in connection with the United States invasion of 1961 was completely chimerical, no matter what Cuban exiles said or felt about the situation, and that the fiasco and its aftermath, in which the United States became involved, was predictable.[16]

These data were public, and were dutifully provided to United States Government agencies. (The Cuban Embassy sent for ten copies.) It is difficult not to think that the information in the public opinion survey might have had greater impact had it been classified. In a culture of secrecy, that which is not secret is easily disregarded or dismissed.

A culture of openness will never develop within government until the present culture of secrecy is restrained by statute. Let law determine behavior, as it did in the case of the Administrative Procedure Act. A statute defining and limiting secrecy will not put an end to overclassification and needless classification, but it will help. At present, apart from atomic energy matters, there is almost no statutory basis for this regulatory regime; it has flourished of its own and without restraint.

The Commission, accordingly, judges that the first priority is to give a firm statutory base to the secrecy system. Classification should proceed according to law. Classifiers should know that they are acting lawfully and properly. We need to balance the possibility of harm to national security against the public's right to know what the Government is doing, or not doing. We should establish by statute that secrecy is the realm of national security and foreign policy. It is not a badge of office or a status symbol.

This latter point is to be stressed. To return to an earlier point, organizations emulate one another, especially if they are competitive. The technical term is "isomorphic": being of identical or similar form. After 80 years, half the buildings in Washington have an intelligence bureau tucked away somewhere. Too much. Wasteful and absurd in an information age that gives you most anything you want from open sources.

Accordingly, we propose a statute establishing a general classification regime and creating a national declassification center:

> Sec. 1 Information shall be classified only if there is a demonstrable need to protect the information in the interests of national security, with the goal of ensuring that classification is kept to an absolute minimum consistent with these interests.

> Sec. 2 The President shall, as needed, establish procedures and structures for classification of information. Procedures and structures shall be established and resources allocated for declassification as a parallel program to classification. Details of these programs and any revisions to them shall be published in the Federal Register and subject to notice and comment procedures.

> Sec. 3 In establishing the standards and categories to apply in determining whether information should be or remain classified, such standards and categories shall include consideration of the benefit from public disclosure of the information and weigh it against the need for initial or continued protection under the classification system. If there is significant doubt whether information requires protection, it shall not be classified.

> Sec. 4 Information shall remain classified for no longer than ten years, unless the agency specifically recertifies that the particular information requires continued protection based on current risk assessments. All information shall be declassified after 30 years, unless it is shown that demonstrable harm to an individual or to ongoing government activities will result from release. Systematic declassification schedules shall be established. Agencies shall submit annual reports on their classification and declassification programs to the Congress.

> Sec. 5 This statute shall not be construed as authority to withhold information from the Congress.

> Sec. 6 There shall be established a National Declassification Center to coordinate, implement, and oversee the declassification policies and practices of the Federal Government. The Center shall report annually to the Congress and the President on its activities and on the status of declassification practices by all Federal agencies that use, hold, or create classified information.

This is our core recommendation. But the statute, if enacted, will succeed only if there are enough persons in government, in and *out* of government, who believe in it. The declassification center will succeed only if individual agencies are willing to cede some control over their horde of hoary testaments. This will not come readily. The culture of secrecy in place in the Federal Government will moderate only if there comes about a counterculture of openness; a climate which simply assumes that secrecy is not the starting place. (As in the "Born Classified" material of the Department of Energy.) One which asks what the purpose is of the organization, and how that purpose is best served in the radically new environment of an information age, in which almost any information is open and accessible.

In one direction we can reach out and touch the time when the leaders of the Soviet Union thought that the explosion at the nuclear reactor in Chernobyl could be kept secret from the rest of the world. In the other direction we can see a time—already upon us—when fourteen-year-old hackers in Australia or Newfoundland can make their way into the most sensitive areas of national security or international finance. The central concern of government in the future will not be information, but *analysis*. We need government agencies staffed with argumentative people who can live with ambiguity and look upon secrecy as a sign of insecurity.

Or worse. Secrecy can be a source of dangerous ignorance. The great discovery of Western science, somewhere in the 17th century, was the principle of openness. A scientist who judged he had discovered something, published it. Often to great controversy, leading to rejection, acceptance, modification, whatever. Which is to say, to knowledge. In this setting science advanced, as nowhere else and never before.

Clearly, there are scientific discoveries that can be kept secret, for a period at least, especially where weapons systems are involved. But these often verge on the technological, and whilst frequently spectacular, they do not stay secret long. Someone else gets onto the idea.

By contrast, secrecy in the *political* realm is always ambiguous. Some things should never be made secret. Some things should be made secret, but then released as soon as the immediate need has passed. Some things should be made secret and remain that way. The problem is that organizations within a culture of secrecy will opt for classifying as much as possible, and for as long as possible.

Observe the aftermath of Executive Order 12958, the most recent in a long series of such orders, issued by President William J. Clinton in 1995. Under the Order there are at present twenty officials, including the President himself, with the power to classify as Top Secret "information, the unauthorized disclosure of which could be expected to cause exceptionally grave damage to the national security." This authority to classify Top Secret information has been delegated under that Order to 1,336 "original classifiers." However, some two million government officials, in addition to one million industrial contractors, have "derivative classification" authority. According to the Information Security Oversight Office, in 1995 there were 21,871 "original" Top Secret designations and 374,244 "derivative" designations. Many of these "derivative" designations involve "sources and methods," one of the subjects concerning intelligence mentioned in the National Security Act of 1947. A report about troop movements might reveal that we have satellite photography in the region; such like matters. But consider: can there really have been some 400,000 secrets created in 1995, the disclosure of any one of which would cause "exceptionally grave damage to the national security"?

What can happen is that the failure of information to be accessible throughout the Government, much less to the public, can cause damage in its own right. An organization with a secret will hold onto it unless there is some exchange for releasing it. The Government becomes a market. Sometimes the exchange is quite palpable: I will exchange my secret for your secret. Sometimes less tangible: the willingness to bring along secrets can provide access for other purposes. But whatever the coinage, there are considerable transaction costs, as economists use this term. These are sluggish markets and highly imperfect ones; true prices are rarely known and impossible to determine.

As was to be predicted, power in a culture of secrecy frequently derives from withholding secrets. This was most evident in the poisonous period following World War II when the United States Army Security Agency's VENONA project began breaking the code of Soviet messages recounting espionage activities.[17] Beginning in 1948, this information was passed to the Federal Bureau of Investigation where, having been further analyzed, it was in the main kept in the Director's vault. The Central Intelligence Agency was not informed about VENONA until 1952. Soviet cables indicated that the Office of Strategic Services (OSS) in World War II had been thoroughly infiltrated with Communists. As the CIA was widely regarded as the successor to the OSS, the Army and the FBI apparently were simply not willing to entrust it with their secrets.

Nor was President Truman himself informed of VENONA. In their recently published 450-page official history, *VENONA: Soviet Espionage and the American Response, 1939-1957,* Robert Louis Benson and Michael Warner write of the charges of espionage and treason in that era:

> Truman's repeated denunciations of the charges against [Alger] Hiss, [Harry Dexter] White, and others—all of whom appear under covernames in decrypted messages translated before he left office in January 1953—suggest that Truman either was never briefed on the Venona program or did not grasp its significance. Although it seems odd that Truman might not have been told, no definitive evidence has emerged to show he was. In any event, Truman always insisted that Republicans had trumped up the loyalty issue and that wartime espionage had been insignificant and well contained by American authorities.[18]

President Truman was almost willfully obtuse as regards American Communism. In part this was a kind of regionalism in an era before television and airlines produced a much more homogeneous polity. There were no Communists in Kansas City politics. Communists were in New York City, and these places were far apart. (It may be noted that the "machine" Democratic politicians of New York were fairly shrewd on this subject, and made their views known in Washington.) Appendix A to our report, *Secrecy: A Brief Account of the American Experience*, relates the ethnic component that has typically accompanied periods of heightened concern about security and secrecy. In the First World War the object of greatest concern was the loyalty of German-Americans. Citizens of Indiana and Wisconsin (as, for example, Congressman Victor L. Berger of Milwaukee) found themselves under suspicion. In the Second World War Japanese-Americans joined German-Americans. In the Cold War the typical suspects, and indeed the typical spies, were of Central European ancestry, with an overlay of graduates of elite American universities. No person active in New York City politics of the 1930s could have failed to know Communists, or know of them. But in Kansas City and Washington, D.C., it was quite possible to see the "Communist conspiracy" as a Chamber of Commerce plot.

To this cultural distance, if it may be called that, add the singular difficulty posed by the personality of the then-Director of the Federal Bureau of Investigation, J. Edgar Hoover. By the mid-1940s, Hoover saw Communists everywhere. Possibly this reflected a mild paranoia; he gave that impression in person. But more likely it may be called the "Pearl Harbor Syndrome." No one would ever be able to say that *his* bureaucracy did not give the Commander-in-Chief timely warning.

In point of fact, Hoover was on to some important things. Thus, on May 29, 1946, he sent George E. Allen, a confidant of the President and head of the Reconstruction Finance Corporation, a four-page letter—PERSONAL AND CONFIDENTIAL BY SPECIAL MESSENGER—George from Edgar. (The first two pages of the letter are reproduced below.) The Director reported that a reliable source had revealed "an enormous Soviet espionage ring in Washington." Of some fourteen names listed, Alger Hiss was there, as was Nathan Gregory Silvermaster. But these names were well down the list. The name at the top was "Undersecretary of State Dean Acheson." The third name was "Former Assistant Secretary of War John J. McCloy." Further on was "Bureau of the Budget—Paul H. Appleby." To have known any of these men is to know that Hoover's suggestion was, well, clinical. Further, that it automatically discredited the other accusations, which happened to be on target. (Withal, neither Hiss nor Silvermaster was at that time in a sensitive government post.)

Benson and Warner continue:

> The tacit decision to keep the translated messages secret carried a political and social price for the country. Debates over the extent of Soviet espionage in the United States were polarized in the dearth of reliable information then in the public domain. Anti-Communists suspected that some spies—perhaps including a few who were known to the US Government—remained at large. Those who criticized the government's loyalty campaign as an over-reaction, on the other hand, wondered if some defendants were being scapegoated; they seemed to sense that the public was not being told the whole truth about the investigations of such suspects as Julius Rosenberg and Judith Coplon. Given the dangerous international situation and what was known by the government at that time, however, continued secrecy was not illogical. With the Korean war raging and the prospect of war with the Soviet Union a real possibility, military and intelligence leaders almost certainly believed that any cryptologic edge that America gained over the Soviets was too valuable to concede—even if it was already known to Moscow.[19]

For the Soviets *had* learned: an American cipher clerk, William Weisband, passed the information on to them in 1948, although he was not discovered until 1950. (Nor prosecuted. "Never reveal sources and methods.") By 1949, the Soviet spy Kim Philby had joined the British mission in Washington as an intelligence liaison officer. Philby received summaries of VENONA translations. The Soviets quickly changed codes.

Time was short, but what if, say, early in 1949 Washington, busy testing new weapons, had told the American public to expect that the Soviets would get their own bomb, and sooner rather than later—that they had gotten hold of many of our plans. (Their first device was almost an exact copy of ours.) Suppose further that the U.S. Government had told the public that even without our secrets, the Soviet scientists were plenty good enough to figure it out in time.

Of course, we did no such thing. In 1956, Edward A. Shils captured the aftermath in his fine, small study, *The Torment of Secrecy: The Background and Consequences of American*

OFFICE OF THE DIRECTOR

Federal Bureau of Investigation

United States Department of Justice

Washington 25, D. C.

May 29, 1946   PERSONAL AND CONFIDENTIAL
                      BY SPECIAL MESSENGER

Honorable George E. Allen
Director
Reconstruction Finance Corporation
Washington, D. C.

Dear George:

        I thought the President and you would be interested in the following information with respect to certain high Government officials operating an alleged espionage network in Washington, D. C., on behalf of the Soviet Government.

        Information has been furnished to this Bureau through a source believed to be reliable that there is an enormous Soviet espionage ring in Washington operating with the view of obtaining all information possible with reference to atomic energy, its specific use as an instrument of war, and the commercial aspects of the energy in peacetime, and that a number of high Government officials whose identities will be set out hereinafter are involved. It has been alleged that the following departments and agencies of the United States Government handle the problem and current development of atomic energy and among these departments and agencies, the United States secret of atomic energy is held in trust. The names of the individuals in each department or agency who control such matters have been furnished as follows:

        State Department – Under Secretary of State Dean Acheson
                           Assistant to the Under Secretary of State Herbert Marks
                           Former Assistant Secretary of War John J. McCloy

    War Department – Assistant Secretary of War Howard C. Peterson

    Commerce Department – Secretary of Commerce Henry A. Wallace

    Bureau of the Budget – Paul H. Appleby
                           George Schwartzwalder

    Bureau of Standards – Dr. Edward U. Condon

    United Nations Organization – Alger Hiss
                                  Abe Feller
                                  Paul Appleby (who is being considered for
                                                transfer from the Bureau of the
                                                Budget to the United Nations
                                                Organization)

Hoover to Allen Letter, May 29, 1946, Page 1

Chairman's Foreword

Honorable George E. Allen

Office of War Mobilization and Reconversion - James R. Newman

Advisors to the Congressional Committee
on Atomic Energy - James R. Newman
Dr. Edward U. Condon

The individual who furnished this information has reported that all of the above individuals mentioned are noted for their pro-Soviet leanings, mentioning specifically Alger Hiss of the United Nations Organization, Paul Appleby and George Schwartnwalder of the Bureau of the Budget, Dr. Condon of the Bureau of Standards, and John J. McCloy of the State Department.

The informant has stated that the McMahon Committee headed by Senator Brien McMahon of Connecticut is charged with formulating the policy concerning atomic energy and serving as advisors to the Committee are Dr. Condon of the Bureau of Standards, who, the informant states, is nothing more or less than an espionage agent in disguise, and James R. Newman, an employee of the Office of War Mobilization and Reconversion who is known to the informant to be a personal friend of Nathan Gregory Silvermaster, who, you may recall, is one of the principal individuals known to have operated as an agent of the Soviet Government in U. S. Government offices for a considerable time until December, 1944. It is known that Silvermaster obtained information through his associates in a Russian espionage network and such information was turned over to the Soviet Government. The informant has indicated that Newman is also a friend of the news commentator Raymond Gram Swing and columnist Marquis Childs. Newman is also reported to be the so-called ringleader of this particular Soviet espionage network and through his employment with the Office of War Mobilization and Reconversion, he had access to material flowing from the White House. The informant stated that through Dr. Edward Condon at the Bureau of Standards, Newman has access to technical data concerning atomic energy. The informant further stated that Secretary of Commerce Henry A. Wallace knows of the background of Dr. Condon but condones his further employment in this highly strategic and important position.

James Newman allegedly obtains from the War Department through the cooperation of Assistant Secretary of War Peterson highly technical information on the atomic bomb itself and all matters relating generally to atomic energy. According to the informant, Newman has a direct line to Assistant Secretary Peterson's office.

With reference to the State Department, it was reported that Newman is in personal and daily contact with Dean Acheson, Herbert Marks, and on some occasions with John J. McCloy, and therefore, any knowledge of atomic energy and international relations with reference to it are immediately known to him.

- 2 -

Hoover to Allen Letter, May 29, 1946, Page 2

Security Policy. "The American visage began to cloud over," Shils wrote. "Secrets were to become our chief reliance just when it was becoming more and more evident that the Soviet Union had long maintained an active apparatus for espionage in the United States. For a country which had never previously thought of itself as an object of systematic espionage by foreign powers, it was unsettling."

The larger society, Shils continued, was "facing an unprecedented threat to its continuance." In these circumstances, "The phantasies of apocalyptic visionaries now claimed the respectability of being a reasonable interpretation of the real situation."[20] A culture of secrecy took hold within American Government, while a hugely divisive debate raged in the Congress and the press.

That was then, and it was a long time back. The public today is not the least concerned about the infiltration of the Government by ideological enemies of the United States. To the contrary, the Government itself is increasingly the object of the "phantasies of apocalyptic visionaries." It is time to change.

A culture of openness can, and ought to, evolve within the Federal Government. The historical appendix to this report observes the salience of ethnicity at times of perceived national danger, a disposition which appears to remain with us. It is not too soon to note the growing suspicion of Muslim citizens, given our adversarial relations with several Islamic nations. Religious doctrine can be an equally powerful source of arousal. If the age of totalitarianism is behind us, "the clashes of civilizations" is seemingly just now resuming. And, as glum experience has taught us, there are ever those who can be corrupted for nothing more than money.

The more, then, to keep our system open as much as possible, with our purposes plain and accessible, so long as we continue to understand what the 20th century has surely taught, which is that open societies have enemies, too. Indeed, they are the greatest threat to closed societies and, accordingly, the first object of their enmity.

Finally, there is the interest of history. The secrecy system has systematically denied American historians access to the records of American history. Of late we find ourselves relying on archives of the former Soviet Union in Moscow to resolve questions of what was going on in Washington at mid-century. This is absurd. (And, if you are a secrecy buff, hazardous; suppose some commissar, sensing the end was nigh, placed forged KGB documents in the files implicating people he didn't like on both sides of the Iron Curtain? Or suppose some disgruntled American slipped misinformation to the KGB, knowing it would one day reveal the (fictitious but damning) treachery of a one-time colleague who had risen above him!)

And it is unnecessary. Whatever else comes of our Commission's work, we will have the great satisfaction in knowing that it encouraged the National Security Agency at long last to release the extraordinary account of Soviet espionage revealed by the VENONA project and the legendary men and women who broke the code and made the connections. We hope this will provide an example for other agencies. It has brought great credit on the agencies involved, and on the individuals who carried out the often impossible tasks. Impossible, that is, until the likes of Meredith Knox Gardner of the Army Security Agency and Robert J. Lamphere of the FBI came along. This is a history of intellectual dedication that Americans have a right to know about. And to celebrate.

It is time also to assert certain American fundamentals, foremost of which is the right to know what government is doing, and the corresponding ability to judge its performance.

****

It remains to express profound gratitude to our Vice Chairman, the Honorable Larry Combest, for his large perspective and singular attention to detail. This bipartisan effort could never have succeeded without his commitment and openness.

---

[1]Edward A. Shils, *The Torment of Secrecy*, with an introduction by Daniel Patrick Moynihan (Glencoe: The Free Press, 1956; reprint, Chicago: Ivan R. Dee, Inc., 1996), 26.

[2]Senate Select Committee on Intelligence, *U.S. Actions Regarding Iranian and Other Arms Transfers to the Bosnian Army, 1994-1995,* 103rd Cong., 1st sess., 7 November 1996, 27.

[3]Senate Committee on Foreign Relations, *Mark-up of Fiscal Year 1994 Foreign Relations Authorization Act: Hearing Before the Subcommittee on Terrorism, Narcotics and International Operations*, 103rd Cong., 1st sess., 1993, 32.

[4]Commission on Government Security, *Report of the Commission on Government Security* (Washington, D.C.: Government Printing Office, 1957), xvi.

[5]Ibid., xvii.

[6]Ibid., xx.

[7]Ibid., xxiii.

[8]David Wise and Thomas B. Ross, *The Invisible Government* (New York: Random House, 1964), 6.

[9]*Report of the Commission on Government Security,* xvii.

[10]R. Jeffrey Smith, "Having Lifted CIA's Veil, Deutch Sums Up: I Told You So," *Washington Post*, 26 December 1996, A25.

[11]Commission on the Roles and Capabilities of the United States Intelligence Community, *Preparing for the 21st Century: An Appraisal of U.S. Intelligence* (Washington, D.C.: Government Printing Office, 1996), B-8.

[12]In fact, the Joint Security Commission's recommendation to restructure the three-tier classification system was *not* adopted in the new Executive Order. Chapter II of this report discusses the reasons this recommendation was not implemented, and why, in the views of this Commission, the proposed change would not have addressed the core problems of the present system.

[13]*Preparing for the 21st Century*, 101.

[14]Ibid., 131.

[15]Lloyd A. Free, "Attitudes of the Cuban People Toward the Castro Regime," Institute for International Social Research (Princeton: July 1960), 26.

[16]Hadley Cantril, *The Human Dimension: Experiences in Policy Research* (New Brunswick: Rutgers University Press, 1967), 5.

[17]The VENONA project began in 1943, although the first message was not broken until December 20, 1946.

[18]Robert Louis Benson and Michael Warner, eds., *VENONA: Soviet Espionage and the American Response, 1939-1957* (Washington, D.C.: National Security Agency, Central Intelligence Agency, 1996), xxiv.

[19]Ibid., xxix.

[20]Shils, *Torment*, 70-71.

VICE CHAIRMAN'S FOREWORD

The Honorable Larry Combest
United States Representative from Texas

Protecting National Security Secrets
in a "Culture of Openness"

The difficulty of the challenge faced by the Commission is immediately apparent from the Commission's title. In Title IX of the Foreign Relations Authorization Act for Fiscal Years 1994 and 1995, Congress established a commission to *both protect and reduce government secrecy.* These goals are divergent at best, and in some respects they actually conflict. Reasonable access to information is a prerequisite for maintaining an informed citizenry, and for maintaining public confidence in the institutions of government. Thus, it was the task of this body to find ways to reconcile the public's legitimate need for access to information with the Government's legitimate need to protect vital national security secrets.

This is a thoughtful and well-intentioned effort, and the recommendations in the report are basically sound as they strive to achieve a balance between security and openness. But no fallible human institution can achieve perfect balance, and this Commission is no exception. I unequivocally endorse the public's right of access to much government-held information, and I concur in the Commission's finding that too much information is classified and kept too long in secret. But I also believe this report may genuflect too far toward the "culture of openness."

If the government's information security and classification system must lean one way or the other, it should err on the side of secrecy. The question is how far the ship of state can list to one side or the other without taking on water and capsizing. Only time and experience can tell if the tilt is too great or too slight in this instance. But lawmakers and policymakers, as well as members of the general public who read this report, must be aware that this is not an abstract intellectual issue. The U.S. Constitution charges the Federal Government with the duty of providing for the common defense and securing the blessings of liberty. Because the Government must pursue those vital purposes in a dangerous world—even more volatile and uncertain than ever in this "Age of Chaos"—the Government must be able to keep secrets. Failure to do so, even out of a well-intentioned desire to open up the processes and archives of government, may cause irreparable harm to the nation, and may cause loss of life. Openness and heightened access are laudable in themselves, but in the act of enshrining them as public policy we also have to beware of the Law of Unintended Consequences.

Protecting Secrets: A Cold War Legacy or Abiding National Interest
The correct balance between security and openness can be achieved only if we think clearly about the underlying reasons for both. First, we have to dispense with the false notion that protecting the secrecy of sensitive national security information is exclusively a result of the Cold War; in effect, that the impulse to secrecy is an aberration, a practice that can be safely dispensed with now that the Soviet threat is gone. Espionage directed against the United States has not ended. Threats to the continental United States, to our citizens and troops abroad, and to our vital interests have not ended.

If anything they are proliferating, so that the dangers, while perhaps less lethal than those of the former Soviet Union, are more widespread and less manageable.

As Chairman Moynihan correctly points out, the government secrecy system did not start with the Cold War, but began during another conflict, with the Espionage Act of 1917. That history should be instructive to those who would seek to cripple or dismantle the nation's ability to keep secrets on the grounds that "the Cold War is over." In one sense, the cold war of struggle and competition between nations is never over. Intelligence collection and the corresponding need to protect vital information, and the need to ensure the reliability and loyalty of government officials who handle that information, will not cease as long as the United States remains a free and independent nation. Indeed, this remains a fundamental requirement of statecraft of any nation in today's world, not just the United States.

Secrecy and National Security

The great English critic and lexicographer Samuel Johnson once said that "patriotism is the last refuge of a scoundrel." We should keep that in mind when national security is invoked as a reason to perpetuate government excess or abuse. But common sense also says that some demands of national security are very real and necessary. National security is not simply one among many government concerns. It should be foremost; it is the primary reason why government is created.

But defense of the nation is not something the citizen can do on his or her own. Only a collective effort under the leadership of competent government can provide for the common defense, and this of necessity includes some modest limits on our collective freedom, including the right to know everything the Government needs to know to carry out this essential function. It is true that too much secrecy, and the abuse of the public's right to know, can erode respect for government. On the other hand, failure to carry out the vital mission of protecting the nation and the American people will undermine the legitimacy of government far more quickly and surely.

The Moral Imperative of Keeping Secrets

In addition to keeping secrets that could affect national security, the Government also has a solemn moral obligation to protect those individuals who provide information valuable to the United States, especially those who do so at risk to their lives. This obligation extends to protecting the methods used to gather the information as well as the sources, so that nothing points back to endanger them. Skilled intelligence professionals can deduce almost as much from the method as from the content. And the more material they have to work with, the easier it is to discern the patterns in the way the United States gathers sensitive information. This is one risk, a potential unintended consequence, in the hasty declassification and bulk release of government documents not sufficiently acknowledged in this report. Some things that might not be apparent to the U.S. Government in the act of bulk declassification could become clear to a hostile intelligence service sifting though a mass of documents; for example, the modus operandi of U.S. intelligence, the matters of greatest interest to the Government, and perhaps even the compromise of specific "sources and methods" are inevitable in a hasty, bulk declassification.

The moral obligation to protect U.S. informants has to be constantly balanced against the public's right of access. This commitment is at least on a par with the moral claims asserted by the "culture of openness."

Is Secrecy a Burden?

The Commission was confronted on many levels with the lack of credibility and loss of respect for the Government system of secrecy, born in part through overclassification, too much complexity, and the well-known phenomenon of self-perpetuating bureaucracy.

It is true that secrecy is a form of regulation, and the American citizen labors under far too many burdensome regulations as it is. But we have to draw a proper distinction between regulation that is necessary and serves an agreed-upon purpose, one connected with the legitimate and necessary function of government, and regulation which is not necessary. Good judgment is the only arbiter, and that judgment has to be informed by an understanding of history, and of the "first principles" which undergird this nation, especially those embodied in the Constitution.

The zeal to open up the process and to declassify information flows in part from a commendable desire among the American people to restore confidence in their government. However, compromising sensitive information through excessive haste to declassify and release will engender a loss of confidence of a different kind. American citizens have a great deal of common sense. They do not want their government withholding information they need to make an informed decision about national policy. But neither do they want their government revealing things that ought to be concealed. They accept the proposition that some things must be kept hidden. They are perfectly capable of understanding that a violent shaking of the security and classification system could compromise vital information and capabilities, and make it harder for the United States to collect information in the future. Informants and allies abroad would be much more reluctant to confide in U.S. intelligence or government officials for fear of being compromised in a rush to declassify.

The citizen is right to be concerned about a government that fosters a dark, closed, and oppressive culture of secrecy. This was, after all, one of the most detested aspects of Communist culture in the former Soviet bloc. But in the final analysis, it must also be said that a government that remains within its proper Constitutional limits, that focuses on its proper Constitutional priorities, and that does not attempt to meddle in the daily lives and routine affairs of its citizens, should not be feared if it also attempts to keep some things secret. The growing fear of government secrecy is linked directly to the growth of government power and intrusiveness. The Commission report does not address this problem per se, but I believe this implication is clear to those not already biased in favor of big government.

The Cost Factor

It will cost many millions to declassify rapidly and release the huge store of currently classified material. Every government expenditure ought to have a cost-benefit. But it is difficult to justify an extraordinary expenditure that goes beyond the costs of routine declassification as a benefit to the taxpayer. Ramping up costs for bulk declassification might benefit special interests; for example, historians, academic researchers, archivists, and policy groups who believe it is the government's duty to radically alter its handling of classified material. But I am hard pressed to see how such an expenditure will benefit taxpayers as a whole.

To be sure, the amount of classified material in government hands is enormous, too enormous. Some of it is more than 25 years old, and presumably much can be released without jeopardizing the nation's security or exposing intelligence sources and methods. But President Clinton's 1995 Executive Order 12958 requires the automatic declassification of all documents over 25 years old by the year 2000. Five years may seem like ample time for this process, but the amount of classified material subject to the executive order means this five-year deadline will impose a huge and costly burden on the Intelligence Community. Trained specialists and limited resources will have to be diverted from intelligence functions far more vital to national security. From a cost-benefit stand-point, an "issue-driven" approach would make more sense than the bulk declassification envisioned under the Executive Order. Issue-driven declassification would focus on releasing documents with public policy or historic significance, rather than engage in a heroic and costly effort to release the entire store of classified documents in haste.

A Statutory Solution?

When confronted with a problem or an abuse, it is the natural tendency of Americans to pass a law. We are great believers in the redemptive power of law; and, after all, that is what Congress does. And, while I support many of the statutory recommendations in this report, I also acknowledge that there is a limit to what can be achieved through a statute.

Any statute that emerges from the give-and-take of Congress might well end up having little or no relation to what this Commission has recommended. It might be watered down in the consensus-building process to the point where it provides no real reform or corrective action. And inadequate legislation could be worse than none at all, for it would create the illusion that the problem was being addressed, while doing little except breeding a dangerous complacency, or creating a new centralized process that merely adds another layer of bureaucracy and cost.

We should pursue statutory solutions, but remain aware that there is no statutory substitute for sound leadership, good management, commitment, competence, and accountability. Flawed and fallible human beings will have to implement the law on a daily basis, so the matters at issue are subject to daily pressures, judgments, biases, and human error. Handling classified information and protecting vital secrets is a fluid, dynamic process subject to the vagaries of human nature. What is required are people who have the competence and good judgment to operate in the zone of tension between divergent goals—reducing secrecy (which includes limits on the ability of government officials to classify documents) while protecting what needs to be protected.

A commendable feature of this report is its emphasis on accountability. Better accountability, whether it comes through statute or through executive order, will work both ways: making sure that unnecessary classification does not happen, and also that a sudden zeal for openness does not inadvertently compromise highly sensitive information.

Personnel Security

The need to clear people for access to sensitive information may have been based, quite legitimately, on fear of subversion by Communist agents in the Cold War. But the end of the Cold War does not end that concern. Today America has enemies just as implacable in their hatred of the United States, if not as threatening in their means, as the former Soviet Union.

Government officials, members of the Intelligence Community, and military personnel are still the targets of attempts to "turn" them. The blandishments of foreign intelligence services may be even more numerous because the end of the Cold War has spawned many new sources of possible subversion. Of course, attempts to subvert are now based less on ideological recruitment, as was common in the Cold War, than on simple greed, as we are already seeing in this supposedly post-ideological age. In streamlining and standardizing the personnel security system, the U.S.

cannot afford to compromise in any degree the requirement for stability and loyalty in the people who will have access to classified material.

Security of Information Systems

The most valuable service of this Commission may prove to be its emphasis on the security of automated information systems, a crucial area of national vulnerability. It is in this area where the countervailing goal of openness may have the most destructive effects if we are not careful. Computer intrusions and attacks on the data banks of the Pentagon and U.S. Government laboratories are now common. The communications and transportation infrastructure, as well as the entire banking and financial structure of the United States, are computer-based and potentially vulnerable to hackers or hostile powers. Successful attacks on America's automated data handling and storage systems could wreak more havoc than a conventional military attack.

This area of concern will be the most difficult to address through legislation because the problems are highly technical and because information technology is not static, but subject to fast-paced change. Legislation that attempts to protect the security of information systems is likely to be too broad or too specific. If too broad, it will be useless; if too specific, it will soon be outmoded by the rapid march of technology. Nevertheless, we must try to steer a course through these two shoals, revisiting the issue annually in Congress if need be to ensure that our vital computer-based and automated information systems are protected.

Conclusion

In public policy there is often an equal and opposite reaction to government abuse. Because government secrecy has been abused, we must not overreact and send the pendulum swinging too far in the opposite direction. The government must be made to discharge its superfluous secrets and behave in a more open manner. Government officials must be more subject to limits on what they can classify. But in our rush to widen access, we must not compromise vital secrets, nor betray those who have risked their lives and fortunes to confide in us. We must make sure greater access and openness do not become a remedy more deadly than the disease they purport to cure.

The task of this Commission was not easy; it required maintaining a balance between conflicting obligations. Walking the fine line between greater openness and safeguarding the nation's security took sound judgment, a discerning knowledge of America's history, and a deep appreciation of the citizen's need for information in a self-governing society to make sound decisions. The nation was immensely fortunate to have just such a man in Senator Daniel Patrick Moynihan to chair this Commission. I commend and thank him for his fine leadership. I also commend and thank my Commission colleagues and the outstanding staff for their dedication to the nation's highest interests which made the success of the Commission, and this report, possible.

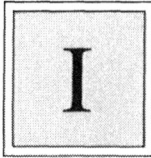

I Overview: Protecting Secrets and Reducing Secrecy

Commission Purposes and Objectives

Congress established the Commission on Protecting and Reducing Government Secrecy in Title IX of the Foreign Relations Authorization Act for Fiscal Years 1994 and 1995 (Public Law 103-236) to make "comprehensive proposals for reform" that are designed "to reduce the volume of information classified and thereby to strengthen the protection of legitimately classified information," as well as to improve existing personnel security procedures. In meeting these objectives, the Commission seeks to promote both the effective protection of information where warranted and the disclosure of information where there is not a well-founded basis for protection or where the costs of maintaining a secret outweigh the benefits.

From the beginning of the American republic, and especially over the past half century, a tension has existed between the legitimate interest of the public in being kept informed about the activities of its Government and the legitimate interest of the Government in certain circumstances in withholding information; in short, between openness and secrecy. This report analyzes the grounds for this tension and suggests means for reconciling the dual "protecting" and "reducing" objectives that are part of the Commission's name and authorizing statute.

It is essential to define the appropriate spheres of protecting and reducing secrecy to avoid perpetuating a system that was identified more than forty years ago as "so overloaded that proper protection of information which should be protected has suffered" and one in which "the mass of classified papers has inevitably resulted in a casual attitude toward classified information, at least on the part of many."[1] The challenge of reducing secrecy overall and protecting secrets more effectively has increased since that time with the broadening reach of national security concerns. Even as the Freedom of Information Act (FOIA) has created a means for the public to obtain government information, consistent with security requirements, the reach of government secrecy has expanded in line with broadened conceptions of what must be protected in the name of national security. Moreover, although the current executive order on classification places a greater burden on those who seek to classify information, existing incentives still tend to promote secrecy over openness.

The result today is a system which neither protects nor releases national security information particularly well. Substantial concerns exist with respect to both the ability of the classification system to protect secrets effectively and the adequacy of the procedures in place to make information available to those outside the Government. In part, this is because the protection of government secrets and the reduction of government secrecy too often have been viewed as competing objectives, instead of being seen as able to reinforce one another when practiced effectively.

This Commission is the first body established by Congress to examine government secrecy in four decades. The only prior body created by statute, the Commission on Government Security, was established in 1955 and issued its final report in 1957. Other commissions and task forces have examined elements of the security system; the most significant of these are described in Appendix G. Some of these previous bodies concluded that incremental changes to the classification system and other security procedures would suffice, while others—most notably the Seitz Task Force of the Defense Science Board in 1970—proposed broader reforms. Several also addressed the problems that arise from inadequate protection of classified information by government officials.

In each case, however, any changes that followed did not alter significantly the basic structure and underpinnings of the security system that developed primarily during the early years of the Cold War. (Although implementation of the recommendations made three years ago by the Joint Security Commission is still an ongoing process, most of the changes made concern specific security practices and procedures; they have little consequence for those outside of government, aside from industrial contractors, and have not affected the functioning of the system overall.)

Indeed, the central finding of the Commission on Government Security that there existed a "vast, intricate, confusing and costly complex of temporary, inadequate, uncoordinated programs and measures designed to protect secrets and installations vital to the defense of the Nation against agents of Soviet imperialism" still rings true today. Many of those programs and measures have proven to be anything but "temporary," however, remaining in place even as the overarching threat to U.S. security posed by the Soviet Union and its ideological supporters within the United States dissipated and gave way to a new set of very different and less monolithic security challenges. To a significant degree, and despite the various studies and a succession of executive orders on classification, today's system remains deeply rooted in the concepts and principles examined thoroughly by the Commission on Government Security four decades ago.

This is particularly striking in view of the National Security Agency's release, beginning in July 1995, of the VENONA intercepts describing Soviet espionage in the United States during the 1940s. Those documents provide historians with a new opportunity to analyze the Commission on Government Security's conclusion that "the Communist threat is both real and formidable." They also reveal how far the United States has come from an era of espionage activities based mainly on ideological motives. Yet even as the global Communist threat is now being analyzed as a historical phenomenon, the security classification and personnel security system that grew up largely in response to it has yet to adapt to new realities.

The revolution in information technology, which has changed the landscape of how the government creates, manages, and protects its information, accentuates this failure of the system to adapt. The estimation that the amount of available information in the United States will grow nineteen times between 1992 and 2000 highlights both the opportunities and the challenges in the years to come.[2] The United States possesses the world's most highly connected and at the same time most vulnerable information infrastructure; a denial or disruption of service could have a significant negative impact, not only on the protection of classified national security information, but more broadly on the functioning and credibility of the Federal Government as a whole.

Moreover, as more records are created and distributed electronically, it will be essential to focus additional attention on how to prevent information from being manipulated or modified in a manner that would alter its basic content or render it unavailable— problems that were much less likely to arise in a "paper-based" world. In light of these varied new challenges, this report also describes key information security issues which relate to both the "protecting" and the "reducing" elements of the Commission's charter.

Secrecy Issues Not Addressed by the Commission

In view of the breadth of its title, the Commission also had to decide which issues relating to government secrecy *not* to address. First, the Commission did not try to examine every facet of the security system. For example, the report does not discuss the myriad of physical and technical security measures used to safeguard information, ranging from facilities protection to document control to operations security requirements. Many of these were addressed in the Joint Security Commission's 1994 report and several of the changes recommended in that report have since been reviewed within the interagency Security Policy Board structure (although the implementation record to date has been mixed).

Nor does this report detail how secrecy is maintained in the Legislative and Judicial Branches (for example, through secrecy oaths and disclosure orders), except in areas that relate to the classification, declassification, personnel security, and information systems security criteria and procedures developed by the Executive Branch. The report also does not examine the impact of various government security requirements on the private sector—including patent, trade secret, and other invention secrecy rules, and export control laws and regulations—except where they relate directly to the protection of *government* secrets.

The Commission also does not address certain issues that, while obviously related to government secrecy, are best considered in the context of a broader examination of intelligence roles and missions. Thus, the appropriate status of the U.S. intelligence budget, role and conduct of covert actions, procedures for intelligence sharing with allies and international organizations, and relationship between intelligence and law enforcement objectives are not addressed in this report. These were among the matters reviewed in the past year by the Commission on the Roles and Capabilities of the United States Intelligence Community in its report, *Preparing for the 21st Century: An Appraisal of U.S. Intelligence*, by task forces on intelligence reform organized by the Council on Foreign Relations and Twentieth Century Fund, and in the report of the House Permanent Select Committee on Intelligence, *IC21: Intelligence Community in the 21st Century*. This Commission has explored government secrecy by analyzing the basic policies and procedures through which it is developed and maintained—not by examining particular secret operations.

Finally, the Commission has drawn a distinction between "secrecy" and "privacy." In *The Torment of Secrecy* (originally published in 1956 and reissued last year with an Introduction by Chairman Moynihan), Edward A. Shils contrasted "secrecy," which he defined as "the compulsory withholding of knowledge, reinforced by the prospect of sanctions for disclosure," from "privacy," which he termed "the voluntary withholding of information reinforced by a willing indifference."[3] The report does not analyze the requirements of the Privacy Act of 1974 nor evaluate the balancing of governmental policies and individual rights, although it does cite privacy interests in discussing subjects such as personnel security procedures and the difficult effort to attempt to develop an updated encryption standard.

Defining Government Secrecy

Scholars have struggled with the general concept of secrecy for centuries. Philosopher and ethicist Sissela Bok has defined a secret as anything that "is kept intentionally hidden, set apart in the mind of its keeper as requiring concealment."[4] A secret may either be kept from everyone or shared on the condition that it go no further. The key element is intentional concealment: the action by one or more "insiders" of keeping something hidden and set apart from any "outsiders." Secrecy is, in turn, the resulting concealment. Edward Shils's definition of secrecy, cited above, adds the element of "sanctions for disclosure" to the framework. As discussed below, however, one of the fundamental problems over the past few decades has been the absence of any clear relationship between the rules for keeping secrets through classification and those for imposing effective discipline when the established safeguards are breached.

> "Three may keep a secret if two of them are dead."
>
> Benjamin Franklin

There is nothing particularly unique about the general means by which the U.S. Government seeks to ensure effective protection of its secrets. The process rests on three pillars. First, an official must identify what information is to be kept secret and then the means for maximizing the likelihood that it will remain secret; in short, the rules for classification and physical security. As the universe of those with whom the information is communicated increases, however, so does the likelihood of an unwanted disclosure. Thus, the second pillar of effective secrecy is to ensure that the secret is shared only with those viewed as trustworthy: a combination of personnel security rules and the principle of "need-to-know." Finally, as Shils's definition reflects, there is a third pillar: rules that those who breach the commitment to maintain secrecy will be subject to some type of sanction. In the context of protecting national security information, this means enforcement through the espionage laws as well as through applicable administrative procedures.

Where any one of these pillars is weak or otherwise not utilized effectively, the secrecy system is not likely to function well. Moreover, the inadequacy of one element may well lead those responsible for the system's administration and management to "compensate" by expanding application of the other pillars. Thus, the perception that the system of sanctions for violating the rules for protecting information is ineffective may contribute to a tightening of the other measures intended to provide security: namely, the rules governing personnel security and classification.

The Means for Protecting Government Secrets

Five major categories of information are protected through some form of government secrecy: (1) national defense information, encompassing military operations and weapons technology; (2) foreign relations information, including that concerning diplomatic activities; (3) information developed in the context of various law enforcement investigations; (4) information relevant to the maintenance of a commercial advantage (typically proprietary in nature); and (5) information pertaining to personal privacy. Of these, the first two categories together define the sphere of "national security information" covered by security classification executive orders and are the primary subjects of this Commission's inquiry.

The U.S. Constitution includes only one explicit reference to "secrecy," and it concerns procedures of the Congress, not the Executive Branch. Article I, section 5 provides "Each House shall keep a journal of its Proceedings, and from time to time publish the same, excepting such Parts as in their Judgment require Secrecy." The authority of the Executive Branch to maintain secrecy has been based in part on four statutes: the Espionage Act, the National Security Act, the Atomic Energy Act, and the Freedom of Information Act.

Nevertheless, as it has developed in the United States over the past eight decades, government secrecy can be understood best as a form of government regulation. With the exception of the procedures for classifying "nuclear-related information" under the Atomic Energy Act and protecting intelligence "sources and methods" under the National Security Act, the mechanics for protecting national security information have evolved through a series of executive orders. Over the past half century, the Congress has played only a limited role in any consideration of how the system should function, limiting itself to occasional oversight hearings. The Executive Branch has assumed the authority both for structuring the classification system and for deciding the grounds upon which secrets should be created and maintained. Thus, what commonly is referred to as "government secrecy" more properly could be termed "administrative secrecy" or "secrecy by regulation."

The series of six executive orders since 1951, however, does not represent the full range of secrets protected through some form of regulation. A great deal of information is protected by the Government *outside* the formal national security classification system. One especially confounding matter has been the uncertain scope of "sensitive unclassified information": information not meeting the criteria for classification but that is considered by the Government to warrant some form of protection. This category (or, more accurately, categories) of information has remained difficult to define, in part because of the greatly varied rationales used to justify its protection.

In 1971, a House subcommittee found no fewer than 62 different control markings being used to restrict the distribution of sensitive unclassified information. Use of these markings was not linked to any explicit statutory authority. In fact, unlike the tiers of Confidential, Secret, and Top Secret security classification, they also were not expressly authorized by executive order. The Commission's own inquiry reveals that, while certain markings have been eliminated and others narrowed since 1971, in most respects little has changed. The numerous markings—more than 50—still used today continue to produce considerable confusion both inside and outside the Government. Chapter II discusses this issue of sensitive unclassified information in greater detail.

The Importance of Protecting Secrets

Effective secrecy has proven indispensable to the functioning of government, serving the interests not only of the officials in power but of the governed as well. Secrecy permits policymakers to freely explore and debate different options, consider alternatives, and weigh the consequences of each; aids in providing the critical element of surprise with respect to a chosen policy; and protects individuals from the possible harm that could arise from publicity.

The primary objective of government secrecy in the national security realm, including its application through the classification system, is to protect U.S. interests by controlling information that provides an advantage (including the element of surprise) over an adversary or prevents that adversary from gaining an advantage that could damage the United States. As the Senate Select Committee on Intelligence noted in its 1986 report reviewing U.S. counterintelligence and security programs, the main rationale underlying classification of national security information must be to ensure that "a hostile element whose goal is to damage the interests of the United States should not have use of the information."[5]

The maintenance of secrecy has proven essential to the successful development, implementation, and completion (or, conversely, the abandonment) of plans and missions. World War II affords several notable examples of successful secrecy in protecting key cryptologic programs from the Germans and the Japanese. (Most of the more recent examples of successful secrecy during wartime remain classified, making it difficult to cite more contemporary cases of such successes.) Secrecy obviously is essential in maintaining the element of surprise that is so critical to the success of particular military missions.

The successful conduct of plans and missions in turn may depend on protecting key technologies. A notable success in this regard was the protection of the efforts, beginning in the 1950s, at Lockheed's Skunk Works facility to rapidly develop an aircraft capable of providing reliable intelligence on Soviet activities. That facility came to be seen as a model for its successful protection of several highly classified aircraft development programs in the years that followed.[6]

Secrecy also is essential to the effective conduct of diplomatic negotiations. The secret diplomacy that preceded President Nixon's trip to China in 1972 provides one well-known example of how secrecy was maintained successfully with regard to a major diplomatic undertaking. More routinely, preserving the secrecy of the specific elements of ongoing negotiations is regarded as essential to their ultimate success.

Closely linked to the protection of plans and missions and the conduct of diplomatic negotiations is the protection of internal policy deliberations: the negotiations among government officials that precede and accompany the development of the plans, missions, and external negotiations cited above. Policy often is shaped only gradually, and the process of developing a coherent official government position often is marked by long periods of disagreement and conflict. Indeed, in *Federalist No. 64*, John Jay cited "preparatory and auxiliary measures" relating to negotiations as the matters that "usually require the most secrecy and the most dispatch."[7]

As one scholar has noted:

> If administrators had to do everything in the open, they might be forced to express only safe and uncontroversial views, and thus to bypass creative or still tentative ideas. As a result, they might end by assuming hasty and inadequate positions. Chances to learn might be lost; premature closure with respect to difficult issues would become more likely. In order to create a pattern out of chaos and avoid haphazard choices, administrators must be able to consider and discard a variety of solutions in private before endorsing some of them in public; the process of evolving new policies requires a degree of concealment.[8]

Thus, drafts and memoranda used in negotiations often remain classified even when the final positions and statements do not. Secrecy also may aid those within government who oppose a particular policy. Of course, this is a benefit to the extent that it enables government to function effectively at a given point in time. However, there also are dangers in the continued maintenance of secrecy that "obscures from the public the divisions and dissensions comprising the administrative history of most important Executive decisions," as well as the fact that, when policies end in failure, there may have been "heroes" who opposed them.[9]

Finally, secrecy is essential in protecting confidential relationships with individuals. The protection by the Government of individuals' identities may take several forms and arise in varied contexts, but probably the best known basis for safeguarding confidential relationships is that enshrined in the National Security Act of 1947 concerning the protection of intelligence sources and methods. This rationale for protection is based primarily on the concern that revealing identities would present substantial risks both to the individuals themselves, to their families, and more broadly to the nation's interests. As evidenced by the actions of Aldrich Ames and other notorious spies, the failure to keep secrets in this context—whether deliberate or unintentional—can have lethal consequences. Moreover, the loss of even a single source in turn may have a chilling effect on the ability to utilize others in the future.

The Intangible Costs of Secrecy

Notwithstanding the compelling interests summarized above, secrecy also carries a range of costs for those responsible for maintaining the secrets and those from whom they are kept. Secrecy has the potential to undermine well-informed judgment by limiting the opportunity for input, review, and criticism, thus allowing individuals and groups to avoid the type of scrutiny that might challenge long-accepted beliefs and ways of thinking. Some form of "sunlight" that permits views to be challenged while they are still in the formative stage can help reveal any institutional biases or preconceived ideas about how to approach a particular issue.

Related to the above, and particularly relevant in the scientific arena, is the impact when secrecy does not permit the sharing of information on new applications of technology. This was a chief interest of the Task Force on Secrecy, established by the Defense Science Board and chaired by Dr. Frederick Seitz, which found, in its July 1970 report, that as a general matter "the classification of technical information impedes its flow within our own system, and may easily do far more harm than good by stifling critical discussion and review or by engendering frustration."[10]

In addition, the failure to ensure timely access to government information, subject to carefully delineated exceptions, risks leaving the public uninformed of decisions of great consequence. As a result, there may be a heightened degree of cynicism and distrust of government, including in contexts far removed from the area in which the secrecy was maintained.

Secrecy can also have significant consequences for the functioning of government itself. Information is power, and it is no mystery to government officials that power can be increased through controls on the flow of information.

One persistent problem in this context has been the intermingling of secrecy used to protect carefully defined national interests with secrecy used primarily to enhance such political or bureaucratic power. This creates the potential that some officials, welcoming insulation from outside scrutiny, will seek means to develop and maintain secrecy beyond what is authorized in a statute or regulation. (An example is when sources and methods protection under the National Security Act is used to deny access to information that does not reveal a particular intelligence source or method.) Such actions obviously have significant consequences for relationships between different parts of government.

As the scope of secrecy grows and the system for protecting secrets becomes more layered and complex, the prospect for leaks—deliberate releases of classified information, nearly always on an anonymous basis—grows as well. Secrets become vulnerable to betrayal, often from high in the chain of command; this in turn promotes greater disrespect for the system itself. Those condemning leaks may, at the same time, be using them in their own self-interest for any number of reasons (ranging from the desire to gain a bureaucratic advantage to using leaks as "trial balloons" for possible policy initiatives). The anonymous leak, often at a senior level, "has become an important tool of governing" and a form of "instant declassification" (although the information leaked is likely to remain officially classified notwithstanding its publication).[11]

> "Leaking has a symbiotic relationship with secrecy. Without secrecy there would be no need to leak information. As government secrecy grows and comes to involve more people, the opportunities to leak from within expand; and with increased leaking, governments intensify their efforts to shore up secrecy."
>
> Sissela Bok, *Secrets*

The leaking of secrets has important consequences for the quality of information made available to the public, as well as for the ability to verify the information. Leaking creates a double standard that may, at times, pit political and career government officials against one another. To the extent that leaking gains any legitimacy, it complicates efforts to impose sanctions on officials for overclassification or other abuses of classification. Leaks that result in changes in policy would appear to reward those within the Government whose motivations may be the most dubious—not those interested in a more sustained and consistent approach to promoting greater openness. Finally, and perhaps most importantly, leaking can greatly damage the integrity of and public respect for the overall classification system, including those efforts by the Government to control the information that is most vital to the nation's security. Leaks undermine the credibility of classification policies and other restrictions on access to information, making it harder to differentiate between secrecy that is needed to protect highly sensitive national security information and that which is not well-founded.

Efforts to Quantify the Costs of Secrecy

Understanding the financial costs associated with keeping information secret is essential to any effort to begin scaling back the scope of secrecy and making protection more efficient. Efforts to measure the costs of classification and related security measures have increased significantly in the past three years. While the U.S. General Accounting Office (GAO) first attempted to measure such costs in a 1972 study and issued a second report in 1993 on the costs "directly applicable to national security information," the Joint Security Commission in 1994 described security costs as "an elusive target" for which there was not a coordinated approach to a uniform cost accounting methodology. [12]

Today, the Government and industry still are not well-positioned to analyze the cost data collected in order to make better-informed decisions on allocating resources. However, progress has been made in quantifying at least the overt costs of classification and related security measures. This has occurred primarily as a result of two surveys mandated by the Congress and carried out under Office of Management and Budget (OMB) guidance, in which Federal agencies have reported on their "classification-related" security costs. The surveys focused on the costs associated with the protection of classified information, and did not include costs related to unclassified information considered to be sensitive, nor costs for the protection of proprietary business information, property, and other assets, nor costs for counterintelligence activities. In addition, declassification costs are not listed separately.

The first survey, released in April 1994, estimated the total security costs of reporting agencies and departments for the preceding year at approximately $2.27 billion; the classified submission of the Central Intelligence Agency (CIA) was not included. A second cost survey was developed in 1995, with a better defined set of reporting categories; issued in April 1996, it reported total security classification costs of roughly $2.7 billion annually for Fiscal Year 1995 and Fiscal Year 1996. As in the earlier survey, the CIA did not provide its cost data in unclassified form.

Efforts to quantify security costs in industry have proceeded more sporadically since a 1989 Aerospace Industries Association (AIA) survey reported $13.8 billion in industry costs (extrapolating from data submitted by fourteen large firms) relating to the protection of national security information. Under Executive Order 12829 of January 1993, which established the National Industrial Security Program (NISP), the Information Security Oversight Office (ISOO) must report to the President on the costs associated with the NISP's implementation. However, there has been considerable debate on the proper approach to accounting for industry costs, and industry has shown reluctance to collect such information.

In 1995, government and industry officials jointly developed a one-page "data collection worksheet" on estimated industry costs. The data submitted in June 1996 estimated, based on a sample of 23 companies, total industry costs relating to protecting national security information for 1995 of more than $2.9 billion. Thus, taking the most recent government and industry cost estimates together, over $5.6 billion was spent in 1995 to protect classified national security information.

The Commission strongly endorses the efforts to attempt to quantify the costs of secrecy. Considerable progress already has been made in a short time in calculating the costs of security classification, and the Commission urges the continued development and refinement of methodologies to help determine these costs, as well as to better calculate the costs of different methods of declassifying information. At the same time, the Commission notes that even these improved cost accounting efforts do not attempt to measure the various intangible costs associated with classification and related activities. Such costs are difficult, if not impossible, to quantify with any degree of precision, yet they must be taken into account in any meaningful evaluation of the secrecy system.

Evolving Concepts of National Security

Under the series of executive orders that have been the cornerstone of the Government's information protection system over the past half century, the concept of national security has formed the basis for classifying information. In practice, however, the breadth of the definition—first referenced in the 1951 Truman Order and then reintroduced in the 1972 Nixon Order—has left those holding the "classification stamp" with great flexibility to decide what national security means in a given context.[13]

Over the years, various government officials and scholars have attempted to provide a theoretical underpinning to national security. Professor Arnold Wolfers, writing in the 1940s and 1950s, produced a framework for viewing it as "the ability of a nation to protect its internal values from external threats," but this definition still left a great deal of leeway for interpreting just what the relevant "internal values" actually are.[14] Are they, for example, limited to the defense sphere and primarily the maintenance of military strength? If so, then why the prevailing use of the term "national security" rather than the narrower "national defense" generally used earlier, including in the espionage laws? Do "internal values" also encompass the ability to maintain an advantageous foreign relations position? To sustain a productive domestic economy? To protect the environment (a matter of growing national and international concern)?

What seems clear is that, given the realities of modern government, with an increasingly complex relationship between matters of defense, foreign policy, and economic policy, and with the expansion of the subject areas considered important to the protection of U.S. national interests, the concept of national security now ranges well beyond the traditional military dimension alone. The President, the Congress, and other senior officials are likely to regard a broad range of matters as directly relevant to the country's security.

This is not to suggest that the expanded framing of national security alone can explain the growth of government secrecy over the past half century. Indeed, it is far from clear that working-level classifiers even consider the meaning of the underlying term "national security," as opposed to simply trying to fit particular information into one of the categories of the applicable classification order. Still, the scope of the term does have implications both for what officials can be expected to treat as classified and for the distinctions drawn between the categories of information deemed to require classification, information protected in other ways, and information not subject to any form of governmental protection.

A Statutory Basis for the Secrecy System

The Case for a Statutory Approach

Many of the problems described in the following chapters, particularly the poor record of implementing classification and declassification policies, derive from the absence of a stable and consistent classification regime. The classification system has been subjected to six different executive orders since 1951, four of which have been issued in the last quarter century alone.

The rules governing how best to protect the nation's secrets, while still ensuring that the American public has access to information on the operations of its government, past and present, have shifted along with political changes in Washington. Over the last 50 years, with the exception of the Kennedy Administration, a new executive order on classification was issued each time one of the political parties regained control of the Executive Branch. These have often been at variance with one another both with respect to the front-end process for classifying and the back-end process for declassifying—at times even reversing outright the policies of the previous order.

As a result, the classification system has undergone repeated adjustments (and, in some cases, major shifts in emphasis) without corresponding improvements in effectiveness. The three executive orders issued since 1978 highlight the problem. As discussed in Chapter II, in many ways President Clinton's Executive Order 12958 closely resembles President Carter's Executive Order 12065—following a thirteen-year interval under President Reagan's Executive Order 12356, which differed from the other two in significant ways. The classification policies of today are similar, in

several respects, to what they were in 1978. So are many of the basic shortcomings
of the system that officials were trying to deal with two decades ago.

Repeated changes both disrupt the efficient administration of the classification system
and can be very costly. Each new order has required that agencies devote significant
time and resources attempting to make personnel aware of how policy changes affect
their work. Although the resources needed to implement new policies can be substantial, rarely are the requirements coordinated with the budget process to ensure that
adequate funds are allocated. In 1983, officials from the Information Security Oversight Office (ISOO) noted that the "frustration" throughout the Government over
having to implement the Reagan Order less than four years after the issuance of the
Carter Order was similar to that experienced when the Carter Order replaced President Nixon's Executive Order 11652 after only six years.

The costs of repeated changes will only increase as more documents are prepared and
used on electronic media. For example, the high cost of making changes to computer
systems, together with the fact that further revisions were expected due to other policy
changes, led NSA officials to postpone updating programs to comply with Executive
Order 12958 so that all changes could be made simultaneously at a lower overall cost.
The result was that well over a year after the Order was issued, nearly every NSA
intelligence report reviewed by the Commission was still being issued with the marking
"OADR" (Originating Agency's Determination Required), even though that marking
had been abolished by the new Order.[15]

Aware that classification orders are regularly replaced, some officials opposed to the
specifics of a given order have resisted complying with and enforcing policies, essentially waiting out an administration in the hope that the order will be replaced. For
example, the declassification provisions of President Carter's Executive Order 12065
were never fully implemented before being scaled back under Executive Order 12356.
This highlights an important shortcoming in the way classification rules currently are
issued and carried out.

The process of developing these classification orders also does little to promote a
system that encourages a balanced assessment of the need for secrecy. Although
there was some opportunity for public comment before the issuance of Executive
Order 12065 in 1978 and Executive Order 12958 in 1995, classification orders have
been developed to a large extent by agency representatives in venues not open to the
public. A senior official involved with one such effort noted that "a group of this kind
has a limited perspective" and that there is "no way to bring balance to the process
from within the Government because there are no institutional advocates for reform of
the classification process within the agencies."[16]

Many of the changes proposed in this report for improving classification and declassification practices probably could be achieved within the current regulatory system.
However, past efforts that relied on those inside the Government to change the system
from within did not result in significant long-term improvements. A more stable
foundation is required for the entire classification and declassification system, with
more consistent application of established rules across all agencies that classify and
less ability to "opt out" where there is disagreement with particular rules. Providing a

legislative basis for the classification and declassification system offers a much likelier means for achieving these types of meaningful changes.

The statute described below is intended to respond to the numerous concerns raised, both directly with this Commission and in the course of previous examinations of the classification and declassification system, about the absence of a stable, coherent regime. It is designed to promote greater attention by the Congress to the dual interests of reducing secrecy overall and better protecting that which should remain secret, while leaving the day-to-day administration of the system in the hands of the Executive Branch. One intended objective of this heightened scrutiny is development of a clearer understanding of the scope of what should be protected under the security classification system. At the same time, however, the Commission does not view this proposed statute as the vehicle for all of its suggestions for improving the current system; indeed, the implementation of most of the recommendations in Chapters II through V would require only Executive Branch action.

Even so, enactment of this general, overarching statute would have the laudatory effect of increasing the likelihood of oversight and, thereby, of promoting greater accountability on the part of the officials within the Executive Branch responsible for setting policies and making decisions on classification and declassification matters. As noted above, while many of the changes proposed throughout this report could be accomplished even without a new law, adoption of a statute affords the best prospect for developing a new approach to the management of classified national security information—an approach characterized by an improved understanding of how best to reconcile and balance the objectives of protecting secrets and reducing secrecy.

A Proposed Statute

The basic rules governing classification and declassification should be the product of an open discussion that weighs both the advantages and disadvantages of secrecy and that is not restricted to the views of those charged with implementing regulations. The Congress can provide such a forum. In addition, there must be incentives for senior agency officials to comply with established policies, coupled with an expectation that they will be held accountable if they do not. The increased likelihood of oversight by the Congress under a statutory framework would provide such an incentive for senior officials to exert greater leadership to ensure the appropriate use of classification and better protection of classified information. In fact, numerous officials from different agencies acknowledged to the Commission that they would be more likely to implement policies backed by the force of a law passed by the Congress.

Recommendation

The Commission recommends enactment of a statute establishing the principles on which Federal classification and declassification programs are to be based.

The Commission proposes the following as the framework for such a statute:

Sec. 1   Information shall be classified only if there is a demonstrable need to protect the information in the interests of national security, with the goal of ensuring that classification is kept to an absolute minimum consistent with these interests.*

Sec. 2   The President shall, as needed, establish procedures and structures for classification of information. Procedures and structures shall be established and resources allocated for declassification as a parallel program to classification. Details of these programs and any revisions to them shall be published in the Federal Register and subject to notice and comment procedures.

Sec. 3   In establishing the standards and categories to apply in determining whether information should be or remain classified, such standards and categories shall include consideration of the benefit from public disclosure of the information and weigh it against the need for initial or continued protection under the classification system. If there is significant doubt whether information requires protection, it shall not be classified.

Sec. 4   Information shall remain classified for no longer than ten years, unless the agency specifically recertifies that the particular information requires continued protection based on current risk assessments. All information shall be declassified after 30 years, unless it is shown that demonstrable harm to an individual or to ongoing government activities will result from release. Systematic declassification schedules shall be established. Agencies shall submit annual reports on their classification and declassification programs to the Congress.

Sec. 5   This statute shall not be construed as authority to withhold information from the Congress.

Sec. 6   There shall be established a National Declassification Center to coordinate, implement, and oversee the declassification policies and practices of the Federal Government. The Center shall report annually to the Congress and the President on its activities and on the status of declassification practices by all Federal agencies that use, hold, or create classified information.

---

* The term "national security" is used in the current classification order (Executive Order 12958, issued by President Clinton in April 1995 and effective in October 1995), as well as in previous classification orders. As Section 2 of the proposed statute makes clear, the President retains the authority and the discretion to determine which categories of information should be open to classification. Nevertheless, having considered this issue in detail, the Commission proposes several categories of information that it believes should be considered for classification. The list of those categories is set out in Chapter II of this report at pages 22-23.

In calling for enactment of a statute, the Commission is aware of the likely difficulties in securing its passage. This is not the first time that a legislative approach to classification management has been advanced, and the fate of past efforts is a testament to the Congress' general reluctance to involve itself in an area often perceived as the exclusive domain of the President. Even so, a half century of near-total deference to the Executive Branch to both design and implement secrecy standards through regulation has resulted in a system that is long overdue for change.

The U.S. Supreme Court has held that the President's authority to "classify and control access to information bearing on national security . . . flows primarily from th[e] constitutional investment of power in the President" as Commander in Chief.[17] At the same time, the Necessary and Proper Clause in Article I, section 8, of the Constitution, which grants the Congress the authority to "make Rules for the Government and Regulation of the land and naval forces," provides a strong basis for Congressional action in this area. As an area in which the President and the Congress "may have concurrent authority, or in which its distribution is uncertain," the security classification system may fall within the "zone of twilight" to which Justice Robert H. Jackson referred in 1952 in his famous concurring opinion in *Youngstown Sheet and Tube v. Sawyer* (the "steel seizure" case).[18]

Moreover, there are clear precedents for Congressional action in this area. In the Atomic Energy Act of 1954, the National Security Act of 1947, and the Assassination Records Collection Act of 1992 (which established broad standards for the declassification of records concerning the assassination of President Kennedy), Congress prescribed standards to govern elements of the classification and declassification process. None of these statutes infringed on the ability of the Executive Branch to administer the classification system, nor have they compromised the ability of agencies to protect sensitive information. In fact, statutory authority for protecting information routinely is cited by agency officials as helping promote sound information management programs. The power of a statute also could assist future administrations in implementing policies on classified information.

Because the proposed statute would provide only the basic principles under which the classification system would operate, it should not raise concerns about separation of powers. The President would retain the authority to implement the law in the manner deemed most appropriate in light of the particular national security concerns existing at the time, as long as such procedures remained within the general boundaries of the law.

Section 1 of the proposed statute provides, consistent with recent executive orders, that classification shall be based upon "interests of national security." Section 2 provides that the President would retain the authority to specify which kinds of information come within the scope of national security. The Commission envisions that the statute also would establish the general procedures governing the declassification of information, consistent with the objective of developing a government-wide "life cycle" approach to the management of classified information. As explained in Chapter III, the statute would include a government-wide program for the declassification of classified information after definite time periods, subject only to specific exemptions. Part of this program would also involve establishment of a

National Declassification Center within an existing agency, most logically the National Archives and Records Administration.

Conclusion

The twelve Commissioners have brought to this inquiry a diverse range of perspectives drawn from varied backgrounds in the Executive and Legislative Branches and in the public and private sectors. Yet despite varied philosophies and work experiences, the Commissioners all agree with the need to change the system in place today for protecting government secrets in response to the dramatic transformations that have occurred since the only prior statutory commission completed its work some four decades ago. New approaches are needed not only because of changing security threats and risks, but also because costs must be contained; while redundancies perhaps could be tolerated in the past, today's realities require much more efficient, prioritized, and cost-effective procedures.

Chapters II through V amplify on the general observations outlined above in the four areas of classification, declassification, personnel security, and information systems security. Each chapter also explores the historical roots of current practices and the consequences for both the dissemination of government information to the public and the sharing of information within the Federal Government. Among the key themes addressed, which transcend the specific findings and recommendations in each chapter, are the functioning of the bureaucracy that has developed over the past half century to protect government secrets; the efforts to promote greater oversight and accountability; and the various costs associated with both protecting secrets and reducing secrecy.

The Commission recognizes the obstacles to achieving substantial improvements, at least in the short term. At the same time, it believes that there now exists a heightened opportunity to propose and build support for changes intended to reduce secrecy and improve the protection of what remains secret. The chapters that follow detail the changes that the Commission recommends to meet both of these objectives.

---

[1] Department of Defense, Committee on Classified Information, *Report to the Secretary of Defense by the Committee on Classified Information* (Washington, D.C.: Department of Defense, 8 November 1956), 6.

[2] Thomas Lipscomb, *"American Competitiveness in the Information Age,"* presentation at the National Policy Forum Conference (Washington, D.C., 25 October 1995), quoting James Billington, the Librarian of Congress.

[3] Edward A. Shils, *The Torment of Secrecy* (Glencoe: The Free Press, 1956, reprint with an Introduction by Daniel Patrick Moynihan, Chicago: Ivan R. Dee, Inc., 1996), 26.

[4] Sissela Bok, *Secrets* (New York: Vintage Books, 1989), 5.

[5] Senate Select Committee on Intelligence, *Meeting the Espionage Challenge: A Review of United States Counterintelligence and Security Programs*, 99th Cong., 2d sess., 1986, Rpt. 99-522, 78.

[6] At the same time, as Lockheed Martin Skunk Works President Jack S. Gordon made clear in a letter and an accompanying "white paper" sent to the Commission on September 18, 1995, the firm worked to ensure that its security practices protected technological capabilities without imposing unnecessary costs or imposing counterproductive restraints on its own officials (Jack S. Gordon, letter to Commission staff, 18 September 1995).

[7] Thomas M. Franck and Edward Weisband, "Dissemblement, Secrecy, and Executive Privilege in the Foreign Relations of Three Democracies: A Comparative Analysis," in *Secrecy and Foreign Policy*, ed. Thomas M. Franck and Edward Weisband (New York: Oxford University Press, 1974), 400-01.

[8] Bok, *Secrets*, 175.

[9] Ibid., 9.

[10] Defense Science Board Task Force on Secrecy, *Report of the Defense Science Board Task Force on Secrecy* (Washington, D.C.: Office of the Director of Defense Research and Engineering, 1 July 1970), 9.

[11] William S. Moorhead, "Operation and Reform of the Classification System in the United States," in *Secrecy and Foreign Policy*, 90. At the time of his writing, Representative Moorhead was Chairman of the Foreign Operations and Government Information Subcommittee of the House Government Operations Committee.

[12] General Accounting Office, *Classified Information: Costs of Protection Are Integrated With Other Security Costs*, NSIAD-94-55 (Washington, D.C.: Government Printing Office, October 1993), 1; Joint Security Commission, *Redefining Security* (Washington, D.C.: 28 February 1994), 115.

[13] Harold C. Relyea, "National Security and Information," *Government Information Quarterly* 4, no. 1 (1987), 11, 19.

[14] Arnold Wolfers, "'National Security' As An Ambiguous Symbol," *Political Science Quarterly* 67 (December 1952), 481-502, cited in Relyea, "National Security and Information," 12.

[15] Commission staff visit to National Security Agency and review of approximately 100 classified documents, 11 September 1996.

[16] Richard M. Neustadt, letter to Chairman Glenn English, 5 May 1982 (House Committee on Government Operations, *Executive Order on Security Classification: Hearings Before a Subcommittee of the Committee on Government Operations*, 97th Cong., 2d sess., 10 March 1982 and 5 May 1982, Appendix 5).

[17] *Department of the Navy v. Egan*, 384 U.S. 518, 527 (1988).

[18] *Youngstown Sheet and Tube Company v. Sawyer*, 343 U.S. 579, 637 (1952).

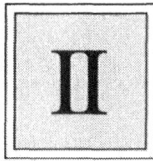

Rethinking Classification: Better Protection and Greater Openness

To the credit of the 29 departments and agencies that currently possess the authority to classify information, there have been serious efforts in recent years to improve classification management practices. There has been a growing recognition of the need to replace a risk avoidance approach to security, which seeks to anticipate *all* risks in the protection of assets, with a risk management approach, which seeks to concentrate limited resources on those assets the loss of which would have the most profound effect on the national security. Today, fewer individuals are authorized to classify information in the first instance than ever before, and efforts are underway to better ensure that these classifiers are more aware of their responsibilities and are evaluated on their classification decisions. The number of special access programs and compartments designed to provide additional protection beyond that of the Confidential, Secret, and Top Secret levels has been reduced. Progress has been made in moving large quantities of information out of the remaining compartments and programs and into the three classification levels, where it is more easily used by a broader range of "customers." Most importantly, the number of classification actions continues to decline and today is at its lowest point since the Information Security Oversight Office (ISOO) began compiling classification statistics in 1979.[1]

Notwithstanding these efforts and results to date, more information continues to be classified than national security needs require. Risk management continues to be more of a goal than an operative philosophy guiding today's security decisions. Serious questions remain about the process by which classification decisions are made, and about the oversight, training, and accountability of those who make classification decisions. Particularly disturbing is the continued perception among many inside the Government that the current classification system simultaneously fails to protect the nation's core secrets while still classifying too much. Justice Potter Stewart's observation that "when everything is classified, then nothing is classified" remains very relevant today.[2] As long as more information than necessary is classified, the long-term benefits of the progress cited above will be limited—benefits such as the enhanced protection of the nation's core secrets, the cost savings that will come from limiting classification, and the value of the American public knowing about the operations and activities of its government. This is particularly true given the information explosion in which the amount of data overall will increase dramatically in the years ahead.

If the progress already made is to continue, there must be a renewed focus on the all-important initial decision of whether to classify at all. Avoiding unnecessary classification in the first place should allow for a more efficient use of already-limited resources by focusing on that which truly needs protection. Combined with the proper implementation of classification practices, this also should lessen the burden of subsequent declassification efforts, contributing to a more orderly and cost-efficient review and release of information to the public. And finally, a more thoughtful and balanced consideration of the need for secrecy should enable government officials to better understand the importance of a particular piece of information and why it needs to be protected, leading to enhanced safeguarding of the nation's secrets.

This chapter describes the current classification system and recent improvements to it, and highlights those areas that the Commission finds most ripe for attention as the decades-old struggle between secrecy and openness proceeds into the Information Age. Commission recommendations in this area attempt to reorient the classification decisionmaking process from one that perpetuates a "default" to classification, in which personnel tend to classify more by rote than by reason, to one that involves a more balanced assessment of the need for secrecy.

Toward a Life Cycle Approach to Classification Management

A meaningful assessment of the need for protection over the long term requires revisiting the initial decision to classify throughout the period in which the information is of value (i.e., throughout the life cycle of that information). Viewing information, and the records in which that information is contained, as having a "life span" is not a novel approach. The Information Resources Management Service of the General Services Administration, for example, maintains that "each type of record has its own distinct life cycle; records are born, reproduced, . . . processed, consulted, reviewed, sent to the sidelines, brought back for consultation, may be reborn into another document, and eventually end up in the trash or permanent storage."[3] Likewise, in developing policy for its management of electronic records, the National Archives and Records Administration incorporated "traditional records management theory . . . reflecting the life cycle of records—creation and receipt, maintenance and use, and disposition."[4]

Such management concepts, however, have been applied only to very limited areas of the Government. The various stages of the life cycle still often are viewed as distinct from one another with respect to the management of classified information. The disjointed nature of current information management practices has a range of troubling consequences. Decisions concerning up-front classification practices (such as portion marking, which designates the parts of a record that are classified and the degree of protection needed) often proceed without any real consideration for how these practices will affect subsequent use of the records or efforts to declassify them. In fact, the tremendous backlog of records currently being encountered in the systematic review of older documents, discussed in Chapter III, is in large part the result of poor records management practices at earlier stages of the records' life cycle.

> Despite being required to mark documents to indicate which portions are classified and which are not, employees in some agencies continue to mark materials "Entire Text Classified," increasing the difficulty of distinguishing which parts truly need protection and which might later be declassified.

Despite recent initiatives being developed by the National Archives, the Federal Government as a whole still lacks any coordinated plan to oversee the creation and management of electronic records, which encompass a rapidly growing share of the documents and images now being created and classified.

This life cycle approach recognizes that both classified and unclassified information (and the records in which that information is contained) exists throughout a life span in which decisions must be made with respect to creation, management and use, and final status (typically either destruction or preservation and release). Unlike other information, however, the management of classified information should include the important initial consideration of whether the information should be classified at all. Yet classifiers continue to consider the benefits of classification without giving equal weight to its costs, an unbalanced approach that has led to too much classification and weakened protection of the nation's core secrets. The life cycle approach thus incorporates the more general "risk management" approach to security which, as the Joint Security Commission (JSC) stated in 1994, includes an appraisal of "asset valuation, threat analysis, and vulnerability assessments . . . along with the acceptable level of risk and any uncertainties, to decide how great is the risk and what countermeasures to apply."[5]

The "life cycle risk assessment" of classified information should encompass an analysis at each stage of the information's "life" of: (1) whether the information requires protection (given the risks, threats, and vulnerabilities to it) and, if so, how much and for how long; (2) the public's right to know about the functioning of government and whether this outweighs the need for protection in a given instance; and (3) the cost of protecting or declassifying the information. This approach also recognizes that consideration of these criteria may lead to different results at different stages of the life cycle. For example, the public benefit in knowing the information initially may be outweighed by the need for its protection, but later may carry greater relative weight and may require its release.

Success in institutionalizing such an approach at all stages in the management of classified information would result in significant benefits. These include helping to foster a better understanding and acceptance of why information was classified in the first place, enhancing the protection of information, and improving the efficiency with which resources devoted to information management are used, thus reducing costs.

The Secrecy System

Bases for Classification

A Half Century of Executive Orders
Executive Order 12958, like prior orders, lays out the rules governing the identification and protection of information, the unauthorized disclosure of which could cause "damage to the national security." The now-common practice of specifying categories of information eligible for classification began in 1978 when President Carter's Executive Order 12065 set out seven such categories, an approach seen at the time as a possible way to reduce initial classification actions. Examination of the Carter Order and subsequent orders, however, reveals only the slightest difference in the *kinds* of information eligible for classification under each. Two categories (confidential sources and cryptology) under President Reagan's Executive Order 12356 were combined with other categories under Executive Order 12958. The so-called "catch-all"

category that allowed agency heads to classify "other categories"of information was rarely invoked, and was deleted under Executive Order 12958.

There has been no shortage of suggestions on how to reduce classification by restructuring the definitions of the categories of information eligible for classification. The Joint Security Commission, for example, proposed several "limited categories" of information that would qualify for its "Specially Protected" category. The review effort that led to Executive Order 12958 also considered narrowing existing definitions, but the interagency group charged with drafting the Order was unable to reach consensus on

> One official involved in drafting Executive Order 12958 acknowledged that anyone seeking to classify a piece of information not explicitly covered by the Order would have to be "unimaginative" not to be able to "fit" the information into one of the seven categories.

how to narrow the criteria. Although the categories as provided in Executive Order 12958 could be more narrowly drawn, at the same time they must be broad enough to allow different departments and agencies latitude to interpret them according to their diverse needs. The Commission cautions, however, against viewing changing the scope of these categories as a "silver bullet" that alone will reduce unnecessary classification.

Despite the difficulties inherent in trying to adjust classification criteria, a different approach—one based on the need for genuine risk assessment—can complement the more deliberative process of classification decisionmaking and focus classification on the core secrets that must remain protected. The categories of information eligible for classification should be narrowly defined, allowing exemptions only in specific, carefully-defined instances requiring approval by the National Security Council (NSC). Under the statute proposed in Chapter I, the President would retain the authority to determine which categories of information should be open to classification.

Classification categories that should be considered are:

- Technical information on the design, development, vulnerability, capability, or use of weapons systems, cryptologic systems, and imagery.

- Names/identities of those individuals or organizations that provide information to the U.S. Government with the expectation that the information will be held in confidence or, if further disclosed, would pose a substantial risk of harm to the individual or organization that provided it.

- Foreign relations or foreign activities of the United States, that, if disclosed, would impair foreign policy.

- Plans for or conduct of military operations that, if disclosed, would impair the effectiveness of present or future operations or jeopardize human life.

- Sources and methods used to collect, process, and analyze information included under the traditional disciplines of signals intelligence (SIGINT), imagery intelligence (IMINT), measurement and signature intelligence (MASINT), and human-source intelligence (HUMINT).

- Foreign government information, the protection of which is specified by the terms of a treaty, agreement, or other international obligation.

What distinguishes some of the above categories from past proposals and the current executive order is that, for the first time, they include *thresholds* for classification. For example, in past executive orders, any information concerning the "foreign relations and foreign activities of the United States" could be considered for classification. Under this suggested approach, such information would still be eligible for classification, but only if it would *impair* those "relations" or "activities," requiring classifiers to make a reasoned evaluation of whether the information truly warrants classification. While the Commission recognizes that those determined to classify information will not allow definitional hurdles to stand in their way, the proposed approach at least should prompt classifiers to think more carefully before doing so, resulting in more reasoned decisions and, perhaps, less classification.

Protection of Sources and Methods

The National Security Act of 1947 tasks the Director of Central Intelligence (DCI) to "protect intelligence sources and methods from unauthorized disclosure." Since 1978, executive orders have specifically authorized the classification of sources and methods information. While charging the DCI with a statutory obligation to protect "sources and methods" may seem redundant, the extensive classification system of today did not exist when the Act was passed half a century ago; the first government-wide executive order on classification came four years later. Classification thus has been the tool by which the DCI (and by extension the intelligence agencies under his authority) has met this statutory obligation.

However, neither the National Security Act nor any of the relevant executive orders has defined what constitutes a "source" or a "method," and the use of these provisions has been the subject of frequent criticism. Protection of sources and methods has been used to justify the classification of a range of information sometimes only indirectly related to a specific source or method. Sometimes included in this are "open sources" such as books, newspapers, and public broadcasts, which can in some areas (such as economic analysis) account for up to 95 percent of the information collected by the Intelligence Community.[6] The view that even such open sources can reveal the methods by which analysts process information and reach their conclusions has also affected agencies' responses to public requests for information, as discussed in Chapter III.

Protection Under the Atomic Energy Act

The Atomic Energy Act of 1954 (AEA), as amended, authorizes an entirely separate system for protecting information from that established by executive order. This distinct system arose from the desire to establish a special regime for protecting highly sensitive nuclear-related information, coupled with the absence of any formal classification system among civilian agencies immediately after World War II. The AEA serves as the basis for between 80 and 90 percent of all classification decisions made by the Department of Energy (DoE), according to Department officials.

The AEA provides for the classification of information, termed Restricted Data (RD), covering "the design, manufacture or utilization of atomic weapons . . . the production of special nuclear materials . . . or the use of special nuclear material in the production of energy." Unlike national security information, which must meet certain criteria before being classified, no affirmative decision is required on the part of the DoE to classify information as Restricted Data: if information fits within the above definition, then it is considered classified from its origin and is said to be "born classified." Statutory authority for the classification of such information also has implications for oversight of DoE classification practices, as discussed below.

While authority for declassifying Restricted Data lies solely with the DoE, the approval of the Department of Defense is required when moving out of the RD category ("transclassifying") information that "relates primarily to the military utilization of atomic weapons." Although not specified as such in the AEA, this transclassified information is referred to as Formerly Restricted Data (FRD). In almost every respect (with the exception that it cannot be shared with another country absent an agreement authorized under the AEA), FRD is treated and handled in the same way as national security information classified under executive order. Like national security information, RD and FRD can be classified Confidential, Secret, or Top Secret.

The separate statutory basis for protecting nuclear information also has affected the process for declassifying this information. This process has been criticized as burdensome, inflexible, and costly by many scientists, environmental researchers, and other scholars. These critics contend that the system for declassifying RD fails to take into account scientific and technological changes, to allow reasonable access to information about environmental hazards caused by nuclear-related activities, or to consider the voluminous information now in the public domain on atomic energy and related matters.[7] The DoE's comprehensive, agency-wide effort to increase public confidence through a policy of greater openness has aided progress toward decreasing the amount of information remaining classified. Its Fundamental Classification Review (discussed further below) used a panel of leading nuclear scientists, historians, and agency representatives to reevaluate the extent to which information now classified as RD or FRD can be made publicly available. Attention to these matters should continue through the DoE's Openness Advisory Committee, composed of distinguished professionals who are responsible for advising the DoE on issues related to declassification and openness.

Since 1992, three studies—all commissioned by the DoE itself—and the draft of the still-pending Fundamental Review have called for eliminating the FRD category, asserting that information within it can be adequately protected by either the traditional classification system or the RD category.[8] One of these studies, issued in 1995 by a National Academy of Sciences task force, explicitly encouraged this Commission to consider "whether there is any continuing justification for two separate and parallel classification systems."[9] The Commission concludes that, as long as RD and FRD are controlled by a separate statute, legislative action will be required to bring meaningful changes to the DoE's current classification system and to bring it into greater harmony with the overall system for controlling access to national security information.

Living With Ambiguity: The Levels of Classification

Individuals who have already decided to classify a piece of information then must decide on the level at which to do so. Executive Order 12958 preserves the three classification levels of Confidential, Secret, and Top Secret that have long served as the foundation for protecting classified information. While elements of the definitions of these three levels have varied over time—Executive Order 12958, for instance, is the first to require classifiers to be able to "identify and describe" the damage to the national security if the information were disclosed—they have remained based on the concept of "damage" since the 1950s. If the unauthorized disclosure of the information could potentially cause damage, it may be classified Confidential; Secret if "serious damage;" or Top Secret if "exceptionally grave damage." Most classifiers employ the middle option: 71 percent of all classified information is Secret; only 20 percent and 9 percent of all classified information is Confidential and Top Secret, respectively.[10]

> The three classification levels are commonly referred to as the "collateral" system—a term meaning "ancillary"—a revealing point, since these three levels are intended to be the core of the classification system.

The difficult task of differentiating between such vague standards has long been criticized by many classifiers, recognizing that reasonable people may well disagree over the degree of damage certain information might cause if disclosed and, thus, over the level at which it should be classified (as well as whether it should be classified at all). This subjectivity has been one of the major factors leading to calls for reducing or consolidating these levels.[11] Most recently, the Joint Security Commission recommended the creation of a "one-level classification system" in which, according to the JSC, the only difference between information with the potential to cause different degrees of damage would have been the type of physical protection it received. Yet even under the JSC's "one-level" proposal, classifiers still would have been required to select and apply one of two "degrees of [physical] protection." In addition, although changing the number of levels may simplify the classification system, the Commission has found no evidence that such a change would reduce the amount of classification.

Controlling Access to Secrets: The "Need-to-Know" Principle

The granting of a security clearance for a certain level of classified information is not supposed to mean that an individual gains *access* to all information classified at that level. The dissemination of classified information is intended to be limited to those who both (1) hold the appropriate clearance, and (2) need the information in order to properly perform their duties. The extent to which the "need-to-know" principle is adhered to in practice, however, has been the subject of debate and disagreement for decades.[12] The placing of classified information on automated information systems presents additional challenges in this regard, as a growing number of cleared personnel are able to access classified information for which they may not have a genuine need. Intelink—the Intelligence Community's version of the Internet, which allows cleared personnel access to a range of classified information—provides one notable example of how need-to-know is becoming harder to enforce in the Information Age.

The difficulty of discerning who truly needs access to classified information has contributed to the rise of a host of methods for limiting such access. A variety of control markings and handling caveats restricts the dissemination of information and has added extra layers to the classification system. For example, thirteen access categories (known as Sigmas) limit access to Restricted Data, and within the Intelligence Community the control marking "ORCON" (Dissemination and Extraction of Information Controlled by Originator) prohibits further dissemination without the specific approval of the originator of the information.

Clarifying Security in Special Access Programs

Access to information considered to be particularly sensitive is controlled through a range of special access programs, which involve access controls and security measures typically in excess of those normally required for access to classified information. (Unless specified as Department of Defense (DoD) Special Access Programs (SAPs), the term "special access program" is used throughout this report to denote any program that limits access beyond that of the three-tiered collateral classification system.) These include programs within the Departments of Defense, Energy, and State, as well as the plethora of compartments within the Intelligence Community designed to protect intelligence information and material referred to as Sensitive Compartmented Information (SCI). The legal basis for creating such programs flows from successive executive orders and, in the case of SCI, from the National Security Act of 1947 and Executive Order 12333 (which lays out the responsibilities of various intelligence agencies). Other special access programs, such as those relating to the protection of the President, the continuity of government operations, and covert action (all known as "national programs"), are operated from within the Executive Office of the President.

> **A Special Access Program**
>
> The Congressional Emergency Relocation Site (located under the Greenbriar Hotel in West Virginia and built to house the entire Congress and some of their staff in the event of a national security emergency) was designed, constructed, and maintained as a special access program for more than thirty years until 1994 when its existence was declassified.

Additional security requirements to protect these special access programs can range from mere upgrades of the collateral system's requirements (such as rosters specifying who is to have access to the information) to entire facilities being equipped with added physical security measures or elaborate and expensive cover, concealment, deception, and operational security plans. Such measures often have been justified as the only way to provide the security necessary to protect information considered especially sensitive. Programs can concern research, development, and acquisition activities; intelligence; or military operations. They can be funded by one agency but managed by another, which often leads to difficulty in simply accounting for how many programs exist and how much money is spent on them.

Publicly acknowledged programs are considered distinct from unacknowledged programs, with the latter colloquially referred to as "black" programs because their very existence and purpose are classified. Among black programs, further distinction is made for "waived" programs, considered to be so sensitive that they are exempt from standard reporting requirements to the Congress. The chairperson, ranking member, and, on occasion, other members and staff of relevant Congressional committees are notified only orally of the existence of these programs.

There are approximately 150 DoD-approved SAPs (the exact number is classified and others have been created but not yet formally approved), down from 200 in the late 1980s, and roughly 300 SCI compartments, compared with an estimated 800 in the late 1980s.[13] These numbers, however, do not include the many subcompartments, perhaps best termed "SAPs within SAPs," that further limit the extent to which personnel have access to various parts of the same program.

A notable example of the declining use of such programs to protect information considered especially sensitive is the reevaluation of how to best protect certain imagery capabilities (which also led to the declassification of large amounts of imagery dating from the 1950s and 1960s). Since 1995, an estimated 95 percent of all imagery derived from electro-optical image systems and once restricted to a highly classified SCI compartment has been produced and disseminated at the Secret level. As a result, this information can now be more widely disseminated to government "consumers," such as the military, which has relatively few individuals cleared above the Secret level.

In 1994, the DoD created the Special Access Program Oversight Committee (SAPOC) to standardize and formalize the approval, termination, revalidation, and restructuring procedures for DoD special access programs. As required by Executive Order 12958, the SAPOC annually reviews and validates all previously identified DoD special access programs for continued special access program status. The review process is intended to validate the need for continued security compartmentation or to restructure a program into either another special access program or a "collateral" program, and seeks to eliminate redundancy among programs. The SAPOC is intended to provide senior leadership, oversight, and management of all DoD special access programs, to ensure compliance with applicable executive orders and other policies and procedures, and to ensure that required information is provided to the Congress. Within the Intelligence Community, the Controlled Access Program Oversight Committee (CAPOC) performs much the same function as the SAPOC, including annual review of all such programs as required by Executive Order 12958 and a report to the Congress. The CAPOC includes within its review the SCI control system compartments and special access programs funded by the National Foreign Intelligence Program.

> Many of the industrial contractor representatives who attended Commission Roundtables noted that there appear to be unlimited budgets for security in many special access programs and a failure to weigh the value of additional security against its costs.

However, while carefully assessing program cost, schedule, and performance, these reviews have not always focused on the special security features imposed and their associated costs. Despite the improvements described above, concerns have been raised that the SAPOC is too senior a body to have the necessary working knowledge and expertise to adequately address the security procedures and costs associated with DoD special access programs.

More generally, the lack of standardized security procedures for special access programs contributes to high costs and other difficulties. The Joint Security Commission (JSC) recommended a "single, consolidated policy and set of security standards" for such programs, but nearly three years later this recommendation has not been implemented.

Industrial contractors performing classified contracts are governed by the National Industrial Security Program (NISP), created in 1993 by Executive Order 12829 to "serve as a single, integrated, cohesive industrial security program to protect classified information." A Supplement to the NISP operating manual (NISPOM) was issued in February 1995 with a "menu of options" from which government program managers can select when establishing standards for contractors involved with special access programs. However, industrial contractors report that wide variations still exist in the standards applied by government program managers of different SAPs. The "menu of options" continues to allow conflicting and costly security requirements. For example, a senior security officer from a large industrial contractor presented the Commission with a thick set of supplemental forms—all prepared by different program managers and often requesting the same information—that frequently are required before contractor employees can be granted access to certain special access programs.

Within the Intelligence Community, special access programs have been standardized by DCI directives, while those within the DoD continue to operate based on a menu with a wide variety of choices. Some military services continue to increase security regulations for SAPs, while others try to do the opposite. To address this problem, many industry representatives suggest establishing a clearer "baseline" standard and then requiring a specific justification before any additional security can be imposed.

Recommendation

The Commission recommends that the Security Policy Board (SPB) implement within one year the JSC recommendation on establishing a single set of security standards for SAPs. The SPB, in conjunction with the DoD, should examine whether the NISPOM Supplement should continue to allow individual SAP program managers to select the security measures for their program rather than conform to a single standard. Industrial contractors should be included in this review and in the development of a single set of standards.

Protecting Other Government Information

It is impossible to understand how the classification system regulates classified information without taking a broader look at the entire process of protecting all government information. Although by definition not part of the classification system, unclassified information viewed by government agencies as needing protection has implications for the amount of information that is classified. Though sensitive information has never been addressed by executive order, the Computer Security Act of 1987 defines it as "information, the loss, misuse, or unauthorized access to or modification of which could adversely affect the national interest or the conduct of Federal programs." Responses to a Commission questionnaire revealed at least 52 different protective markings being used on unclassified information, approximately 40 of which are used by departments and agencies that also classify information.[14] Included among these are widely-used markings such as "Sensitive But Unclassified," "Limited Official Use," "Official Use Only," and "For Official Use Only."

Agencies protect some unclassified information in response to legal mandates (such as the Privacy Act) or specific agency regulations. Most specify the types of information that fall into this category, ranging from the very broad and general (e.g., "adverse effect upon the national interest" if disclosed) to the very detailed and specific (e.g., particular aspects of atomic energy defense programs). Agencies control access to this information through a need-to-know process, store it in locked desks or cabinets, and provide at least rudimentary protection when used in automated information systems. Still, there is little oversight of which information is designated as sensitive, and virtually any agency employee can decide which information is to be so regulated.

Moreover, the very lack of consistency from one agency to another contributes to confusion about why this information is to be protected and how it is to be handled. These designations sometimes are mistaken for a fourth classification level, causing unclassified information with these markings to be treated like classified information.

> Some officials admit to classifying information that should not be classified so that it would fall under the more clearly defined boundaries of the classification system and receive greater protection.

Numerous officials expressed concern to the Commission about the protection and handling of their agencies' information by other agencies; some even admitted to classifying information inappropriately to ensure its protection. A related concern arises from U.S. compliance with agreements under which it is obligated to protect information provided by foreign governments at a level at least equal to that provided by those governments. Lacking any clear level of protection for unclassified sensitive information, the U.S. Government must protect a great deal of unclassified foreign information as though it were classified, thus incurring the accompanying security costs.[15]

In 1986, the Government attempted to address concerns that easy access to multiple databases made it increasingly likely that adversaries could piece together highly sensitive technical information from unclassified sources by proposing creation of a new category of sensitive but unclassified information. However, the resulting outcry over the specter of government control of information in commercial databases caused the proposal to be quickly dropped, but not before the term "sensitive but unclassified" came to be associated by many with unwarranted government attempts to control unclassified information. Over a decade later, the Commission finds that the problems associated with ensuring both the protection and public availability of sensitive information continue to complicate the efficient administration of the classification system and believes that the Executive Branch should examine more thoroughly whether resolution of this problem is possible.

The Classifiers

Original Classification Authorities: The Linchpin of Classification
Under Executive Order 12958, Original Classification Authorities (OCAs) are defined as the only individuals permitted to "classify information in the first instance." Typically

department or agency heads, or other senior government officials, OCAs are designated in writing by the President.

In response to studies that identified the number of original classifiers as a contributing factor to the amount of classification and noted that many individuals possessed the ability to classify originally simply because it was viewed as a measure of status, many agencies have dramatically reduced the number of people with that authority.[16] As of 1995, there were fewer than 5,400 individuals specifically authorized to classify information in the first instance, the smallest number since such statistics were first collected in the early 1970s (when almost 60,000 persons had that authority).[17]

While OCAs account for only six percent of all classification actions in any given year, this does not provide an accurate measure of their influence on the overall amount of information classified. As the only individuals actually designating what information is classified, their decision to classify particular information constitutes the first stage of its life cycle as national security information. Many original classifiers also are responsible for the classification guides that others use in the course of their daily work. A decision to include a piece of information in such a guide thus can lead to a multitude of subsequent "derivative" classification actions.

Until recently, very little was required of any classifier when making a classification decision. Executive Order 12958 for the first time requires OCAs to justify their decisions by completing a classified "why line," in which they must explain why the information warrants classification (a requirement that can be satisfied by citing a relevant category of classifiable information). In addition, the Order requires original classifiers to identify themselves on the materials they classify. Added attention to proper classification should also come as a result of the Order's requirement that "management of classified information" be included as "a critical element or item to be evaluated in the rating" of original classifiers.

> A single decision by an OCA to include a piece of information, data, or technology in a classification guide can lead to thousands of subsequent "derivative" classification actions.

Because the original classification decision is the linchpin on which all other subsequent decisions depend, extreme care should be taken in making this initial decision. The current practice of merely citing one of the categories of classifiable information on the "classified why" line does little to lessen the tendency to classify by rote and does not adequately reflect the long-term consequences of an original classification decision. Requiring all original classifiers to provide a more detailed justification for each original classification decision would assist in this regard. Such a statement could include: (1) the damage to the national security that might result from the unauthorized disclosure of the information, as well as the other criteria (discussed below) used in making the decision; (2) how the information differs from information already classified; and (3) the classification guidance consulted in determining that the information was not already classified.

Both the Central Intelligence Agency (CIA) and the DoE already have such a requirement and report no significant administrative burden in its implementation; the DoE notes that it allows for enhanced oversight by permitting internal review of original decisions. Requiring such a written justification would prompt original classifiers to think more carefully about their decisions and make a more concerted effort to consult existing classification guidance. A written record of original decisions might have the added benefit of encouraging the preparation or updating of classification guides. Finally, an explanation of the intent behind a decision should assist both in oversight of classification decisions and the life cycle management of information by helping others determine subsequently whether the information still warrants classification.

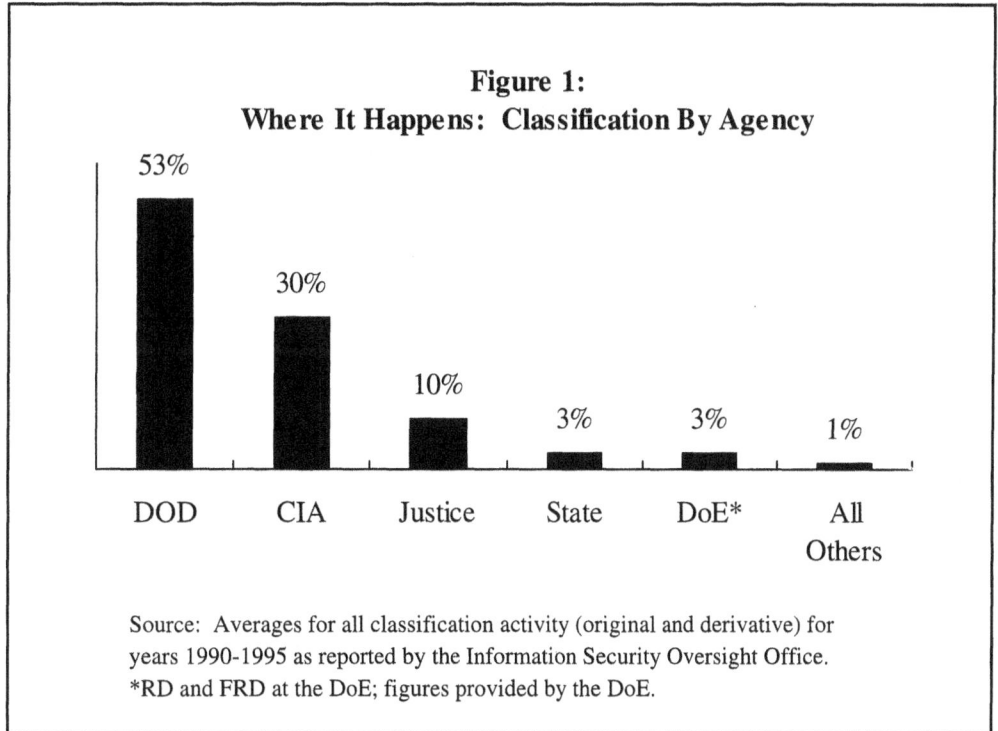

Figure 1:
Where It Happens: Classification By Agency

53%

30%

10%

3%

3%

1%

DOD   CIA   Justice   State   DoE*   All Others

Source: Averages for all classification activity (original and derivative) for years 1990-1995 as reported by the Information Security Oversight Office.
*RD and FRD at the DoE; figures provided by the DoE.

Derivative Classifiers: Enhancing Accountability Where it Matters

Ninety-four percent of all classification actions in the last six years have occurred when personnel have classified "derivatively" by extracting or paraphrasing information in already-classified materials or by using their own interpretation of what they believe requires classification, including the use of classification guides.[18] Unlike original classifiers, those who classify derivatively are almost never designated in writing (the DoE being an exception). Virtually anyone with a security clearance, from the entry-level soldier to an employee of an industrial contractor to a political appointee, can classify information derivatively; the CIA and the National Security Agency (NSA) are but two examples of agencies where nearly all employees are potential derivative classifiers. While over 80 percent of all classification occurs within the DoD and the CIA alone (Figure 1), an estimated three million government and industry employees today have the ability to mark information as classified.[19]

> An estimated three million government and industry employees today have the potential ability to mark information as classified.

Many of the individuals who classify derivatively remain unfamiliar with the proper procedures and even are unaware that it is something in which they are engaged, raising fundamental questions about the accountability, oversight, and training of those making the majority of all classification actions. When there is little chance anyone will be able to determine the source of a classification action and hold the classifier accountable for it, the derivative classifier has little reason to think seriously about whether classification is really justified.

Requiring the identification of derivative classifiers could help begin to change this mindset. Some agencies—such as the CIA, DoE, National Reconnaissance Office (NRO), and Treasury Department—already require that all personnel identify themselves on the documents they classify, and they report few administrative problems. A separate line for classification would distinguish responsibility for classification from responsibility for content, assist with agency oversight of classification management and classification challenges, and help with processing Freedom of Information Act (FOIA) requests. Furthermore, knowing that they would be associated with the classification of a document over its life cycle, derivative classifiers might become more likely to consult classification guides, seek guidance from superiors, and properly portion mark documents—in short, to weigh the classification decision more carefully.

In contrast to Original Classification Authorities, most derivative classifiers are not required to be evaluated on their classification actions. Although Executive Order 12958 states that such performance ratings should be given to those "whose duties significantly involve the creation or handling of classified information," most agencies have not applied this requirement to those who classify derivatively. As a corollary to improved training for derivative classifiers (recommended below), long-term benefits could accrue by including the proper classification of information (the classification of only that information required for the legitimate protection of national security) as a critical element in the performance evaluations of *all* those authorized to classify. Knowing that one will be evaluated based, in part, on careful attention to classification responsibilities would provide a positive incentive to exercise this duty responsibly.

Developing Better Classification Guides

That so many government and industry employees are engaged in classification raises numerous issues with respect to the guides used by derivative classifiers—guides which equate to a delegation of classification authority.[20] The quality of guides can have an enormous impact on the quality of the entire classification system; approximately 94 percent of all classification decisions are based on these guides, or on other previously classified material. There are thousands of classification guides throughout the Government, many of them hundreds of pages long, and many themselves classified. The vast majority are found within the DoD, which reports over 2,000 guides, most covering weapons systems.

With different agencies (and different programs within agencies) preparing guides, they can sometimes contradict one another. Another problem is the failure of some agencies to regularly update these guides, a matter of particular concern to industrial contractors who must rely on guides often prepared without their input and which, at times, fail to consider information already in the public domain. As required by Executive Order 12958, many agencies now are reviewing and updating their classification guides, a development that may improve the quality of these guides.

Those who classify must have a clear understanding of how their senior managers view classification management and how they want them to approach their classification responsibilities. Some agencies attribute a decrease in original classification decisions to the increased use of classification guides. For the successful implementation of a life cycle approach to information management, and given the exponential effect of guides on subsequent derivative decisions, it is imperative that guides be reviewed frequently. Equally critical is that these reviews include a risk assessment analysis to determine whether information still requires the same level of protection or whether protection is still needed at all. Those guides pertaining to industrial programs could benefit from the input of contractors. More up-to-date guides should also assist with the declassification of information, as discussed in Chapter III.

Improving the Training and Education of Classifiers

The subjective nature of classification decisions accentuates the need for effective training and education to ensure that classification is employed only when truly necessary. Yet the vast majority of derivative classifiers receive little, if any, formal training, and OCAs often are able to avoid training altogether. Although numerous executive orders have called for general security training, none has required agencies to ensure that derivative classifiers receive initial training or remain proficient in classification throughout their careers. Declining budgets have further limited the ability of agencies to provide training programs, which tend to be both resource and personnel intensive.

Executive Order 12958's requirement that original classifiers "receive training in original classification" constitutes an important step in attempting to improve the quality of classification decisions. However, while offering suggestions as to what agencies *might* include in this training, neither the Order nor its implementing directive establishes minimum standards for this training, and there are no current plans to consider such minimum standards. Moreover, no training is required for derivative classifiers. To their credit, several agencies maintain formal training programs for those authorized to classify, although these vary widely and the number of personnel involved remains small.

Emphasizing Training

The Headquarters Army Materiel Command in June 1996 mandated that its 800 personnel (all but two of whom were derivative classifiers) attend a series of briefings on Executive Order 12958.

Quality training can play a significant role in developing more proficient classifiers and better life cycle management of government information. As the ISOO has recognized, training would "reduce the volume of information unnecessarily classified by improving the competence . . . of classifiers" and would "increase uniformity in the application of classification principles and marking."[21] Information can be better protected when classifiers understand what they are protecting and why. Initial training would ensure that classifiers have the basic tools to perform their duties, and ongoing education would reinforce that training. Internal computer services such as the NSA's "Policy On Line," which encourages the two-way flow of information between agency personnel and classification management specialists, offer one way to provide enhanced employee awareness of and proficiency in classification practices.

Expanding the training mandated in Executive Order 12958 for original classifiers to include derivative classifiers, and requiring periodic attendance at agency programs on classification designed to ensure continued proficiency over time, are but two ways to improve the practices of classifiers. Training, subject to minimum Executive Branch standards, could also serve as a prerequisite for being evaluated on one's approach to classification, as suggested below.

Recommendation

The Commission recommends that agencies take several steps to enhance the proficiency of classifiers and improve their accountability by requiring additional information on the rationale for classification, by improving classification guidance, and by strengthening training and evaluation programs.

Elements of this approach should include:

- Original classifiers shall provide a detailed justification for each original classification decision;
- Derivative classifiers shall be required to identify themselves on the documents they classify;
- Classification guides shall be better developed, more definitive, and updated regularly, and industry shall participate in the preparation of guides affecting industrial programs;
- Training shall be expanded to include derivative classifiers and shall conform to minimum Executive Branch standards; and
- Proper classification of information shall be included as a critical element in the performance evaluations of *all* employees authorized to classify.

The Key to Better Classification: The Initial Decision to Classify

The Importance of the Initial Decision

As a result of the system described above, classifiers must engage in a two-step process of first determining whether the information qualifies as one of the categories of information eligible for classification, and then whether its unauthorized disclosure could reasonably cause damage to the national security. In reality, however, these two steps often are compressed into one, in which all information falling into the eligible categories is classified. In part, this is a reflection of Executive Order 12356, which for over a decade directed that such information "*shall* be classified" (emphasis added). Yet under Executive Order 12958, simply because information *could* cause damage does not mean it *must* be classified; the new Order makes it clear that information falling into one of the categories of classifiable information *may* be classified, and that "if there is significant doubt about the need to classify information, it shall not be classified."

The task of deciding which information is to be classified, at which level, and for how long remains in large part a subjective judgment open to a range of interpretation. The absence of widespread training and the unavailability or lack of clarity of some classification guides only make appropriate classification decisions all the more difficult. Experts in classification management have pointed out that this first step of the classification management process—the identification by original classifiers of information that should be protected, coupled with derivative classifiers' interpretation of those decisions—tends to be the weakest link in the process of identifying, marking, and then protecting the information.

To reduce this subjectivity, several agencies are developing or already using technologies that attempt to quantify the damage that information might cause if disclosed and then actually make decisions for the classifier. However, even the most advanced programs cannot reduce entirely the subjectivity inherent in classification. Of potentially much greater benefit are "decision tools" that can assist classifiers in making classification decisions. These tools, such as one being developed at the NRO, guide classifiers through the process step-by-step, permitting a computer-generated document to be classified only after the preparer has gone through all the necessary steps and certified that the information contained within the document satisfies the criteria for classification. The National Security Council has taken this approach one step further, applying it to electronic mail; "masks" prevent NSC personnel from sending or printing internal electronic mail messages until they have certified whether classification is needed, a reform that, according to one former official, has contributed to a recent decrease in the amount of classification at the NSC.[22]

The importance of the initial decision to classify cannot be overstated. Classification means that resources will be spent throughout the information's life cycle to protect, distribute, and limit access to information that would be unnecessary if the information were not classified. Classification also means that those who need the information in the course of their work have to be investigated and adjudicated for access. Classification further means that a document may have to be edited to remove some of the most sensitive details if it becomes necessary for the information to be more widely distributed. Finally, classification means that some form of review will have to take place if and when the document is considered for declassification, archiving, or long-term storage.

One official involved with the drafting of Executive Order 12958 expects it to "do little" to reduce the amount of information that is classified.

All too often, however, attention has focused on other aspects of the classification process, such as the level at which the information is to be protected after it is classified. The JSC's call for a "one-level classification system" was only the most recent in a long line of proposals to restructure the levels of classification or overhaul the entire three-tier classification structure. Yet even the JSC made clear that its proposal was designed primarily to streamline the system and reduce costs, and not to reduce the amount of information classified at the outset (although it argued that this could be a by-product of a less complicated system).[23] In addition, key officials involved in the development of Executive Order 12958 have acknowledged that the Order focuses more on the declassification of already classified information than on policies that would reduce the amount of information classified at the outset.

Despite the significance of this initial decision, relatively little is known about exactly how much information is classified. Much of this uncertainty derives from the fact that over two decades of statistical reporting by the ISOO and its predecessor, the Interagency Classification Review Committee, have chronicled classification "actions" (the individual act of designating a document as classified by either an original or derivative classifier) rather than the actual amount of classified materials generated. These actions are based on extrapolations of samplings that often take place at different times and vary in duration from agency to agency. The more than 3.5 million actions reported in 1995 are an extremely rough estimate of the number of actions that may have occurred that year. Nor does this estimate necessarily correlate to the number of pages, computer diskettes, or images classified that year, since a single action can result in the classification of a one-page memorandum or a document hundreds of pages long.

Given this uncertainty, it should not be surprising that there is little agreement on the extent of *over*classification. For over a decade the ISOO has estimated that between one and ten percent of all classified documents are unnecessarily classified.[24] In 1995, a White Paper prepared by the DoD Inspector General concluded that the classification process at the DoD is "fundamentally sound" and that "the present size of classified holdings is not the result of too much information being needlessly classified."[25] In contrast, a 1985 preliminary study prepared by the staff of two House subcommittees proposed a classification system in which "roughly nine-tenths of what is now classified" would no longer qualify for classification.[26] More recently, former NSC Executive Secretary Rodney B. McDaniel estimated that only ten percent of classification was for "legitimate protection of secrets."[27] Given the uncertainty surrounding the breadth of classification, however, efforts to quantify with any precision the extent of unnecessary classification not only may be futile, but are unlikely to help in understanding its causes or possible remedies.

It may be more meaningful to recognize that the perennial problem of unwarranted classification attests to the continued failure of classifiers to engage in a rigorous assessment of the need for classification. For instance, in seeking to protect information about certain weapons systems (the classification of which has been permitted under successive executive orders), many of the support functions associated with these systems, such as information concerning logistical and administrative support, have also been classified even though it was doubtful that their disclosure could have caused any damage to the national security. In the Commission's review of one intelligence agency's documents, a memorandum to employees of the agency describing an upcoming "family day" in which family members could visit the agency was classified Confidential because the person who signed the memorandum was under cover. By simply omitting the name of that individual, the memo would have been unclassified. The entire agenda for a Commission meeting at one intelligence agency was classified because one word—not crucial to the topic being discussed—revealed a classified relationship. At other meetings, Commission staff inquiries as to why certain briefing slides were classified were met with responses such as "I'm not sure," or "This is just the way we prepare our materials."

Improving the Initial Decision

To the credit of many officials, there has been a growing recognition of the need to replace a risk avoidance approach to security, which seeks to anticipate *all* risks in the protection of assets, with a risk management approach, which seeks to concentrate limited resources on those assets the loss of which would have the most profound effect on the national security. This perspective was reflected in the Joint Security Commission's conclusion that security managers "must make tradeoffs during the decision phase between cost and risk, balancing the cost in dollars, manpower, and decreased flow of needed information against possible asset compromise or loss." Some agencies have taken the initiative to go beyond what is required of them and have reevaluated the extent to which they employ classification. For example, the Department of Energy recently engaged in a thirteen-month Fundamental Review of its classification policies, its first such review ever, and in its draft report recommends that a number of topical areas no longer be classified.

These exceptions aside, three years after the JSC report, risk management continues to be more of a goal than an operative philosophy guiding today's security decisions. The desire to avoid any and all possible loss too frequently continues to be the predominant approach to security in general and to classification management in particular. However, the JSC's proposal to apply risk management to the classification system by restructuring that system entirely is only one way to reform the system. Concentrating on the initial decision of whether or not to classify—the point at which classifiers decide whether to place the information in that three-tiered classification structure—holds greater potential for improving the classification process and reducing the amount of information classified than does restructuring the entire system.

Costs vs. Benefits

The Navy requires that "the advantages and disadvantages of classifying . . . be weighed." Among the factors the Navy encourages its classifiers to consider are: cost, the "net national advantage" (to include the benefits of not classifying), and the ability of other nations to know or possibly to learn about the information.

Neither of the two steps for deciding whether or not to classify serves as a significant deterrent to unnecessary classification. Moreover, the emphasis on damage to the national security can contribute to unnecessary secrecy. Although some agencies, such as the Department of the Navy (see box), have gone beyond these criteria, the vast majority of classifiers still employ an approach that fails to reflect the magnitude of the decision to classify. Classifiers, instead, should consider a range of factors when making the decision to classify and, in so doing, undertake a more balanced analysis of whether classification is necessary. In this regard, the Commission seeks to build on the 1995 report of the National Research Council which, in its review of the classification and declassification practices of the DoE, recommended that before such decisions are made, "the benefits of classification [must] clearly outweigh the costs."[28]

The consideration of additional factors during the classification decision could reduce or eliminate the need for classification in a given instance. These could include the following factors:

- actual intention and ability of an adversary to inflict damage (threat);
- ability to defend assets in the event of an attack (vulnerability);

- probability of loss given threat and vulnerability (risk);
- resources required to avoid or minimize risk (cost);
- interest of adversaries in obtaining this information (value of information); and
- expected benefit of the information being publicly available (public release).

Such factors could be considered when original classification decisions are made, during the preparation of classification guides, and when derivative classifiers find themselves in situations where guidance is unclear.

Considering these factors could lead an official to conclude that while information may fall within one of the specified categories eligible for classification and might cause damage to the national security if disclosed, the actual threat to that information or likelihood of compromise may be so low or nonexistent that classification is not necessary. The costs of protecting a particular piece of information may be so high that they outweigh the possible advantages to be gained from its protection. In other cases, the sensitivity of information, or its value to the national security, may be so great that protection—no matter the cost—would be warranted.

Introducing these additional factors into the classification decisionmaking process may, in some cases, make this initial decision somewhat more difficult. However, given the long-term implications of the initial decision, a more deliberative process is necessary. This should allow for a more efficient use of classification in the short-term and lead to savings in both time and resources in subsequent reviews for downgrading or declassification.

The consideration of additional factors should not be viewed as an invitation to embark on intensive efforts to quantify these factors into complicated mathematical formulas or intricate computer programs. Patterned after the National Research Council's call for costs and benefits of secrecy at the DoE to be considered in their "broadest sense," the Commission believes that simply having to *think more* about whether classification is necessary may cause classifiers to give their decisions greater care—a process that should lead to more reasoned classification and may, in many cases, lead to less classification.[29]

Recommendation

The Commission recommends that classification decisions, including the establishment of special access programs, no longer be based solely on damage to the national security. Additional factors, such as the cost of protection, vulnerability, threat, risk, value of the information, and public benefit from release, could also be considered when making classification decisions.

Enhancing Implementation and Oversight

Ultimately, a policy is only as good as its implementation. The fact that classification decisions will remain subjective judgments makes the need for meaningful oversight of implementation all the more critical. Yet responsibility for ensuring judicious classification today rests almost entirely within individual agencies, which rarely view reducing classification as a priority. Improved oversight requires renewed attention at three levels: the Congress, the Executive Branch as a whole, and the departments and agencies themselves.

A Greater Role for the Congress

Congressional oversight of how agencies implement classification policies pursuant to executive order has been virtually nonexistent. The Congress periodically has considered what the classification policies of the Executive Branch *should* be, but it has been far less active in reviewing whether the classification provisions of a given executive order are being implemented appropriately. Any congressional attention to how much classified information is generated has been mainly a by-product of hearings on how the failure to release already-classified documents has affected public access to information, as well as of recent efforts to focus on the costs of the system as a whole.

> Responsibility for ensuring meaningful classification today rests almost entirely within individual agencies, which rarely view reducing classification as a priority.

Greater congressional attention to agency classification and declassification practices would come through enactment of a statute, as recommended in Chapter I. Periodic oversight hearings would be an important start; holding senior agency officials accountable for their agency's classification practices would prompt greater attention to the long-standing problems described above. Furthermore, the Congress could use the confirmation hearings of senior officials to question them on their plans and approach concerning both access to and protection of government information. Of course, use of budget authority would be the ultimate leverage, and would offer a powerful incentive for senior agency officials to reduce the amount of information they classify, to protect more efficiently the information they do classify, and to make continued improvements to their overall information management programs.

The Focal Point: Executive Branch Policy Development and Oversight

Executive orders are the most visible element in the larger process of developing classification policies and then overseeing their implementation. However, confusion over the proper roles of the two organizations charged with policy development and oversight, the Security Policy Board (SPB) and the Information Security Oversight Office, combined with shortcomings in how each organization operates, have hampered the development and oversight of sound classification policies and practices.

Policy Development: Who's in Charge?

Responsibility for policy development lies primarily with the SPB, established within the National Security Council by Presidential Decision Directive (PDD) 29 in September 1994. The main impetus for creating such a body came from the Joint Security Commission, which found that the lack of a coherent framework for formulating, implementing, and overseeing U.S. security policies was the "prime cause of the problems . . . associated with security policies, practices, and procedures." Emphasizing the need for "a unifying structure" capable "of pulling . . . disparate [government] elements together and overcoming bureaucracies' traditional resistance to innovation and change," the JSC called for a security executive committee to develop security policies across the Defense and Intelligence Communities and oversee their implementation. Because the JSC envisioned that this new body would also perform oversight, it noted that existing groups, such as the ISOO (tasked by executive orders since 1978 with conducting oversight of agencies' classification practices) could be consolidated under the new structure.

> Confusion over the proper roles of the SPB and the ISOO has hampered the development and oversight of sound classification policies and practices.

Although somewhat different from the body envisioned by the JSC in that it includes agencies outside the Defense and Intelligence Communities, the SPB is intended as the "principal mechanism" for the "coordination, formulation, evaluation and oversight of security policy."[30] Now composed of representatives from 35 agencies, the SPB is a multi-tiered structure of five permanent committees supported by a host of ad hoc steering committees and working groups; a Security Policy Forum composed of agency representatives at the Assistant Secretary level; and the senior-level Board itself, now co-chaired by the Deputy Secretary of Defense and the Director of Central Intelligence.

Under the SPB umbrella, many areas of security policy, such as personnel security, are coordinated more effectively than before. Representatives from various agencies now have a common venue to discuss matters of mutual concern. In contrast, however, responsibility for developing, implementing, and overseeing classification and declassification policies prescribed by executive order is not clearly defined, and is fragmented between the SPB and the ISOO. Less than a year after the SPB was created, Executive Order 12958 continued the practice of charging the ISOO with not only overseeing agency classification and declassification practices, but with leading "interagency meetings to discuss matters pertaining" to the Order—in other words, classification policy. In an effort to deal with this jurisdictional overlap, the ISOO Director serves as chair of the SPB's Classification Management Committee, a group which also serves as an advisory committee to the ISOO.

Officials of both the ISOO and the SPB acknowledge that this arrangement has been far from satisfactory and, on numerous occasions, has worked to the detriment of timely and coherent information security policy. For example, confusion over the roles of the two organizations resulted in some disagreement over the extent to which the SPB could influence the specifics of the directive implementing Executive Order 12958, a directive the President tasked to the ISOO. In addition, there was intense debate between the ISOO and the SPB staff over the degree to which agencies could "opt out" of certain provisions of the Order's safeguarding directive (laying out how agencies are to physically protect classified information), for which the SPB is responsible. Concerns raised by the ISOO were overruled, and member agencies moved to exempt themselves unilaterally from parts of the directive.

> Since its creation two years ago, the SPB has yet to issue a workable definition of risk management, failing to achieve agreement among the member agencies.

Nor are these problems restricted to the classification management arena. Significant problems remain with regard to the SPB's overall functioning. The SPB has failed to make meaningful progress on several key issues, such as developing an effective framework for applying (or even a workable definition of) risk management principles to security decisions, as well as implementing JSC recommendations to standardize the security rules applicable to special access programs. Despite this, several monthly meetings of the Security Policy Forum have been canceled because there reportedly were an insufficient number of agenda items or no substantive issues ready for decisionmaking.

Sound and coherent security policies have also suffered because the SPB process is premised on obtaining the agreement of all affected agencies through consensus policymaking, an approach explicitly criticized by the JSC. Member agencies have retained the ability to delay and dilute policies with which they disagree. Not only has this approach delayed progress, but it has meant that SPB products often go no further than the extent that the least supportive agencies will accept. As discussed in Chapter IV, although the SPB has produced adjudicative standards and investigative guidelines to improve clearance reciprocity between government agencies, these are only *minimum* standards; agencies may go beyond these standards, thus limiting the extent to which there is genuine reciprocity of clearances. And as of the printing of this report, the SPB had yet to produce the safeguarding directive cited above—nearly two years after being tasked to do so by the President. It seems reasonable to question whether this is what the JSC had in mind when it called for a group capable "of pulling . . . disparate elements together and overcoming bureaucracies' traditional resistance to innovation and change."

In addition, the SPB's plethora of committees and working groups has left the early crucial stages of policy development in the hands of less-senior representatives who may not even be aware of the positions advocated by the agencies' more senior officials. Indeed, these representatives have at times spent months negotiating consensus products, only to have these overturned by their own senior management at higher levels within the SPB structure. Moreover, the fact that the SPB staff, which also plays an influential role in policy development, is detailed from and will return to the very agencies affected by these policies is yet another example of how difficult it is for the SPB to represent anything more than the collective will of the government security bureaucracy.

With the exception of the access granted to the Commission staff, the SPB process remains largely isolated from outside observers. Because there is the potential that information of a classified nature may arise, meetings at all levels of the SPB structure are usually held in secure facilities, requiring attendees to possess security clearances. As a result, while certain industry group representatives with clearances have been permitted to attend meetings, other nongovernmental representatives without clearances cannot. Although a draft legal opinion by the Justice Department has affirmed this practice, the result is that policies developed within the SPB are debated and promulgated out of view of the public and of the Congress. All of this directly contradicts the JSC's vision of an organization that would "provide a focal point for Congressional and public inquiries regarding security policy or its applications."

41

Nor are the two entities that were designed explicitly to serve as venues for public input to the policymaking process actually doing so. In the same directive that established the SPB, the President (as the JSC recommended) created a five-member Security Policy Advisory Board to provide ongoing "non-governmental and public interest" input into the SPB process. More than two years later, however, only three positions have been filled, and there appears to be no active effort to fill the remaining two. Moreover, while these individuals carry impressive credentials, all come from government security and intelligence backgrounds. In addition, the Advisory Board deals only with issues referred to it by the SPB. Similarly, although an Information Security Policy Advisory Council (ISPAC) was created under Executive Order 12958 to "advise the President" on the policies contained in the Order, over a year and a half later none of the Council's seven seats have been filled, no meetings have been held, and none are expected for the foreseeable future.

Oversight: The Critical Missing Link

The SPB and the ISOO must also contend with overlapping mandates with respect to oversight. Although explicitly charged with oversight by Presidential Decision Directive 29, the SPB has devoted little or no time to such responsibilities. Yet even if it had done so, the value of such oversight would be questionable. Any such oversight would be conducted by the SPB staff, which lacks the resources to actively review agency practices and has little, if any, expertise on classification management issues. The unlikely prospect of the SPB staff aggressively reviewing the classification practices of their own agencies raises doubt about the independence and effectiveness of such oversight.

The potential consequences of the SPB's failure to pursue its oversight obligations, however, have been mitigated by the ISOO's continued activity in this area. As directed by Executive Order 12958, the ISOO continues to oversee agency classification practices. The ISOO has achieved some success, notwithstanding its limited resources and personnel and the fact that it has been shuffled among three different agencies in as many years.[31] Although questions have emerged concerning its ability to act independently of its new parent agency, the National Archives and Records Administration, the ISOO has remained independent of the agencies generating the bulk of classified information.

Nevertheless, Executive Branch oversight of classification practices has been and remains largely ineffective. In many respects, the ISOO has been reduced to a body that highlights ongoing agency practices rather than one that attempts to effect change in those practices. The height of the ISOO document reviews in the mid-1980s consisted of approximately one visit to each agency per year. The ISOO did not conduct a single on-site review of any agency's classified product for the two years between 1994 and late 1996. Moreover, despite its enhanced authority to oversee special access programs under Executive Order 12958, the ISOO has not yet done so. In addition, because the ISOO is limited to oversight of national security information, there is no

> The ISOO has achieved some success in the face of limited resources and personnel and being shuffled among three different agencies in as many years. Still, the ISOO has been reduced to a body that highlights ongoing agency practices rather than one able to effect change in those practices.

independent oversight of the 80 to 90 percent of DoE classification activity involving Restricted Data and Formerly Restricted Data under the Atomic Energy Act.

Given all of the above, it is not surprising that the ISOO's own Director has characterized its work as "overseeing agency oversight."[32] Yet the absence of more aggressive oversight by the ISOO may simply be an acknowledgment of its inability to enforce agency compliance with established rules. Although the ISOO has always possessed the authority to report on improper classification, acting on those reports remains the prerogative of the agencies themselves. In fact, while the ISOO often has been able to resolve disagreements by working with agencies, only once has it issued a formal report on abuse of classification to an agency.

Instead, the ISOO has directed much of its effort to describing agency classification practices in its annual report. This report has evolved significantly in recent years to include an array of statistical data on classification and declassification activity and, as of 1995, the costs associated with classification. Yet even this report, which is the ISOO's primary oversight tool, is widely considered within agencies to be more of an externally-imposed requirement than a helpful internal management tool—a point that has been confirmed by the ISOO Director himself. In addition, several agencies admit to doing little to ensure the accuracy of the data they report, further calling into question the value of these annual reports in their present form.

A New Approach to Policy Development and Oversight

Clearly, there needs to be a resolution of the respective roles of the SPB and the ISOO, as well as a strengthening of both policymaking and oversight functions in the classification management arena. Failure to do so risks compromising the quality of the policies themselves and their implementation at a time when institutionalizing sound information management policies is critical to the long-term credibility and success of the system for protecting the nation's secrets.

There are certain prerequisites if policymaking and oversight in this area are to succeed. With respect to policymaking, any specific rules promulgated by the Executive Branch need to comply with the key principles of the statute and must not be solely the product of the implementing agencies. While agencies should be allowed to contribute to the development of these rules, final authority must reside elsewhere, in a forward-thinking body of innovative members engaged in continual reassessment of the appropriateness and effectiveness of these policies. Recognizing the critical role of staff in such an organization, this body would benefit immeasurably from a permanent staff with the necessary expertise and independence from affected agencies.

The policymaking process must also become more open. Only on the rarest of occasions when classified information must be discussed should representatives of outside organizations be prohibited from attending. In addition, the President should work to fill the remaining positions on the Security Policy Advisory Board with individuals who would bring the "non-governmental and public interest perspective" that the President intended the Advisory Board to provide. Likewise, the President should promptly appoint the Information Security Policy Advisory Council so that it may begin to advise the President on Executive Order 12958.

Oversight should be the responsibility of a strong and active organization, independent of the agencies that classify, perhaps modeled after agency inspectors general offices. To be truly effective, such an organization should also possess the means to compel agency compliance with established policies. One possibility would be to empower it with some form of limited budgetary authority—such as the review and certification of agencies' expenditures for classification and declassification activities before they are submitted to the Office of Management and Budget (OMB). A greater willingness on the part of both the National Security Council and OMB officials to question the classification of the documents they receive could provide an additional incentive for senior agency officials to address classification matters more seriously. Equally critical is that such a body have adequate resources, whether through a budget line item or the reallocation of resources from the principal classifying agencies.

The Commission believes that classification and declassification policy and oversight should not be viewed solely as security matters. Instead, they should be viewed primarily as information management issues which require personnel with subject matter and records management expertise. In addition, classification and declassification are unique in that, unlike many security issues, they profoundly affect numerous individuals and organizations outside the Government.

Under the statutory approach recommended in Chapter I, the President would retain the authority to establish policymaking and oversight mechanisms to fulfill the basic principles of the legislation. Therefore, the Commission envisions that this recommendation could be achieved by an executive order modifying either Executive Order 12958 (which sets out the responsibilities of the ISOO) or Presidential Decision Directive 29 (which sets out the responsibilities of the SPB), or both.

Recommendation

The Commission recommends that responsibility for classification and declassification policy development and oversight be assigned to a single Executive Branch body, designated by the President and independent of the agencies that classify. This entity should have sufficient resources and be empowered to carry out oversight of agency practices and to develop policy. Based on its oversight findings, this body would then make recommendations for policy and implementation of classification and declassification issues directly to the National Security Council. The Security Policy Board would have an opportunity to comment on these policy recommendations through the NSC process.

Strengthening Implementation and Oversight Within Agencies

Beyond restructuring the incentives for individual classifiers, as suggested above, oversight within agencies can be enhanced through periodic audits and reviews by agencies of their own classified product. However, executive orders have long failed to distinguish clearly between oversight and review of classification management practices and oversight of security practices generally. Those that do occur still focus more on the *safeguarding* of already classified information than on whether the information was properly classified in the first place or whether classification is still warranted at later stages of a document's life cycle.[33] The past decade has seen a steady decline in even these limited inspections.

Agencies are now required by Executive Order 12958 to institute ongoing self-inspection programs, including the periodic review and assessment of their classified product. Under the Order's implementing directive, however, such reviews are only one of several options that agencies "may include" in their program. Many agencies still fail to devote sufficient resources and personnel to reviewing their own practices and classified product. In contrast, the recently developed Information Management Audit and Improvement Program at the CIA serves as a model for how to implement an oversight program. Following audits to evaluate compliance with classification and records management policies, auditors intend to work with staff in a non-punitive manner to improve compliance. Citing the "many benefits" they provide, the ISOO has pointed out that "document reviews highlight an individual agency's performance in classifying and marking documents and suggest areas in need of improvement."[34]

Each agency with the authority to classify would benefit from an established program, subject to minimum Executive Branch standards, for regular evaluations of its classification and declassification decisions, including the review of representative samples of agency classified materials. Such evaluation programs would help foster a nonpunitive approach to improving the quality of classification decisions. Improved agency evaluations, which could be implemented by an agency ombudsman (as suggested in Chapter III), could serve as the basis for outside review of an agency's classification program. In addition, a greater willingness on the part of agency executive secretaries to question the classification assignments of the documents they receive could provide an additional incentive for personnel throughout those agencies to classify properly.

Conclusion

As in the past, the ability of the United States to defend its national security interests in the future will depend, in part, on its ability to maintain the confidentiality of certain information. The ability of the public to obtain information about the activities and operations of its government will depend, in part, on limiting that secrecy to only those activities that truly require it. Paradoxically, today's secrecy system fails to meet either of these goals effectively.

To improve existing practices, senior officials across all the agencies that classify must exert greater leadership and make it clear to subordinates that reducing secrecy, consistent with national security concerns, is a priority. Policies that either implicitly or explicitly encourage classification without much thought to the consequences of that decision must give way to those that encourage a more balanced consideration of the need for secrecy. Those who classify must be instructed and then evaluated on how they approach their classification responsibilities. Classifiers must be aware that classification means that resources will be spent throughout the information's life cycle to protect, distribute, and limit access to information that would be unnecessary if the information were not classified. The tools designed to assist those classifiers, including classification guides, must be readily available and reflect current national security realities. Underlying all these reforms is the need for a more stable and consistent classification regime, which over fifty years of Executive Branch regulation has been unable to provide.

The age-old struggle to find the proper equilibrium between the need for secrecy in certain instances and the need for open government will by no means end with this Commission. Still, the proposals set out above have the potential to reorient the secrecy system to reflect the fact that reducing secrecy and protecting core national secrets are not exclusive of, but instead dependent upon, one another.

---

[1] The President has designated the following 29 officials (including himself) as having the authority to classify originally: Vice President, Chief of Staff to the President, Director of OMB, National Security Advisor, Director of the Office of National Drug Control Policy, Chairman of the President's Foreign Intelligence Advisory Board; Secretaries of State, Treasury, Defense, Army, Navy, Air Force, Energy, Commerce, and Transportation; Attorney General; Chairman of the Nuclear Regulatory Commission, Director of the Arms Control and Disarmament Agency, Director of Central Intelligence, Administrator of the National Aeronautics and Space Administration, Director of the Federal Emergency Management Agency, U.S. Trade Representative, Chairman of the Council of Economic Advisors, Director of the Office of Science and Technology Policy, Administrator of the Agency for International Development, Director of the U.S. Information Agency, President of the Export-Import Bank of the United States, and the President of Overseas Private Investment Corporation; and Information Security Oversight Office, *1995 Report to the President* (Washington, D.C.: Information Security Oversight Office, 1996), 16.
[2] *New York Times Co. v. United States*, 403 U.S. 713, 729 (1971) (concurring opinion).
[3] Peter Hernon, "Information Life Cycle: Its Place in the Management of U.S. Government Information Resources," *Government Information Quarterly* 11, no. 2 (1994): 147, quoting General Services Administration, Information Resources Management Service, *Applying Technology to Record Systems: A Media Guideline* (Washington, D.C.: May 1993), 45.
[4] National Archives and Records Administration, *Draft "Requirements for Electronic Recordkeeping in the Office Environment* (College Park: National Archives and Records Administration, 1996), 4.
[5] Joint Security Commission, *Redefining Security* (Washington, D.C.: 1994), 5.
[6] Commission on the Roles and Capabilities of the United States Intelligence Community, *Preparing for the 21st Century: An Appraisal of U.S. Intelligence* (Washington, D.C.: Government Printing Office, 1995), 88.
[7] National Academy of Sciences Panel on DoE Declassification Policy and Practice, Committee on International Security and Arms Control, *Review of the Department of Energy's Response to the Recommendations in the National Research Council Study of DoE Declassification Policy and Practice* (Washington, D.C.: National Academy of Sciences, July 1996), 15-21.
[8] Meridian Corporation, *Classification Policy Study* (Washington, D.C.: Department of Energy, 4 July 1992), 56; National Research Council, *A Review of the Department of Energy Classification Policy and Practice* (Washington, D.C.: National Academy Press, 1995), 90; Department of

Energy, *Openness...Creating a Legacy: Fundamental Classification Policy Review, Draft Report for Public Comment* (Washington, D.C.: Department of Energy, 2 February 1996), 22. In a 1996 follow-up to their 1995 report, the National Research Council explained that an additional problem with FRD is the difficulty of obtaining interagency agreement on which information is to be transclassified and declassified. According to the NRC, "relatively low-ranking staff members from other [non-DoE] agencies may be able to block proposed. . . actions for inappropriate reasons." (National Academy of Sciences Panel on DoE Declassification Policy and Practice, Committee on International Security and Arms Control, *Review of the Department of Energy's Response,* 9).

[9] National Research Council, *A Review of the Department of Energy Classification Policy and Practices,* 48.

[10] Averages for years 1990-1995, as reported by the Information Security Oversight Office.

[11] Among the first was the 1957 Commission on Government Security, which called for the outright abolition of the Confidential level (The Commission on Government Security, *Report of the Commission on Government Security* [Washington, D.C.: Government Printing Office, 1957], 176). Although it did not call for its abolition, the 1970 Seitz Task Force called the Confidential level "probably useless" as applied at the time to research and development (Defense Science Board, Task Force on Secrecy, *Report of the Defense Science Board: Task Force on Secrecy* [Washington, D.C.: Office of the Director of Defense Research and Engineering, 1 July 1970], 10). The initial draft of what would later become Executive Order 12958 also eliminated the Confidential level. However, it was retained out of concerns that (1) the military services, which use a great deal of Confidential information, would be forced to spend enormous sums of money replacing safes so that the information could be protected at the Secret level, and (2) doing so could jeopardize prior or pending prosecutions under the Espionage Act.

[12] The 1957 Commission on Government Security pointed out disagreement over how effectively the need-to-know principle was being implemented (Commission on Government Security, *Report of the Commission on Government Security,* 313). By 1984, ISOO found "widespread indifference" to the principle (Information Security Oversight Office, *Annual Report to the President for FY 1984* [Washington, D.C.: Information Security Oversight Office, 1985], 23). In 1994 the Joint Security Commission stated that the classification system "does not adequately enforce the `need-to-know` principle" (Joint Security Commission, *Redefining Security,* 8).

[13] Controlled Access Program Oversight Committee (CAPOC), Community Management Staff official, interview by Commission staff, June 1996; Office of the Under Secretary of Defense for Policy Support officials, interview by Commission staff, June 1996.

[14] This Commission requested information from all thirteen Cabinet-level departments and 34 agencies thought most likely to generate sensitive unclassified information. Of the twelve departments and 32 agencies that responded, nine departments and 30 agencies stated that they generate such information.

[15] Office of the Assistant Deputy to the Under Secretary of Defense (Policy) for Policy Support officials, interview by Commission staff, 22 May 1996.

[16] A 1956 report commissioned by the Secretary of Defense recommended that DoD reduce the number of individuals with the authority to classify information as Top Secret (Department of Defense, Committee on Classified Information, *Report to the Secretary of Defense by the Committee on Classified Information* [Washington, D.C.: Department of Defense, 8 November 1956], 6). The 1985 Stilwell Commission report called for "further reductions" in the number of Original Classification Authorities at the Department of Defense (The Commission to Review DoD Security Policies and Practices, *Keeping the Nation's Secrets: A Report to the Secretary of Defense by the Commission to Review DoD Security Policies and Practices* [Washington, D.C.: Department of Defense, 1985], 49).

[17] Information Security Oversight Office, *1995 Report to the President,* 11.

[18] Average for years 1990-1995, as reported by the Information Security Oversight Office.

[19] Information Security Oversight Office official, interview by Commission staff, June 1996.

[20] The General Accounting Office first stated in 1979 that the practice of allowing personnel to classify derivatively through the use of guides "seriously weakens control over the classification process because it allows thousands of individuals who are not designated as classifiers to be involved in the process without being personally accountable" (General Accounting Office, *Improved Executive Branch Oversight Needed for the Government's National Security Information Classification Program*, LCD-78-125 [Washington, D.C.: General Accounting Office, 9 March 1979], iv).

[21] Steven Garfinkel, letter to Chairman Lee Hamilton, Subcommittee on Europe and the Middle East, Committee on Foreign Affairs, Washington, D.C., 4 August 1989. The letter responded to inquiries by Chairman Hamilton concerning the operation of the classification system.

[22] Morton Halperin, meeting with Commission staff, 19 October 1995.

[23] The Joint Security Commission argued that a "less complicated system can help correct the current approach that has led to classifying too much at too high a level and for too long" (*Redefining Security*, 10).

[24] Steven Garfinkel, Director, Information Security Oversight Office, stated at a May 5, 1982, congressional hearing that "about 5 percent of the documents [ISOO] review[s] clearly don't merit classification" (House Committee on Government Operations, *Security Classification Policy and Executive Order 12356, Committee on Government Operations,* 97th Cong., 2d sess., 12 August 1982, 44). In 1992 ISOO reported that its review of nearly 11,000 classified documents revealed that only 1.5 percent should not have been classified, and the need for another 1.7 percent was "questionable" (Information Security Oversight Office, *Report to the President for FY 1992* [Washington, D.C.: Information Security Oversight Office, 1993], 9). In 1996 Director Garfinkel stated to Commission staff that the problem of unnecessary classification ranges between 5 and 10 percent "at most" (interview by Commission staff, 15 May 1996).

[25] Inspector General, Department of Defense, *White Paper: Classification and Declassification Within the Department of Defense* (Washington, D.C.: Department of Defense, May 1995), letter of transmittal and page i.

[26] Subcommittee on Civil and Constitutional Rights, House Committee on the Judiciary and Subcommittee on Civil Service, Committee on Post Office and Civil Service *Preliminary Joint Staff Study on the Protection of National Secrets,* 48.

[27] Thomas P. Coakley, ed., *C³I: Issues of Command and Control* (Washington, D.C.: National Defense University Press, 1991), 94.

[28] National Research Council, *A Review of the Department of Energy Classification Policy and Practices*, 89.

[29] National Academy of Sciences, *A Review of the Department of Energy's Response,* 6.

[30] President, Presidential Decision Directive 29, "Security Policy Coordination" (15 September 1994), 2.

[31] When created by President Carter's Executive Order 12065, the ISOO was placed within the General Services Administration and received general policy direction from the National Security Council. In FY 1995, the ISOO was moved to the Office of Management and Budget (OMB) as a result of an attempt within Congress to place the office within the NSC—a move that sparked concerns that the ISOO's oversight activities would conflict with the NSC's policymaking role. However, some OMB officials strongly opposed having the ISOO based within the OMB, and Congress in turn transferred the ISOO to NARA beginning in FY 1996. During FY 1996, the ISOO operated on funds earmarked for NARA, which did not receive any additional appropriation to accommodate the ISOO's activities.

[32] Steven Garfinkel, telephone conversation with Commission staff, August 1996.

[33] The three most recent executive orders on classification (Executive Orders 12065, 12356, and 12958) highlight this particularly well. All three orders directed agencies to establish security education and/or training programs to ensure their implementation, but none specified that classification management (to be distinguished from security generally) be included in this training.

[34] Information Security Oversight Office, *Annual Report for FY 1992* (Washington, D.C.: Information Security Oversight Office, 1993), 4.

III Common Sense Declassification and Public Access

Why Public Access Matters

In a democratic society, the citizens both choose their governors and are the governed. This dual role of the public has produced a tension between the need for secrecy and the need to keep government accountable. Broad access to information is critical for government officials to shape well-reasoned policies and for the public to monitor those it has elected to act on its behalf. However, expansion of the Government's national security bureaucracy since the end of World War II and the closed environment in which it has operated have outpaced attempts by the Congress and the public to oversee that bureaucracy's activities.

As Chapter II made clear, core secrets do exist that need the highest level of protection. There is widespread agreement, even by those who most vigorously support broad declassification, that there are many types of government information that will always require zealous protection—for example, sources whose exposure would jeopardize human life; signals intelligence or imagery, the loss of which would profoundly hinder the capability to collect data; information that would assist chemical, biological, or nuclear proliferators; and details about special military capabilities. However, these types of information are only a portion of the universe of information that now is classified. This chapter focuses on the rest of the classified world, including policy, analysis, factual, and historical data, and how to ensure its public availability when it no longer needs protection.

Ensuring public access to information that does not require protection is a key to striking the balance between secrecy and the openness that is central to the proper functioning of this country's political institutions. There has been a gradual but encouraging shift in recent years on the part of many agencies that use classified information toward declassifying and releasing more of that information to the public. Some agencies realize that better relations with the public can grow from easier access to agency records that no longer need protection. Openness can also demonstrate to the world, especially newly-emerging democracies that are beginning to open their own countries' archives, the strength of our free institutions.

Other benefits flow from moving information that no longer needs protection out of the classification system. Broad access to information promotes better decisions. It permits public understanding of the activities of government and promotes more informed debate and accountability. It increases the Government's ability to respond to criticism and justify its actions to the public. It makes possible the free exchange of scientific information and encourages new discoveries that foster economic growth. By allowing a better understanding of our history, it provides opportunities to learn lessons from the past, and it makes it easier to quash unfounded speculation about the

Government's past actions. Reducing the amount of information in the classification system allows for better management and cost controls of that system and increases respect for the information that needs to stay protected. Greater access thus provides ground in which the public's faith in its government can flourish.

Chapter II addressed the problem of overclassification of information at the beginning of its life cycle. This chapter focuses on what happens at the end of that life cycle, discussing recent attempts to provide more public access as well as the barriers that persist for effective ways to declassify. It makes recommendations designed to ensure that, in making declassification decisions, agencies use resources efficiently, apply accurate data in making judgments about release, and interact effectively with the public. The Commission supports the appropriate protection of truly sensitive information while establishing wiser ways to handle the rest. In short, this chapter is about managing declassification consistent with principles of good government.

Promising Developments: Declassification Success Stories

There has been notable progress by agencies in providing public access to government information that no longer requires the protection of the classification system. For example, public release of the VENONA intercepts in 1995 provided an unprecedented glimpse into the world of codes and codebreaking and revealed new insights into controversial aspects of our nation's history. In 1992, the National Reconnaissance Office's (NRO's) existence was declassified and in 1996, the NRO for the first time publicly announced the planned launch of a reconnaissance satellite. The NRO's stated goal in ending its policy of keeping such launches secret was: "We want to spend our resources protecting the things that are worth protecting."[1] The Intelligence Community also has begun declassifying under Executive Order 12951, which was

In addition to the key insights furnished by release of the VENONA intercepts, declassified information has played a central role in our understanding of, or actions in, times of crisis. For example:

- The declassification of U-2 photographs of Soviet missiles in 1962 shortly after they were taken allowed their use as a centerpiece of U.S. efforts to resolve the Cuban Missile Crisis;

- Nearly thirty years after the end of World War II, revelations of signals intercepts and codebreaking successes (the Ultra project in the European theater and Magic in the Far East) produced a fundamental re-evaluation of the conduct of that conflict; and

- Public release in 1995 of imagery demonstrated evidence of genocide in Srebrenica that helped garner international support for U.S. diplomatic efforts in Bosnia.

issued under the leadership of Vice President Gore, imagery collected from satellites. The eventual result is to be the public release of over 886,000 satellite reconnaissance images (some of which the Government has posted already on the Internet).

In recent years, agency task forces have searched for, reviewed, and declassified large volumes of records on issues involving past government actions about which there is great public interest. After passage of the President John F. Kennedy Assassination Records Collection Act of 1992 and the establishment of a Review Board to monitor implementation of the law, agencies undertook intensive searches for and reviews of relevant records. The result has been to make publicly available over three million pages of previously secret records related to that key event.

In response to the creation of a Senate select committee to investigate the fate of Americans who were prisoners of war or missing in action in past military conflicts, the Department of Defense (DoD) in 1991 established a Central Documentation Office that began a process of coordinating broad searches, declassification reviews, and public releases of records. In 1993, the DoD also established a task force to assist the Gulf War Illnesses Advisory Committee by locating, declassifying, and posting on an Internet site records that might help explain the physical ailments reported by veterans of the Persian Gulf War. Some critics have charged that neither of these two projects has yet released all relevant records. The Gulf War project also came under scrutiny when intelligence reports that had been placed on-line were removed but later reinstated after their removal drew complaints. Nevertheless, both have succeeded in making much more declassified information available to the public than would otherwise be the case.

Agencies have shown initiative in providing public access in other ways. In recent years, the State Department has worked closely with a statutorily created historical advisory committee to more regularly review, declassify, and publish records on key foreign policy events for its *Foreign Relations of the United States* series. In 1996, the Defense Department and the Central Intelligence Agency (CIA) each established formal working relationships with advisory groups of prominent scholars to obtain advice on their declassification efforts, although it is not yet clear what the continuing impact these citizen committees ultimately will have on those agencies' public access policies.

In addition, the Department of Energy (DoE) in 1993 began an "Openness Initiative" to increase public confidence in the DoE and to make more declassified information publicly available. The DoE also established an advisory committee in response to reports of government-sponsored human radiation experiments. In 1995, that advisory committee issued a comprehensive report and assembled over 1.6 million pages of relevant records from numerous sources, most of which had not been easily accessible before; these records are now available at the National Archives and on the Internet as well. Another consequence of the DoE's attempts at greater openness was that an environmental group that had been on the verge of suing the Department (and that had sued it in the past) decided to refrain from legal action and give the Department additional time to respond to the problems it had identified.

Unnecessary Secrecy Persists

Although some agencies show promising signs of more openness than in the past, public access to government information that no longer needs protection is not yet universally recognized as an important agency mission that deserves priority. Despite the increased access to government information that resulted from the projects just described, it is important to understand that none was created solely due to agency initiative; all were compelled by pressure on the Executive Branch from the public, the media, and the Congress. Where government activities have stayed shrouded in secrecy, sometimes for many years, that secrecy at times has contributed to widespread public speculation of government wrongdoing. Sometimes this has resulted in the eventual declassification of records, but often the perception that the Government is using classification to hide its misdeeds has already taken root and is difficult to dispel.[2] Public mistrust of the reasons information is classified is illustrated by a 1994 DoD survey, which found that a majority of Americans believe that "given the world situation," too much information still is kept secret by the Government.[3]

> According to a former government historian, weather reports produced by an aide to General Eisenhower during World War II were still classified thirty years after the fact.

Skepticism about agency motives can also arise from the way in which an agency declassifies and publicly disseminates information. When agencies selectively declassify only a handful of records on an event but do not make entire files available, it can lead to the impression that the Government is more interested in self-justification of its actions than in a full airing of the historical record.

Secrecy is a tool that can help government officials reach policy goals, but too often a secret can become self-perpetuating even after the reason for maintaining it has been achieved or abandoned. Solving the problem of the growing backlog of classified documents, discussed in more detail below, requires the acceptance of declassification as a routine government activity. The dictionary defines "classify" as simply "to organize or arrange according to class or category." Thus, providing public access to government records that no longer need protection, or "declassifying," means finding sensible, cost-effective, and routine ways to separate the categories of materials no longer warranting protection from those needing to stay secret. One historian active in recent debates about the appropriate boundaries of government secrecy has observed that "the whole process of security classification itself is a Cold War artifact; we need to distinguish what of the process can be jettisoned and what we need to keep."[4]

> Journalist and former hostage Terry Anderson filed FOIA requests for agency records on his capture and release. After waiting many months for responses to his requests, he received copies of his own press clips that had been kept in classified government files. Nearly everything else in those files was denied to him as still secret.

Sensible Risk Management

Chapter II discussed the Joint Security Commission's (JSC's) recommendation in 1994 that agencies practice sensible risk management as an integral part of deciding whether information should be classified. Although many government officials claim to practice risk management in making declassification decisions, their analytic approach often more closely resembles absolute risk avoidance. Risk management, as applied to declassification, means that the information at issue is assessed to determine what harm is likely to occur from release. There is some highly sensitive information that requires zero tolerance of risk from its potential release. However, other information that required protection at an earlier point in its life cycle may later be amenable to a risk assessment that would result in a decision that the information can be released.

Thus, applying risk management principles to declassification is closely tied to the type of information involved; not all classified information should be treated alike when it is being considered for release. For example, information that would encourage nuclear proliferation needs careful protection. However, a decades-old report analyzing a foreign country's political situation or in which policymakers are advised of possible options may not pose any risk to national security from public release. Evaluation of the potential harm from release based on current and realistic risk assessments is critical to managing declassification well.

Continuing Barriers to Declassification and Public Access

Agencies are making more declassified information available than before, and in the process they are discovering positive aspects to increased public knowledge about what they do. However, it remains very difficult for the public, and sometimes for the Congress, to get access to information about certain government activities when information related to them has been protected at some point by classification. Scholars, historians, journalists, scientists, and individual citizens cite many problems in obtaining access to even very old or widely known information because it is still classified. Many who try to use the Freedom of Information Act (FOIA)—even to get information in government files about themselves—routinely wait up to several years before they receive a response. Even when records are eventually released, they are often riddled with excisions (frequently called "redactions"). Outside the FOIA context, scientists who wish to exchange information with their colleagues have been threatened at times with the loss of their clearances or instructed by government officials not to discuss certain matters that an agency asserts are classified, even though the information in question is based on what already is publicly known.[5]

> Information Security Oversight Office Director Steven Garfinkel has observed that "the major failing of all our security classification systems up to now has been the absence of a viable declassification program that could adequately address the huge buildup of older, permanently valuable classified records."

Despite some successes in increasing public access, the vast majority of classified information, including many very old records that might provide key insights into our nation's history, remains inaccessible to the public. Sensible, cost-effective processes do not currently exist to distinguish between the material that would and that would not harm national security if it were released. Now, it simply is easier to classify information and keep it classified than to move it out of the system when it no longer requires protection.

Persistent declassification problems include:

- How to handle the huge amount of classified material accumulating across the Government;
- Limited resources and lack of expertise within agencies to implement effective, sensible, and well-managed public access policies;
- Internal agency resistance to mandated declassification responsibilities;
- No identification, to date, of a method or process to protect our most sensitive secrets in a cost-effective way;
- A legacy of poor agency records management of information; and
- A lack of leadership insistence that recordkeeping and declassification should be priority agency missions.

Ensuring proper and timely public access to still-classified government records requires focus, discipline, and good records management. These fundamentals are particularly important given the impact of new technologies on the creation of records, making it all the more critical that the Government find sensible and cost-effective ways to act in this area. As some in government already recognize, the basic challenge is to simultaneously manage two transitions: from paper-based to electronic records systems, and from performing declassification on an ad hoc basis to doing so in systematic, efficient, and cost-effective ways.[6] Recognizing these challenges is the first step but, as described below, most agencies have not yet begun to adequately address them.

Declassification Under Past Executive Orders

Declassification has been addressed in some degree of detail in every national security executive order since President Eisenhower's Executive Order 10501. Certain requirements have been imposed repeatedly on agencies with the intent of ensuring that records no longer needing protection were regularly moved out of the classification system and made available to the public. Chief among these requirements, as illustrated in Table 1, are:

- Identifying and marking declassification dates or events when classifying;
- Portion marking to indicate varying degrees of sensitivity within records;
- A balancing test directing that information be declassified if the public interest outweighs the need to protect it;
- Establishing appeals processes and oversight structures;
- Establishing schedules (of time periods ranging from ten to thirty years) for systematically requiring a record's declassification review or release based on the type of information it contains; and
- Providing mandatory review procedures under which agencies or the public can request declassification of individual records.

However, when agencies perceive that implementation of these key elements is largely optional, experience has shown that the goal of promoting more effective declassification is not achieved. For example, Executive Order 12356 instructed that rather than assigning a date or event for declassification at the time a record was created, a new marking—"Originating Agency's Determination Required"—could be used. When OADR was applied to a record, no scheduled deadlines for declassification review applied. OADR soon became the default marking that classifiers across the Government used as a declassification instruction.[7] By 1992, 95 percent of all documents classified that year were marked OADR.[8] Executive Order 12356 also allowed, but did not require, systematic declassification. Agencies thus devoted few resources to it, contributing to a vast growth in the amount of classified records.

Table 1: Provisions in Past Executive Orders Promoting Public Access to Information

PROVISIONS	Executive Orders					
	10501	10964	11652	12065	12356	12958
Declassification date or event on document at time of classification	YES	YES	YES	YES	Optional	YES
Portion marking of paragraphs in a document	NO	NO	YES	YES	YES	YES
Balancing test of the public's right to know and need to protect	NO	NO	NO	YES	NO	NO
Appeals or oversight structure	YES	NO	YES	YES	YES	YES
Scheduled automatic declassification review or release	NO	YES	YES	YES	NO	YES
Formal mandatory review procedures	NO	NO	YES	YES	YES	YES

Executive Order 12958: A Renewed Focus on Declassification

In 1995, with the stated goal of "seeking to bring the system for classifying, safeguarding, and declassifying national security information into line with our vision of American democracy in the post-Cold War world," President Clinton signed Executive Order 12958. Under this Order, records over 25 years old will be presumed declassified beginning in the year 2000 unless an agency acts to keep them classified based on an exemption provided in the Order. Agencies were given five years to complete their review of these older records, and in the Order's first year were to complete a declassification review of 15 percent of the records subject to the Order.

Although agencies were required to submit declassification plans and proposals for the file series they intended to exempt from automatic release, not all submitted timely plans or provided many details about how they intend to implement the Order.

Moreover, without feedback on those plans from the National Security Council or the Information Security Oversight Office (to which the plans were submitted), agencies have proceeded to implement those plans as originally drafted even if they might not fully reflect the letter or spirit of the Order.

In addition, the Federal Bureau of Investigation (FBI) and the DoE received waivers from compliance with the automatic declassification provisions of the Order in exchange for their assurances that they would, on an expedited basis, undertake comprehensive reviews for possible release of their older records that are not classified pursuant to an executive order but nevertheless are unavailable to the public. However, to date no FBI records have been released under this agreement. The waiver for the FBI was based on its claim that privacy interests preclude public access to its older law enforcement records (although the Privacy Act does not apply to records that have been deposited at the National Archives, which is where many FBI records over 25 years old reside). The DoE's waiver was based on the fact that most of its records are not classified under an executive order but separately under the Atomic Energy Act. Thus, the FBI and the DoE have numerous records in which the public is interested that are not subject to the declassification provisions of this Order at all.

Declassification under the Order in other agencies is occurring slowly. Many agencies have chosen to start with their least sensitive records. Others are reviewing and declassifying their most sensitive documents first, reasoning that if the Order's five-year deadline is not met, the remaining records potentially subject to automatic declassification will present a lower risk of damage upon release. One year after the Order took effect, certain agencies had done almost nothing to comply with its declassification provisions. On the other hand, within a year after the Order was issued the Commerce Department already had reviewed and released nearly all of its classified records subject to the Order (although its situation is not completely comparable to that of other agencies subject to the Order because it classifies very little information in the first place).

The President's stated intent when signing Executive Order 12958 was that its provisions should result in "large-scale declassification [that] won't be dependent on the availability of individuals to conduct a line-by-line review." Nevertheless, most agencies indicate that they intend to implement the Order by doing the costly line-by-line review (discussed more fully later in this chapter) that the Order sought to avoid. This approach is driven in part by the discovery that file descriptions only vaguely or sometimes incorrectly describe the contents and their classification levels. It also is being used because line-by-line review is the only way most agencies have ever processed records for public release.

Declassification and the Freedom of Information Act

The link between the FOIA and declassification of records is not always understood by government officials responsible for implementing the declassification provisions of executive orders. The FOIA originally was intended to serve primarily as a means of access to individual, relatively current records of the Government, not to large numbers of decades-old records of permanent historic value. However, due in part to the failure of agencies over the years to implement executive order provisions for regular release of records that no longer need protection, the FOIA by default became (along with mandatory declassification review under executive orders) one of the few means available to the public to get access to those materials.

The primary experience most agencies have had with declassification has been through conducting line-by-line reviews of records in response to FOIA requests. The FOIA establishes a statutory right for any person to obtain copies of Federal agency records and is the primary vehicle for the public to obtain access to government records. Thirty years after its enactment, the FOIA's continuing significance and vitality stem from the legally enforceable rights it creates for requesters and the presumption of release that it establishes, limited only by the exemptions it provides that agencies may invoke to deny access.

However, requesters and agencies alike find the FOIA an imperfect tool for obtaining the declassification of records. Effective use of the FOIA requires considerable patience and, often, significant financial and legal resources. Problems posed by the FOIA's current use as a primary mechanism for declassifying records include:

* Long delays that regularly occur and often stretch to years before agencies answer requests;
* Lack of public access to clear guidance on how files are kept, as well as to indexes to those files, which would encourage the filing of more specific requests and assist agencies in locating responsive records;
* Broad application of the FOIA's exemptions, particularly the interpretation of the Act's national security exemption (which allows only the withholding of information "properly classified" under an executive order); and
* Inadequate support of senior officials for agency FOIA operations, including a lack of resources to respond to the huge volume of FOIA requests filed each year.[9]

Some archivists and historians believe that an overreliance on the FOIA as the means for declassification of historical records also hinders effective research. For example, the FOIA process makes individual records available to the person who requested them, but does not guarantee that the declassified records will be more widely released because there is no requirement that copies be placed in agency reading rooms, on-line, or at the National Archives. Additionally, the process of retrieving and reviewing individual records rather than declassifying entire record groups can skew the historical context of the records that are released.

In enacting the Electronic Freedom of Information Amendments (EFOIA), signed into law on October 2, 1996, the Congress and the President took a step toward improving agency responsiveness to FOIA requests. These amendments clarify that the Act applies to records in electronic as well as paper format, while also giving agencies relief from some of the Act's administrative requirements. In the words of one of the Act's sponsors, the EFOIA is intended to "deliver common-sense efficiency and government accountability to the American people."[10] Still, because of the sheer volume of classified material that has accumulated in agencies over the years, these recent amendments will not wholly cure the FOIA's shortcomings for public access to classified records.

How Much Is Still Classified?

The amount of classified material that the Federal Government has accumulated, much of which is more than a quarter-century old, is enormous. To comply with the mandate in Executive Order 12958 to process for automatic declassification all documents over 25 years old by the year 2000, agencies for the first time are comprehensively surveying their classified records holdings. In the process, they are discovering more and more records than were previously thought to exist. Many of these have never been evaluated to determine whether they are of permanent value (the threshold under the Federal Records Act for which agency records must be preserved for posterity) and are thus required to be processed for declassification under the Order. For example, the Washington National Records Center, a regional government storage facility, has between 4.3 and 5 million pages of documents that agencies have never assessed to determine whether they are permanent records.[11]

As Figure 2 illustrates, based on data provided by individual agencies, the Commission estimates that there are over 1.5 billion pages of records 25 years old and older still classified by the Federal Government.[12] Of this amount, agencies currently plan to review less than one-half—approximately 719 million pages—under the automatic declassification provisions of the Order, meaning that agencies are exempting from automatic declassification over three quarters of a billion pages. A little over a year after Executive Order 12958 took effect, agencies had declassified about 57 million pages, less than one-tenth of what they had identified for review. Unless current agency plans change, public access to the hundreds of millions of exempted pages will occur either through the systematic declassification procedures required by Executive Order 12958 (which have yet to be established in most agencies), or through the current but inadequate system of individual requests filed under the Order's mandatory review process or the FOIA.

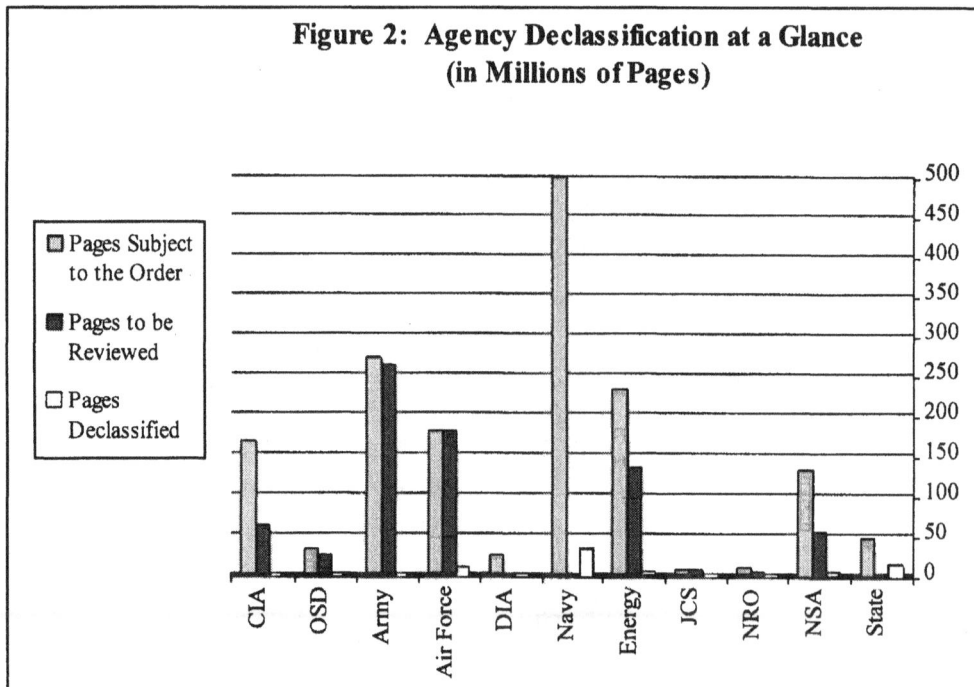

Figure 2: Agency Declassification at a Glance (in Millions of Pages)

Although these numbers seem overwhelming, it is important to understand that they are only estimates based on initial surveys of the numbers of file boxes that appear to contain classified records. For example, unclassified records often are commingled with classified material when stored, or an entire box may be marked as classified even if it contains only a single classified document. In addition, many classified documents have numerous attachments that are themselves unclassified. Many older records are duplicates of others: copies may already have been declassified. Some file boxes turn out to be partly empty. Some boxes contain other items, such as shoes, plastic bags, office supplies, and drug samples. In one case, a file box was found to contain a mock hand grenade used for military exercises. While the review task facing agencies under Executive Order 12958 is significant, these insights into how records actually are stored indicate that agency estimates may overstate the amount of permanent records that needs to be reviewed. Thus, the ultimate declassification burden on agencies may turn out to be less onerous than the numbers currently suggest.

How Long Does It Take Before Information Is Declassified?

So large an amount of information has stayed classified for so long partly because of the past failure of agencies to employ adequate and reliable means to move some of it out of the classification system when it no longer needs protection. The requirement in Executive Order 12958 that classifiers mark documents with a date or event for future declassification is a step toward dealing with this problem. However, past executive orders also have included this requirement, with little apparent effect on the duration of classification past the point it is required. One reason the requirement of denoting declassification dates or events seems not to have worked in the past is that many government officials simply resist implementing it, arguing that it takes a "crystal ball" to determine when information will no longer need protection. They may also resist because they have not been trained in how to make such judgments or because such requirements are rarely enforced, making it easy for them not to do even the minimal extra work that the Orders have required.

However, some who regularly create and use classified records understand that there is a life cycle for such materials; these officials acknowledge that there is a predictable "expiration date" for much classified information that can be determined when the information is created, based on experience with similar types of data. For example, certain portions of military plans requiring a high level of secrecy before an operation takes place often can be declassified shortly afterward because those elements of the plan have become common knowledge. Similarly, much information dealing with foreign policy may require initial classification because the matters discussed or identities of those involved are sensitive, but at some point in the future—ranging from months to years—the information may no longer need protection. In addition, even when declassification dates have been placed on records, they rarely have been enforced when that date has passed. Moreover, those markings can be invalidated by a future executive order, as occurred when Executive Order 12065 was replaced in 1982 by Executive Order 12356, causing the effort that had been expended under the previous Order to assign declassification dates essentially a waste of time and money.

How Much Does Declassification Cost?

Closely tied to an agency's decision on how to implement declassification procedures is the cost of those procedures. Declassification can be very expensive, especially for line-by-line reviews of records that some agencies estimate cost a dollar or more per page.[13] Given the huge numbers of pages now awaiting declassification review under Executive Order 12958, other approaches to declassification besides line-by-line review are being considered.

Declassifying records without reviewing them line-by-line is commonly referred to as "bulk" declassification, a process often misunderstood to mean the release of records without any review of their content at all. A more accurate description of this process as it is used by trained archivists is "high-volume review." This approach involves the use of reliable survey techniques to accurately determine the contents of record groups and to assess whether they contain material that would damage national security if released. The age of the records, their subject matter, and the extent to which they were properly and accurately stored and indexed all contribute to how that review is conducted. In contrast to the costs associated with line-by-line review, the National Archives estimated that in 1992 the average cost to declassify using reliable sampling techniques was about seven cents per page.

Recent experience has shown that high-volume review for declassification can be a valid, reliable, and cost-effective way to process older historical records for potential public release. In 1994, President Clinton issued Executive Order 12937, ordering the declassification of millions of pages at the National Archives dating back to World War II and some as recent as the Vietnam War. After assessing the content and sensitivity of the records, the National Archives and agencies jointly identified and excluded from release file groups that contained highly sensitive material. Through this high volume review, 40 million pages were declassified, with no indication that any information still needing protection was inadvertently released in that process. Moreover, these materials were processed for release at an average cost of less than $400 per million pages—a fraction of a cent per page.[14] In addition, as mentioned earlier in this chapter, Executive Order 12951's mandate to review and declassify satellite imagery is another vehicle by which classified materials that at one time were never expected to be viewed by the public are being made available in cost-effective ways that do not risk current methods of collecting sensitive information.

> **Declassification Can Save Money**
>
> The Department of the Air Force found that it could save millions by declassifying information about space shuttle flights that carried Air Force research and development equipment. The savings came from eliminating information and physical systems security that were unnecessary in an unclassified environment.

Resource issues have been a primary factor in the slow pace at which agencies have implemented automatic and systematic programs for declassification as required by Executive Order 12958. Many officials who were tasked by their agency to implement those provisions of the Order attribute their delay in doing so to their agency's failure to earmark new funds for this purpose. Moreover, congressional oversight committees have scrutinized agency budget requests and limited the amount that can be spent on declassification until the cost estimates on which those requests are based were adequately justified.

Yet resource availability alone does not explain why some agencies conduct successful declassification programs while others do not. Some agencies have shown that creative and effective implementation of declassification need not depend upon receipt of additional funds. For example, in August 1996, the Department of the Air Force won the Hammer Award (presented as part of the Clinton Administration's National Performance Review) for the efficient and creative implementation of its declassification program. It achieved these results not through an infusion of new funds but by finding the resources needed through other means, including using computers discarded by other offices, staffing the project with reservists, and developing internal computerized training and guidance.

New technologies hold promise as efficient tools for less costly declassification. The National Security Agency found that simply by implementing basic automation tools in its processing of POW/MIA documents, it saved over $330,000 in three and a half years, largely by replacing manual redaction with machine-aided processing.[15] Some agencies, including the State Department, have for some time used computers to aid in declassification and in responding to FOIA requests; others continue to declassify pieces of paper laboriously by hand, using markers or tape to mask text. Many agencies have hired contractors to help them develop technological solutions for reviewing classified documents and, if necessary, redacting them for release, especially for records that exist in electronic, film, or other formats. However, much of this technology is either still in prototype, not fully operational, or is proprietary and cannot be shared with other agencies that would find it useful. Moreover, despite the allure of electronic wizardry, the most advanced technological solution is not always the most efficient and cost-effective one for declassifying.

There are also significant social and political costs when an agency does not routinely implement a means for public access to records that no longer need protection. Not only does the volume of classified documents that needs to be stored, accounted for, and protected continue to grow, but the costs associated with not understanding and learning from past events can be high. For example, historians have noted that it became increasingly difficult after the issuance of the 1982 Executive Order to get access to agency records from the 1940s and 1950s—the critical formative years of the Cold War. Currently, the Office of the Secretary of Defense has at least 30 million pages of records more than 25 years old.[16] The Joint Staff has 4.7 million more pages of classified information from the 1940s and 1950s to be declassified.[17] This backlog of materials means that it is likely to be some time before records from these offices are available to enhance public understanding of the past 50 years.

The Impact of Agency Equities:
Multiple Agency Reviews Mean Multiple Delays

A recurring problem agencies face in conducting declassification reviews concerns how best to declassify documents containing other agencies' "equities" (information originating in those other agencies). The current process for resolving agency equities may be a major obstacle to implementing the automatic declassification provisions of Executive Order 12958. At the State Department, up to one-third of the declassification workload involves referrals of records to and from other agencies.[18] The Defense Intelligence Agency estimates that 90 percent of its product requires referral to outside agencies before a final declassification decision can be made.[19] A related obstacle to timely declassification is how the records of agencies that no longer exist or have merged into others are processed. In such cases, it can be difficult to find anyone willing to devote resources or who has the expertise to evaluate the current sensitivity of such records, with the result that the information is not referred anywhere and often stays classified even though it no longer requires protection.

Current procedures for processing records with multiple equities are expensive and complex. An agency referring classified records to another agency for its review must make copies of the records and specially package and transport them in compliance with security procedures (which, depending on the records' classification levels, can range from sending them via registered mail to having them personally transferred to a government courier by a staff person with appropriate clearances). This process is repeated for every record that contains agency equities and can occur multiple times if a single document needs to be referred to more than one agency and also when that record is returned to the referring agency only partly declassified. At every step of this process, additional costs are incurred. Not only is the process burdensome and costly for agencies, but there are no deadlines by which agencies must respond to such referrals. The result can be lengthy delays before a review is completed and information released to the public (see box below).

Some encouraging steps toward more cooperative, creative ways to deal with agency equities have emerged from the implementation of automatic declassification under Executive Order 12958. Concern that its own equities might not be protected led the CIA to initiate the Remote Archive Capture project, designed to reproduce on CD-ROMs all classified documents at the presidential libraries for distribution to agencies likely to have equities in the records. Similarly, concerns that nuclear-related information classified under the Atomic Energy Act is embedded, but not identified as such, in

---

Access Delayed Can Be Access Denied

A journalist who filed a FOIA request with the Department of State in 1984 seeking information on oil production in Saudi Arabia during the 1970s finally received a reply in 1993 — nine years later. That reply consisted of a one-page chart that the State Department had retrieved and referred to the originating agency, the Department of Energy. In 1989, the DoE sent it to the Central Intelligence Agency for further review. It was then returned by the CIA to the DoE in 1993, and finally sent to the journalist with half of its numbers deleted and a notation on the document that it had actually been declassified in 1992. After nearly a decade of waiting, the journalist had long since moved on to another story.

documents that were classified under an executive order has prompted at the DoE an understanding of the need for interagency coordination and communication in declassification. The DoE has agreed to provide comprehensive guidance and training to other agencies to help them recognize such information and to speed resolution of any questions so that records containing such sensitive information can be processed more easily.

Thus, interagency use of accurate and up-to-date declassification guidance is one way to streamline the process of resolving agency equities. Some agencies already provide the National Archives with such guidance, and National Archives' officials, in turn, have encouraged agencies to share with each other any guidance they use in making declassification decisions. With some exceptions, agencies have been slow to embrace this approach, partly because some seem to be unfamiliar with using even their own agency's guides. This reluctance also seems due to a belief that others will not understand how to use the guides that do exist. However, the DoE's recent experience indicates that some types of information can be protected better if other agencies are better informed, through guides or through training, about how to recognize sensitive information.

The Current State of Agency Records Management

When agencies properly manage records containing national security information based on a life cycle concept, it creates the organizational and contextual framework for efficient declassification. In order for agencies to make informed decisions as to what records can be made publicly available, there must be adequate and accurate information available on (1) what records exist and where they are located; and (2) the contents of collections. Neglect of records management has resulted in a widespread lack of this information.

The link between poor records management and the ability of agencies to provide access to the huge backlog of still-classified records became apparent as agencies began to take steps to comply with Executive Order 12958's automatic declassification requirements. For many agencies, it is impossible to retrieve information promptly, to make informed decisions about whether it needs continued protection, and to refer back to previous declassification decisions. Together, these result in duplicative and inconsistent releases of information.

A survey of offices within the Defense Department found that the standard instructions providing records management guidance for all agency employees were in almost every case unknown to all except the secretarial staff.

Lack of access to government records no longer needing protection is inextricably tied to the legacy of poor records management practices across the Government. Unorganized files and vague, unreliable, or nonexistent finding aids have impeded the task of locating and identifying documents subject to declassification under Executive Order 12958. Few agencies have devoted significant time, attention, and resources to good records management and to systematic declassification reviews of older records; as a result, many are unfamiliar with basic declassification techniques and do not have either personnel trained in these processes or an infrastructure to support effective and efficient declassification. As a consequence, agencies have been compelled to conduct a more complicated search for records than the Order's provisions seem to have anticipated. As one government official observed in connection with the issuance of Executive Order 12958, agencies "must integrate classification management more closely with information and records management. If we had been following that advice from the beginning, the tasks ahead of us would be far, far simpler to accomplish."[20]

Current and former government officials, scholars, and records management experts all cite the poor state of the Government's records management practices as a major impediment to declassifying the millions of pages of still-secret older records. Records management principles must also be clearly defined and implemented in order for agencies to manage records created using emerging technologies. If, as one report concluded, "the goal must be to reduce the volume of classified information before it arrives in the archives, not after," then the long-term solution is to make records management and declassification requirements a routine daily administrative practice, just as classification is now.[21]

The Federal Records Act grants the National Archives substantial authority over government records management, but in the past it has not consistently exercised that authority. Under that law, the National Archives has the authority to require all agencies to review their records and to establish the conditions under which they must be turned over to the National Archives when they are no longer needed for current agency operations. The Archivist's consent also is required before any agency can destroy records. The primary mission of the National Archives is to ensure that the Government's permanently valuable records are kept and, where possible, made available to the public. In order to exercise these functions and ensure active coordination and oversight of agency declassification, storage, and disposition of Federal records, the National Archives must—although it has not always done so in the past—exert a strong leadership role within the Government. To do so requires the ongoing commitment of top leadership at the National Archives and also will require that it have adequate resources to exercise this function. In a strategic plan issued in July 1996, the National Archives already has indicated its intent to "work in partnership" with agencies to implement classification and declassification policies and to develop records management programs based on the information's life cycle. This approach can be a significant step toward improving the current state of records management in the Government.[22]

> One individual familiar with the Federal Government's track record for implementing records management practices observed that in many agencies, records management employees are seen as less important to the agency's mission than those who order supplies.

Agency Attitudes Affect Public Access

Also crucial to ensuring due attention to public access at the end of the life cycle of government information is the attitude of those who implement records and information policy. Many agency personnel are implementing declassification programs under Executive Order 12958 in innovative ways. Others, unfortunately, appear more resourceful in finding ways to evade their declassification responsibilities. For example, at one interagency meeting of officials charged with implementing Executive Order 12958, much of the discussion focused on ways to interpret the Order's language to escape its portion marking requirement and to apply its automatic declassification exemptions in ways designed to avoid scheduled declassification in the future.

An example of how the access system can remain dominated by security concerns, despite efforts at reform, is the Department of Energy's Office of Declassification. This Office, until recently called the Office of Classification, has the authority to classify information but cannot declassify information. It can only recommend declassification to the Office of Security Affairs, which makes the final decision and to which the Office of Declassification reports.

In addition, many officials simply do not see public access as part of their agency's mission. As one agency employee noted in the context of explaining the attitude some officials have toward the FOIA, members of the public who request declassification often are considered "the enemy," those officials view the effort required to process requests as "a disruption" in their duties, and they feel that providing public access "is not what we get paid for."

The differing attitudes that agency employees display toward declassification seem to stem in part from their past training. Those who press hardest for the ability to discard agency records to avoid declassifying them often were trained strictly as security professionals and do not have policy or records management backgrounds or training in history. Thus, they often are not best equipped to assess the significance and value of older records to the public. The focus of their jobs has been to think about how to keep information secret, not how it might be made more available if it no longer needs protection. For example, at one DoE laboratory many applications for classification officer positions (which also involves declassification responsibilities) are from security guards seeking promotion.

However, the DoE has shown an awareness of the need to move beyond a solely security focus in declassification by commissioning a fundamental review to reevaluate standards for what can be declassified. Playing a major role in that process are professionals who have substantive program expertise, not just security officers. This fundamental review was undertaken with support from senior agency officials and included public input. It is a model mechanism other agencies could adopt, in which justifications for declassifying particular categories of information are publicly debated in a thoughtful way without compromising sensitive information, and attitudes toward declassification are reshaped through a comprehensive approach to forming an agency's public access policies.

Not only are agency records management programs weak, but seldom do the various offices involved in public access and declassification communicate or coordinate with each other, either because they are not organized under the same reporting structure or because of turf battles. In many agencies, several offices—including the records management staff, historian's staff, FOIA staff, security personnel, and public affairs officials—are all engaged in some aspect of declassification, but traditionally these persons have not regularly worked together or notified one another of their decisions. Declassification works best when coordination *within* an agency is maintained. Good communication among the different offices that handle classified information, and in some cases the centralization of these offices, can lead to cost savings and efficiency by eliminating redundant functions and better enabling offices to assist one another in making informed decisions.

Public Access in the Information Age

Another issue that needs to be addressed is how to ensure access to records created in other media when the technology itself is obsolete. For example, punch cards on which agencies recorded computer data many years ago are now unreadable because there are no machines available through which the data can be retrieved. Also, a GAO report describes archival problems with certain magnetic tapes that can no longer be read because the hardware no longer exists.[23] These problems have raised concerns for the future management and preservation of electronic records and imagery.

Developing technologies are already playing a key role in aiding declassification and will continue to do so in the future. However, while some have begun to grapple with these issues, there are few coordinated efforts to share technical knowledge, to make systems interactive, or to use these systems across the Government in the most effective manner. Moreover, many agencies are spending large sums independently to obtain technology to assist them in declassification, some of which may prove ineffective or simply duplicative of what exists elsewhere.

Aside from the recent electronic FOIA amendments discussed earlier, the effect of technology on access to classified Federal records has received inadequate attention to date. The use of computers, photocopiers, and fax machines that easily create, copy, and transmit multiple copies of records is constantly growing, and the number of government records generated grows accordingly. Agency databases used for records management, declassification, and tracking of declassified information (where these functions exist) are not interoperable across the Government and sometimes not even within a particular agency. These databases also are not always constructed in ways that make them most useful. For example, the State Department maintains a database it shares with the presidential libraries, listing documents that are still classified; the database has not, however, in the past contained information that a library would find far more useful, such as lists of documents that have been reviewed and released.

The U.S. Army Center of Military History deployed historians to both Somalia and Haiti to ensure the preservation of historically important records created as part of the operations conducted there. These historians collected the information not on paper but in electronic form and then transferred it to a database at Fort Leavenworth, Kansas.

Adequate Oversight Is Crucial to Sensible Declassification Policies

Similar to the problems of inadequate oversight of the classification process discussed in Chapter II, oversight of agency implementation of declassification policies and practices barely exists. Too often, oversight occurs only when a congressional committee is refused access to information or when news reports raise public interest in specific records being withheld from the public because they are classified.

Chapter II's description of the shortcomings of the current mechanisms for oversight of classification applies equally, if not even more so, to declassification. In part, this absence of oversight is due to mixed signals from senior Executive Branch officials about the importance of a vigorous declassification program across the Government.

Most notably, the National Security Council played an active role in the drafting, coordination of agency and public input, and issuance of Executive Order 12958. Since then, however, it has paid little attention to agency implementation of the Order's declassification provisions. Declassification policies will only be as effective as the oversight of the agencies that implement those policies. That oversight must come from the Congress and the highest levels of the Executive Branch.

Recommendations for Improving Declassification and Public Access

> "The time to repair the roof is when the sun is shining."
>
> President John F. Kennedy

As the discussion above demonstrates, the Federal Government's process for dealing with information that no longer needs the protection of the classification system is badly in need of repair. It would be difficult, in fact, to devise a system that works less effectively and at a greater cost than the one now in place. The Commission makes three key recommendations, described below, to remedy the current situation and to avoid repeating past mistakes in the future.

Establishing A National Declassification Center to Coordinate Public Access Policy

Because few agencies see declassification as a primary mission to which resources and expertise should be devoted, timely and cost-effective declassification of older government records of permanent historical value does not occur. As one study observed, agency information security programs have "lost sight of the fact" that the purpose of these programs is twofold: to satisfy the public's right to know and to safeguard information from unauthorized disclosure for national security reasons. That study concluded that "a better balance between the two purposes is needed."[24] For public access and declassification, that "better balance" remains to be achieved across the Government.

The backlog of decades-old classified records described earlier in this chapter is due at least in part to defects in the way the Federal Government is organized to provide access. Declassification procedures are needed that take into account the fact that the resources available for it are finite. There are few incentives for agencies to declassify, little accountability for the ways in which they do provide access, and a lack of cost-effective, sensible procedures to accomplish the release of classified records that no longer need protection.

After examining the practices of a variety of agencies, the Commission concludes that declassification will work most efficiently and effectively when the direction of that activity is centrally coordinated. The process needs to be tied closely to an under-standing of how records are kept, the context in which they were created, and how changing circumstances over time may (or may not) affect their continued need for protection. Those who declassify need to be motivated and to have the expertise, resources, and support to do their jobs well.

Recommendation

The Commission recommends the creation by statute of a central office—a National Declassification Center—at an existing Federal agency such as the National Archives and Records Administration to coordinate national declassification policy and activities. This Center would have the responsibility, authority, and funds sufficient to coordinate, oversee, and implement government declassification activities. The Center would monitor agency declassification programs and provide annual reports on their status to the Congress and the President.

This recommendation establishes within an existing agency a central coordination function lacking in the currently fragmented approach to agency declassification. The logical agency to administer the Center is the National Archives and Records Administration, which is already charged under the Federal Records Act with implementing many of the functions that this Center would perform. The National Archives has an understanding of how records are kept, what needs to be retained, and what can be discarded. The National Archives also can provide expert, educated, and cleared staff to review records; it has successfully done so in the past when agencies have provided sufficiently detailed guidance to do so, and at a minimal cost. (In 1995, the component of the National Archives responsible for declassification reviewed and released 111 million pages of permanently valuable records with a budget of only $2 million.) Because the National Archives has as its primary mission the management and public dissemination of federal records, it is an organization that could administer the Center.

An important aspect of the Center's coordination of declassification across the Executive Branch would be to facilitate exchange among agencies of detailed declassification guidance to resolve the equities concerns discussed earlier in this chapter. Certain categories of highly sensitive information, such as compartmented programs, human intelligence sources, and signals intelligence, could be generally exempted from declassification processing at the Center and from the sharing of declassification guidance except in circumstances where the agency head at his or her discretion may choose to do otherwise. Confidence in the Center's operations would also be enhanced by inclusion of a mechanism for agencies and the public to appeal declassification decisions made under the Center's direction. In creating the Interagency Security Classification Appeals Panel (ISCAP), Executive Order 12958 does provide an appeals mechanism for declassification decisions. However, the ISCAP operates currently in a limited fashion and does not reach all declassification activities across the government. An effective appeals mechanism made a part of the Center should have a broader reach that includes interagency appeals, FOIA requests, and other declassification projects undertaken by agencies.

The Center would perform a variety of services that would streamline declassification and assist agencies in processing records for release. It could, for example, coordinate search and review of records across agencies in response to particular public or congressional interest. However, this recommendation does not envision that the Center's primary function would be the compilation of specialized collections. Rather, the Center's mission would be to help direct government-wide declassification policy and to ensure that agencies follow basic records management and archival principles in implementing declassification. This would include efforts to keep file series intact in order to preserve the evidentiary value of the records and the historical context in which they were created.

> One agency official observed that if individuals can derivatively classify using guides or other documents, there is every reason to believe that, with training, they can in many cases also effectively use guides to derivatively declassify.

Another key function of the Center would be to administer declassification functions on behalf of agencies, assuming the Center was provided resources sufficient to undertake that task. Agencies would be encouraged to send their classified records of permanent historical value to the Center for processing and public release. Thus, agencies would be able to take advantage of the Center's expertise while retaining substantive control over what is declassified through providing detailed guidance to be applied to the records that they send to the Center. Agencies would also be encouraged to detail employees to serve on interagency declassification review teams coordinated by the Center. These teams would, as appropriate based on the sensitivity of the records, conduct joint declassification reviews of records containing multiple agency equities that had been sent to the Center or were still housed at particular agencies.

The Center also would be responsible for establishing and coordinating agency pilot projects for records management and declassification review, especially those involving the use of new technologies. It could serve as a central government clearinghouse for procurement of, specifications for, and use of new declassification and archival storage and retrieval technologies. The Center would promote the coordinated use and sharing among agencies of new technologies, ensure greater interoperability, avoid the procurement of duplicative or proprietary systems, and employ new technologies that respond to researcher demand in cost-effective ways.

Under this approach, agencies likely would need to devote fewer of their program resources to declassification. An initial outlay of funds would be required for the Center's start-up costs and ongoing activities. However, this investment should pay substantial dividends in future years, both in financial savings and with regard to the larger opportunity costs discussed earlier in this report that lack of access to information has generated in the past.

The Commission also believes that an important component of the Center would be a permanent advisory panel to provide for regular public input and advice on agency declassification priorities. This advisory panel could serve as a liaison both with other historical advisory groups established by individual agencies and with the public as well. Experience shows that advisory bodies created by statute and composed of distinguished scholars, researchers, and other members of the public can help expedite the release of records important to informed public debate on significant policy and historical issues. The active participation of advisory bodies can also bring credibility to agency declassification activities, especially those that may be vulnerable to charges that the agency is selectively declassifying only records that show it in a favorable light. The Center could also perform a support and coordination role with agency ombudsman offices, the establishment of which is discussed below.

Clarifying Protection of Sources and Methods Information

The Intelligence Community has made progress in the declassification of certain sensitive sources and methods, such as some limited types of signals intelligence and information about imagery (as well as the images themselves) collected from satellites. A benefit of these efforts has been that such information should not need to be subject to systematic or automatic declassification reviews or require FOIA requests for its public release, thereby saving significant resources.

Underlying many sources and methods claims is the fact that the secret being protected is not the content of the information itself, but instead how it was obtained. Yet the public and historians generally do not care how information was collected; they want to know how it was used and what decisions it informed. The National Security Act of 1947 requires that intelligence sources and methods are to be protected "from unauthorized disclosure." Over the years, this very general language has come to serve as a broad rationale for declining to declassify a vast range of information about the activities of intelligence agencies. Thus, sources and methods information is not treated like other types of classified information. In practice, the sources and methods rationale has become a vehicle for agencies to automatically keep information secret without engaging in the type of harm analysis required by executive orders as a prerequisite to keeping other kinds of information secret. The statutory requirement that sources and methods be protected thus appears at times to have been applied not in a thoughtful way but almost by rote.

Recommendation

The Commission recommends that the use of sources and methods as a basis for the continuing classification of intelligence information be clarified through issuance of an Intelligence Community directive by the Director of Central Intelligence, explaining the appropriate scope of that protection.

Clarifying the scope of and reasons for sources and methods protection would not put at risk information that is truly sensitive, but would remove the ability to apply this rationale to withhold automatically all information that could be construed as relating in any manner, however indirectly, to an intelligence source or method. This recommendation would not in any way diminish the authority of the Director of Central Intelligence to protect sources or methods. A directive could, for example, provide guidance that analysis and information drawn from open sources should not routinely be included in the scope of that protection. Such a directive would be consistent with and would preserve the intent of the National Security Act of 1947 that highly sensitive information—for example, human intelligence—is not placed in jeopardy but continues to get the protection it deserves.

Improving Records Management and Other Agency Practices to Promote Public Access

To address the numerous problems described earlier in this chapter and to achieve the goal of integrating good records management into agency operations, agencies should make that goal a regular responsibility for *every* employee, including senior management and political appointees. Individual accountability could be enhanced through means such as including this responsibility in the evaluation and promotion process. Agencies should devote resources to comprehensive and up-to-date training for all employees in their records management responsibilities. Cooperative working partnerships among agencies and the National Archives are integral to achieving the effective records management programs necessary to ensure that the Government's declassification practices work well.

A significant element currently missing from the declassification activities of many agencies is a vigorous, systematic declassification program. A program based on a comprehensive plan with established deadlines and benchmarks to measure performance would alleviate many of the problems discussed above. Other elements of a successful program include adherence to duration limits for protection of classified information (declassifying documents according to the date or event marked on a document and no later) and the compilation of a regularly updated database of all agency declassification guidance. Another key component is to prioritize records for declassification, based on public input, according to record groups and not according to topics. In the past, declassification by topic has been very costly, and it can skew understanding of the context in which the records were created.

Recommendation

The Commission recommends that agencies better structure their records management and systematic declassification programs to maximize access to records that are likely to be the subject of significant public interest.

Elements of this proposal should include:

- Complying with the dates or events for declassification, including through the use of new technologies;
- Consolidating and regularly updating declassification guidance that is easily

accessible to those authorized to declassify within the agency;

- Prioritizing declassification according to entire record groups selected through active consultation with the public and outside scholars, and regularly informing the public of systematic review results;
- Requiring all offices with any declassification-related activities to demonstrate that they are operating in partnership with others in the agency involved in related activities; and
- Establishing ombudsman offices in each agency that has original classification authority or engages in declassifying records: these offices would intervene in and resolve classification and declassification issues upon request, act as a conduit for public concerns about access to records, and, where appropriate, refer issues to the agency's Inspector General.

Creating ombudsman offices in every agency that is involved in classification and declassification of information would promote more effective records management and access policies. Some agencies, such as the CIA, already use such an office to broker other types of complaints about internal agency action (in the CIA's case, to address charges that analysis has been politicized). Although the Joint Security Commission recommended the creation of an ombudsman function, it was seen only as applying to the classification of information and did not include a role for that office regarding declassification. Moreover, the JSC's more limited ombudsman recommendation has not been implemented to date.

As recommended here, the ombudsman office would be headed by a senior officer whose full-time job would be to oversee the process of classification and declassification and to deal with concerns about particular actions. This official would also be empowered to intervene in disputes between agencies and FOIA requesters before they escalate into expensive, time-consuming litigation. Thus, the ombudsman office would work closely with all agency personnel involved in the life cycle of information, including records managers, training officers, classifiers, declassifiers, FOIA officers, and general counsel offices. The office would be required to submit to the agency head regular reports on cases undertaken, activities observed, and the status of agency cooperation and compliance with relevant statutes, executive orders, and other directives.

Conclusion

Not all classified records should be released, but most eventually can be. As with the previous chapter's recommendations to restructure classification policy, this chapter's recommendations are premised on making the declassification of government records at the end of their life cycle a more focused, disciplined, cost-effective, and well-managed process. Better management of declassification means that more resources and attention can be devoted to protecting our nation's core secrets.

Deregulating classified information at the end of its life cycle through appropriate declassification, whether that occurs 5 days or 50 years after it is created, must be based on a common sense understanding of the need to constantly strike a delicate balance between secrecy and openness. Although resources to accomplish declassification are finite, these judicious calculations are nevertheless vital to a vigorous democracy and to an accountable government. Finding the fulcrum of that balance is critical to fostering both sounder security practices and greater public confidence in government. These goals can be met through sensible, cost-effective ways of keeping within the classification system all information, but *only* that information, that truly needs protection.

[1] "U.S. Spy Satellite Ready for Launch," *New York Post* (19 December 1996): 37.

[2] For example, Oliver Stone's movie "JFK" and its allegations of agency involvement in President Kennedy's assassination led to creation of the Assassination Records Review Board and the declassification of over a million pages of agency records. Assertions of a cover-up of the crash of extraterrestrial spacecraft in New Mexico in the 1940s led to declassification of records about Department of Air Force activities in the area during that period. See Headquarters U.S. Air Force, *The Roswell Report: Fact versus Fiction in the New Mexico Desert,* stock no. 008-070-00697-9 (Washington, D.C.: Government Printing Office, 1995).

[3] See Department of Defense Personnel Security Research Center, *Public Attitudes Towards Security and Counter-Espionage Matters In The Post Cold War Period*, prepared by Tom W. Smith, National Opinion Research Center, for the Security Awareness Area of the Personnel Security Research Institutional Award Program (Monterey: November 1994).

[4] Interview by Commission staff, 6 November 1995.

[5] Dr. Alexander DiVolpi, statement at the Commission's Public Access Roundtable, National Archives and Records Administration, Washington, DC, May 16, 1996 (describing problems he and colleagues have encountered in publishing and discussing scientific information in the public domain that the DoE later claimed was classified). See also Glenn T. Seaborg, "Secrecy Runs Amok," *Science* (3 June 1994): 1410 (former chairman of the Atomic Energy Commission discusses his experience with DoE assertions that his personal diary was classified and its seizure of his personal papers even though he had previously sought and obtained verification from the AEC that they contained no classified material).

[6] See, e.g., Central Intelligence Agency, "CIA Briefing for the Commission on Protecting and Reducing Government Secrecy" (18 August 1995, chart 3), on file with the Commission.

[7] Department of State official, interview by Commission staff, 21 August 1996. That official called OADR a potential "time bomb" because of its implicit requirement that every classified document marked OADR—no matter how innocuous or highly sensitive—equally required review by the originator before it could be declassified and released.

[8] General Accounting Office, *Classified Information: Volume Could Be Reduced by Changing Retention Policy*, GAO/NSIAD-93-127 (Washington, D.C.: Government Printing Office, May 1993), 16-17.

[9] In 1992, the last year for which complied statistics are available, 575,424 FOIA requests were filed and nearly $108.5 million spent to implement the law. "Costs Go Up But Requests Go Down in 1993 Annual Reports," *Access Reports* (17 August 1994): 4-5.

[10] House of Representatives, Rep. Randy Tate (R.-Washington) speaking for the Electronic Freedom of Information Act Amendments of 1996, H.R. 3802, 104th Cong., 2d sess., *Congressional Record* (17 September 1996), 142, pt. 128: H10450. Senator Patrick Leahy (D.-Vermont) first introduced this bill in 1991, held hearings in 1992, and was one of its key proponents through its final passage in 1996.

[11] National Archives and Records Administration official, letter to Commission staff, 29 July 1996. One cubic foot is about 2,500-3,000 pages. (National Archives and Records Administration official, telephone conversation with Commission staff, 29 July 1996.)

[12] Data gathered by the Commission staff from government agencies on the numbers of pages subject to declassification under Executive Order show the following:

Agencies	Pages 25 years old and older subject to Executive Order 12958	Pages to be reviewed for declassification (excluding exemptions)	Pages declassified as of January 1997
CIA	165,900,000	59,300,000	19,600
Defense, Office of the Secretary	30,235,000	21,450,000	unknown after 476,104 pages reviewed
-Army	270,000,000	same	0
-Air Force	176,495,000	same	7,503,781
-DIA	21,005,000 (not including 201,000 cans of aerial film)	unavailable	unavailable
-Navy	500,000,000	unknown	33,120,000
Energy	230,000,000	132,000,000	1,600,000
JCS	4,675,625	same	570,000
NRO	6,500,000	1,300,000	0
NSA	129,300,000	53,300,000	1,900,000
State	45,000,000	unavailable	12,500,000
TOTAL	**1,579,110,625**	**718,520,625**	**57,213,381**

[13] Department of the Navy, "Declassification Plan for Navy and Marine Corps Records Under Executive Order 12958," (16 April 1996), on file with the Commission.

[14] National Archives and Records Administration, *Declassification Projects: Time & Cost To Process 1,000,000 Pages* (on file with the Commission).

[15] National Security Agency, "Estimated Cost Saving for Declassification Effort" (9 February 1996, briefing sheet, on file with the Commission).

[16] Department of Defense staff, telephone conversation with Commission staff, 24 September 1996.

[17] Ibid.

[18] Department of State officials, interview by Commission staff, 19 September 1995.

[19] Defense Intelligence Agency officials, interview by Commission staff, 30 August 1995.

[20] National Classification Management Society, "Virtual Interview With The Director, Information Security Oversight Office," *Viewpoints* 1 (1995): 31.

[21] Inspector General, Department of Defense, *White Paper: Classification and Declassification Within the Department of Defense* (Washington, D.C.: Department of Defense, May 1995), *ii*.

[22] National Archives and Records Administration, *Ready Access To Essential Evidence: The Strategic Plan Of The National Archives And Records Administration, 1997-2000*, 13.

[23] General Accounting Office, *Environmental Data: Major Effort Is Needed to Improve NOAA's Data Management and Archiving*, GAO/IMTEC-91-11 (Washington, D.C.: Government Printing Office, November 1990), 26-27.

[24] Inspector General, DoD, *White Paper, i*.

IV Personnel Security: Protection Through Detection

The personnel security system was put in place following World War II as a means of supporting the classification system and of implementing the Truman and Eisenhower Administrations' programs to investigate the loyalty of Federal Government officials. Over the past half century, a variety of directives and additional regulations have been issued to tailor the system to specific needs and respond to particular concerns (at times on an agency-specific basis), creating a layering of rules and, in turn, certain redundancies and other inefficiencies.

Even so, the fundamental standards and criteria around which personnel security policies and procedures are organized remain those set out in an executive order that is now nearly 44 years old. Although President Clinton's Executive Order 12968, issued on August 2, 1995, provides for common investigative and adjudicative standards to improve clearance reciprocity, strengthens appeal procedures, and improves the means of ensuring non-discrimination, it does not supersede Executive Order 10450, issued by President Eisenhower in 1953. Thus, in effect, it simply adds another regulatory layer to the personnel security system.

Personnel security in the future must be better integrated throughout the workplace, with managers and line officers accepting greater responsibility for security. High-profile examples of espionage arrests and poorly-administered procedures reduce confidence in the overall system and reinforce the Commission's view that the existing approach to personnel security is in need of substantial reform.

An updated personnel security system also must allocate more attention and resources to monitor, assess, and assist current employees, in particular those in positions of greatest sensitivity and those who have become at risk as a result of changes or difficulties in their lives. The Commission also believes that the personnel security process must be better understood. Many employees and applicants who have passed through the process have little understanding of what it actually involves. Greater security awareness and understanding should lead to a more secure working environment, as personnel become more knowledgeable about the key security concerns and significant threats, and what mechanisms exist to respond to these challenges.

Overview of the Personnel Security Process

The Background Investigation

The chief objective of the personnel security process is to attempt to determine whether past behavior is a matter of concern for future reliability. Before prospective Federal employees (both military and civilian) and contractors' employees who work in the national security arena can have access to national security information, they must undergo an investigation and adjudication to determine whether they should receive a security clearance. As Figure 3 shows, according to a 1995 General Accounting Office (GAO) report, more than 3.2 million government employees and contractors held security clearances in 1993 (the last year for which full data are available).[1]

A security clearance indicates that a person has been investigated and deemed eligible for access to classified information based on established criteria set out in regulations. Although in limited instances agency heads may grant a clearance without an investigation, employees normally receive access to classified information only when they have been "cleared" and a "need-to-know" justification has been provided. In practice, however, the "need-to-know" principle is seldom applied strictly, except in specific areas such as most special access programs (SAPs), which maintain access rosters.

Figure 3: Number of Federal and Contractor Employees with Clearances

2,299,000

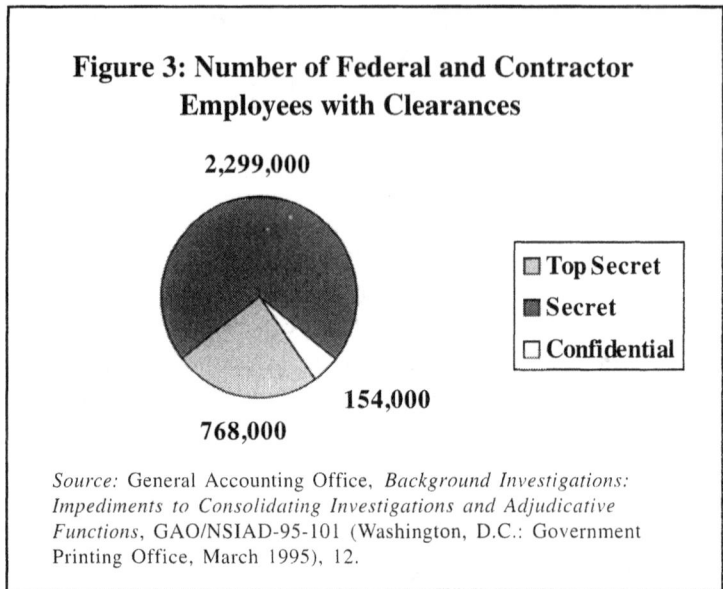

154,000

768,000

Top Secret
Secret
Confidential

Source: General Accounting Office, *Background Investigations: Impediments to Consolidating Investigations and Adjudicative Functions*, GAO/NSIAD-95-101 (Washington, D.C.: Government Printing Office, March 1995), 12.

The clearance process begins with the submission of a personal history statement detailing past residences, educational and employment background, criminal history, relatives, and other personal information. An investigation is then requested and conducted by a government agency such as the Defense Investigative Service (DIS)—which is the largest investigative agency in the Federal Government—or by a private contractor on behalf of an agency.

The length and complexity of the background investigation varies depending on the level of clearance (or the access) needed. In most agencies individuals are vetted for Confidential, Secret, or Top Secret clearances, and possibly for access to Sensitive Compartmented Information (SCI) as well. The Department of Energy (DoE) has a separate system pursuant to the Atomic Energy Act; most of its employees receive either an "L" clearance, which equates to a Confidential or Secret clearance, or a "Q" clearance, which equates to a Top Secret clearance.

Types of Investigations

There are three types of personnel security investigations: a National Agency Check (NAC), which includes, but is not necessarily limited to, a check of FBI name and fingerprint records; Office of Personnel Management (OPM) investigations on all applicants for Federal service; and, when appropriate, review of Department of Defense (DoD) records of cleared military and civilian employees or contractors. The NAC has served as the basis for Confidential and Secret clearances, primarily for U.S. military personnel.

When the NAC is supplemented by a credit check and written inquiries, the investigation is termed a NAC with Written Inquiries (NACI). Written inquiries are sent to schools, employers, and local law enforcement agencies to verify information submitted by the person under investigation. This has been the standard procedure required for Confidential and Secret clearances for Federal civilian employees in most agencies, as well as "suitability determinations" for applicants seeking Federal employment in positions not needing a security clearance. (It is notable that applicants for non-national security positions traditionally were subject to investigative steps for a "suitability" determination that *exceeded* those for military applicants who needed a Secret-level security clearance.) Those requiring access to Secret special access programs, however, usually require a review process similar to that for a Top Secret clearance.

A Single-Scope Background Investigation (SSBI), incorporating the NAC but using investigative interviews in lieu of written inquiries, is required for Top Secret clearances, for many SAPs designated Secret or Top Secret, for "Q" clearances, and for access to SCI data. As part of the background investigation process, investigators interview the applicant, current and former neighbors, character references, former educators, former spouses, and current and former employers; undertake local and national law enforcement record checks; and obtain credit reports and military and medical records. In addition, some agencies such as the CIA and the NSA require the applicant to undergo a polygraph examination, a medical examination, and a psychological evaluation.

Government employees and contractor personnel with security clearances are also subject to reinvestigations (covering the period beginning with the date of the last investigation) throughout their careers. The timing of reinvestigations can be random, but for Top Secret clearances they must be completed not less than once every five years. While the primary difference between initial investigations and reinvestigations is the period of time covered, some reinvestigation components may vary from the initial investigation. For example, during an initial polygraph examination, the NSA and the CIA cover counterintelligence issues (sabotage, espionage, and foreign intelligence) as well as additional issues such as possible use of drugs and any criminal activity, which are not included in subsequent tests. The Departments of Energy and Defense require regular in-house reviews as part of their "personnel reliability" programs for employees in extremely sensitive positions (such as those having access to nuclear devices); these reviews are conducted annually and consist of an interview, urinalysis, psychological testing, and a credit check.

Investigative Costs

As shown in Figure 4, according to a March 1995 GAO report surveying 51 different agencies, the total cost of background investigations in 1993 (the latest year for which such figures are available) was $326 million.[2] The individual costs for a standard field investigation vary considerably, depending upon both the investigative agency and the priority of the investigation. OPM charges $3,425 for service within 120 days and $3,995 for 35-day service.[3] The Defense Investigative Service, in contrast, to date has not

Figure 4: Total Investigation Costs (in Millions)

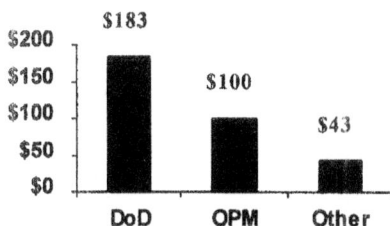

Source: General Accounting Office, *Background Investigations: Impediments to Consolidating Investigations and Adjudicative Functions,* GAO/NSIAD-95-101 (Washington, D.C.: Government Printing Office, March 1995).

been permitted to charge its customers for investigations or reinvestigations, although this restriction is now being reexamined.

The Adjudication

The information collected during the investigative process is then forwarded to an adjudicative office, where an adjudicator evaluates all of the data collected in order to make a clearance determination. This decision is based on established guidelines. An adjudicator who believes that the investigation is incomplete usually has the opportunity to request additional information from the investigator.

When an already cleared employee is transferred or detailed to another agency or special access program, that individual's file is reviewed again by an adjudicator at the receiving agency or by a program security officer prior to the acceptance of the employee's clearance. As a result, even though the individual's clearance may be up to date, additional security vetting is usually required before the clearance will be accepted by the receiving agency or special access program.

Improving the Current System

Modernizing the System's Cold War Foundations

Prior to the Cold War, the Federal Government's efforts to maintain a trustworthy and reliable civil service were based primarily on the Civil Service Act of 1883. The Act included a core principle of "suitability" for Federal employment, defining this as "a requirement or requirements for government employment having reference to a person's character, reputation, trustworthiness, and fitness as related to the efficiency of the service." Seventy years later, Executive Order 10450 imposed an additional requirement for Federal employment: "that all persons privileged to be employed in the departments and agencies of the Government, shall be reliable, trustworthy, of good conduct and character, *and of complete and unswerving loyalty* to the United States" such that ". . . *employment and retention . . . is clearly consistent with the interests of national security*." (Emphasis supplied.)

The criteria applied to "suitability" and "security eligibility" determinations today are largely redundant. All civilian Federal Government employees, regardless of whether they need access to national security information, must be found suitable for government service through use of at least a NACI. Those requiring access to national security information must also be found security-eligible as defined by Executive Order 10450. However, the two-step process of determining suitability and security eligibility is not applied uniformly across agencies, frequently involves duplicative steps and long delays, and is poorly understood by applicants and many agency officials alike. In addition, both the responsibilities and the criteria for suitability and personnel security determinations may differ from agency to agency. Some agencies place responsibility for both evaluations in the same office, while others maintain separate offices for making suitability and security determinations, at times with minimal coordination between the offices.

While the fundamental principles of the personnel security system remain based on Executive Order 10450, numerous other authorities have modified the specific language set out in the Order for issuing security clearances, either because the Order needed further amplification over the years or because it did not fit the needs of a particular agency. For example, the Order does not mention "classified information"

Table 2: Major Personnel Security Authorities Since EO 10450

The Atomic Energy Act	As amended in 1954, set out the restricted data classification system, with an entirely separate structure from national security clearances.
Executive Order 10865 (1960)	Established standards governing access for industry employees.
Title 5 of the Code of Federal Regulations	Authorized heads of departments to prescribe regulations for determining the suitability of applicants for Federal service.
Public Law 88-290 (1964)	Amended the Internal Security Act of 1950 to specifically address personnel security concerns of the NSA.
DoD Directive 5200.2-R (1979)	Combined all Department of Defense personnel security programs, including DoD Directive 5210.9, which established the military personnel security program requiring the military to abide by the same loyalty oath as civilians.
National Security Directive 63 (1991)	Established single scope background investigative standards for access to Top Secret and Sensitive Compartmented Information.
Executive Order 12829 (1993)	Created the National Industrial Security Program (NISP), a consolidation of Federal industrial security programs and relevant regulations.
Director of Central Intelligence Directive 1/14 (revised 1994)	Provided adjudication standards for access to Sensitive Compartmented Information.
Executive Order 12968 (1995)	Updated standards governing access to national security information.

or include the words "clearance," "access," or "need-to-know." Some of the many laws and regulations pertaining to the investigation of applicants and employees for suitability or security eligibility determinations are summarized in Table 2.

A 1988 RAND Corporation report, *To Repair or Rebuild*, identified some of the key problems in the current personnel security process. Among the important issues raised was how to define the *basic purpose* of the personnel security system; that is, should it focus on responding to the loss of secrets through espionage, or should it look more broadly at how to address behavioral problems of cleared personnel ranging from alcoholism and drug use to financial problems? According to the report, the broader the definition of personnel security, "the more difficult it becomes to separate personnel security problems traditionally associated with personnel management, or to prevent them from lapping over into other security areas, such as counterespionage or physical security." The report concluded:

> Modest changes and incremental improvements to the current program are not likely to produce a significantly more effective personnel security program. Major investments in improving the effectiveness or efficiency of current procedures should be deferred until the theoretical foundations of the program are thoroughly examined to provide a clearer understanding and more complete description of the personnel security problem.[4]

In the nine years since that report was issued, however, any changes have been modest and any improvements incremental in nature. It is essential that a personnel security system for the post-Cold War era include new guiding principles reflecting updated needs and priorities. These guiding principles must be common across the Government to help officials implement specific personnel security procedures that enhance both national security and the understanding of operational needs, that are sensitive to individual rights, and that are supportive of employees' needs.

Recommendation

The Commission recommends five guiding principles as the essential elements of an effective personnel security system. Most already are part of the current system (including under Executive Order 12968), but too often they are not actually practiced throughout the Federal Government. The Commission recommends that these standards be incorporated into a new statute or regulation that would supersede Executive Order 10450.

While specific processes and tools may change over time, there must be consistent guiding standards underpinning the overall system.

The five guiding principles are:

- **Openness and clarity of standards:** All applicants for government employment, as well as those seeking contractor positions that require government review, must be provided with clear information in writing about the security vetting process. Currently, applicants, employees, and contractors typically are provided little information on the process. Promoting a greater understanding of the process should help to improve overall accountability, both for employees and for those responsible for administering security programs. For example, creating a standard brochure to explain the clearance process and address the most common questions would bring greater clarity to the system for applicants, employees, and contractors.

- **Balanced, "whole-person" standards:** The goal of an investigation and adjudication should be to develop a balanced picture of the individual, based on both positive and negative factors, including evidence that past problems have been overcome.

- **Reciprocity for classified access:** When a government employee or contractor transfers or is detailed to, or is directly hired by another agency or private contractor, that individual's clearance should be accepted by the receiving agency if it is equivalent to or higher than that required for the new position and if the previous investigation and adjudication occurred within the established timeframe. Agency or program-specific supplemental forms should be eliminated.

- **Nondiscrimination principles:** Denials and revocations of access should not be based on arbitrary or capricious standards. The U.S. Government is not permitted to discriminate on the basis of race, color, religion, sex, national origin, disability, sexual orientation, or mental health counseling in granting access to classified information. Although Executive Order 12968 represents a significant step forward in this regard, it has not yet been fully implemented across the Government.

- **Assurances of due process:** Applicants and employees should be immediately informed in writing of the reasons for suspensions, denials, or revocations of clearances and access, and should be given the opportunity to appeal an adverse determination to a senior official or panel not involved in the original determination. A person who has been denied a clearance or had a clearance revoked should be allowed to reapply after a determined period of time.

Increasing Clearance Reciprocity and Standardization

Agencies often do not accept the clearances of government employees who transfer from one agency to another, or of contract employees who wish to work on projects

The Defense Department has estimated that by the year 2001, without additional resources or major system improvements, SSBIs will take an average of 278 days. Currently, DIS completion time for SSBIs is between 175 days and 220 days.

for multiple agencies. Agencies frequently criticize the quality of each other's investigations and adjudications. As one result, they insist on duplicating lengthy and costly procedures even though an individual's clearances are current. Representatives of industry have expressed frustration over the frequency with which contractors are investigated and adjudicated, with some citing cases in which individuals were reinvestigated repeatedly during a single year because they required access to multiple programs.

In order to improve clearance reciprocity between government agencies, the interagency Security Policy Board has agreed on minimum investigative standards across the Federal Government; these have been forwarded to the White House for review. However, a significant exception to this policy remains because these are only *minimum* standards. Thus, agencies are still permitted to retain specific additional security requirements, thereby limiting the extent to which there can be genuine reciprocity of clearances.

In addition to this lack of clearance reciprocity, the system is also made less efficient by the failure to standardize the personnel security questionnaires that are used. An April 1995 OMB memorandum prescribed one form, Standard Form 86, for use by Federal agencies in security clearance background investigations.[5] This new requirement has yet to be fully implemented, however, because the form was written for a background investigation covering seven years, while the standards for investigative components for a Top Secret clearance with access to Sensitive Compartmented Information (SCI) have since changed and now vary from three to ten years. As a result of these differences, several agencies continue to use agency-specific forms. The longstanding objectives of greater uniformity, reciprocity, and cost effectiveness in the clearance process appear to be a considerable distance from actually being realized.

Recommendation

The Commission recommends that individuals in both Government and industry holding valid clearances be able to move from one agency or special program to another without further investigation or adjudication. The single exception to this true reciprocity of security clearances shall be that agencies may continue to require the polygraph before granting access.

This approach would reduce the "dead time" often facing cleared employees and contractors when they transfer to other agencies or projects. The Government would no longer have to pay for employees to sit idle and there would be less likelihood of losing quality personnel who do not want to wait long periods for the completion of additional clearance procedures.

Enhancing Investigative Quality

Standards vary widely for the hiring, training, and continuing education of personnel security investigators, adjudicators, and security officers. This can contribute to inconsistent quality in both investigations and adjudications.

The standards for personnel security investigators and adjudicators have changed over time. At one point, the Justice Department's Bureau of Investigation (later the FBI) had the authority to conduct all investigations of those in sensitive positions, and almost all of its agents, who conducted the investigations, were required to have a degree in either law or accounting. As the number of personnel requiring background investigations rose substantially following World War II (pursuant to President Truman's Executive Order 9835 in 1947 and then President Eisenhower's Executive Order 10450 six years later), and as the chief responsibility for investigations shifted to the Civil Service Commission, hiring requirements for investigators were eased. Today, despite the great emphasis placed on the background investigation, standards for investigators and adjudicators are minimal; usually a bachelor's degree in any field will suffice, though it is not a requirement.

In addition, there are no common standards for training or continuing education: initial training usually consists of four weeks of classes and is followed by varying periods of on-the-job training. The Defense Investigative Service, for example, has had a hiring freeze since 1991 and only conducts sporadic training for its investigators. Although the DIS is reviewing its continuing education practices, senior DIS officials recognize that they face, as one acknowledged, "a crisis situation because we know our people are not receiving training."[6] The OPM has no continuing education requirements. And the Federal Government, because it recently privatized its investigations division, must monitor the standards set for hiring qualifications, training, and education by the successor to its Federal Investigations Service, the U.S. Investigation Service, Inc.

Reducing Inefficiencies in the Processing of Cases

According to a 1993 study by the Defense Department's Personnel Security Research Center (PERSEREC), over 96 percent of all DoD personnel security adjudications were favorable.[7] Even so, cases with either no or only minor derogatory information usually are reviewed closely by *two* officials: an adjudicative specialist and a supervisor. This procedure is applied even after a case has had an initial review for investigative sufficiency by two officials, the specialist directing the investigation and a supervisor, before being forwarded to the adjudication office. Because of large caseloads and first-in, first-out processing, even cases without derogatory information (termed "clean" cases) are sometimes held up behind cases with substantial derogatory information that take much longer to adjudicate.

Time delays can inconvenience applicants and waste significant resources. Both the Government and private industry can lose qualified applicants who do not have the patience or resources to wait, sometimes up to a year or more, to find out whether or when they can begin work. The GAO has estimated that these processing delays cost the Government $920 million a year in productivity losses;[8] these costs will only increase as delays worsen.

To alleviate the delays in the clearance process, adjudicative offices should consider establishing fast-track procedures by handling clean cases first, rather than holding them in line behind cases with derogatory information that require more detailed analysis and processing. If the required level of investigation has been undertaken and no derogatory information has been revealed, the adjudicative office would issue a clearance immediately with only one review.

Establishing fast-track adjudications would eliminate a second adjudicative review, thus saving time and resources, reducing adjudicative backlogs (which are extensive and growing in several agencies), and permitting adjudicators to focus more time on serious derogatory cases. Expedited processing of clean cases would provide a good example of applying risk assessment principles in an era of diminishing personnel security resources. The NRO, for example, already uses this method successfully, contributing to its average processing time of under 60 days.

> **Derogatory Information**
>
> **Minor Derogatory:** Information that, by itself, is not of sufficient importance or magnitude to justify an unfavorable administrative security clearance determination.
>
> **Moderate Derogatory:** Information on the basis of which an unfavorable administrative security clearance determination may not necessarily be made, but which obligates the investigative agent to pursue its development.
>
> **Significant Derogatory:** Information that could, in itself, justify an unfavorable administrative action, or prompt an adjudicator to seek additional investigation or clarification.

Addressing Transparency and Due Process Concerns

Most agencies make little effort to disseminate any information regarding the personnel security process to applicants, contractors, and employees subject to investigation or reinvestigation. These individuals thus remain largely uninformed with respect to basic, unclassified information concerning the overall process, the length of time it takes, the standards applied, and their own status.

For example, personnel security officials from one agency reported that approximately 10 percent of applicants withdraw from consideration after having applied for a security clearance—often because they can no longer afford to wait. Contractors also voiced concerns that the system is not accountable to its customers. For example, if the contractor calls to check on the status of an employee, the agency in question often cannot determine where the individual stands in the clearance process. In addition, those subjected to the clearance process often do not understand it. Some assume, for example, that they will be denied a clearance for reasons that are not actually grounds for rejection. Moreover, security officials in many agencies often do not know or understand the investigative or adjudicative processes of other agencies.

While Executive Order 12968 attempts to address other concerns about the fairness of the personnel security process, it does not include provisions that are designed to improve the basic understanding and transparency of the process. Applicants or employees who have their clearances denied, suspended, or revoked, and who are not provided a reason, are effectively denied due process, even though Executive Order 12968 explicitly calls for improvements in this regard.

Allocating Resources More Effectively

Shortcomings in the initial screening process appear to account, at least in part, for the hiring of two spies: Karl Koecher, arrested in 1984, and Larry Wu-Tai Chin, arrested in 1985, both of whom were agents of foreign intelligence services when hired.[9] These cases, however, are the rare exception; other spies, including those responsible for the most damaging espionage incidents in recent years, turned to espionage only after many years of trusted Government service, and very rarely with ideological motivations.

Data from the PERSEREC and Project SLAMMER, a study of post-World War II espionage cases, confirm that few persons join the Government or begin contractor employment with the intent of committing espionage.[10] The main threat instead comes from trusted "insiders," those who already hold clearances and only much later in their careers decide to commit espionage. Even so, the personnel security system estab-lished under Executive Order 10450 consistently has allocated most resources to the initial clearance process, based on the once-prevailing concerns about the Soviet Union and its allies placing espionage agents inside the U.S. Government.

The Difficulties of Talking to Neighbors

"The neighbors are never at home unless it is in the evening or on the weekend, and often do not want to talk to strangers, regardless where they say they are from. Single women often will not open their doors for someone they don't know, regardless of whether he or she has a badge. Possibly the biggest problem is that neighbors do not want to say anything that can potentially subject them to a lawsuit."

-- Intelligence Community Investigators

This focus on the initial clearance has shortchanged the allocation of resources and attention to reinves-tigations and continuing assessment programs. Continuing assessment programs and reinvestiga-tions often are the first areas subjected to budget cuts. For example, the DIS announced in 1995 that, due to diminishing resources, it could no longer conduct periodic reinvestigations on a routine basis and would establish an annual 5 percent ceiling on all counterintelligence-scope polygraphs for current employees. While this policy was later modified to place decisions on initiating reinvestigations with the heads of agencies (after senior NSA officials voiced concern), questions regarding the *quality* of reinvestigations have not been addressed.

In a period of declining resources, the Federal Government also should target its security dollars toward the most productive elements of the investigation: those that yield the most substantial information relevant to the clearance decision. The most productive source overall for developing derogatory information, according to a 1996 PERSEREC report, was the person under investigation: the report noted that in 81 percent of the cases in which incriminating information was uncovered, the individual subject provided such information through the interview or on the personnel security questionnaire.[11]

Some elements of an initial background investigation are much more productive than others; those that are the most productive include interviews with former spouses and employers, medical professionals, relatives, and listed or developed character references.[12] The least productive sources include neighborhood interviews, which are also the most expensive and time consuming.[13] Interviews with education references also are not productive, according to this and other studies.

The limited utility of neighborhood interviews should not be surprising. The practice of interviewing neighbors is based on a vision of America as it once was—with individuals living in the same geographic areas most of their lives, enabling investigators to glean useful information from local sources with relative ease. Today, this is less often the case, given greater personal mobility, privacy concerns, and the litigiousness of society. When the difficulty of gaining access to neighbors and the time and substantial expense of the procedure are also factored in, the notion that neighborhood interviews should be done routinely as part of every background investigation requires reassessment.

The Security Policy Board has implicitly acknowledged the limited usefulness of neighborhood interviews by agreeing to limit their scope to three years for Top Secret/ SCI clearances. The Commission believes that the time has come to go further; in view of the limited resources often available and the need to prioritize, it is important to focus on the most productive elements of the personnel security investigation. The Commission recommends the following steps to reallocate investigative resources and focus on the most productive aspects of the investigation.

Recommendation

The Commission recommends that current requirements for neighborhood interviews and for interviewing educational references in every investigation be eliminated.

Under the above proposal, neighborhood interviews and checks of educational references still would be allowed where personnel security officials believe that the information yielded from these interviews would be productive; they simply would not be *required* in every investigation. This proposed approach is consistent with the critical objective of achieving increased reciprocity through greater standardization of personnel security procedures; it would promote common standards across the Government that make sense in view of existing resource constraints.

Greater attention needs to be directed toward making continuing evaluation programs more effective. For example, using existing public and private data bases—with the express advance permission of the individual under review—to periodically scan for criminal history, as well as for credit, travel, and business history, normally would provide more accurate information at less cost than standard field reinvestigations.

Personnel security professionals could monitor the behavior and activities of cleared personnel on a continuous basis in a more effective, cost-efficient, and nonintrusive manner. Given the evidence that there is little likelihood of catching spies through the current standard investigative or reinvestigative process, better continuing assessment programs could enhance the probability of deterring or identifying espionage activities.

Recommendation

The Commission recommends that greater balance be achieved between the initial clearance process and programs for continuing evaluation of cleared employees.

Most of the information needed is already available on existing databases; private industry experiences suggest that efforts to utilize automation to access such data can be very cost-effective as well as productive. Nevertheless, because some automated tools can be expensive, a cost-benefit assessment should be completed prior to utilizing them.

Resources should be focused on those individuals in the most sensitive positions or where there is some evidence of suspect behavior; in an era of diminishing resources and frequent budget cuts, more effective continuing assessment can be accomplished only by concentrating on the areas of greatest vulnerability. In addition, those holding what are identified as the most sensitive positions could be subjected to more frequent, "in house" reviews similar to the personnel reliability programs used by the Defense and Energy Departments, as described above. These measures provide a cost-effective way to monitor and assess employees with greater regularity and frequency, but without necessarily having to direct additional resources toward the traditional field investigation.

Strengthening Employee Assistance Programs

The focus on the initial investigation has also limited the attention and resources given to programs intended to assist current employees. These programs, generally termed Employee Assistance Programs (EAPs), are critical in ensuring that employees can receive professional assistance if they face serious personal problems. Despite a requirement in the Federal Employee Substance Abuse Education and Treatment Act of 1986, as well as evidence of their benefits, standards for EAPs across the Federal Government do not exist. Furthermore, it is often not clear to the employee whether attending an EAP would harm his or her career. Both the quality of such programs and the resources made available for them also vary widely from agency to agency. The Commission therefore supports efforts to strengthen these programs.

According to 1994 figures, 79,742 employees turned to EAPs for help.[14] The cost for EAPs varies considerably, ranging from $8 to $50 per employee.[15] Although some employees may never seek the help that they need, others may seek or can be directed to seek mental health or job counseling, as shown in Figure 5. While the number of individuals who did not commit espionage as a result of successful counseling is impossible to quantify, helping cleared employees cope with their personal problems almost certainly will deter some incidents of espionage and other major security breaches.

The maintenance of confidentiality is and should remain a key element of such programs. Employees having emotional and financial difficulties are less likely to seek counseling if there is a perception that confidentiality is either nonexistent or poorly maintained, and that reprisals from security officials are possible. For example, convicted spy James Hall reportedly had sought help for his alcoholism from a military EAP, but declined to return after a counselor warned that attending one could damage his career. Confidentiality policies for EAPs should include nondisclosure of files and information garnered during the course of counseling, except in cases where confidentiality is prohibited by law (such as when there is admission of child abuse, intent to do harm, or other criminal activity).

One additional issue with respect to EAPs is whether contractor employees should be eligible. Most government agencies are prevented under the Federal Employee Substance Abuse Education and Treatment Act of 1986 from offering any EAP services to contractor employees and their families. While some larger firms are able to fulfill this function in-house, smaller companies often do not have the resources to create an EAP. Because contractor employees may have access to the same national security information as Federal employees, agencies that work with them should have the option of offering the services of EAPs to contractor employees in certain circumstances (without being required to do so). NSA officials, for example, have said that they would like to be able to provide EAP services to contractor employees from smaller companies, but cannot do so at present because of the legal restriction.

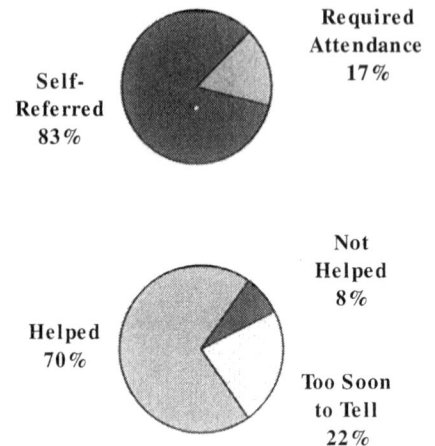

Figure 5: Federal EAP Statistics

Required Attendance 17%

Self-Referred 83%

Not Helped 8%

Helped 70%

Too Soon to Tell 22%

Source: Office of Personnel Management, *Fiscal Year 1994: Report to Congress Title VI of Public Law 99-570* (Washington, D.C.: Government Printing Office, September 1995), 5-7.

Assessing the Value of Financial Disclosure

Under the 1995 Intelligence Authorization Act, all Executive Branch employees with access to "particularly sensitive classified information" must complete a financial disclosure form. In April 1995 (while what became Executive Order 12968 was still under interagency review), Acting Director of Central Intelligence William Studeman announced that all CIA employees and agency contractors would be required to submit annual financial disclosure forms. Executive Order 12968, issued in August 1995, requires that the "head of each agency" designate those employees (including industrial contractors, members of the Armed Forces, and civilian employees) who would be subject to this reporting requirement.

Studies, including Project SLAMMER, demonstrate that interest in financial gain is one of the leading motivations for espionage and other criminal activities.[16] Primarily as a result of the Aldrich Ames case, the Congress (through the 1995 Intelligence Authorization Act) and the Executive Branch (through Executive Order 12968) determined that a new financial disclosure form was needed for those who have access to very sensitive information. The form would be used in addition to credit reports, other financial information collected, and the consent form that individuals sign, which allows access to an individual's financial information provided the investigator can show cause.

The requirement for a new financial disclosure form has generated considerable debate among those responsible for its implementation. For example, nearly all members of the SPB's Personnel Security Committee have expressed the view that using such a form would not meaningfully enhance personnel security and that the concerns raised over the past two years by industry (including cost, use of the data collected, and maintenance of the data's confidentiality) have not been addressed adequately.

While Executive Order 12968 provides fairly specific guidelines to assist agency heads in deciding who is required to fill out a financial disclosure form, agency officials, employees, and contractors have voiced concern over how officials will interpret the Order's provisions. They also are concerned that collecting the financial data by this method will be a costly endeavor with limited returns. The CIA and the Customs Service, two agencies that have been using a financial disclosure form, have not yet quantified the effectiveness of their forms. Furthermore, once the information has been collected, there is continued uncertainty over whether the Government has the resources or technical capability to analyze it in a meaningful way.

Finally, there is still considerable uncertainty concerning whether the financial information collected should be used as an analytical or investigative tool. If investigators use the form simply as an investigative tool, it may provide very little added value to the consent forms that all employees with security clearances already are required to sign. If it is used as an analytical tool, adjudicators would use that information in their security eligibility determinations, as they currently use credit reports and other available information.

Recommendation

The Commission recommends that both the Congress and the Executive Branch reevaluate the requirement to utilize a new financial disclosure form and consider staying its implementation until there is further evaluation concerning how it would be used and whether its benefits exceed its costs. The Congress and the Executive Branch should review alternative approaches to improving data collection, including utilization of the expanded access to certain financial and travel records provided for under Executive Order 12968.

Advancing Polygraph Research

Senior officials from agencies that use the polygraph see it as a significant tool because of its utility in generating admissions of wrongdoing, either during the pre-test, test, or post-test period. The polygraph saves time and money, and it serves as a deterrent by eliminating some potential applicants from seeking a highly sensitive position in the first place. The polygraph examination is conducted before the background investigation, saving additional resources should the applicant be rejected as a result of polygraph admissions. According to a May 1993 NSA letter to the White House, "over 95% of the information the NSA develops on individuals who do not meet federal security clearance guidelines is derived via [voluntary admissions from] the polygraph process."[17]

Because disparities exist in the procedural safeguards employed by different agencies for those employees requiring access to highly sensitive information, full reciprocity of security clearances between the agencies cannot be achieved. While the polygraph is used to screen employees at the CIA, NRO, DIA, NSA, and FBI (which resumed screening in 1993), the White House, NSC, State Department, and Congress have traditionally resisted adopting polygraph screening. Even among the agencies that use the polygraph, the scope, methods, and procedural safeguards may diverge.

Although the polygraph is useful in eliciting admissions, the potential also exists for excessive reliance on the examination itself. A related concern is that too much trust is placed in polygraph examiners' skills, creating a false sense of security within agencies that rely on the polygraph.[18] The few Government-sponsored scientific research reports on polygraph *validity* (as opposed to its utility), especially those focusing on the screening of applicants for employment, indicate that the polygraph is neither scientifically valid nor especially effective beyond its ability to generate admissions (some of which may not even be relevant based on current adjudicative criteria).[19] Many senior intelligence community officials, however, have told Commission members that they believe the polygraph is scientifically valid.

Agencies that Use the Polygraph for Employment Screening

Central Intelligence Agency
Defense Intelligence Agency
Drug Enforcement Agency
Federal Bureau of Investigation
National Security Agency
National Reconnaissance Office

A 1989 Department of Defense Polygraph Institute (DoDPI) study found that 60 percent of subjects were incorrectly cleared in a test that measured the subject's knowledge or guilt of a crime. The results of this test concluded that the ability to identify those guilty or knowledgeable of a crime "was significantly worse than chance."[20] The DoDPI study, however, was conducted in a controlled setting, and, therefore, may not accurately reflect the conditions under which a polygraph is normally taken. (Another report, a detailed 1991 FBI study entitled "Polygraph Examinations in Federal Personnel Security Applications," is classified in its entirety, and so the Commission cannot reference any of its substantive findings or recommendations in this unclassified report.)

Past commissions, an internal CIA working group, and several other studies have also called for additional research concerning polygraph accuracy.[21] However, comprehensive research into the accuracy of the polygraph has not been funded, despite the fact that the President's Foreign Intelligence Advisory Board in 1988 recommended that the Director of Central Intelligence fund all future requests for studies on screening accuracy. Moreover, despite DoDPI's efforts to manage an effective research program in recent years, little support for it appears to exist within the broader scientific community, primarily because there is no open and objective peer review of DoDPI's research.

The Commission believes that the following would improve understanding of both the polygraph's utility and its scientific validity, thereby promoting better informed decisions concerning its use.

Recommendation

The Commission recommends that:
(1) the director of scientific research at the Department of Defense Polygraph Institute (DoDPI) establish a committee that includes cleared, outside scientific experts to develop a coherent research agenda on the polygraph; initiate and participate in a small grant program to stimulate independent research outside the Government; and review and comment on scientific progress and the quality of government-sponsored research in this field; and (2) independent, objective, and peer-reviewed scientific research be encouraged as the best means to assess the credibility of the polygraph as a personnel security tool and identify potential technological advances that could make the polygraph more effective in the future.

Making the Clearance Process More Efficient Through Automation

Although steps have been taken to automate elements of the personnel security process within various agencies, there is no overall vision of how the personnel security system should operate in the Information Age. Most of the system still remains tied to a slow-moving, paper-based world, rather than functioning through a sophisticated system of interconnected computers.

Recently developed, and potentially very promising, innovations include the pre-screening software program "Military Applicant Screening System" (MASS), developed at the PERSEREC, which leads military applicants through a series of questions to determine whether or not they would be eligible for a clearance. If the applicant would be ineligible for a clearance, military recruiters can direct the applicant to another position for which a clearance is not required, thereby saving scarce investigative resources.

Other new developments include PERSEREC's "Adjudicator's Desktop Reference Guide," which stores a broad array of guidelines, laws, and statistical information to help adjudicators make final clearance decisions. Under review within the Security Policy Board is a common identification badge that will allow personnel from one agency to travel to another agency without having to undergo the traditionally cumbersome process of passing clearances.

The Commission endorses these and other examples of automation of the personnel security system, and recommends a more coordinated approach to developing additional programs. For example, building on the progress already made, a "Personnel Assurance System" index could be developed to rank employees by the degree of harm they could inflict, based on the sensitivity of their position and an assessment of the relevant threat, as well as on their level of clearance. Those in the most sensitive positions would be subject to more frequent and more detailed adjudication.

In addition, improved computer programs could be created that are capable of continually scanning different databases (e.g., that of the Treasury Department, consumer credit reports, national criminal databases, and other commercially available databases) for suspect behavior or other indicators of potential problems. Existing public databases today include vast amounts of information on all facets of personal finances and holdings. Consistent with applicable privacy requirements, officials should use these databases as valuable open source information to assist in personnel security decisions.

The Commission believes that a more efficient, partially automated personnel investigative process could be created using already-available technologies. The Defense Investigative Service and the OPM Federal Investigations Processing Center already have embarked on multimillion-dollar projects that will automate much of the initial personnel security investigative process for civilian, military, and industrial contractor employees; the objective now is to find a way to integrate these automation projects into the entire personnel security process.

Conclusion

From the time of its inception following World War II, the personnel security process has remained vital to the protection of national security information. Unfortunately, the process has not evolved to meet current national security needs.

A number of problems prevent the personnel security system from operating efficiently and effectively. For example, the authorities governing the clearance process are disjointed and outdated, which leads to confusion both for the administrators and for customers of the process. Attempts to revamp the system have resulted in ad hoc or piecemeal solutions, such as the financial disclosure form inspired by the Aldrich Ames espionage case, that tend to address only the most recent high-profile espionage cases rather than the underlying problems of the system. Fewer government resources have led to a dangerous focus on initial investigations at the expense of reinvestigations, even though recent studies have shown that individuals now typically turn to espionage only after years of government service. Moreover, too many of the remaining resources are being used for less productive investigation elements, such as neighborhood checks or redundant investigations for contractors and Federal employees who transfer between agencies.

The solutions for these problems must come from a fundamental reevaluation of the personnel security system, rather than from temporary fixes. A successful security clearance process commences when an applicant applies for a security clearance, but it must continue with frequent and productive reinvestigations, better employee assistance programs for troubled employees, and improved general security awareness by managers and coworkers. Some recent innovations have demonstrated how automation can improve the system; a coordinated approach to developing further such programs is desirable.

The Commission believes that the proposals set out above will move the personnel security system in the desired direction. Guiding principles will lead personnel security officials to a better understanding of their mission and responsibilities. Increased reciprocity will allow employees to transfer more easily between agencies without redundant investigations. Reallocating resources based upon the need for greater balance between the initial clearance process and continuing assessment programs will provide more protection against "trusted" insiders who can cause serious damage to our nation's security. Finally, an evaluation of the tools of the personnel security system, such as the polygraph, will help ensure that they further the aims of the overall process.

---

[1] General Accounting Office, *Background Investigations: Impediments to Consolidating Investigations and Adjudicative Functions*, GAO/NSIAD-95-101 (Washington, D.C.: Government Printing Office, March 1995), 12.

[2] Ibid., 11.

[3] Office of Personnel Management, Federal Investigations Notice 95-4, 1 August 1995.

[4] Carl Builder, Victor Jackson, and Rae Starr, *To Repair or Rebuild: Analyzing Personnel Security Research Agendas,* R-3652-USDP (Santa Monica: RAND, September 1988), 11.

[5] Office of Management and Budget, Memorandum for Senior Information Resource Management Officials: Approval of Standard Suitability and Background Investigation Questionnaires (Office of Management and Budget, Washington, D.C., 11 April 1995).

[6] Defense Investigative Service Official, telephone conversation with Commission staff, 20 June 1996.

[7] Defense Personnel Security Research Center, *Report on Personnel Security* (Washington, D.C.: Department of Defense, 1994), 20.

[8] Comptroller General, *Report to the Congress of the United States: Faster Processing of DOD Personnel Security Clearances Could Avoid Millions in Losses*, GGD-81-105 (Washington, D.C.: General Accounting Office, 15 September 1981), ii.

[9] Department of Defense Security Institute, *Recent Espionage Cases: Summary & Sources* (Richmond: Department of Defense Security Institute, July 1994), 12, 15.

[10] Suzanne Wood and Martin Wiskoff, *Americans Who Spied Against Their Country Since World War II*, PERS-TR-92-005 (Monterey: Defense Personnel Security Research Center, May 1992), 26.

[11] Ralph M. Carney, *SSBI Source Yield: An Examination of Sources Contacted During the SSBI* (Monterey: Defense Personnel Security Research Center, 1996), 6.

[12] Ibid., 15.

[13] Personnel Security Working Group et al., *Evaluation of DCID 1/14 Investigative Requirements* (Washington, D.C.: Director of Central Intelligence, April 1991), 31.

[14] Office of Personnel Management, *Fiscal Year 1994: Report to Congress on Title VI of Public Law 99-570* (Washington, D.C.: Government Printing Office, September 1995), 1.

[15] Ibid., 12-20.

[16] Willis Reilly and Paul Joyal, *Project SLAMMER: A Critical Look at the Director of Central Intelligence Directive No. 1/14 Criteria* (Washington, D.C.: Director of Central Intelligence, 1993), 25-28. Project SHADOW is the name given to a current DoD Security Institute project to reinterview the subjects of Project SLAMMER and produce new videotapes for the purpose of developing better security education and awareness information. Department of Defense official, telephone conversation with Commission staff, 12 January 1997. See also Jeff Stein, "Treason on Their Minds: 'Project Shadow' Aims to Spot Moles Earlier," *Washington Post*, 12 January 1997, C2.

[17] National Security Agency, letter to Holly Gwin, White House Office of Science and Technology, 4 May 1993.

[18] House Permanent Select Committee on Intelligence, Report on *United States Counterintelligence and Security Concerns* (1986).

[19] See Office of Technology Assessment, *Scientific Validity of Polygraph Testing: A Research Review and Evaluation—A Technical Memorandum,* OTA-TM-H-15 (Washington, D.C.: Office of Technology Assessment, November 1983); House Permanent Select Committee on Intelligence, *United States Counterintelligence and Security Concerns*; Department of Defense Polygraph Institute, *Study of the Accuracy of Security Screening Polygraph Examinations.* For additional information and examples of studies that found the polygraph was scientifically valid in certain applications, see Department of Defense Polygraph Institute, *Bootstrap Decision Making for Polygraph Examinations,* final report of DOD/PERSEREC Grant No. N00014-92-J-1795 prepared by Charles R. Honts and Mary K. Devitt (Grand Forks: University of North Dakota, 24 August 1992); Charles R. Honts, *Theory Development and Psychophysiological Credibility Assessment* (Boise: Boise State University, 1996); Charles R. Honts, *1994 Final Report: Field Validity Study of the Canadian Police College Polygraph Technique,* Science Branch: Supply and Services Canada, contract #M9010-3-2219/01ST (Grand Forks: C. Honts Consultations, 1994); Christopher J. Patrick and William G. Iscono, "Validity and Reliability of the Control Questions Polygraph Test: A Scientific Investigation," SBR Abstracts, *Psychophysiology* 24, no. 5 (September 1987):604-05.

[20] Gordon Barland, Charles R. Honts, and Steven Barger, *Studies of the Accuracy of Security Screening Polygraph Examinations* (Fort McClellan: Department of Defense Polygraph Institute, 24 March 1989), iii.

[21] Office of Technology Assessment, *Scientific Validity of Polygraph Testing*, 102.

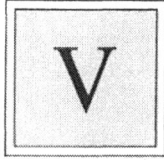

V | Information Age Insecurity

The Information Age is irrevocably altering the means by which the Government must approach the challenge of protecting its information. Protection no longer equates to placing documents in filing cabinets with strong combination locks. Instead, information vital to the security and continued prosperity of the United States resides in a series of increasingly interconnected classified and unclassified systems. The Commission believes that the findings and recommendations noted below provide policymakers the means to begin protecting information properly now and into the next century.

This is an era of extraordinary change not only in information technology, but also in the very way in which individuals communicate with one another. The Commission's goal is not to predict the future that these technological changes will help mold. Rather, it is to better understand the nature of the new threats, so that the Government, with the full support of the private sector, can mitigate or prevent them.

At present, there exists what appears to be a growing gap between technological change and the human capacity to adapt to that change. The risk is that the Government will make bad decisions not because it has too little information, but rather because it has too much information about the wrong things. In such a rapid-paced and changing environment, it is only natural to fall back on old biases, protocols, and shortcuts. Convictions, as Nietzsche once noted, can be "more dangerous enemies of truth than lies."

Federal Government Information Security and the National Information Infrastructure

The information revolution, characterized by the growing convergence of computer and communications technologies, requires a fundamental rethinking of traditional approaches to safeguarding national security information. Those responsible for the protection of national security face new, increasingly difficult challenges presented by the proliferation of computer networks linked by telephone lines, cable, direct broadcast service, and wireless communications, and by the replacement of the traditional computer mainframe by personal computers. In this new electronic world—the National Information Infrastructure (NII)—best symbolized by the steadily growing global Internet, it is not clear what responsibility the Federal Government has to protect the infrastructure that stores, carries, and transmits nearly all of the Government's unclassified and classified information.

The NII within the United States is only one portion of the Global Information Infrastructure (GII) that connects public and private computer networks around the world. For the Federal Government to assume a leadership position in protecting the NII, which is critical both to maintaining economic security and to promoting electronic commerce, would require the dedication of significant resources and effort.

While government involvement in protecting the nation's information infrastructure today is limited, the Preamble to the Constitution makes clear that its citizenry expects government to have a responsibility and means "to insure domestic tranquility [and] provide for the common defense." Even a partial disruption of America's critical infrastructures would, by any account, erode "domestic tranquility." A major incentive for increased government responsibility for protection of the National Information Infrastructure is the degree of reliance by both the civilian and military sectors of government on the infrastructure to carry vital communications, both classified and unclassified.

Both the NII and the GII are evolving at an exponential pace, and there appears to be little agreement concerning how best to shape their development, as well as a lack of existing institutions capable of leading such an effort. Standards for protecting and managing information systems contained within the NII do not currently exist. Furthermore, there is no visible national forum that exists to promote consistent and coordinated international cooperation in defining protection needs or standards, nor is there any comprehensive legislative framework for protecting information and information systems that addresses the variety of perspectives representing law enforcement, national security, the commercial sector, and privacy interests.

Moore's Law

"In 1965 Gordon Moore, who later co-founded Intel, predicted that the capacity of a computer chip would double every year. He said this on the basis of having examined the price/performance ratio of computer chips over the three previous years and projecting it forward. In truth, Moore didn't believe that this rate of improvement would last long, but ten years later his forecasting proved true. And then he predicted the capacity would double every two years. To this day, his predictions have held up, and the average—a doubling every 18 months—is referred to among engineers as Moore's law."

Bill Gates, *The Road Ahead*

The Commission has identified four critical means for improving information systems security: (1) greater Executive Branch oversight and accountability; (2) increased congressional oversight and accountability; (3) improved education, awareness, and training; and (4) upgraded capabilities for responding to new and emerging threats. These are discussed following a review of why the Government must take the lead in enhancing information systems security.

The Growing Threat to Information Systems Security

Information technology costs for the Federal Government exceeded $25 billion in 1995. Within its civilian agencies, the Government employed 120,000 information technology workers, and operated 25,000 medium and large mainframe computers and more than two million individual work stations.[1] The Department of Defense has over two million computers, 10,000 local area networks, and 100 long-distance networks. The civilian sector has a critical responsibility to maintain privacy and services for the public using automated data processing and relying on the National Information Infrastructure. Just as critical to the Department of Defense is its ability to carry out any mission that is dependent on information carried on and supported by the NII. If key responsibilities of both the civilian and military sectors of government are heavily dependent upon an unsecured, potentially unavailable Internet, the Government must address whether this reliance on the NII (and GII) is acceptable and, if so, how to manage the risks involved.

Notwithstanding considerable expenditures on information technology, there exists a widening chasm between the security requirements of and the protection provided for unclassified systems government-wide and those applied to the classified systems that are located principally within the Defense and Intelligence Communities. For example, in the civilian sector, the integrity and availability of information are primary concerns; however, in the Defense and Intelligence Communities, the confidentiality of information has been the traditional concern. Thus, the Executive Branch justifiably remains reluctant to impose upon unclassified networks a classified information systems security standard of confidentiality, primarily because of additional costs and other administrative burdens.

The NII itself is vulnerable to many disruptive forces, including natural events, mistakes, technical failures, and malicious acts. For example:

> A lightning strike on a critical node in a network may cause node failure; an earthquake or hurricane may not only physically disrupt the network but also cause network congestion, another source of disruption. . . . Cutting a fiber optic cable with a backhoe may result in the loss of a primary telecommunications link. A power failure at a critical network node may cause a significant loss of data and information and may isolate portions of the network. Corrupting of key network management data by a network manager can cause many networks to fail. Viruses introduced by [adversaries domestic or foreign] can cause a network to become overloaded and ineffective or to break down at a critical juncture.[2]

'This is a stickup . . .'

Source: *The Los Angeles Times*, December 10, 1974. Reprinted with permission of *The Los Angeles Times*.

The disruptive nature of such occurrences, however caused, was demonstrated in 1988, when a self-replicating software "worm" was released into the Internet and infected over 6,000 host computers worldwide in less than two hours. By the year 2000, it is estimated that the Internet will have 250 million users worldwide operating on 96 million host computers. The potential threat posed by such growth will be a major source of concern, particularly to the Defense Department, which is using the NII to improve its information sharing and its communications connectivity.

> **Malicious Data & Computer Security**
>
> "Traditionally, computer security focuses on containing the effects of malicious users or malicious programs. As programs become more complex, an additional threat arises: malicious data. . . . In general, the outlook is depressing: as the economic incentives increase, these vulnerabilities are likely to be exploited more frequently."
>
> W. Olin Sibert, 19th National Information Systems Security Conference (October 1996)

The General Accounting Office (GAO) has pointed out the national security threat implicit in the relatively inexpensive advantages provided to potential enemies by Internet connections.[3] Disruptions of military operations or denial of service from critical communications nets and power systems to a deploying or deployed U.S. expeditionary force could be the "electronic Pearl Harbor" that some have been forecasting. Nor does the threat emanate only from potential "conventional" information warfare foes. Terrorism has the potential to greatly damage any society that is increasingly dependent on electronic means of creating, storing, and disseminating most or all of its information. The terrorist threat has multiple potential targets, all of which are "on-line," including the Department of Defense, government agencies, private industry, health care organizations, airlines, stock markets, banks, and law enforcement agencies.

Given the costs of damage that has been caused by mere "hackers" in the way of fraud, theft, and denial of accurate information, the threat posed by "cyber terrorists" cannot be dismissed. As Professor Walter Laqueur wrote in a Spring 1996 article in *Foreign Affairs*, the difference between the range of threats posed by hackers on the one hand, and cyber terrorists on the other, is that the latter have the will and the capabilities to destroy or render unusable the NII.

However, being on-line does not necessarily imply a universal vulnerability. Those who understand security and use it effectively also are growing in numbers and sophistication. Many new and evolving defensive tools are available already and more will become available once the private sector becomes more cognizant of emerging threats and the need to better protect information systems, especially when conducting electronic commerce.

The range of threats to national information systems is well catalogued. The National Institute of Standards and Technology (NIST) lists threats and associated losses based on their prevalence and significance in the current computing environment and their expected growth.[4] The GAO noted in its May 1996 report (Figure 6) that the sophistication of attacker tools is increasing while the required knowledge of the attackers is decreasing.[5] The Department of Justice and the FBI estimate that while only ten percent of the criminal community was computer literate in 1996, this rate will climb to 70 percent by 2010.[6] According to the National Research

> Commercial telecommunications carriers, part of the Public Network and, in turn, part of the NII, provide over 95 percent of the DoD's worldwide telecommunications needs.

Figure 6: Trends in Hacker Tools

Sophistication of Attacker Tools

High

Tools with GUI

Packet Spoofing

Stealth Diagnostics

Sniffers

Sweepers

Hijacking Sessions

Disabling Audits

Exploiting known Vulnerabilities

Password Cracking

Self-replicating Code

Low

Password Guessing

Required Knowledge of Attackers

1980   1985   1990   1995

Source: Defense Information Systems Agency, Briefing to Commission staff, March 21, 1996.

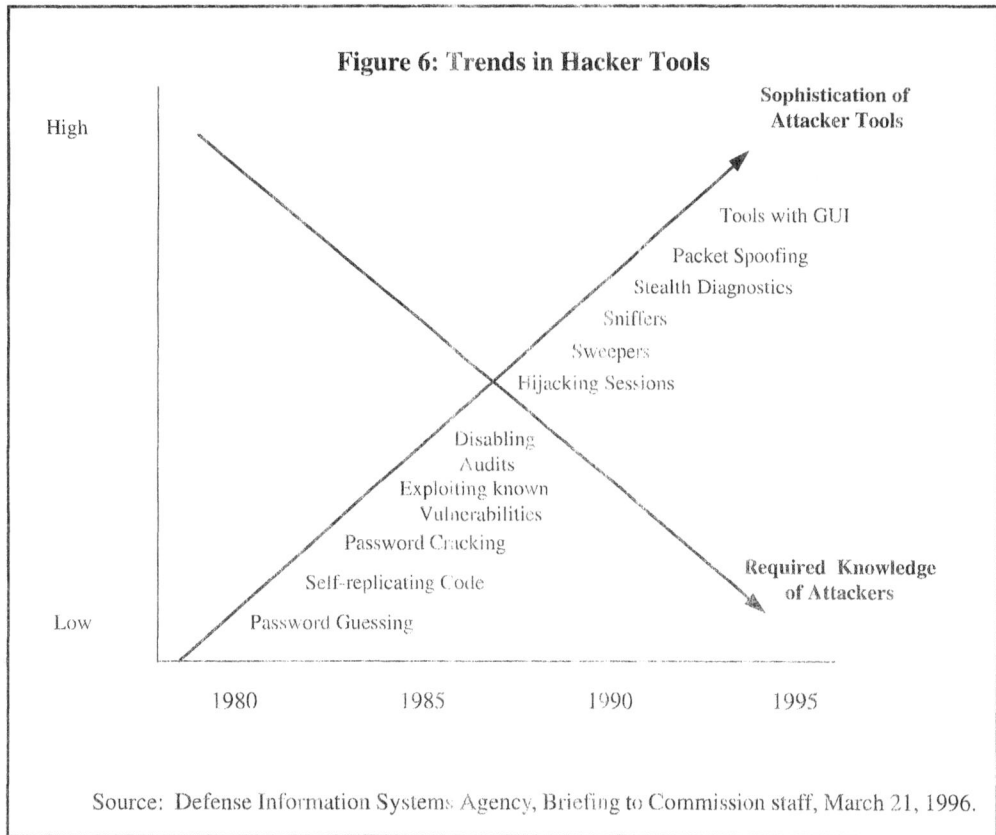

Council report of May 1996, "Of all the information vulnerabilities facing U.S. companies internationally, electronic vulnerabilities appear to be the most significant." The report identifies four principal threat sources to U.S. businesses: "Foreign national agencies (including intelligence services); disgruntled or disloyal employees that work 'from the inside'; network hackers and electronic vandals; and thieves."[7]

In December 1995, the President's National Security Telecommunications Advisory Committee assessed the risks to the nation's Public Network (PN), which includes any switching system or voice, data, or video transmission system that is used to provide communications services to the public, noting that ". . . computer intruders are using increasingly advanced software tools and techniques to attack the PN; . . . the PN is the means for providing access to other desirable targets; . . . and the PN is rapidly evolving to incorporate many different emerging technologies and services, and additional security standards are needed."[8]

The Improving Federal Response

The increased threat to national information systems has not gone unnoticed by the Executive Branch and the Congress. In July 1996, President Clinton issued Executive Order 13010, "Critical Infrastructure Protection," which established the Commission on Critical Infrastructure Protection to study the threats to and develop national policy for protecting critical infrastructures. The Commission will present its findings by July 1997. The Order also created an interim Information Protection Task Force, chaired by the FBI, "to identify and coordinate existing expertise, inside and outside the

Federal Government … in order to coordinate existing infrastructure protection efforts to better address and prevent crises that [will] have a debilitating regional or national impact."[10]

The Subcommittee on Investigations of the Senate Committee on Governmental Affairs, at the urging of former Senator Sam Nunn, held a series of hearings in May, June, and July 1996 regarding the threats to and potential solutions for protecting the NII. Government and industry officials, together with Members of Congress, proffered opinions for identifying and countering both existing and emerging threats. The Subcommittee also heard testimony regarding Executive Order 13010.

Despite past and continuing problems, recent Executive Branch initiatives demonstrate that information systems security is becoming a primary national security concern. For example, on July 16, 1996, Deputy Secretary of Defense John P. White testified before the Senate Government Affairs Committee's Permanent Subcommittee on Investigations regarding security in cyberspace. In the course of his testimony, he described a proposal to create a Joint Defense and Intelligence Community Information Warfare Technical Center that would be located at the National Security Agency. The Center would have the "responsibility to bring the expertise of the intelligence and military communities to define common problems and provide community-specific solutions that will contribute further to information and infrastructure assurance through employment of advanced technology."[11] The Commission believes that centers such as this one could serve as bridges to industry to garner their support in solving this burgeoning problem.

The Federal Government attempts to balance two important and often conflicting policy objectives when dealing with information systems security: (1) promoting the development and widespread use of cost-effective information safeguards, and (2) controlling the proliferation of technologies that might impair national security and law enforcement capabilities. Until the arrival of computers, these protective methods or safeguards took the form of secret codebooks, passwords, and seals to authenticate signatures. Today's world of electronic recording, storing, and transmittal features the mathematical analogues of these systems. The most successful of these safeguards are based on cryptography, which is the technique of concealing the contents of a message by code or cipher.

In 1992, the Computer System Security and Privacy Advisory Board, established by the Department of Commerce pursuant to the Computer Security Act of 1987, recommended a broad national cryptographic policy review before any new or additional cryptographic solution is approved as a U.S. Government standard.[12] The following year the Board noted that any approved standard must address issues of national security and law enforcement protection, the protection of commercial sector computer and telecommunications interests, and the protection of individual liberty interests. It also stated that "the Congress of the United States must be involved in the establishment of cryptographic policy." More recently, the Board endorsed the May 1996 National Research Council's *CRISIS* report, which found that the primary problem in dealing with cryptography is a policy vacuum: to date it has proven impossible to develop a consensus for a coherent national cryptography policy.

Currently, the United States is in an information protection quandary, best exemplified by the ongoing debate regarding cryptography and the commercial export of strong encryption algorithms. The existing national protection standard, developed by the Department of Commerce in 1977, is the Data Encryption Standard (DES). The DES is a published Federal encryption standard, developed jointly with industry, that is used to protect unclassified computer data and communications.

The DES certification period as the Federal Information Protection Standard expires in 1998, with no apparent "public" algorithm alternative in sight. However, the NIST is initiating a process that is intended to lead to the selection of an encryption algorithm for government use as an eventual successor to the DES. While there is no prohibition on the use of DES within the United States, under current export control laws it may not generally be exported by U.S. firms as part of a computer's operating system. The most notable exception is its exportability to financial organizations worldwide.

Until recently, the Executive Branch had failed to develop a new plan for protecting information transmitted across electronic systems. This failure was based on the setback experienced with the rejection of the "Clipper Chip" proposal in 1994 that would have permitted the decoding of encrypted data by U.S. Government officials if warranted by law enforcement or national security concerns. However, on November 15, 1996, the President issued Executive Order 13026, entitled "Encryption Export Policy." This new policy removes encryption products from the U.S. Munitions List regulated by the Department of State, and places them on the Commerce Control List of the Department of Commerce.[13] Although not fully embraced by industry, this policy change is designed to encourage global adoption of a key recovery system and development of a key management infrastructure, as well as allow for the use of strong encryption while protecting public safety and national security.

Improving Oversight Mechanisms

Enhancing Executive Branch Oversight and Policy Formulation

A chief shortcoming in any effort to address the range of important information systems security issues is the persistent lack of effective Executive Branch oversight and the consequent scarcity of resources devoted to information systems security. The Executive Branch lacks centralized focus and direction in developing oversight mechanisms for protecting both unclassified and classified data in Federal information systems, and for ensuring that the development of technology necessary to provide security for information systems keeps pace with the development of the systems technology itself.

The Commission believes that more focused oversight, coupled with better guidance from key components of the Government, would improve the current situation. There is no department of information or information security to oversee the government information infrastructure, much less the national information infrastructure. There is no information technology official equivalent to the Surgeon General to advise the public and government officials alike of the perils from the latest strains of "cyber-diseases." There is no Information Systems Security "911" to call when any number of problems could arise. There is no single policy formulator within the Executive Branch for information systems security. Inspector General offices, with few exceptions, lack the personnel, skills, and resources to address and oversee information systems security within their respective agencies. The President cannot turn to an "Information General" and ask how U.S. investments in information technology are being protected from the latest viruses, terrorists, or hackers.

Over the last ten years, a convoluted information systems security policymaking structure has developed. The Computer Security Act of 1987 and the subsequent National Security Directive (NSD) 42 divided the responsibility for information systems security between the classified and unclassified worlds. If, however, the objective of the 1987 Act was to develop a clear system of policy development and oversight, the result has been just the opposite. In this confusing system, merely ascertaining the correct total number of computer units requiring protection within the Federal Government has proven problematic.

The NIST's Computer Security Division in its Computer Systems Laboratory is charged with developing standards and guidelines for unclassified information systems security, but it has been given relatively few resources to complete this task. In addition, the OMB should wield considerable authority in its role of enforcing information resources management policies and accounting for security in information technology procurement by civilian agencies. However, with only limited resources devoted to this task, the OMB has been unable to effectively monitor agency compliance with either legislative or regulatory requirements.

For classified information systems, policymaking is bifurcated. The Security Policy Board (SPB) reports to the President through the Assistant to the President for National Security Affairs. The National Security Telecommunications and Information Systems Security Committee, created under NSD 42, reports to a Steering Group consisting of fourteen heads of various departments and agencies, each having significant interaction with national security information systems. Both have policymaking responsibilities. The SPB has been unable to create a formal interagency committee structure for discussing information technology issues, largely because it focuses primarily on security issues dealing with classified information within Defense and the Intelligence Community. Information systems security concerns all branches of the Government, and the private sector as well. A previous attempt by the SPB in December 1994 to address sensitive but unclassified information met with great resistance by both the civilian side of the Government and industry.

There are additional examples that illustrate the diffusion of policymaking responsibilities. The Defense Department has the responsibility for implementing policies and procedures for protecting classified information systems. The Director of the National Security Agency is responsible for performing sixteen different tasks, the most significant of which involve: (1) providing technical assistance in protecting classified information systems; (2) upon request, providing assistance in protecting unclassified information systems; and (3) coordinating research and development of techniques and equipment to secure national security systems. The Director of Central Intelligence creates overall guidelines for the Intelligence Community.

In September 1993, the Clinton Administration created several new organizations in an attempt to shape both the development and the security of the NII. These groups included the Information Infrastructure Task Force and its subset, the NII Security Issues Forum, as well as the U.S. Advisory Council on the National Information Infrastructure and its security working group. The work of the Task Force is coming to a close, and the U.S. Advisory Council issued its last report in March 1996.

However, the Task Force report of September 1995 failed to address organizational issues, resources, policy, proposed legislation, and authorities for the agencies to act in protecting the NII. Although the groups have succeeded in generating public discussion of information systems security issues, critics from industry allege that their efforts have been chaotic, disorganized, and lacking in direction. The Commission received comments from the private sector urging that policy development in this area, including the best means of protecting sensitive unclassified information in automated information systems, should be guided by a group located outside the Defense and Intelligence Communities, in light of the fact that approximately 90 percent of all government information is not classified.[14] Such a group would need the authority to develop new rules and policies governing information systems security. (For further discussion of sensitive but unclassified information see Chapter II.)

Table 3: Potential Legislative Jurisdiction for Information Systems Security

Senate Committees
- Committee on Appropriations
- Committee on Armed Services
- Committee on Banking, Housing, and Urban Affairs
- Committee on Commerce, Science, and Transportation
- Committee on Foreign Relations
- Committee on Governmental Affairs
- Committee on the Judiciary
- Select Committee on Intelligence

House Committees
- Committee on Appropriations
- Committee on Banking and Financial Services
- Committee on Commerce
- Committee on International Relations
- Committee on Government Reform and Oversight
- Committee on the Judiciary
- Committee on National Security
- Committee on Science
- Permanent Select Committee on Intelligence

Enhancing Congressional Oversight and Policy Formulation

There will be no substantive, long-term improvements in security policy without a unifying structure to provide leadership, focus, and direction on information systems security matters.[15] The Congress should play a key role in developing such a policy. As discussed both in the 1995 Office of Technology Assessment report and in the May 1996 report of the National Research Council, the Congress has vital roles to play in areas such as cryptographic policy, safeguarding of information, protecting personal privacy in a network-based society, and reform of export control laws.

However, as Table 3 shows, a diverse array of committees and subcommittees have potential responsibility for information systems security issues. The Congress, therefore, appears poorly organized at present to assist in formulating policy and conducting effective oversight in this area. Partly as a result of this lack of a clear structure, the Congress has failed to develop overarching policy and guidance that ensure sufficient focus and direction on these and other important information security issues.

In addition to these organizational problems, the existing legislative framework for computer security issues is badly outdated. That framework, the Computer Security

Act of 1987, was enacted before the proliferation of connectivity and networked personal computers. The Act called for improving the security and protecting the privacy of sensitive information in Federal computer systems, and it created a means for establishing minimum acceptable security practices for such systems. As noted above, it also provided that protection of classified information systems is the responsibility of the NSA, leaving responsibility for unclassified information with the Commerce Department's NIST. However, the Act failed to provide the NIST with the resources or authority needed to accomplish its mandate. For example, the NIST has never received adequate funding and other support needed to pursue projects to stimulate greater systems security among civilian agencies.

The Computer Security Act of 1987, by maintaining clear lines of authority between classified and unclassified information systems and by assigning responsibilities to separate bureaucracies, failed to foresee today's world of computer connectivity and the threats posed to and by that world. Now, a decade later, the Act should be revised to reflect the realities of today's Information Age and to provide a focal point for a comprehensive effort to implement a national information infrastructure policy that takes account of the numerous and complex interests at stake. An updated statutory framework could also help replace the disparate regulations and legislative proposals that have emerged over the past decade. The reallocation of existing resources to safeguard national information systems properly should be accompanied by a clarification of the threats faced by the civilian parts of the Federal Government.

Recommendation

The Commission recommends revising the Computer Security Act of 1987 to reflect the realities of information systems security in the Information Age.

Some of the changes to the Act might include:

- Moving the Computer Systems Laboratory from the NIST to a higher visibility position within the Commerce Department, thereby increasing the likelihood of funding and personnel to support the civilian side of Government;
- Directing agencies to set aside specific funds, perhaps as a budget line item, for information systems security training; and
- Requiring the Office of Personnel Management to create a career path for information systems security professionals that includes network administration and computer crime investigation.

As with the Executive Branch, promising recent developments reflect heightened Congressional attention to the above concerns. For example, beginning in May 1996, the Senate's Permanent Subcommittee on Investigations held a series of hearings to focus on information systems security. The Subcommittee assembled panels of high-ranking government officials and private sector experts to attest to the weaknesses and vulnerabilities of both government and private sector information systems. In addition, the GAO, at the request of the Subcommittee, submitted a report that made public the increasing vulnerabilities of unclassified Department of Defense computer systems.[16]

However, to date efforts to develop legislation in this area remain fragmented. Subjects encompassed by recent bills include encryption, copyright protection, threat assessments, criminal computer activity, and espionage through computer systems. The FY 1997 Defense Authorization Act addressed information systems security by calling for the President to submit to the Congress a "description of the national policy and plans to meet essential Government and civilian needs during a national security emergency associated with a strategic attack on elements of the national infrastructure" and to "assign responsibilities to Federal departments and agencies in the event of a strategic attack on the information systems-dependent national infrastructure."[17] The Commission believes that the initiative by the Administration, outlined in Executive Order 13010, is a good first step in response to that legislative mandate.

Addressing Current Problems

Preventing Redundancies in Technology Development

The Federal Government has no standardized mechanism for coordinating and informing agencies of technology developments. As a result, agencies often duplicate efforts and waste resources by overlooking or ignoring technological tools existing elsewhere in the Government. Although it would save money to simply adapt to one form or another, many agencies distrust the quality of products developed at other agencies, or believe that their own specialized needs require some duplication of effort. For example, the Departments of Defense and Energy each developed separate electronic personnel security questionnaires, despite knowing that all government agencies eventually will use a standardized form. The limited resource base of the future will necessitate more cooperation and free exchange of ideas and technology and less of an attitude of "not invented here."

However, there are positive signs that more cooperative research and development efforts are starting to emerge. For example, at Fort Leavenworth, Kansas, the U.S. Army, with advice from other Government organizations, has constructed an electronic records management "test bed" that incorporates many features of this cooperative approach. It is available to all Federal agencies: the Army shares insights from its experience with the test bed and offers without charge all software used in the system to any agency. This is an example of the cooperative spirit that is needed to establish a sound electronic records management structure in the Federal Government.

In addition, the Congress and the Executive Branch recently have established guidelines for developing new information systems that may impose some order on the creation of information systems security tools and avoid wasteful expenditures. However, both the Information Technology Management Reform Act and Executive Order 13011, "Federal Information Technology," fail to create a central mechanism that coordinates the Government's focus on emerging technologies. The Commission believes that creating a central technology clearinghouse to coordinate all research and development regarding information technology and to standardize government information technology acquisitions might lessen the burden on departments and agencies. The need for this approach is already implicit within the context of Executive Order 13011.

Promoting Government-Industry Cooperation

Government and industry cooperation in the world of information technology is not a new concept. More than twenty years ago, a partnership between government and industry solved that generation's need for strong encryption with the Data Encryption Standard. At that time, the security offered by DES was sufficient for protecting sensitive unclassified information within the Government. Due to technological advances in encryption-breaking techniques, however, certain protective technologies, such as DES now are too weak to adequately protect banking and other extremely sensitive information.

With a growing national and global need for new information protection standards, government and industry must reinvigorate their partnership. Maintaining a U.S. leadership role in developing and promulgating international standards is dependent upon such cooperation both domestically and internationally. Moreover, a government oversight role in developing and promulgating safeguarding standards is highly desirable. Information systems products mutually developed by government and industry carry an implied guarantee of integrity and reliability that no private firm alone can provide.

Advocates of renewed government-industry cooperation to solve information protection problems recognize that there must be incentives, such as indemnification, in order for industry to cooperate with the Government. Information systems security problems will not be "just" government or "just" industry problems; they will be shared by all who need information protection. Only the Federal Government, however, has the resources to invest on the scale needed to ensure functioning large-scale systems and can provide the forums necessary to permit public debate on the concerns of the different equities involved: privacy, law enforcement, national security, and commercial interests.

Discouraging the Use of Classification as an Alternative to Effective Information Systems Security

Studies conducted in the last several years, including those by Defense agencies, private companies, Congressional committees, and the General Accounting Office, have shown that Federal information systems are extremely vulnerable to attacks by both foreign governments and hackers. The publicity created by these investigative efforts has heightened concern about protecting certain sensitive but unclassified data that reside on computer systems.

Because of these high-profile reports and other expressions of concern regarding unauthorized access to and potential destruction of Government information systems, some Members of Congress have suggested that sensitive information stored on computer systems should be incorporated into new or existing classification levels to provide an extra measure of protection. Classification, however, addresses the *symptoms* rather than the causes of existing problems. Extending classification to potentially millions of sensitive but unclassified documents would both be costly and run directly counter to the intent in Executive Order 12958 and other efforts to reduce the scope of classification. The Federal Government instead should work toward developing and implementing more effective and coordinated computer security measures.

Improving information systems security is preferable to and less costly than the very expensive process of classifying millions of sensitive documents that do not currently warrant such form of protection and control. This approach would require agencies to address the real problem: computer system vulnerabilities throughout the Federal Government and the inadequate response thus far.

Encouraging Greater Accountability and Leadership

In light of the more than $25 billion spent for information technology in 1995, it is reasonable to question what type and quality of information systems security the Federal Government has obtained in return for its investment. It appears clear that there has been neither adequate leadership nor accountability with respect to agency investments in information systems security technology. Under provisions of the new Information Technology Management Reform Act enacted in February 1996, Chief Information Officers at agencies are now specifically responsible for making proper decisions on technology acquisitions. With rare exceptions, however, the management of information technology resources is not specified in the job descriptions of agency heads. Nor is the required successful and comprehensive security for these assets mentioned in the job descriptions of the security officers whom senior officials may place in charge of information technology acquisitions and operations. Often, security officers are assigned to implement and oversee computer security requirements as a third or fourth additional duty.

Furthermore, the OMB has assigned only two people to oversee the entire information systems infrastructure of the Federal Government (excluding the DoD and the Intelligence Community). The NIST's Computer Systems Laboratory has 25 people and a $4 million budget to "secure" the Federal Government's unclassified information systems. There is no oversight of research and development and acquisitions among agencies to avoid redundancies and duplications. Agencies thus are left to implement their security programs with little regard for the correct mix of security required. Information systems decisionmaking is budget-driven, and security appropriations often are the first line items to be eliminated or reduced.

On the legislative side, the disparate and overlapping committee and subcommittee jurisdictions make it difficult to coordinate leadership in the Congress on matters of information systems security. Moreover, the entire world of information systems and systems security remains unexciting to many; as a result, Members of Congress for the most part have not given it much attention.

The Congress needs an independent, focused research and analytical capability if it is to make informed judgments on the direction the Executive Branch chooses to take concerning information technology and other related issues. This is especially true when Congressional committees must exercise oversight of individual departments and agencies that are developing information resource management approaches in response to statutory requirements. Greater expertise would provide the Congress with the information necessary to make decisions on technology issues in a rapidly changing technical environment. Such expertise can be developed by using existing resources within the Congressional Research Service and the Government Accounting Office to advise the Congress on policy formulation, oversight, and other duties in the area of information technology.

Planning for the Future

The requirements of the next century will demand that the Federal Government and industry work more closely than ever before to develop technologies that address the problems that accompany the rapid proliferation of information systems within the Federal Government. Prioritizing and dedicating the necessary resources are essential in each of the areas listed below.

Disseminating Threat Information

In spite of recent attempts to facilitate and encourage broader dissemination of threat information produced by elements of the Intelligence and Law Enforcement Communities, much of the information available still is provided in paper form or through briefing of individuals. There exists no systematic means for informing government agencies or private industry about the threats to the National Information Infrastructure. Accurate and timely threat information, available on-line, could assist interested parties in focusing limited resources to counter key threats and encourage industry to provide threat information to other firms as well as to the Government.

While a fully automated threat dissemination process would place an additional burden on the Intelligence and Law Enforcement Communities, the benefits derived from such a process would far outweigh any additional costs, especially if the change encourages private industry to become a full partner in addressing the threats to the NII. However, prior to expanding the existing automated intelligence information systems to include new industry customers, current as well as potential users must be aware of and understand the concerns raised by the Intelligence Community in potentially providing certain extremely sensitive intelligence information to industry customers. With innovations such as INTELINK, an Internet-like database that contains classified information for the Defense and Intelligence Communities, this isolation of classified computer systems has begun to diminish. The costs to the Government and industry for establishing a contractor version of a database, such as INTELINK, can range from as little as $5,000 for a basic computer and secure telephone unit to $500,000 for a complete system that includes audio and video capability for Top Secret/Sensitive Compartmented Information.[18]

Increasing Awareness of Computer Attacks

At present, there is no national-level computer incident response center that is able to receive, analyze, compare, collate, and disseminate to appropriate authorities incidents of computer attack, "denial of service," or computer crime. The Commission believes that current technology offers potential means for addressing shortcomings in the detecting and reporting of computer attacks or attempted intrusions. For example, the Federal Emergency Management Agency has an existing state and local information infrastructure in place to support a national computer incident response center, thus reducing the need for substantial investment in additional bureaucracy and spending. Any effort to establish a national response center could capitalize on existing infra-structures, until such time as a clear need for a more permanent structure and reporting system emerges.

A national computer incident response center could build upon experiences gained from existing computer emergency response entities. A response center would utilize mainly existing infrastructure and lines of communication, keeping new costs down. Reporting received, including that from state and local levels, would help focus agencies on the need to manage risks and would encourage the development of a database that promotes more accurate threat assessments.

To be effective, such a center would require cooperation from the private sector as well as from state and local governments. This cooperation may be difficult to achieve, however, especially from corporations and financial institutions reluctant to acknowledge losses from computer attacks. An expressed promise of confidentiality in protecting information received from both government and nongovernment sources would be essential for private industry to provide attack information.

Friendly Greetings?

One company whose officials met with the Commission warned its employees against reading an e-mail entitled "Penpal Greetings." Although the message appeared to be a friendly letter, it contained a virus that could infect the hard drive and destroy all data present. The virus was self-replicating, which meant that once the message was read, it would automatically forward itself to any e-mail address stored in the recipient's in-box.

Developing Auditing and Intrusion Detection Capabilities

The exponential increase in computer network interconnectivity has made automated information systems simultaneously more powerful and more vulnerable to attacks or intrusions. Attempts to compromise the confidentiality, integrity, or availability of information in these systems tend to exploit flaws in either the operating system or the application programs. The degree to which these intrusions are prevented, or at least diverted, is directly related to the amount of resources and time devoted to building and maintaining the system's defenses. Improvements are needed both in detection and in the collection of data on intrusions. An intrusion detection system does not, in and of itself, stop an intrusion in progress; it merely serves as a mechanism to alert system security officials. Intrusion detection systems must be combined with timely assessment and response capabilities in order to achieve effective systems security. As stated at the National Information Systems Security Conference in October 1995:

> Computer and Internet misuse has become a frequent topic of today's
> mainstream media, and the demand for anti-intrusion technology is
> exploding. However, intrusion detection products are as yet esoteric
> and not well integrated to work together with complementary ap-
> proaches such as intrusion preventing "firewalls."[19]

One encouraging sign is that the technological advances that have occurred since that
Conference now do provide some limited means of scanning for system vulnerabilities.

An intrusion detection system must identify, preferably in real time, unauthorized use,
misuse, or abuse of computer systems. More reliable data collection also would permit
more reliable assessments of the dangers posed by these intrusions. One reason
computer intrusions into unclassified systems are not reported within the Federal
Government is that most agencies do not mandate that incidents be reported. In the
private sector, there is great reluctance to report anything to the Government. These
reasons include fear of loss of client base if the information is revealed; lack of
indemnification by the Government for failing to protect information owned by others;
and a presumptive drain on limited resources to obtain protective measures with no
incentives to do so.

Just as in the private sector, many Federal agencies are reluctant to make the investments required in this area because of limited budgets, lack of direction and
prioritization from senior officials, and general ignorance of the threat. Without
spending mandates, managers will not prioritize in favor of protecting extremely
vulnerable unclassified databases. An additional problem is that detection of intrusions
in classified information systems still may not be able to eliminate the possibility of
unauthorized copying of classified data. As the May 1996 GAO report on DoD
intrusions stated, attacks are exploiting basic vulnerabilities such as poor password
usage. Improved intrusion detection systems cannot be a cure for careless and
ineffective computer security procedures or techniques.

Including Security in Automation Projects

All Federal Government agencies today are using automation, including the Internet, to
increase their productivity, efficiency, and visibility to the public, and to achieve cost
savings. However, at present there are few security standards available to guide
agencies in creating and implementing automation projects. As a result, the degree of
information security varies from project to project, sometimes leaving sensitive information susceptible to interception, duplication, or malicious alteration. In addition, most
operating systems within a given computer have many security features that are not
turned on automatically when the system is activated or started. These features, once
activated, would markedly improve the overall security posture of the system without
spending additional resources, if officials had the training and awareness to utilize the
systems to the fullest extent possible.

If agencies fail to implement adequate security during the initial stages of an
automation project, they may be forced to add security, usually at far greater cost and
in the glare of public scrutiny, during a later crisis. Estimates in the Joint Security
Commission report suggest that incorporating security into a computer system during

the planning stages costs between 5 and 10 percent of the entire project budget. In contrast, the cost can rise to 25 percent of the project's budget if security is not implemented until after problems arise, as is usually the case.[20]

Professionalizing Information Systems Security

The Federal Government must promote greater awareness of the vulnerabilities of national information systems. One way to do so is to create, support, and promote an information systems security career field within the Government. The NSA's National Computer Security Center has made significant advances in defining the knowledge, skills and abilities, curriculum requirements, and on-the-job experience required to produce information systems security specialists. Its program for developing a professional cadre to secure the classified systems can serve as a model for protecting the unclassified systems of the Government and the private sector.

Despite the need, there currently is no government-wide speciality or career field for computer security personnel, network administrators, or computer crime investigators. Nor are there any universities or colleges offering a doctoral program in Computer Security; while the NSA's National Computer Security Center is in the process of promoting such a program, it is expected to take years to fully develop.[21] Focusing more attention on the development of a computer security career path, within both the Government and the private sector, would ensure the continued presence of personnel and resources devoted to safeguarding information systems—critical in an era of increased connectivity and heightened system vulnerabilities.

Agencies should be prepared to refocus existing resources on the training needed to create information systems security specialists. The direction must come from the top for creating a career path as an incentive for improving the quality of the computer security force expertise. Senior managers and leaders must be made aware of the need for a quality force to protect national information systems and must provide the guidance, authority, and direction necessary to meet this need.

> **Recommendation**
>
> **The Commission recommends developing an information systems security career path across the Government.**

Strengthening Information Technology Training and Awareness

Senior Executive Branch and Congressional officials, users of Federal computers, and overseers of information systems security all need continuing education and training to remain abreast of developments in information systems technology and understand how to protect the contents of those information systems.

The first element of such education and training efforts concerns the basic rules for use of information systems. No coordinated Federal Government effort exists to teach computer ethics or rules of behavior to employees working on Federal computer systems. A 1996 survey of Federal agencies and private corporations showed that few employees even had a working knowledge of current laws on the misuse of computer systems. The results of that survey are shown in Figure 7.

A 1994 report by the Office of Technology Assessment noted that "unauthorized use of computers by authorized users is estimated to be the second largest source of computerized losses," following only human error.[22] If agencies wish to focus on the critical issue of training, automated courses on computer ethics and safeguarding would allow large numbers of government employees to receive training more cheaply than through traditional classroom instruction; recently, several government agencies have begun to develop such computerized training courses.

The second element of training focuses on security awareness. The Computer Security Act of 1987 requires agencies to improve the security and protect the privacy of sensitive information in Federal computer systems. The Act cites mandatory Federal computer security training as a means of attaining improved security awareness and accepted computer security practices. Yet despite the increased threats and vulnerabilities present in today's national information infrastructure, there is little evidence of serious attempts to increase training and education programs. The 1987 Act does not ensure that agencies budget sufficient resources to safeguard information assets, and, in reality, the training provision of the 1987 Act was an unfunded mandate.

Information exchange that is automated and accessible at low cost is the third element of security education, training, and awareness. Such information exchange must provide a communication infrastructure that reflects the technological advances of the next century. The recent efforts of the Defense Advanced Research Projects Agency (DARPA) to automate a customer-driven information exchange database are noteworthy. DARPA's experience and expertise in creating and supporting the forerunner of the Internet has served as the basis for creating a private network (Intranet)

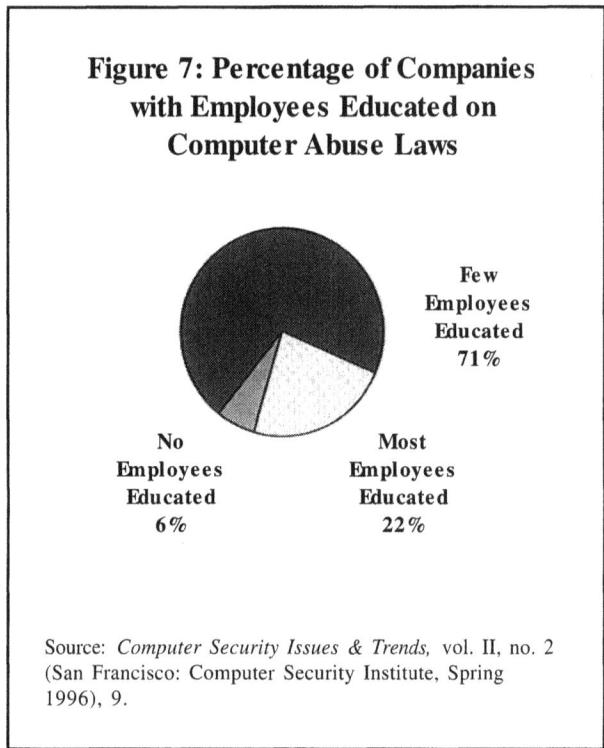

Figure 7: Percentage of Companies with Employees Educated on Computer Abuse Laws

Few Employees Educated 71%

No Employees Educated 6%

Most Employees Educated 22%

Source: *Computer Security Issues & Trends,* vol. II, no. 2 (San Francisco: Computer Security Institute, Spring 1996), 9.

that provides security officials, both within Government and industry, such a communications link for problem solving. DARPA's know-how and objectivity in efforts such as this security-focused Intranet can help foster additional progress on information exchange.

Conclusion

The Federal Government has a clear responsibility to protect its own information infrastructure. Less clear is what the Government should be doing to protect the overall National Information Infrastructure. The transmittal of both classified and unclassified Government information depends upon the privately-created NII lines of communication, but the Government has no claim or right to control the private, commercial, and proprietary information moving across the same systems. In the event of an attack on the NII resulting in significant damage to the security of the nation as a whole, to selected elements of the population, or to critical infrastructures, policies and procedures that are well-founded and well-tested must be in place.

Leadership is lacking, however, throughout the Federal Government in the area of information systems and systems security, and as a result, agencies have not dedicated the resources needed to protect information systems adequately. If senior officials were made more aware of the magnitude of the problem and held more accountable for information systems security, the necessary prioritization of resources probably would follow.

Solutions do not lie in the creation of new government bureaucracies. In fact, many of the tools needed to create coherent policy, advise agencies, and educate system users and protectors already exist. The fact that Inspectors General do not pursue oversight of information systems security does not mean that they cannot, given greater emphasis and resources from their respective agencies' leadership. The fact that the NIST's Computer Systems Laboratory has not vigorously pursued security solutions and standards does not mean that it cannot, given dynamic leadership and the funds needed to do its work. The fact that the NSA has been viewed as a traditional protector of classified information does not mean that it cannot devote more of its considerable resources to advising about protection of the unclassified government information systems. The fact that the Computer Security Act of 1987 is ill-suited for a world of connectivity does not mean that the law cannot be amended or replaced to reflect today's needs.

In summary, the security of the Government's information systems would be enhanced as a result of increased attention in three broad areas: (1) national policy development, application, and oversight; (2) threat recognition and crisis management; and (3) professionalization of the information systems security career field. This Commission believes that the existing Presidential Commission on Critical Infrastructure Protection is ideally suited to expand upon this report's findings in the area of information technology and, through its own recommendations, to educate the Government and the public on the preferred approaches to efficient protection of information systems.

---

[1] Office of Management and Budget, "Security of Federal Automated Information Resources" (Washington, D.C., February 1996, briefing sheet), 8.
[2] Department of Defense, Joint Staff, *INFORMATION WARFARE: Legal, Regulatory, Policy and Organizational Considerations for Assurance*, prepared by SAIC, 2nd ed. (Washington, D.C.: Department of Defense, 4 July 1996), 2-18.

[3] General Accounting Office, *Information Security: Computer Attacks at Department of Defense Pose Increasing Risks,* GAO/AIMD-96-94 (Washington, D.C.: Government Printing Office, May 1996), 11-12.

[4] National Institute of Science and Technology, *An Introduction to Computer Security: The NIST Handbook*, 800-12 (Washington, D.C.: Government Printing Office, October 1995), 21.

[5] General Accounting Office, *Information Security*, 13.

[6] Interview by Commission Staff, 12 September 1996.

[7] National Research Council, *Cryptography's Role in Securing the Information Society (CRISIS)* (Washington, D.C.: National Academy Press, 30 May 1996), 1-25.

[8] National Security Telecommunications Advisory Committee, Network Security Information Exchange, *An Assessment of the Risk To the Security of Public Networks* (Washington, D.C.: National Communications System, December 1995), ES1-ES2.

[9] Department of Defense, Joint Staff, *INFORMATION WARFARE: Legal, Regulatory, Policy and Organizational Considerations for Assurance*, prepared by SAIC (Washington, D.C.: 4 July 1995), 1-1.

[10] President, Executive Order 13010, "Critical Infrastructure Protection," *Federal Register* 61, no. 138 (17 July 1996): 37345 - 37350.

[11] Senate Committee on Governmental Affairs, *Security in Cyberspace: Hearings before the Subcommittee on Investigations*, 104th Cong., 2nd sess., 16 July 1996.

[12] Office of Technology Assessment, *Information Security and Privacy in Network Environments*, OTA-TCT-606 (Washington, D.C.: Government Printing Office, 1994), 176-177.

[13] President, Executive Order 13026, "Encryption Export Policy," *Federal Register* 61, no. 224 (19 November 1996): 58767-58768.

[14] National Security Telecommunications Advisory Committee, Network Security Information Exchange, *An Assessment of the Risk to the Security of Public Networks*, 2.

[15] Joint Security Commission, *Redefining Security* (Washington, D.C.: 28 February 1994), 2, 102, 106. For further discussion on sensitive but unclassified information, see also Chapter II, pages 28-29 of the report.

[16] General Accounting Office, *Information Security*, 2.

[17] Public Law 104-201, 104th Cong., 2nd sess. (23 September 1996).

[18] Office of the Executive Director, Intelligence Community Affairs Staff, telephone conversation with Commission Staff, 4 September 1996.

[19] Lawrence R. Halme and R. Kenneth Bauer, "AINT Misbehaving — A Taxonomy of Anti-Intrusion Techniques," *Proceedings of the 18th National Information Systems Security Conference,* Vol. I (Baltimore: National Institute of Standards and Technology, 10-13 October 1995), 164.

[20] Department of Defense official, telephone conversation with Commission Staff, 30 July 1996.

[21] Department of Defense official, telephone conversation with Commission Staff, 7 June 1996.

[22] Office of Technology Assessment, *Information Security and Privacy in Network Environments,* 25-26.

Appendix A

SECRECY

A Brief Account
of the American Experience

TABLE OF CONTENTS

1. <u>Secrecy as Regulation</u>

Secrecy is a form of government regulation. There are many such forms, but a general division can be made between regulations dealing with domestic affairs, and those dealing with foreign affairs. In the first category, it is generally the case that government prescribes what the citizen may do; in the second category, it is generally the case that government prescribes what the citizen may know.

Again, in the first category, it is generally the case that such regulations derive from statute. Congress makes a law, entrusting its enforcement to a bureaucracy which issues rules and rulings to carry out the law. This is a feature of the administrative state that appeared in the United States in the early 20th century, roughly between the administrations of Theodore Roosevelt and Woodrow Wilson. Thus, the Department of Commerce and Labor was established in 1903; the Federal Reserve Board in 1913; the Federal Trade Commission in 1914. An executive gazette—the *Official Bulletin*—was inaugurated in 1917. (The *Official Bulletin* was published for only two years. It was the precursor to the *Federal Register*, in which all new regulations are published, which began in 1936.)

Secrecy became a persuasive mode of regulation with the advent of the national security state at mid-century, although its origins also go back to the beginning of the century. The statutory base of secrecy is modest; two or three laws, of which the National Security Act of 1947 is emblematic. Withal, its spare reference to the protection of "sources and methods" led to a vast secrecy system almost wholly hidden from view. There would be no *Official Bulletin*.

Three general propositions will emerge from this "Brief Account." The first is that from the time of the First World War, the beginning of the great power conflicts that would continue for the better part of the century, the United States recurrently faced espionage attacks by foreign governments, and on occasion, sabotage of notable proportion. A recurrent pattern of these crises is the involvement of ethnic groups, often first-generation immigrants who have retained strong attachments to their ancestral homes and, not infrequently, to political movements that were prominent at the time of immigration.

The ethnic dimension of international conflict has repeatedly created a fear of internal conspiracy in aid of external threat. This was succinctly stated by Theodore Roosevelt in October 1917:

> The men who oppose the war; who fail to support the government in every
> measure which really tends to the efficient prosecution of the war; and above
> all who in any shape or way champion the cause and the actions of Germany,
> show themselves to be the Huns within our own gates and the allies of the men
> whom our sons and brothers are crossing the ocean to fight.[1]

Arguably, one consequence of the "Hun within" syndrome is that the United States developed a pattern of extensive defensive secrecy far greater than would have been required to deal with an essentially external threat. A kind of backward formation took place. Whereas, in the usual situation (if there is such) the existence of secrets required defensive measures, in the American experience of the 20th century, the secrets came about largely *because* there was a perceived threat. Loyalty would be the arbiter of security. Given that loyalty could not be assumed, a vast secretive security system emerged.

The second proposition is that the statutory basis for secrecy has been, and remains, so elusive that violations of secrecy occur with relative impunity. Edward A. Shils defined secrecy as "the compulsory withholding of knowledge, reinforced by the prospect of sanctions for disclosure."[2] This was written in 1956, when the morale of the Cold War system was high, and discipline was readily maintained. In 1946, as will be discussed, the Army Security Agency (formerly the Army Signal Security Agency) decoded the first of several thousand VENONA[3] messages sent by the KGB [Komitet Gosudarstvennoi Bezopasnosti (Committee for State Security)][4] and other Soviet intelligence agents identifying spies working within the American Government. The consequences for American counterespionage were spectacular; the VENONA project continued until 1980. Early on, the Soviets learned of its existence through a spy in the Army Security Agency itself, but as for the American public, not a whisper was heard until the 1980s, and only with the establishment of the Commission on Protecting and Reducing Government Secrecy has this extraordinary archive been made public.

In time, however, the system degraded, largely in consequences of having grown to grotesque proportions. A specific example would be the celebrated "Pentagon Papers," essentially an official history of the war in Vietnam. Most of which were "Top Secret." The *New York Times*, and later the *Washington Post*, obtained copies and proceeded to publish selections. The United States Government moved to enjoin publication. The Supreme Court overruled the Executive Branch. Soon after, Harold Edgar and Benno C. Schmidt, Jr. published an article on the case in the *Columbia Law Review*. Just what was the law here? they asked. They replied, after 158 pages, that they could not possibly tell.[5]

It has now become routine for information of the highest classification to appear in the press, most commonly as a tactical move in some intra-government policy dispute. There are no sanctions. A fairly routine example of what might be called "deregulation" occurred on October 22, 1996, when the *Washington Times* published details of a "Top Secret" CIA analysis of the control system of Russian nuclear weapons. The following day, the *Washington Post* had a "follow-up" story by Reuters:

CIA Rates 'Low' the Risk of Unauthorized Use of Russian Nuclear Warheads

The Central Intelligence Agency has concluded that Russia's control over its nuclear arsenal has been weakening, but the chance of unauthorized launch or blackmail remains low, CIA officials said yesterday.

"The Russian nuclear command and control system is being subjected to stress that it was not designed to withstand as a result of wrenching social change, economic hardship and malaise within the armed forces," according to a classified report prepared last month, the officials said.

The CIA report, "Prospects for Unsanctioned Use of Russian Nuclear Weapons" and stamped top secret, was disclosed by the Washington Times in its editions yesterday. CIA officials confirmed the accuracy of the material quoted in the article.

Now came the essential part of the story: Who benefited when someone within the government chose to betray this "secret"? The Reuters dispatch continued:

> Disclosure of the CIA report bolstered critics of President Clinton . . . who favor building a costly missile defense system over administration objections that it could undermine the 1972 Anti-Ballistic Missile Treaty.
>
> "It reinforces the urgent need for a missile defense to be put in place as soon as possible for the United States as well as for its allies and friends," said James Lilley . . . who served as U.S. envoy to China and South Korea under presidents Ronald Reagan and George Bush.

This is a fixed pattern. Classified documents are routinely passed out to support an administration; weaken an administration; advance a policy; undermine a policy. A newspaper account would be incomplete without some such reference.

Shils's definition to the contrary, however, *there are now no sanctions for disclosure*. Not, that is, for anyone at the Deputy Assistant Secretary level or above. In the manner of maturing bureaucracies, most agencies involved with security matters have developed a range of publications concerning their activities. The Department of Defense Security Institute publishes *Recent Espionage Cases*. The May 1996 issue recorded all cases since 1975. It is melancholy reading. Of 89 such cases, 55 involved persons who on their own decided, typically, to try to sell secrets to the Soviets. Only fifteen were "recruited" successfully and there were only nine real-life foreign agents. Hardly a "Hun within" in the batch. But there is one notable case, that of a civilian analyst with the Office of Naval Intelligence who supplied Jane's Publications with classified photos showing a Soviet nuclear-powered carrier under construction. The photographs were subsequently published in *Jane's Defence Weekly* (July 1984). The employee was sentenced to two years' imprisonment. The Defense Security Institute comments that this was "the first individual convicted under the 1917 Espionage Code for unauthorized disclosure to the press."[6]

Along with the *de facto* immunity of senior officials who release classified information, there developed a form of Congressional oversight, beginning with the House Committee on Un-American Activities and the Senate Subcommittee on Internal Security, which could and did protect the intelligence community, as it came to be known, and let out a fair amount of information to the public. But in the process, the public also "learns" a good many things that are not so. As Evan Thomas, the author of a recent book on the early days of the CIA, notes in a recent issue of *Studies in Intelligence*, a publication of the Central Intelligence Agency: "Polls show that nearly 80 percent of Americans believe JFK died as a result of a conspiracy, and about half believe the CIA was somehow involved."[7] Secrecy begets suspicion, which can metastasize into belief in conspiracies of the most awful sort.

Despite the growing frequency of high-level disclosure of classified materials, the public perception is not wrong; the vast proportion of classified material remains classified. This reflects the principled character of the men and women of the Armed Services and the assorted intelligence and related agencies. It also reflects the sheer dimension of the secrecy system. It would be a fair guess that if every page of every newspaper published in the United States on a given weekday were given over solely to reprinting the classified documents *created* that day, there would not be enough space. This, in turn, reflects the criterion of classification, which is to say, *national security*.

Harold C. Relyea, of the Congressional Research Service, notes that, "A perusal of the Federal statutes indicates that *national security* suddenly began to appear with some frequency as the undefined term in laws enacted around the time of U.S. involvement in World War I."[8] National defense was not enough; that had been the concern of admirals and generals: dockyards and arsenals and order of battle. This was something more. The world was a far more dangerous place; ideological conflict was as serious as military conflict: indeed, more so, and far more elusive in its details. For the better part of a century the United States would hardly know a moment's peace of mind. We would gradually see, in Donald L. Robinson's term, "The Routinization of Crisis Government."[9]

The decisive moment in this regard was the enactment in 1947 of the National Security Act, which established the unified Department of Defense, the Central Intelligence Agency, and the National Security Council, the latter a standing committee in the White House designed to deal with emergencies of all sorts. In testifying in support of such legislation before the Senate Committee on Military Affairs, James F. Forrestal, then Secretary of the Navy, was explicit in choosing the term "national security" over "national defense." Unifying the Army and Navy was not nearly enough. Forrestal set out a list of "eight requirements against which to measure any plan for national security":

> (1) Organized means for the integrating of foreign and military policy;
> (2) Organizations in being for directing industrial mobilization and for reconciling industrial mobilization with national resources.
>
> That means in particular that you don't create military demands beyond your capacity to fill them or that will do injury to other great and urgent demands. And that question of balance, in my view, is one of the most important considerations in war.
>
> ****
>
> (3) A more efficient organization for the translation of strategic requirements into requirements for materiel and personnel.
> (4) Provisions for the coordination of military and other war budgets.
> (5) Adequate means for the elimination of waste and duplication in and between the military departments.
> (6) An efficient coordinated intelligence organization serving all Government departments and agencies.
> (7) An organizational means for fostering scientific research and development within the military departments and among civilian organizations.
> (8) Full opportunity of each branch of the military services to develop for its specialized task.[10]

At this time, a report prepared for Forrestal declared that "our international policy in the years ahead looks for national security through a United Nations organization for the maintenance of world peace."[11] This would hardly do today, and yet, in the first war following the Second World War, in Korea beginning in 1950, the United States fought under a United Nations flag. If the United Nations receded as a vehicle for collective security—another term of that time—the North Atlantic Treaty Organization was by now also in place. International venues would vary; what continued ever after was Forrestal's dictum that national security must "bring in every element of our Government."[12]

A succession of post-World War II presidents issued executive orders published in the *Federal Register* asserting this particular form of regulation, but without defining it. Truman in 1951:

> *Classified security information.* The term "classified security information" as used herein means official information the safeguarding of which is necessary in the interest of national security, and which is classified for such purpose by appropriate classifying authority.[13]

Eisenhower in 1953:

> Section 1. *Classification Categories.* Official information which requires protection in the interests of national defense shall be limited to three categories of classification, which in descending order of importance shall carry one of the following designations: Top Secret, Secret, or Confidential. No other designation shall be used to classify defense information. . . .[14]

A 1972 Executive Order by President Nixon was more ambitious:

> Section 1. *Security Classification Categories.* Official information or material which requires protection against unauthorized disclosure in the interest of the national defense or foreign relations of the United States (hereinafter collectively termed "national security") shall be classified in one of three categories, namely "Top Secret," "Secret," or "Confidential," depending upon the degree of its significance to national security. No other categories shall be used to identify official information or material as requiring protection in the interest of national security, except as otherwise expressly provided by statute.[15]

The most recent Executive Order, that of President Clinton in 1995, is exemplary in the succinctness of its core definition:

> *Definitions.* For purposes of this order:
> (A) "National security" means the national defense or foreign relations of the United States.[16]

But succinctness is not the same as clarity. Under these executive orders, "national security" is in the eyes of the "appropriate classifying authority." Of which there are at present roughly 5,300 persons within the Federal Government with the authority to classify "originally," but an estimated *two million* additional persons in the Government who then can classify "derivatively" by citing already-classified documents or by using "classification guides" prepared by their agencies, and another one million in private industry with such ability.[17]

A third and final proposition is that secrecy, unless carefully attended to, is a source of considerable sorrow in government. That there can be a need for it, none should dispute. The Framers so provided in Article 1, Section 5 of the Constitution:

> Each House shall keep a Journal of its Proceedings, and from time to time publish the same, excepting such Parts as may in their Judgment require Secrecy. . . .

But, as Joseph Story wrote in *Commentaries on the Constitution of the United States*, the object of the clause requiring the keeping of a Journal is "to insure publicity to the proceedings of the legislature, and a correspondent responsibility of the members to their respective constituents."[18]

And so, at the very outset we encounter the unavoidable tension between the right of the public to know and the need for government, in certain circumstances, to withhold knowledge.[19] Relyea has observed: "Ideally, all information held by government belongs to the citizenry."[20] And yet, it can be very much in the interests of the same citizenry that some information *not* be generally available, and within the capacity of a mature democracy to make the distinction. Provided only that the system be kept under review.

However, secrecy can confer a form of power without responsibility, about which democratic societies must be vigilant. A disturbing instance occurred after the discovery, beginning with the Army Security Agency's code-breaking in 1946, of a most considerable Soviet espionage *apparat* in the United States, including, by all the evidence, senior officials of the United States Government. The person who most needed to know this was the President of the United States. The issue was national security and he was Commander-in-Chief.

It would appear, however, that President Truman was not told. In their superb account of these events, *VENONA: Soviet Espionage and the American Response, 1939-1957*, published by the National Security Agency and the Central Intelligence Agency (in connection with a major October 1996 conference on VENONA), Robert Louis Benson and Michael Warner write:

> Truman's repeated denunciations of the charges against Hiss, White, and others—all of whom appear under covernames in decrypted messages translated before he left office in January 1953—suggest that Truman either was never briefed on the Venona program or did not grasp its significance. Although it seems odd that Truman might not have been told, no definitive evidence has emerged to show he was. In any event, Truman always insisted that Republicans had trumped up the loyalty issue and that wartime espionage had been insignificant and well contained by American authorities.[21]

Benson and Warner continue:

> The long spate of prosecutions and loyalty hearings coincided with, and helped heighten, the atmosphere of suspicion and accusations now known as McCarthyism. Republicans in Congress were echoing widespread sentiment when they criticized the Truman administration for its failure to prevent Communism from conquering Eastern Europe and China. "Softness" on Communism abroad was portrayed by Republicans as the corollary of laxness at home. Suspicions that the Roosevelt and Truman administrations had neglected internal security fed charges of a Democratic-led coverup of the wartime *Amerasia* affair, as well as Eisenhower administration Attorney General Herbert Brownell's 1953 accusation that then President Truman had ignored FBI warnings about Harry Dexter White in 1946. Republican Senator Joseph McCarthy and allies exploited this confusion and rancor, blaming Communists in the State Department for "losing" China and accusing Federal workers of disloyalty on flimsy pretexts.

The tacit decision to keep the translated messages secret carried a political and social price for the country. Debates over the extent of Soviet espionage in the United States were polarized in the dearth of reliable information then in the public domain. Anti-Communists suspected that some spies—perhaps including a few who were known to the US Government—remained at large. Those who criticized the government's loyalty campaign as an over-reaction, on the other hand, wondered if some defendants were being scapegoated; they seemed to sense that the public was not being told the whole truth about the investigations of such suspects as Julius Rosenberg and Judith Coplon. Given the dangerous international situation and what was known by the government at that time, however, continued secrecy was not illogical. With the Korean war raging and the prospect of war with the Soviet Union a real possibility, military and intelligence leaders almost certainly believed that any cryptologic edge that America gained over the Soviets was too valuable to concede—even if it was already known to Moscow.[22]

The decision to share or to withhold information could be—*can be*—highly personal and political, or purely professional. The Central Intelligence Agency was not informed about VENONA until 1952. The KGB cables indicated that the Office of Strategic Services (OSS) in World War II had been thoroughly infiltrated with Soviet agents. As the CIA was widely regarded as the successor to the OSS, the Army and the FBI were appropriately cautious in sharing their secrets. That is a problem not to be avoided. But when secret information is withheld for personal or political reasons, the democracy can be put at risk.

2. <u>The Experience of the First World War</u>

Much of the structure of secrecy now in place in the United States Government took shape in just under eleven weeks in the spring of 1917. As provided by the Constitution, President Woodrow Wilson on April 2 asked Congress for a Declaration of War against Imperial Germany. That same day, an espionage act was introduced in the House of Representatives; the next day in the Senate. On April 4, the Senate adopted a Declaration of War. On April 5, the United States Civil Service Commission provided the President with a choice of executive orders providing for "excluding from the Government service of any person of whose loyalty to the Government there is reasonable doubt."

On April 6, the House declared war. On April 7, the President signed a "Confidential" executive order concerning the loyalty of government employees. The debate on "the Act to punish Acts of Interference with the Foreign Relations, the Neutrality of the Foreign Commerce of the United States, to punish Espionage, and better to enforce the Criminal Laws of the United States, and for other purposes," known as the Espionage Act of 1917, continued through the spring, and the legislation was signed into law on June 15.[23]

The Espionage Act had an antecedent in the Alien and Sedition Acts of 1798, three Acts dealing with aliens and one with sedition. The bills were passed by a Federalist Congress, as historian Jerald A. Combs writes, "to silence opposition to an expected war with France." Neither country had declared war, but French and American ships had fought many battles. One measure required an alien to live in the United States for fourteen years before becoming a citizen; immigrants at the time were mostly French and Irish who supported the Democratic-Republicans, who in turn tended to support France. Thomas Jefferson and James Madison challenged the constitutionality of the Acts, which were a prominent issue in the 1800 election, won by Jefferson. The Acts thereupon expired, were repealed, or were amended out of existence.[24] It was our first such experience as a nation, and one which was eerily reenacted 119 years later.

It would be too much to state that the Democratic administration of Woodrow Wilson expected war with Germany from the outset of hostilities in Europe in 1914. But its sympathies lay with Great Britain, as would those of the administration of Franklin D. Roosevelt, a spare two decades later. Moreover, Imperial Germany, in the face of proclaimed American neutrality, set about a campaign of espionage aimed at curtailing the American supply of weapons for the Allied forces, and in so doing involved itself with ethnic elements: German and Irish, opposed to support for the Allies; and a new group, Indians, in the main Punjabis, opposed to British rule in India.

The pattern here is the perception of both *external* and *internal* threat, the latter deriving from ideological or ethnic elements, these latter often overlapping. The first statute enacted by the 1st Congress prescribed the Oath of Allegiance taken by officers of the American Government. It was an oath to support the Constitution of the United States. In 1861, four months into the War of Secession, the oath was amended to read "support, protect, and defend the Constitution and Government of the United States against all enemies whether *domestic or foreign*"[25] (emphasis added). Note that domestic comes first. The linkage never thereafter dissolved.[26]

With the 20th century, a new intensity attended the anxieties of state. Normally moderate, reasonable men and women would grow hysterical confronting unnamed, unseen, frequently nonexistent dangers. In Europe, the Great War itself was in great measure the result of such insecurities. It was a civil war, as we can now see it, that all but destroyed the premier civilization of the age, both by itself and, even more, by its vertiginous aftermath. War brought revolution, which brought more war, then more revolution. No state was any longer secure; this in the aftermath of the long and virtually undisturbed stability of the century preceding.

The United States could not escape this; did not. Thus, it came about that on November 20, 1915, Wilson's Secretary of State Robert Lansing, the most moderate of men, experienced prior to the outbreak of war with all manner of arbitral tribunals which had promised an era in which disputes between nations would be settled by law, rather than arms, would write the President urging that he include in the forthcoming State of the Union address:

> [S]ome suggestion as to legislation covering foreign intrigues in our internal affairs such as conspiracies to blow up factories, to encourage strikes, to interfere with industrial operations, to gather information of this government's secrets, etc., etc.[27]

The previous May 10, Wilson, the embodiment of the academic in politics, thoughtful, careful, reasoned above all, had told a Philadelphia audience, "There is such a thing as a man being too proud to fight."[28] Now on December 7, 1915, in his Annual Message on the State of the Union to Congress, he said of the War in Europe, "We have stood apart, studiously neutral." But then *this*:

> There are citizens of the United States, I blush to admit, born under other flags but welcomed under our generous naturalization laws to the full freedom and

opportunity of America, who have poured the poison of disloyalty into the very
arteries of our national life; who have sought to bring the authority and good name
of our Government into contempt, to destroy our industries wherever they thought it
effective for their vindictive purposes to strike at them, and to debase our politics to
the uses of foreign intrigue. . . . A little while ago such a thing would have seemed
incredible. Because it was incredible we made no preparation for it. We would
have been almost ashamed to prepare for it, as if we were suspicious of ourselves,
our own comrades and neighbors! But the ugly and incredible thing has actually
come about and we are without adequate federal laws to deal with it. I urge you
to enact such laws at the earliest possible moment and feel that in doing so I am
urging you to do nothing less than save the honor and self-respect of the nation.
Such creatures of passion, disloyalty, and anarchy must be crushed out.[29]

No President had ever spoken like that; none since. In a half-century of Cold War with the Soviet
Union, when there were indeed persons of foreign birth, living in the United States, actively
involved in seditious activities on behalf of the Soviet Union, no President ever spoke like that.
Others in public life did; *many* others in private life did, including many who knew what they were
talking about. But the telling fact is that the intensity of fear and, yes, loathing of those years was
never later equaled.

Assistant Attorney General Charles Warren was assigned the task of drafting such laws. On
June 3, 1916, *seventeen* separate bills were sent to Congress.[30] The following February 3, 1917,
Germany resumed unrestricted submarine warfare, and the United States broke diplomatic
relations. On February 20, the Senate combined thirteen of the seventeen bills and passed that
measure, but the House did not act. At a cabinet meeting of March 20, Attorney General Gregory
asserted that "German intrigues" were afoot but complained of the "helplessness of his Department under existing laws."[31] In his address asking for a Declaration of War, Wilson cited spying
as an example of the hostile intent of the "Prussian autocracy":

[F]rom the very outset of the present war it has filled our unsuspecting
communities and even our offices of government with spies and set criminal
intrigues everywhere afoot against our national unity of counsels, our peace within
and without, our industries and our commerce. Indeed it is now evident that its
spies were here even before the war began.[32]

In short order, Congress passed legislation based on the original seventeen bills the administration
had proposed, and on June 15, the Espionage Act was signed into law.

****

There was then, as now, a large American population of German ancestry. German culture was
widely admired, the German language taught in public schools, German political traditions viewed
as essentially democratic. Early in the War, the Berlin government set out to use these attachments to influence public opinion to oppose American entry into the War. As the War began in
August, 1914, the German ambassador arrived in the United States with $150,000,000 in German
Treasury notes[33] ($2.2 billion in current dollars) to pursue a propaganda campaign, purchase
munitions for Germany, and conduct an espionage campaign aimed at denying war material to the
Allies. This latter was the province of the Military Attache, Captain Franz von Papen.

In a fateful manner, whilst the British made friends, the Germans made enemies. Early in the morning of July 30, 1916, German agents, probably assisted by Irish nationalists, blew up a munitions dump at the Black Tom railroad yard and the adjoining warehouses in New York harbor. (The site is now Liberty State Park, where tourist boats depart to visit the Statue of Liberty.) It was a stunning event, in both magnitude and consequence.[34] Sabotage became a national issue.

Captain von Papen also provided support for the Ghadar movement (Urdu for "mutiny"), composed principally of Punjabi Indians seeking independence from British rule. It was based principally in California, to which Punjabi agricultural workers had migrated from Canada. Once war was declared on Germany, the United States Government indicted some 105 persons of various nationalities for participating in the conspiracy. From the start it was viewed as the "Hindoo conspiracy." When the first arrests were made, the *San Francisco Chronicle* noted U.S. Attorney John W. Preston's characterization of those indicted as involved in "the Hindoo conspiracy [which] was an offshoot of the German neutrality plots." The article goes on to say that:

> According to the complaint on which the Hindoos were taken into custody they conspired to "Cripple, hinder and obstruct, the military operations of Great Britain" by sending Hindoos to India to stir up a revolt, and to help Germany by forcing Great Britain to withdraw troops from Europe for service in India to quell the revolt.[35]

At the trial, the conspiracy was described as one which "permeated and encircled the whole globe."[36] Twenty-nine defendants were found guilty: fifteen Indians, fourteen German-Americans or Germans. The latter included Franz von Bopp, German Consul in San Francisco. The "Hindoo conspiracy" entered the national imagery.[37]

For all the energy and expenditure, it is not clear what Berlin had to show for its elaborate and extensive espionage activity. At this time, the United States possessed one genuine "national defense" secret—which was that the American military was in no sense prepared for a major war with major adversaries. The Army was so under-equipped that when it got to France it had to borrow French artillery. But this was an open secret, and in that sense, the Espionage Act can be said to have accomplished little or nothing. German espionage, real or imagined, did, however, do great damage to German-Americans, and thereby to the American people at large.

As war approached, Woodrow Wilson had delivered himself of this mordant forecast:

> "Once lead this people into war," he said, "and they'll forget there ever was such a thing as tolerance. To fight you must be brutal and ruthless, and the spirit of ruthless brutality will enter into the very fibre of our national life, infecting Congress, the courts, the policeman on the beat, the man in the street." Conformity would be the only virtue, said the President, and every man who refused to conform would have to pay the penalty.[38]

He seems not to have noticed his own excess, a failing not unknown in university presidents. He had alerted Congress to the intrigues of the foreign-born pouring poison into "the very arteries of our national life." Whether he realized it or not, Wilson was forever showering civil liberties on Germans in Germany whilst taking them away from American citizens of German descent. In his message to the Congress asking for a Declaration of War, he was emphatic: "We have no quarrel with the German people. We have no feeling toward them but one of sympathy and friendship."

The New York Times.

"All the News That's Fit to Print"

THE WEATHER
Partly cloudy and warmer Monday; Partly cloudy, with probable showers Tuesday; moderate southwest winds.

ONE CENT In Greater New York, Jersey City and Newark. TWO CENTS Elsewhere.

VOL. LXV...NO. 21,373.

NEW YORK, MONDAY, JULY 31, 1916.—EIGHTEEN PAGES.

MUNITION EXPLOSIONS CAUSE LOSS OF $20,000,000; 2 KNOWN TO BE DEAD, MANY MISSING, 35 HURT; THE HARBOR RAKED BY SHRAPNEL FOR HOURS

FIRST EXPLOSION TERRIFIC

Earth Torn Away and Great Hole Filled with Blazing Debris.

TWO MEN UNDER ARREST

Barge of High Explosive Alleged to Have Been Moored Against Orders.

87 CARS OF SHELLS FIRED

Heavy Damage in Manhattan and Brooklyn—Statue of Liberty Hit.

View of the Wreck of the National Storage Company's Plant on Black Tom Island

In the right hand foreground, barges and canal boats are moored.

Detailed Estimates of the $20,000,000 Loss by the Fire and Explosion in Jersey City

National Storage Company, plant and contents.....	$12,000,000
Plate glass in Manhattan and Brooklyn..............	300,000
Plate glass in Hoboken.............................	30,000
Plate glass in Jersey City.........................	50,000
Lehigh Valley Railroad, 80 cars, grain elevator, tugs, tracks.	1,000,000
Central Railroad of New Jersey, 12 cars, damage to tracks..	60,000
Ammunition in cars and barges.....................	5,000,000
Moran Towing Company, three barges................	180,000
Buildings on Bedloe's, Ellis, and Governors Islands....	200,000
Other barges sunk, with cargoes...................	200,000
Total	$19,645,000

Glass Damage Exceeds a Million; Few Downtown Buildings Escape

Ellis Island Like War-Swept Town; Damage Estimated at $75,000

Only Six of 607 Persons at Barrage Receive Injuries—Immigrants Taken to Battery Till Danger Is Past
—Strange Freaks of Blast Are Seen.

Insurance Companies Prepare to Pay Heavy Losses, While Small Property Owners Who Are Unsecured Suffer Heavily
—Hospital Roof Caves In.

ALLIES ADVANCE ON 6-MILE FRONT NORTH OF SOMME

British and French Attack at Same Time from Delville Wood to River.

FRENCH REACH MAUREPAS

Capture 200 Prisoners—British Push Their Line East and Take 250 Germans.

DAY OF GREAT BATTLES

Heavy Counterattacks Fail to Win Back Ground—German Losses Reported Very Heavy.

2,567,000 Prisoners Taken by Central Powers

STRIKE TIES UP 3D AV. SYSTEM AND MAY EXTEND

General Manager Hedley Gets Police Protection for N.Y. City Railways' Cars.

ORGANIZING SUBWAY MEN

From Battery to Westchester, Including Crosstown and Belt Lines, No Red Cars Move.

SERVICE IS PROMISED TODAY

System Carries 250,000 Passengers Daily—Union Officials Busy in All Five Boroughs.

AMERICA DEMANDS RIGHTS IN TRADE

Protests "in the Most Decided Terms" in Note to Great Britain.

DENOUNCES THE BLACKLIST

Says It Brushes Aside Safeguards and Condemns Without Hearing and Without Notice.

Throughout the War, he pressed a policy of "war on the German government, peace with the German people." Save such as might have migrated to Milwaukee!

Never before, never since, has the American government been so aroused by the fear of subversion, the compromise of secrets, the danger within. In *The Growth of the American Republic* (1969 edition), Samuel Eliot Morison, Henry Steele Commager, and William E. Leuchtenburg write:

> In 1917-19 the people of the United States abandoned themselves to a hysteria of fear of German conspiracies and of Communist subversion, and the government indulged in greater excesses than at any previous crisis of our history.[39]

Note the linkage of ethnic identity and political radicalism. This was present in Wilson's 1915 message to Congress: "creatures of passion, disloyalty, and anarchy" who "must be crushed out." Now it all broke out. The historians continue:

> The war offered a great opportunity to bring patriotism to the aid of personal grudges and neighborhood feuds. The independent-minded sort of citizen who was known to his conforming neighbors as a 'Tory' in the Revolution, a 'Jacobin' in 1798, and a 'Copperhead' in the Civil War became a 'pro-German traitor' in 1917 and a 'Bolshevik' in 1918, and was lucky if he did not have garbled scraps of his conversation sent in to the Department of Justice or flashes from his shaving mirror reported as signals to German submarines. German-Americans, the vast majority of them loyal to the United States, were subjected to all sorts of indignities. Schools dropped German from their curricula, and even some universities abolished their German departments; German books were withdrawn from public library circulation and German publications driven under cover. The Governor of Iowa decreed that 'conversation in public places, on trains, or over the telephone' should be in the English language. Frederick Stock, distinguished conductor of the Chicago Symphony Orchestra, was deprived of his baton; the patriotic mayor of Jersey City refused to allow Fritz Kreisler to appear on the concert stage; and some universities revoked degrees they had conferred on distinguished Germans, thus giving academic sanction to the doctrine of retroactive guilt.[40]

Fortunately, Dwight D. Eisenhower had graduated from West Point in 1915.

As Congress attempted to restrain the Executive, although faintly, it might better be said to have lagged. *The Encyclopedia of the United States Congress* records:

> The censorship portion [of the Espionage Act] set off a storm of Congressional controversy. House Speaker James Beauchamp (Champ) Clark declared that censorship of the press was "in flat contradiction of the Constitution" and progressive Hiram W. Johnson and conservative Henry Cabot Lodge condemned it. Congress dropped the provision, but the rest of the bill sped through. . . .
>
> Postmaster General Albert S. Burleson and Attorney General Thomas W. Gregory vied with one another in clamping down on what they considered to be treasonable utterances. And within a year the president asked Congress for

amendments to strengthen the Espionage Act by extending its reach to "profane, scurrilous, or abusive language about the form of government . . . the Constitution . . . or the flag of the United States, or the uniform of the Army and Navy." The result—the Sedition Act—became law on 16 May 1918.

Under these statutes some pro-German newspapers and speakers and, far more often, socialist and other radical antiwar voices were suppressed and punished. In its 1919 *Schenck v. United States* and *Abrams v. United States* decisions, the Supreme Court upheld the constitutionality of this legislation. Congress allowed the law to expire in 1921.[41]

Again, the authors of *The Growth of the American Republic*:

> Under these harsh laws the government instituted widespread censorship of the press; banned two Socialist newspapers from the mails; held up circulation of a tax-journal, *The Public*, because it advised that more of the costs of the war should be borne by taxation; and banned Thorstein Veblen's *Imperial Germany and the Industrial Revolution.* . . . A hapless film-producer was sentenced to ten years in jail for producing a film on the American Revolution called *The Spirit of Seventy-six*, because it was thought that it might excite anti-British sentiments; a Vermont minister was sentenced to fifteen years' imprisonment for citing Jesus as an authority on pacifism. . . .[42]

At the now considerable distance, it is difficult to appreciate the force of pacifism as a political movement of the late 19th and early 20th centuries. It was international, based on creed, and given to association with socialism and other such commitments. There was nothing notably exotic in its doctrine, certainly not in the age of The Hague Peace Conferences convened in Holland in 1899 and 1907 by the Czar of Russia, nor of the Hague Peace Palace built there between 1907 and 1913.

William Jennings Bryan, Wilson's first Secretary of State, was a pacifist—in the words of his biographer a "pacifist committed, with remarkably few reservations, to nonviolence in dealings between the nations." To this end, he had set about negotiating some nineteen "cooling-off" treaties providing for international commissions to conciliate disputes when ordinary diplomatic methods failed. (In the Hoover administration, Secretary of State Frank B. Kellogg would negotiate another nineteen).[43] Bryan resigned, gracefully, over the tone of Wilson's response to the German sinking of the *Lusitania* and other ships. Arthur Link observes "it was not so much what the President's note said as what it did not say," that Bryan could not accept. It did not say that the United States would do everything possible "to avert even the possibility of war."[44] Josephus Daniels, Wilson's Secretary of the Navy, was a Bryan supporter, and was certainly dubbed a "pacifist," as his obituary noted.[45] A teetotaler, too. Doubtless also a foe of The Trusts. When, in March 1916, Wilson appointed Newton Diehl Baker Secretary of War, the *New York Times* headline read, "Baker to Be New Secretary of War; He is known as an Ardent Pacifist."[46]

Nonviolence had been advocated by Quakers in America since the 17th century. Of a sudden, such views became subversive, and "foreign," and a penal offense. The United States Government grew reckless in its infringement of liberty. Consider the matter of Eugene V. Debs, who had run for President as the candidate of the Socialist Party of America in 1912. He had received 900,369 votes, 6.0 percent of all votes cast. (Wilson received only 41.9 percent.) On

June 16, 1918, Debs delivered a speech in Canton, Ohio, which had an anti-war theme and expressed solidarity with three men—Wagenknecht, Baker, and Ruthenberg—who were convicted of failing to register for the draft. He also condemned the conviction of Kate Richards O'Hare for obstructing the draft. Such speech was now forbidden under the Espionage Act. Debs was tried, convicted, and sentenced to ten years' imprisonment on each of three counts, to be served concurrently.

The Supreme Court did not consider the constitutionality of the Espionage Act of 1917 and the Sedition Act of 1918 until after World War I was over. The enduring legal precedent established by the Court in its consideration of these Acts comes from *Schenck v. United States*. In writing that opinion on behalf of the Court, Justice Oliver Wendell Holmes articulated the "clear and present danger" test. The ruling affirmed that Congress has a right to limit speech in an attempt to limit certain "evils." Holmes explained:

> The most stringent protection of free speech would not protect a man in falsely shouting fire in a theatre and causing a panic. It does not even protect a man from an injunction against uttering words that may have all the effect of force. . . . The question in every case is whether the words used are used in such a circumstance and are of such a nature as to create a clear and present danger that they will bring about the substantive evils that Congress has a right to prevent.[47]

Subsequent to *Schenck*, Justice Holmes also wrote the opinion, for a unanimous court, upholding the conviction of Eugene V. Debs on March 10, 1919.[48]

As never before, as never since, the American Presidency, with the cooperation of Congress and the courts, was obstructing democracy in the name of defending it.

Not altogether. In 1920, Debs once again ran for President as the candidate of the Socialist Party of America, this time from the Atlanta Penitentiary. He received more votes (915,940), but a lower percentage of the electorate (3.4), than in 1912. On Christmas Day 1921, President Warren G. Harding commuted his sentence. He was provided a railroad ticket from Atlanta to Washington. On December 26, he called first on Attorney General Harry M. Daugherty, and thereafter had a half-hour visit with President Harding at the White House. In the 1920 election, Harding had promised a return to normalcy, and he kept his word. (On Wilson's last day as President, Congress repealed the 1918 amendment to the Espionage Act, known as the Sedition Act.) But nothing would be quite the same again.

3. Loyalty

Loyalty had appeared. The day after the Declaration of War in 1917, President Wilson had issued an executive order in effect requiring government employees to support government policy, both in conduct and sympathy. The Order read:

<u>Confidential</u>

In the exercise of the power vested in the President by the Constitution and the resolution of Congress of April 6, 1917, the following order is issued:

The head of a department or independent office may forthwith remove any employee when he has ground for believing that the retention of such employee would be inimical to the public welfare by reason of his conduct, sympathies, or utterances, or because of other reasons growing out of the war. Such removal may be made without other formality than that the reasons shall be made a matter of confidential record, subject, however, to inspection by the Civil Service Commission.

This order is issued solely because of the present international situation, and will be withdrawn when the emergency is passed.

Woodrow Wilson

The White House
7 April 1917[49]

In the manner of bureaucracy, the "emergency" lingered on. The Civil Service Commission was debarring persons from "future examinations" by reasons relating to "loyalty" as late as 1921, when the United States formally terminated the War.[50]

Clearly, the concept of loyalty predates the 20th century, but loyalty as a qualification determined by large organizations maintaining confidential records was new to American society. Three days after President Wilson asked for a Declaration of War, the Civil Service Commission was ready with a choice of executive orders "excluding from the Government service of any person of whose loyalty to the Government there is reasonable doubt." The Civil Service Commission had been established pursuant to the Pendleton Act in 1883; an act of modernization, under which the Executive Branch of the United States Government was becoming a recognizable bureaucracy. (A century later, efforts would begin to extend this mode of organization to the Legislative Branch.)

It is a distinctive, and seemingly universal characteristic of bureaucracy to conduct affairs by regulation—uniformity being the principle organizational goal. *Save* for the survival and well-being of the organization itself. Organizations are like that. To this end, one form of bureaucratic regulation is secrecy.

Max Weber first described this characteristic in the chapter "Bureaucracy," in his work *Wirtschaft und Gesellschaft* (*Economy and Society*), published after his death in 1920, but most likely written in part prior to World War I. He writes:

Every bureaucracy seeks to increase the superiority of the professionally informed by keeping their knowledge and intentions secret. Bureaucratic administration always tends to be an administration of 'secret sessions' in so far as it can, it hides its knowledge and action from criticism.

> The pure interest of the bureaucracy in power, however, is efficacious far beyond those areas where purely functional interests make for secrecy. The concept of the 'official secret' is the specific invention of bureaucracy, and nothing is so fanatically defended by the bureaucracy as this attitude, which cannot be substantially justified beyond these specifically qualified areas. In facing a parliament, the bureaucracy, out of a sure power instinct, fights every attempt of the parliament to gain knowledge by means of its own experts or from interest groups. The so-called right of parliamentary investigation is one of the means by which parliament seeks such knowledge. Bureaucracy naturally welcomes a poorly informed and hence a powerless parliament—at least in so far as ignorance somehow agrees with the bureaucracy's interests.[51]

Weber describes an "ideal type" that in real life will vary from place to place and time to time. But nearly a century later, it can be agreed that the generalization holds, especially in a setting in which government chooses or is forced to be concerned about the loyalty of some portion of the citizenry.

For the concept of loyalty implied that there was much information within a bureaucracy which could be used to injure the Government or the national interest if revealed by disloyal persons to hostile nations or, for that matter, to internal elements hostile to our "way of life."

Anarchism, "a belief that every form of regulation or government is immoral,"[52] became a proto-international movement in the 19th century. In its terrorist mode, it had set about blowing up czars and such. After the assassination of President William McKinley, the United States by statute barred anarchists from entering the country. The arrest, imprisonment, and deportation to Russia of Emma Goldman was a celebrated case of the later Wilson years. (Poor Goldman had just gotten out of prison for distributing birth control information.) Idealists, no doubt, these were frequently violent persons who threatened the necessary state "monopoly on violence."

Even so, there does not appear to have been any systematic search for anarchists at the Federal level. This began with the Espionage Act, and in short order bureaucracies were compiling dossiers and government officials were classifying information by various degrees of secrecy. It would appear in this regard that the predecessor of today's three-tier gradation of Confidential/Secret/Top Secret (at that time, For Official Use Only/Confidential/Secret) was adopted by the American military from the British forces in France.[53] Again, it all begins in 1917.

4. The Encounter with Communism

If 1917 was an eventful year in the United States, it was a momentous one in Russia. In a cabinet meeting on March 20, following the sinking by German submarines of three American merchant vessels, President Wilson spoke of summoning Congress and, by all implication, asking for a Declaration of War. Secretary of State Lansing recorded that the President spoke of the situation in the belligerent countries, "particularly in Russia where the revolution against the autocracy had been successful. . . ."[54] Lansing took up the point to argue that "the revolution in Russia, which appeared to be successful, had removed the one objection to affirming that the European War was a war between Democracy and Absolutism . . . ." Further, American entry into the War "would have a great moral influence in Russia. . . ."[55] This was a moment all but erased from history by the events that followed.

That autumn, the Bolsheviks seized power and created the world's first totalitarian regime. On October 26 (on the Russian calendar), the day after the "storming" of the Winter Palace in St. Petersburg, Lenin pronounced in *Pravda* that the "dictatorship of the proletariat" had commenced. If hardly a democratic society, Czarist Russia was even so a reasonably open one. (*Pravda*, which began publication on May 5, 1912, was freely circulated.) All this was now supplanted by terror, violence, and above all, secrecy. If something like the Soviet regime had been envisioned, both by those who had great hopes for it and those who instinctively feared it, none seem to have anticipated that secrecy would be its most distinctive feature. Everything that went on in government was closed to public view. Civil society ceased to exist. Only the nameless masses and the reclusive leaders remained.[56]

Soviet secrecy carried over into foreign affairs. The new regime was both threatened and threatening. Early on, American, British, and French expeditionary forces were sent to overturn the new Bolshevik Government and so, somehow "keep Russia in the war." (It could be fairly remarked that the United States took this intervention rather too offhandedly. Nothing came of it, so that we may be said not to have assumed that it would affect Soviet attitudes and conduct. As it was, the United States did not recognize the Soviet government and exchange ambassadors until 1933.)

Even while under attack, however, the Soviets began recruiting secret agents in foreign countries. They saw themselves as leaders of a worldwide movement—the red flag, symbol of universal brotherhood—and anticipated early success as other regimes began to collapse at the close of the War. Some agents were undercover, some quite public, some both.

John Reed, a 1910 Harvard graduate, was of the latter sort. In 1913, he joined the staff of the *Masses*, a socialist journal published in New York. (Its fame is in large measure accounted for by the illustrations of John Sloan and other painters and illustrators of the Ashcan School.) In August, 1917, Reed wrote an article, "Knit a Straight-Jacket for Your Soldier Boy." This brought upon him prosecution under the Espionage Act and, with his acquittal, a measure of fame in his own circles.[57]

But the great event was his trip to Russia, where he witnessed the Bolshevik coup. His account, *Ten Days that Shook the World*, appeared in 1919 (soon after his acquittal in the *Masses* trial) and was a master work of what would come to be known as *agitprop*. He attended the All-Russian Soviet convention in January 1918. In the summer of 1919 he was expelled from the Socialist Party of America at its convention in Chicago and thereupon helped found the Communist Labor Party. He died in Russia of typhus on October 17, 1920, and was buried in the wall of the Kremlin in Moscow, the equivalent—then—of interment in St. Peter's in Rome. Lenin wrote an introduction to one edition of his book, although he did not live to see the movie (*Reds*, 1981).

Reed was a Soviet agent. On January 22, 1920, he received from the Comintern gold, jewels, and other valuables worth 1,008,000 rubles for Party work in the United States.[58] The United States Government did not know this. It has only just been discovered in Soviet archives.

(That and much more.) For the next seven decades the United States Government would be the object of a sustained Soviet campaign of infiltration and subversion. There would be, as with Great Britain, a measure of success among elites, but in the pattern now already seen, an ethnic factor would be the most prominent.

In the beginning, most American Communists would be Russians. The Communist Party of the United States of America (CPUSA) was organized at Moscow's behest in 1921, merging Reed's Communist Labor Party with the Communist Party of America, organized by a former socialist, Midwesterner Charles Emil Ruthenberg. The membership was not large and was overwhelmingly foreign-born.[59] Theodore Draper, in *The Roots of American Communism,* estimates that 10 percent spoke English. Harvey Klehr et al., make that 12 percent.

Draper comments: "It is just to say that the American Communist movement started out as a predominantly Slavic movement. . . ." In a familiar pattern, immigrants brought their politics with them, or responded sympathetically to political changes in their homelands.[60] He goes on to state that this situation changed as "Americans" and "other nationalities" joined the movement.[61] But the ethnic dimension of American Communism never ceased, albeit at times it was overshadowed by the likes of John Reed.

Perhaps a quarter of a million persons passed through the Communist Party between 1919 and 1960—with emphasis on passing through.[62] Nathan Glazer estimates that at the peak of popularity there were "considerably fewer than 100,000 Communists."[63] Nor did the Party, or parties in the first instance, have an auspicious beginning. Fear of radical revolutions got out of hand in 1919-20. There was a good deal of disorder, and no small amount of criminal behavior. On May Day, 1919, some 36 bombs were sent by mail to prominent politicians, judges, and other "enemies of the left."[64] The *New York Times* wrote of a "nationwide bomb conspiracy." The Washington house of Attorney General A. Mitchell Palmer was damaged by a bomb which went off prematurely and blew up the bomber.

All this would appear to have been a last surge of anarchism, but it was generally taken for Bolshevism. "Russian Reds Are Busy Here," ran a *New York Times* headline. Palmer, the "Fighting Quaker," responded with major cross-country raids—the Palmer Raids—on radical organizations, including the New York-based Union of Russian Workers, on November 7-8, 1919, the second anniversary of the Bolshevik Revolution. On January 2, 1920, Federal agents arrested more than 4,000 Communists in 33 different cities as undesirable aliens deserving of deportation.[65] The *Washington Post* warned "[t]here is not time to waste on hair-splitting over infringement of liberty." J. Edgar Hoover, a 24-year old Justice Department official, located a U.S. Army transport, termed the "Soviet Ark," to take a shipload of radicals home, and invited Members of Congress to see them off at Ellis Island. He now emerged as a national figure, whilst his superior, the Attorney General, began making plans to run for President.

The unrest did not last. May Day 1920 passed without incident. With his credibility badly damaged, Palmer saw his presidential aspirations erode. Warren G. Harding, running for President against Democrat James Cox, said that "too much has been said about Bolshevism in America."[66] The Democratic administration, leaderless following Wilson's stroke on October 2, 1919, had become undisciplined and erratic. Such intervals would recur, with both parties involved, but now a sense of civic order returned. Draper observes:

Ironically, the Palmer raids came as a blessing in disguise to the foreign-language federations. More than ever they were able to imagine themselves Russian Bolsheviks in America. Had not the Russian Revolution been forced to work illegally almost to the very eve of the seizure of power? Was there any fundamental difference between Palmer's prisons and the Czar's dungeons, the Bureau of Immigration's deportations and the Ochrana's exiledom in Siberia? If the Russian road to the revolution was right, then the postwar repression in the United States merely offered additional proof that the American revolution was really approaching. The underground character of the movement became the supreme test of its revolutionary integrity. A truly revolutionary organization by definition had to suffer repression, as in Czarist Russia. The Russia hypnosis made a necessity into a virtue.[67]

And now the new rulers of Russia turned their acolytes into agents. Klehr et al., write:

> Soviet intelligence was able to make use of the Comintern and its operatives because from its foundation, the Communist International had encouraged Communist parties to maintain both a legal political organization and an illegal or underground apparatus. Among the twenty-one conditions required for admission to its ranks, the Comintern in 1920 stipulated that all Communist parties create an illegal "organizational apparatus which, at the decisive moment, can assist the Party to do its duty to the revolution." These underground apparatuses were intended both to defend the Communist movement from police repression and to promote secret political subversion.

> Comintern representatives often traveled on false passports, entered countries illegally, and carried large amounts of cash and valuables to distribute secretly to local party leaders and organizations. The Comintern maintained clandestine courier services, secret mail drops, and systems of coded telegraphic and radio communications with foreign Communist parties. Year after year the Comintern issued instructions and pleas to its member parties to form secret units, train cadres to operate illegally, and prepare systems of safe houses and fake identification documents to protect its key officials in case of repression by hostile governments. Communists, in short, were not novices at the kind of work required for espionage. Soviet intelligence agencies quickly recognized that they could piggyback on these activities for espionage operations.

> The United States did not officially recognize the USSR until 1933. Before that date, Soviet money for the American Communist movement had to be sent by way of secret couriers. The earliest known subsidies were sent in 1919. **** Four payments [are recorded as sent to] America; 209,000 rubles to Kotliarov on 16 July 1919, 500,000 rubles to Khavkin on 30 September 1919, [as noted] 1,008,000 rubles to John Reed on 22 January 1920, and 1,011,000 rubles to Anderson on 31 January 1920. ****These four subsidies alone add up to 2,728,000 rubles. The value of the ruble on foreign exchange markets fluctuated wildly from 1919 to 1922 before the Soviets stabilized the "hard" ruble used for international trade at between $1 and $2. The Comintern document records that the subvention for American operations was in "value," a term in Comintern bookkeeping meaning that the sums were transmitted in the form of gold, silver,

or jewels rather than currency. Thus, this account reveals that in this period the Comintern supplied the tiny American Communist movement with the equivalent of several million dollars in valuables, an enormous sum in the 1920s.[68]

In time the size of the subsidies fell off, but even so, they continued.[69]

There were several consequences of the relative isolation of American Communists. Apart from the intellectual circles in Manhattan and a very few other metropolitan centers, and apart from elements in the American labor movement, Communists were almost unknown. Among intellectuals, and especially within the labor movement, the encounter with Communism produced an often fierce anti-Communist response. (From the beginning of the Cold War to its end, the American Federation of Labor was unmatched in its understanding of Communism and its opposition to it.) In time, an opposition appeared in the form of ex-Communists who had broken with "the Party," or disillusioned "fellow travelers." With a sure sense of things to come, Ignazio Silone predicted that the "final battle would be between Communists and ex-Communists"—such was the insight and loathing of the latter.[70]

Even so, there was a measure of social distance on the part of most ex-Communists such that their tales when told often seemed too exotic to be true. They were easily dismissed as fantasists or worse. Klehr et al., write of Benjamin Gitlow, an early Communist leader who was expelled from the Party in 1929, in one of the recurrent purges that followed Stalin's exile of Trotsky:

> A decade later he testified before a congressional committee that in its early years the party often received its Soviet subsidies in the form of diamonds and jewelry, which it then converted to cash with the aid of sympathetic businessmen. But, like so many defectors from communism, Gitlow has frequently been regarded as an unreliable witness and his testimony discounted.[71]

Trotsky was an emblematic figure. He was living in Manhattan when the Bolsheviks came to power in St. Petersburg; rushed home, became foreign minister, commanded armies, might have succeeded Lenin, was exiled by Stalin, and in time was assassinated in Mexico City. In his autobiography, *Out of Step*, Sidney Hook, professor at New York University and a one-time Communist who, with many a New Yorker, followed Trotsky into opposition to Stalin, relates: "Ironically, it was one of my students, Sylvia Ageloff, who unwittingly gave Trotsky's assassin access to commit the murder."[72] Ageloff's sister served for a time as secretary to Trotsky in Mexico City. She visited her sister; Trotsky and his wife grew fond of her. Back in New York, a woman friend casually offered Ageloff a ticket to Paris that she herself could not use. In Paris she met a dashing young Belgian journalist; her first love. He was, in fact, Ramon Mercader, "whose mother was a leading member of the Spanish Communist Party, . . . then living with a general of the NKVD in Moscow."[73] In 1940, with Ageloff's guileless help, Mercader made his way to Mexico City, joined Trotsky's household, and thereupon murdered him.

Back in New York, there now commenced yet another raging battle between Stalinists and Trotskyites. Who/whom into an eternity of commissions, and conventions, and contentions. As ever, the party-line Communists lied about everything; we now know that Mercader was indeed a KGB agent, and that in 1943, the KGB even planned a commando raid to free him from Mexican prison.[74] Life and death issues in New York City; little noticed in the rest of the nation.

In 1948 Whittaker Chambers, at one point in the early 1930s a contributor to the Communist publications the *Daily Worker* and the *New Masses*, later an editor at *Time*, would startle the nation with the assertion that in the mid-1930s he had been an undercover agent of the Soviet Union and a member of a Washington "cell" that included, most prominently, Alger Hiss. A great controversy arose. Could Chambers have possibly been telling the truth? Again to cite Sidney Hook, "everyone" in New York in the 1930s knew his past. (". . . I assumed—and I am confident that I was not the only one—that Chambers was engaged in underground work after he left the *New Masses*.")[75] He broke with the Party; then he realized the penalty for this could be Death.

> Chambers was on the verge of hysteria, convinced that, because he had become
> a faceless, nameless, unknown creature of the underground, his elimination either
> by murder or kidnaping would remain undetected. His goal was to become a
> *public* character again, to emerge under his own name and thus prevent his
> disappearance into the shadows.[76]

Hook advised a complicated "'life insurance' policy" whereby Chambers would "draw up a detailed list of all the Soviet operatives he knew, all the 'sleepers' in Washington and elsewhere, anyone who had given him any information" and send this to Earl Browder, then head of the American Communist Party, with the further information that if Chambers were murdered the list would be made public. Hook continues: "When Chambers first publicly identified his fellow-conspirators in 1948, the names were quite familiar to me." They were the same names he had given to a mutual friend, Herbert Solow, in 1938. They were the same names Chambers had given to Adolph Berle, then Assistant Secretary of State, in 1939.

> Years later, in 1953, I questioned Berle about the incident and its aftermath. He
> painted a very vivid picture of the confusion that prevailed in Washington at the
> time Chambers showed up in his office. World War II had begun, and "the world
> was falling to pieces around us." Nonetheless, despite his initial incredulity at the
> bizarre tale, Berle steadfastly insisted that he had sent word of Chambers' story
> to the White House. Berle himself ended up convinced that it was true. Fortu-
> nately Berle kept his notes of his meeting with Chambers, which listed the names
> Chambers had identified as his confederates.[77]

And so the interval of 1918 to 1939 concluded and the Great War resumed. During that interval the Soviet Union had put in place a fairly elaborate espionage apparatus, more or less reflexively. From the Soviet perspective the United States was a somewhat marginal power, but even so, spies might in time prove useful. As indeed they would, however briefly. For its part, the United States Government was not much interested in such matters. The anti-Communist hysteria of 1919-1920 was seen, especially within the circles of the administration of Franklin D. Roosevelt, as something of an embarrassment. As President Harding had stated, "too much has been said about Bolshe-vism in America."

Looking back on that period, David Riesman wrote in 1952:

> Twenty and even ten years ago, it was an important intellectual task . . . to point
> out to Americans of good will that the Soviet and Nazi systems were not simply
> transitory stages, nor a kind of throwback to the South American way—that they
> were, in fact, new forms of social organization, more omnivorous than even the
> most brutal of earlier dictatorships. At that time, there were many influential

people who were willing to see the Nazis as a menace but insisted that the Bolsheviks were a hope.[78]

Besides, the Bolsheviks were now the established rulers of a major power; potential opponents in the East of the Nazi regime in Germany, which had begun its devastating conquests in the West. And, of course, the great secret of American Government at this time was that, some military matters apart, it had none.

5. <u>The Experience of the Second World War</u>

The Great War resumed in 1939. The combatants were much the same; war, however, was changing with the advent of aerial bombardment. The very idea had once seemed repellent. The First Hague Conference banned bombing from balloons, but the Germans went ahead even so to develop the first strategic bombing force, using dirigibles. Soon actual "bombers" were developed; for which the all-important appurtenance was the "bombsight."

In the 1920s an American inventor, Carl L. Norden, had developed a device that promised precision high-altitude bombing. The "Norden Bombsight" became America's most important secret. By November 1937, German spies had stolen the complete plans. The theft was part of a large German espionage operation that would be known as the "Ritter Ring" for Colonel Nikolaus Ritter, who directed it from Hamburg. The Norden operation was carried out by Hermann Lang, a 36-year-old native of Germany, now a naturalized U.S. citizen living in a German-American neighborhood in Queens, New York. He worked as an assembly inspector at the Norden plant on Lafayette Street in downtown Manhattan. (An equivalent facility today would be located in New Mexico and surrounded by electrified fence. But we were learning!) Lang evidently considered himself a German patriot, and he copied the bombsight plans as an act of German patriotism.[79]

Soon, however, the Federal Bureau of Investigation was onto the operation. Another participant in the Ritter Ring was one Fritz Duquesne, an Afrikaner of Huguenot descent, born in 1877 in the Cape Province, and so a witness to the Boer War. By the 1930s, he was a naturalized U.S. citizen, but was willing to spy against the United States if in so doing he would be "working toward the destruction of his hated enemy, England."[80] On June 29, 1941, 23 members of the Ritter Ring—nineteen in New York and four in New Jersey—were arrested in what J. Edgar Hoover termed for Walter Winchell's broadcast that evening "the greatest spy roundup in U.S. history."[81]

At some level, espionage was becoming entertainment. There would be a movie in 1945, loosely based on the activities of the Ritter Ring, *The House on 92nd Street*. The Federal Bureau of Investigation now acquired a firm place in the national imagery as the nemesis of sovereign subversives, with German and later Japanese spies taking the place of 1920s gangsters. This was partly the personality of the Director, but also intrinsic fascination with the subject of espionage, as evidenced by the spy novel and any number of moving pictures of the 1930s. Much of this was entertainment, and no more; some part reflected anxieties. But also, and with far greater consequence, the United States Government was acquiring—principally in the FBI, but not exclusively—an organized capacity to defend against foreign attack and, most importantly, was beginning to learn the art of infiltration where there was a "domestic" component to the foreign attack.

Note two uniformities. Twentieth century war requires, will be seen to require, measures directed against enemies both "foreign *and* domestic." Such enemies, real or imagined, will be perceived both in ethnic terms and ideological terms.

A further uniformity: Government responds to domestic threats by regulatory measures to ensure the loyalty of the government bureaucracy and the security of government secrets, and by statutory measures to protect against disloyal conduct on the part of citizens and, of course, foreign agents.

We do well to be wary of rules of organizational behavior, much less of political affairs. But then, are we not equally obliged to be mindful of the view of the Framers of the U.S. Constitution that they had discovered, in James Madison's phrase, "a new science of politics" which brings stability to the constitutional government they devised? (As noted, in secret!)

The record of 1917 and the years immediately following is instructive. President Wilson looked up the rules, in this case the law of the sea, and decided that Germany was in gross and criminal violation. Whereupon the United States Government declared war. New laws and regulations were dutifully enacted. But events got out of hand. In time, it was the conduct of the United States Government that approached the illegal. A possible explanation for this is that the Government at this time had no organized means of assessing danger and dealing with it.

It is notable that there was little anti-German hysteria during the Second World War, in great contrast to the First. In measure, this may be accounted for by the success of the first round in suppressing the German presence in American culture, largely defined.

To return for just a moment, the anti-German hysteria—not too strong a term—of the First World War was unlike anything previously known in the ethnic history of the United States. Consider this passage from the *Harvard Encyclopedia of American Ethnic Groups*:

> Public burnings of German books were frequent. By summer 1918 about half of the states had restricted or eliminated German-language instruction, and several had curtailed freedom to speak German in public. The German press suffered under the censorship powers of local postmasters, and pacifist Mennonites endured harsh attempts to force conscription on them.
>
> One German-American response was a decided shift to the Republican party in the elections of 1918 and 1920, but far more significant was the rapid dismantling of the associational structure of German America. The total number of German-language publications declined from 554 in 1910 to 234 in 1920; daily newspaper circulation in 1920 was only about a quarter of its 1910 level. Language shift accelerated rapidly in the churches as elsewhere; in 1917 only one-sixth of the Missouri Synod Lutheran churches held at least one English service a month, while at the end of the war, three-quarters were doing so. The National German-American Alliance dissolved in April 1918 under Senate investigation.[82]

Even so, German Nazis made a considerable effort to establish an American base. The *Harvard Encyclopedia* records: "Recruiting began as early as 1924, but the first large-scale organization was the Friends of New Germany, organized in July 1933 after orders from Berlin dissolved the existing Nazi cells."[83]

A new immigrant, Fritz J. Kuhn, promptly joined. By 1936, Kuhn had become leader of the *Amerika-Deutscher Volksbund*, formed at Buffalo, New York, thenceforth a not insignificant political presence popularly known as "the Bund." On George Washington's Birthday, 1939, Kuhn and his allies organized a mass rally in Madison Square Garden in New York; the newsreel coverage was stunning. A Nazi rally, uniforms, salutes: arouse the masses to the struggle against "Rosenfeld's Jew Republic." Robin Edwin Herzstein estimates that the Bund "probably" consisted of some 6,500 "activists" at this time, with a combined pool of 50,000 to 100,000 sympathizers, family, and friends.[84] In about the same range, that is, of the early Communist Party. The differences were perhaps not that different. Herzstein describes the same immigrant core, with much the same apocalyptic fantasies:

> When the Depression struck, many of these newly arrived Germans found themselves in dire straits. Unemployed or engaged in menial tasks like dishwashing, these disappointed people found solace in the Bund. They could leave their cramped cold-water flats, head for a local *Stube*, and sit around drinking beer. The conversation often turned to the Jews and to the misery of living in Roosevelt's America. Tens of thousands of such people attended Bund meetings and rallies. Better educated leaders, like Fritz Kuhn, found them easy to manipulate.
>
> Kuhn and his associate Gerhard Wilhelm Kunze made themselves the spokesmen of these alienated recent immigrants. Like Hitler, they hoped that the United States would fragment into an ethnic free-for-all. As one of the Bundist put it, "This will happen here. It is inevitable. When that day comes, and it is probably not far-off, we must be prepared to fight for the right kind of government. We must win the masses to our side." When *der Tag* (the Day) arrived, the Bund had to be ready to grab its share of the loot.[85]

There was even the reaching out to other ethnic groups reminiscent of the earlier experience: White Russians, Italians, Irish. The differences, however, were decisive. At the end of 1939, Kuhn was jailed for embezzlement; by 1941, Nazi Germany had declared war on the United States; and by 1945, the Third Reich was crushed. There was not time for the impact Soviet Communism had, nor anything like the range of receptive audiences.

That said, the onset of the Second World War found the United States significantly better *organized* to deal with subversion, real or imagined. After war broke out in Europe in 1939, the government posted FBI agents in embassies in Latin America to compile information on Axis nationals and sympathizers. (A practice that continuously expanded thereafter.)[86] The FBI was, of course, active at home as well as abroad. Within three days of Pearl Harbor, some 1,291 Japanese, 857 Germans, and 147 Italians had been taken into custody.[87] However, the Federal law enforcement agency was much restrained in contrast with the public and some state officials, notably California Attorney General Earl Warren. On February 3, 1942, Director Hoover wrote to Attorney General Francis Biddle:

> The necessity for mass evacuation is based primarily upon public and political pressure rather than on factual data. Public hysteria and in some instances, the comments of the press and radio announcers, have resulted in a tremendous amount of pressure being brought to bear on Governor Olson and Earl Warren, Attorney General of the State, and on the military authorities. . . .

> Local officials, press and citizens have started a widespread movement
> demanding complete evacuation of Japanese, citizen and alien alike.[88]

Which was indeed the case.

On February 13, 1942, Congressman Clarence Lea of California, the senior West Coast Representative, wrote to President Roosevelt on behalf of the Members of Congress from California, Oregon, and Washington:

> We recommend the immediate evacuation of all persons of Japanese lineage
> and all others, aliens and citizens alike, whose presence shall be deemed
> dangerous or inimical to the defense of the United States from all strategic
> areas. . . .
>
> We further recommend that such areas be enlarged as expeditiously as
> possible until they shall encompass the entire strategic area of the states
> of California, Oregon and Washington, and the Territory of Alaska.[89]

Such views prevailed.

On February 19, 1942, President Roosevelt issued Executive Order 9066, "Authorizing the Secretary of War to Prescribe Military Areas." The Order gave the Secretary of War the power to exclude persons from designated areas, in order to provide "protection against espionage and against sabotage to national-defense material."[90]

No group was singled out, but the result was that Japanese aliens, along with American citizens of Japanese descent and Alaskan Aleuts, were prohibited from living, working, or traveling on the West Coast of the United States. Between May 8, 1942, and March 20, 1946, a total of 120,313 persons of Japanese descent living on the West Coast were interned in relocation camps in the West, the last of which was closed on March 20, 1946. In Latin America, some sixteen countries interned at least 8,500 Axis nationals. Where governments were reluctant, the United States did the job for them. In 1942 Peru deported some 1,000 Japanese, 300 Germans, and 30 Italians to the United States. Some Japanese were in American custody as late as 1949.[91]

Some argued that Germans and Italians should be dealt with in much the same way. But the Germans and Italians were far more numerous, making internment prohibitive, and their political influence was more formidable. On May 15, 1942, Secretary of State Stimson recommended to the President at a cabinet meeting that particular individuals should be excluded from militarily sensitive areas, but not entire classes of Germans or Italians.[92] On October 12, 1942, Columbus Day, Attorney General Biddle announced that Italian aliens would no longer be classified as enemies.[93] Germans remained technically enemy aliens, though by January 1943, most restrictions on Germans had been removed.

By comparison with the public arousal and resistance that accompanied the "red-baiting" period of the late 1940s and early 1950s, there was little protest at the internment of Japanese and others during World War II. The Roosevelt administration never experienced any loss of reputation; Earl Warren went on to become Chief Justice of the United States. In time—more than four decades later—Congress made amends by means of the Civil Liberties Act of 1988, which states that the Japanese internment was:

carried out without adequate security reasons and without any acts of espionage or sabotage documented . . . , and was motivated largely by racial prejudice, wartime hysteria, and a failure of political leadership.[94]

The Act provided redress for about 80,000 survivors of the internment, who were eligible to receive $20,000 each. More importantly, they received an apology from Congress, on behalf of the American people.

Extend the term "racial prejudice" to include ethnic and religious prejudice and we see a pattern of response to crisis that seems fairly fixed. In 1943, Lieutenant General John L. DeWitt, Western Defense Commander, issued *Final Report: Japanese Evacuation from the West Coast, 1942*, which contains this passage:

> In the war in which we are now engaged racial affinities are not severed by migration. The Japanese race is an enemy race and while many second and third generation Japanese born on United States soil, possessed of United States citizenship, have become "Americanized," the racial strains are undiluted. . . . There are indications that [West Coast Japanese] are organized and ready for concerted action at a favorable opportunity. *The very fact that no sabotage has taken place to date is a disturbing and confirming indication that such action will be taken.*[95] (Emphasis added.)

The latter statement verges on clinical paranoia, in which the absence of overt threat is interpreted as a means of allaying suspicion in a situation of real danger. This can be the mark of a troubled mind. It can also, however, be the mark of profound insight into the ways of the world. Hence the impulse to secrecy by befuddled minds as well as vigilant ones.

6. <u>The Experience of The Bomb</u>

The Second World War came to a close in August 1945 when the United States dropped two atomic bombs on Japan. The most awesome secret in the history of warfare was now revealed to the world. In time the United States would learn that it was already known to Communist spies.

The atom bomb changed warfare. For the United States, atomic espionage changed peacetime as well. Nothing since has been the same.

Prometheus-like, man stole fire from the gods. Maurice M. Shapiro, now chief scientist emeritus of the Laboratory for Cosmic Physics at the Naval Research Station, in Washington, recalled the scene in the New Mexico desert:

> At precisely 5:30 there was a blinding flash—brighter than many suns—and then a flaming fireball. Within seconds a churning multicolored column of gas and dust was rising. Then, within it, a narrower column of debris swirled upward, spreading out into an awesome mushroom-shaped apparition high in the atmosphere.[96]

Next came "an oppressive sense of foreboding." J. Robert Oppenheimer recalled a line from Hindu scripture:

> We waited until the blast had passed, walked out of the shelter and then it was extremely solemn. We knew the world would not be the same. A few people laughed, a few people cried. Most people were silent. I remembered the line from the Hindu scripture, the *Bhagavad-Gita*: Vishnu is trying to persuade the Prince that he should do his duty and to impress him he takes on his multi-armed form and says, "Now I am become Death, the destroyer of worlds," I suppose we all thought that, one way or another.[97]

The scientists at the site knew that if the test worked it would end the War, as it did within a month, and forever change the nature of warfare. It was the culmination of four years of secret work. Before the next year was out, we would learn that Communist spies had stolen the secret. Our punishment would now begin.

This was a complex fate. But then, so was that of Prometheus. For his audacity he was chained to a mountain where daily his liver (which grew again at night) was consumed by an eagle. He was freed at length by Heracles. So, at length, might the United States be freed from the long torment of secrecy that followed if we will but think more clearly about its uses and its limits.

These were both on display on those hilltops in New Mexico at the moment of the Trinity test. The scientists present had submitted to an unfamiliar and altogether uncongenial secrecy, because they knew what was at stake. Hans Bethe of Germany, Enrico Fermi of Italy, and James Chadwick of Britain would have especially known what was at stake. There was no real scientific secret to atomic fission; German scientists knew it. There *are* no secrets in science. Oppenheimer and his associates had "simply" figured out the techniques and found the resources to build a bomb before our enemies did. Shapiro recorded the openness of scientific discourse even at that moment of profound concealment:

> While waiting for the rain to abate so that the test could begin, Dr. Bethe and I discussed his epochal discovery of the thermonuclear reactions that power the sun and stars. For me it was a memorable dialogue: we were about to witness the first massive fission explosion, yet we talked of controlled fusion—the steady burning of hydrogen in stars. We pointedly did not discuss the prospect of future H-bombs, also based on thermonuclear reactions.

But this would come; it had to come. Thanks to successful espionage, the Russians tested their first atom bomb in August 1949, just four years after the first American test. As will be discussed, we had learned of the Los Alamos spies in December 1946—December 20, to be precise. The U.S. Army Security Agency, in the person of Meredith Knox Gardner, a genius in his own right, had broken one of what it termed the VENONA messages—the transmissions that Soviet agents in the United States sent to and received from Moscow.

The Soviets had the names of the principal scientists working at Los Alamos. This could only mean they were after the secrets of the bomb. It would be some time before we knew they had gotten them, but alarms now rang throughout the American Government. (American scientists knew that in any event the Soviets would have this capability in time.)

BRIDE

TOP SECRET

TO BE KEPT UNDER LOCK AND KEY :
NEVER TO BE REMOVED FROM THE OFFICE.

SUEDE

USSR

RUDAI-2A

Ref No: S/NBF/T193

Issued: Z/C/21/5/1952

Copy No: **205**

1. LIST OF SCIENTISTS ENGAGED ON THE PROBLEM OF ATOMIC ENERGY.

2. UNSUCCESSFUL EFFORTS OF AN UNIDENTIFIED PERSON (POSSIBLY
   "STAR") TO CONTACT NICHOLA NAPOLI AND "HELMSMAN".

From: NEW YORK

To: MOSCOW

No: 1699   2 Dec 1944

Conclusion of telegram No. 940 [sic][i].

    Enumerates [the following][a] scientists who are working on
the problem[ii] - Hans BETHE, Niels BOHR, Enrico FERMI, John NEWMAN,
Bruno ROSSI, George KISTIAKOVSKI, Emilio SEGRE, G.I.TAYLOR, William
PENNEY, Arthur COMPTON, Ernest LAWRENCE, Harold UREY, Hans STANARM,
Edward TELLER, Percy BRIDGEMAN, Werner EISENBERG, STRASSENMAN
               [7 groups unrecoverable]
our country addressed himself to NAPOLI[iii] and the latter, not
wanting to listen to him, sent him to BECK [BEK][iv] as military
commentator of the paper.   On attempting to visit HELMSMAN [RULEVOJ][v]
he was not admitted to him by the latter's secretary.

              ANTON

                         [T.N. and Comments overleaf]

Distribution

The United States Government set out to forestall a nuclear arms race. President Harry S Truman proposed to the United Nations a plan to control atomic weapons, known as the "Baruch Plan" for his representative, Bernard M. Baruch. This was blocked by the Soviet Union, whose leader Joseph Stalin was determined to have his own bomb. The first Soviet A-bomb test took place in August, 1949. It was a near-exact copy of "Fat Man," the American weapon that destroyed Nagasaki in August 1945.

Now the stakes were raised. This sequence was described in a lecture by Hans Bethe, "My Road From Los Alamos," given at the University of Maryland on December 8, 1994. For a period it was not clear whether a fusion weapon was technically possible. The mathematician Stanislaw Ulam and the physicist Edward Teller demonstrated that it was. Dr. Bethe's lecture describes what followed with the succinctness of the historical moment:

> When Truman made his decision [to accelerate the hydrogen bomb project], it was not clear whether the hydrogen bomb actually could be developed. However, early in '51—about a year after Truman's decision—there was an ingenious idea by Ulam and Teller, both of them, just how to make a hydrogen bomb. It was so convincing that it was clear that not only the United States could make it but surely there were competent physicists in the Soviet Union who could do it as well. And this being so, it was then clear that it had to be done and in spite of my apprehension, I agreed to participate for a good half-year in developing the hydrogen bomb. We concluded it had to be done because the Soviets could, we believed, do it too. And indeed it was done by Sakharov and his collaborators.
>
> I have listed here the tests of the hydrogen bomb, beginning in 1952, which were made.
>
> First the U.S. tested a device which could not have been delivered in a war, which consisted of liquid deuterium. And it worked. It worked, in fact, impressively, giving a yield of some 10 megatons.
>
> This was followed in August '53 by a Soviet test which Sakharov called the "layer cake," alternate layers of uranium and liquid deuterium to provide the nuclear fuel which is necessary for a fusion reaction. This would have been deliverable, its yield of energy of four-tenths of a megaton.
>
> In '54 the United States made tests in the Pacific where they tested various variations, all with liquid deuterium, and developed some three or four different hydrogen bombs, each giving about 10 megatons.
>
> And finally in November '55, there was an additional Soviet test. Sakharov had, in the meantime, hit upon the idea of Ulam and Teller, and produced a device just like ours. They deliberately reduced the yield of it so they could deliver this bomb from a plane to the . . . test ground and the plane could get away. This could have been three megatons.

As Bethe's remarks make clear, the Soviets did not steal the "Teller-Ulam method." Their own scientists discovered it, as scientists will do once certain principles are abroad. But the hydrogen

Model of the "Fat Man," the atomic bomb detonated over Nagasaki, Japan on August 9, 1945. (Source: National Archives and Records Administration.)

Iulii Khariton with a copy of the first Soviet atomic bomb, detonated on August 29, 1949. (Source: Dr. A. Iu. Semenov, 1992. Reprinted with permission.)

bomb began, obviously, as a weapon, and as a weapon, for the most obvious reasons, its details were kept as secret as possible.

With, however, an all-important difference. There was no way to keep the whole world from knowing *about* the secret, for the simple reason that the bombs had to be tested. The weapon was new, and there was much to be learned about it, and the only way to do so was to set one off. Thus began a series of "tests" by assorted nuclear powers which continue almost to this day. But none since has quite seized the world's imagination as did the underwater explosion in 1946 on Bikini, a small coral atoll in the Marshall Islands, designed to test the effect of the atom bomb on naval armament and equipment and on certain forms of animal life. The photographs were unforgettable. One caption reads: "An Awe-Inspiring Mushroom Cloud rises above Bikini atoll in an underwater atomic bomb test. The mighty column of water dwarfs huge battleships." One ship captain, apprised of radioactive fallout, ordered the decks swabbed. Captain Cook might have done as much; such was the suddenness with which this new age came upon us. The Bikini tests were followed in 1948 with the tests of three weapons at Eniwetok atoll, two hundred miles west in what was now termed the Pacific Proving Grounds.

The tension between great publicity and even greater secrecy finally led *Life* magazine to "tell all." In lengthy articles, "The Atom" in May 1949, and "The Atomic Bomb" in February 1950, the fundamentals of the science and the particulars of the weapon were set forth in layman's language. Americans were not yet used to this much secrecy. Secrecy, that is, which they *knew* about. The editors of *Life* were clearly upset by the imbalance of what they termed "Necessary security and unnecessary secrecy. . . ." They were, even so, scrupulous. A preface to the article on "The Atomic Bomb" declares: "This article reveals no secrets. It is based on published, unclassified material that can be found by anyone, including the Russians, in public libraries." The text of the article invokes a number of the nation's most respected journalists and commentators to the effect that secrecy was getting out of hand:

> For the past five years the operations and results of the U.S. atomic weapons program have been almost completely unknown to the public. The critical facts about this greatest of all publicly owned enterprises have been withheld, partly because of essential security restriction. But a larger factor behind the present state of public ignorance is the extension of secrecy far beyond the limits of true security.

> This growing disparity between required security and officially imposed secrecy has recently come in for sharp criticism by many of the country's best-informed observers. Joseph and Stewart Alsop, writing about the world strategic situation and the H-bomb, say, "what the President has said [about the bomb] is not one third, or one tenth, of what it is his bounden duty to say." Hanson Baldwin, in the *New York Times*, writes: "facts are the foundation of democracy—and facts we do not have." Physicist J.R. Oppenheimer, in a recent television interview, pointed out that wisdom and truth cannot flourish without the give-and-take of debate and criticism, and added that "the facts [about atomic energy] are of little use to an enemy, yet they are fundamental to an understanding of the issue of policy."

> The extent of public information about atomic weapons must of course be limited. It cannot and should not include a knowledge of facts that could conceivably be of

use to an enemy. It should, but—for reasons of specious security—does not at present include all the facts that are useless to an enemy or known to him.

The article ended with a plea not usual for editors at *Time-Life*:

> It must be assumed that the approximate size of the U.S. stockpile of bombs is no secret. Nevertheless this information, so vitally necessary to the making of policy, is denied to the people who are finally responsible for determining what policy shall be: the citizens of the U.S. and their elected representatives.

> There is no possible justification for this kind of overextended secrecy. Enlightened members of the federal government know this, and they have fought its growth. Two years ago David Lilienthal, then chairman of the Atomic Energy Commission, warned the American people of the harmful effects that such phony security might have: "There is a growing tendency in some quarters to act as if atomic energy were none of the people's business. . . . In my opinion this is plain nonsense, and dangerous nonsense—dangerous to cherished American institutions and for that reason dangerous to genuine national security. . . . If schemers or fools or rascals or hysterical stuffed shirts get this thing out of [the people's] hands, it may then be too late to find out what it is all about."

> The restriction of public knowledge Lilienthal feared is being brought about. So stifling are the effects of all-encompassing security that conscientious publications are unwilling to take the responsibility for presenting conclusions which they themselves could draw from the available, nonsecret literature. The government can and should take that responsibility—now, before it is too late.

But it *was* too late. For a complex of reasons. The most important being that the United States now had reason to fear for its security. Pearl Harbor had seemed devastating, but it represented an external threat which soon passed. Now there appeared an *internal* threat in the form of American Communists serving as agents of the Soviet Union.

Fear of radical revolutionists had gotten out of hand in 1919-20. There was a good deal of disorder and no small amount of government misconduct. Let us say in extenuation that a world war, followed by what for awhile seemed the onset of world revolution, required a fair amount of adjusting. A measure of balance returned, in part, surely owing to the "isolationist" bent that appeared in national politics in reaction to Wilsonian activism. Just as importantly, the legal profession began to brush up on the Bill of Rights. On May 28, 1920, twelve of the nation's most respected lawyers and legal scholars, including Harvard Law School Dean Roscoe Pound, Harvard law professors Felix Frankfurter and Zechariah Chafee, Jr., and Francis Fisher Kane, former U.S. Attorney for the Eastern District of Pennsylvania (who had resigned on January 12, 1920 to protest the January 2 "Palmer Raids"), issued a 67-page booklet entitled *Report upon the Illegal Practices of the United States Department of Justice*. The booklet, which has been termed "the most authoritative denunciation of the anti-Red activities of the Justice Department yet made," documented abuses of the Constitution, in particular the Fourth, Fifth and Eighth Amendments, that had been taking place at the behest of the Justice Department.[98]

Nothing like the Palmer Raids of 1919 and 1920 would happen again in the United States. The Sacco-Vanzetti trial, again involving anarchists, would take place in 1921, but it was a *trial*, not a raid. Following the Second World War, we would go through much torment over Communism and Communist subversion. There was a good deal of public alarm, and a good deal of histrionics, but there were few of the excesses of this earlier period. No president since has sent a rival candidate to prison.

On the other hand, there was to be no return to normalcy.

In 1943, the Army Signal Intelligence Service (later the Army Security Agency) began intercepting Soviet intelligence traffic sent mainly from New York City—assigning the code name VENONA to the project. By 1945, some 200,000 messages had been transcribed, a measure of Soviet activity. As recorded earlier, on December 20, 1946, Meredith Gardner made the first break into the VENONA code, revealing the existence of Soviet espionage at Los Alamos. Steadily, the facts accumulated and identities could be established. In January 1949, the British Government was informed that the VENONA intercepts showed that atomic secrets were being passed to the Soviets from the British Embassy in Washington in 1944 and 1945 by an agent code-named HOMER, later identified as Donald MacLean. In the summer of 1948, Army Security Agency cipher clerk William Weisband passed on information about the VENONA project to the Soviets. This was discovered in 1950. (Weisband also served as a Russian translator, and therefore was working closely with those attempting to decrypt the intercepts.)

Now we entered a period of rising tension. Trials arising from charges of espionage, notably those of Alger Hiss for perjury, were taking place in rapid succession. In Great Britain Klaus Fuchs confessed in January 1950 that he had been a Soviet agent at Los Alamos. On February 9, 1950, in a speech at Wheeling, West Virginia, Senator Joseph McCarthy announced he was in possession of a list of 205 Communists serving in the Department of State. In time, he would accuse George C. Marshall of treason, as described below. In June 1950, the FBI identified Julius Rosenberg as the agent coded named "ANTENNA/LIBERAL" in the VENONA decrypts. Julius and Ethel Rosenberg and Morton Sobell were later tried and convicted, on March 29, 1951, of conspiracy to commit espionage by transmitting atomic secrets to the Soviets. In May 1951, Donald MacLean, along with Guy Burgess, defected to Moscow.

But for every accusation there was a denial. For as many who were willing to believe Whittaker Chambers, there appeared to be a corresponding number convinced of Hiss's innocence. For all who could agree there were Communists in government, there were as many who saw the Government as contriving fantastic accusations against innocent persons.

A balanced history of this period is now beginning to appear; the VENONA messages will surely supply a great cache of facts to bring the matter to some closure. But at the time, the American Government, much less the American public, was confronted with possibilities and charges, at once baffling and terrifying.

The first fact is that a significant Communist conspiracy *was* in place in Washington, New York, and Los Angeles, but in the main those involved systematically denied their involvement. This was the mode of Communist conspiracy the world over. George Kennan would write in his memoirs:

> The penetration of the American governmental services by members or agents
> (conscious or otherwise) of the American Communist Party in the late 1930s was
> not a figment of the imagination . . . it really existed; and it assumed proportions
> which, while never overwhelming, were also not trivial. (*Memoirs 1950-1963.*)

The second fact is that many of those who came to prominence denouncing Communist conspiracy, accusing suspected Communists and "comsymps," clearly knew little or nothing of such matters. And in many instances, just as clearly were not in the least concerned. Hence, the character of the accusers lent credibility to the accused!

There was a political subtext to much of the debate, which only muddled matters more. Often those who were telling the truth about Soviet espionage were discredited or discounted as readily as those who knew little or nothing, but who would accuse others of anything. The ridicule could be devastating, as with the ditty, "Who's going to investigate the man who investigates the man who investigates me?" A fault line appeared in American society that contributed to more than one political crisis in the years that followed, long after President Dwight D. Eisenhower, much in the manner of President Harding, calmed things down.

A compelling question is why the United States Government never let the American public know what *it* knew. By 1950, at least some in the Government were aware that our VENONA "secret" had been compromised. The Soviets knew that we knew, or could surmise. It was the American public that did not know. (It was not until 1986 that the existence of the VENONA project first was made public in a book by the FBI's liaison to the project, Robert Lamphere,[99] and only just now that substantive information is being released.)

It is not even clear how widely the VENONA revelations were shared *within* the United States Government. Thus, a Soviet cable of March 30, 1945 identified an agent, code-name ALES, as having attended the Yalta Conference of February 1945. He had then journeyed to Moscow where, according to the cable, he and his colleagues were "awarded Soviet decorations." This could only be Alger Hiss, Deputy Director of the State Department's Office of Special Political Affairs; the other three State Department officials in the delegation from Yalta to Moscow are beyond suspicion.[100] The party was met by Andrei Vyshinsky, the prosecutor in the Moscow trials of 1936-38. By no later than June 1950, the U.S. Army was persuaded that ALES *was* Hiss.

But . . . did the State Department know of this VENONA message? Did the White House? As noted in Chapter 1, apparently not. What seems increasingly clear is that the entire VENONA project was kept secret from Harry S Truman and his Attorney General, Tom Clark.[101]

Not the least astounding revelations of the VENONA intercepts is that a fair number of Americans who almost certainly were atomic spies were never prosecuted. To do so the Government would have had to reveal what it knew. Secrets are not readily shared. For that matter, Weisband, who passed on to the Soviets that we were breaking their code, was never prosecuted for this crime.

TOP SECRET UMBRA VENONA

MGB

From: WASHINGTON

To: MOSCOW

No: 1822

30 March 1945

Further to our telegram No. 283[a]. As a result of "[D% A.'s]"[i] chat with "ALES"[ii] the following has been ascertained:

1.   ALES has been working with the NEIGHBORS[SOSEDI][iii] continuously since 1935.

2.   For some years past he has been the leader of a small group of the NEIGHBORS' probationers[STAZhERY], for the most part consisting of his relations.

3.   The group and ALES himself work on obtaining military information only. Materials on the "BANK"[iv] allegedly interest the NEIGHBORS very little and he does not produce them regularly.

4.   All the last few years ALES has been working with "POL'"[v] who also meets other members of the group occasionally.

5.   Recently ALES and his whole group were awarded Soviet decorations.

6.   After the YaLTA Conference, when he had gone on to MOSCOW, a Soviet personage in a very responsible position (ALES gave to understand that it was Comrade VYShINSKIJ) allegedly got in touch with ALES and at the behest of the Military NEIGHBORS passed on to him their gratitude and so on.

No. 431   VADIM[vi]

_____

Notes: [a]   Not available.
Comments:
    [i]   A.: "A." seems the most likely garble here although "A." has
           not been confirmed elsewhere in the WASHINGTON traffic.
    [ii]   ALES: Probably Alger HISS.
    [iii] SOSEDI: Members of another Soviet Intelligence organization,
           here probably the GRU.
    [iv]   BANK: The U.S. State Department.
    [v]   POL': i.e. "PAUL," unidentified cover-name.
    [vi]   VADIM: Anatolij Borisovich GROMOV, MGB resident in WASHINGTON.

7. The Cold War

The Cold War, as it has been called, began almost immediately after the end of the Second World War, and is probably best understood as the third in a succession of "civil wars" within Western Civilization that commenced in 1914.

The encounter began in Central Europe, just as had the two earlier conflicts, with the Soviets pressing to expand their dominion in the wreckage of previous regimes. In 1949 Communists triumphed in a civil war in China, and instantly the conflict was global.

With the National Security Act of 1947 the United States had brought its armed forces under unified direction, established a National Security Council "to advise the President with respect to the integration of domestic, foreign and military policies relating to the national security," and also created a Central Intelligence Agency to provide "national intelligence" to the President and agency heads that was to be "timely, objective, independent of political considerations, and based upon all sources available to the intelligence community."[102] In time the CIA's mission would expand to include para-military operations.

The legislation can be seen as one feature of a more general rationalization and modernization that was occurring within American Government at this time. It was a recognition that the United States had become the preeminent world power and would be managing conflict, and very likely engaged in warfare, *around* the world for an indefinite future. A vast peacetime military establishment began to take shape. (After instant demobilization in 1946!) To respond to the threat in Europe, recognizing that if the Soviets were to invade western Germany the United States would inevitably be involved in the aftermath, we chose to become engaged in advance, helping to shape the North Atlantic Treaty. For the first time in history, we entered a peacetime alliance committing us to war if others were attacked.

In 1955 the Soviets organized the Warsaw Pact and the symmetry was complete. Central Powers vs. Allied Powers, Axis Powers vs. Allied Powers, Warsaw Pact vs. North Atlantic Treaty Organization.

The extraordinary fact of the final stage of this Hundred Years' War is that warfare never broke out between the major contesting powers. Proxy conflicts of all sorts did occur. United States forces saw action. Still, this time, global confrontation did not result in global war.

The reason, of course, was the atomic bomb, and the strategic thinking that commenced with the onset of the atomic age. It is for others to say, but surely American strategic doctrine, with the key concept of "second strike" as the key to nuclear stability, achieved just that. But beyond strictly nuclear affairs it is perhaps not too early to suggest that American statecraft—and yes, that of the Soviets also—had evolved. Things had been learned; no party ever reached irrevocably too far.

In the meantime, however, ideological conflict raged, as did efforts to gain strategic or tactical advantage through espionage or subversion. In most of these events we observe the uniformity formulated by the political scientist James Q. Wilson. Organizations in conflict become like one another. Both parties organized alliances, built strategic forces and conventional forces, cultivated dissent among adversaries, as much as possible denied them information, and built up intelligence forces of unprecedented size, scope, and global reach. It could be said that the Cold War brought two innovations to the armamentarium of the great powers: strategic nuclear forces and intelligence services.

We have seen that the Soviet attack in the area of intelligence commenced just after the First World War, and was hugely successful during the Second World War. The Soviets even infiltrated the Office of Strategic Services (OSS), established in June 1942. It would, for example, appear from the VENONA messages that Duncan Chaplin Lee, Special Assistant to OSS Director William J. Donovan, was a Soviet agent.

Lee, of the Lee family of Virginia, was a 1935 graduate of Yale University. He then spent three years as a Rhodes Scholar at Oxford—dangerous years—returning to Yale for law school. Thereafter he joined Donovan's law firm in New York, and in July 1942 joined the OSS. He appears regularly in the KGB cables that began to be intercepted in 1943, and thereafter were decrypted by those involved in the VENONA project.

The complicity of Alger Hiss of the State Department seems settled. As does that of Harry Dexter White of the Treasury Department. White, the closest advisor to Secretary Henry J. Morgenthau and later Assistant Secretary, headed the American delegation to the Bretton Woods Conference of 1944, which shaped postwar financial institutions such as the World Bank and the International Monetary Fund.

And so to an irony that only now begins to emerge. It would appear that by the onset of the Cold War the Soviet attack in the area of espionage and subversion had been blunted and turned back. There would be episodic successes in the years to come, but none equal to earlier feats. New York of the 1930s. Los Alamos. Some unions. The State Department. The Treasury Department. By the close of the 1940s, Communism was a defeated ideology in the United States, with its influence in steep and steady decline, and the KGB reduced to recruiting thieves as spies.

At this distance it is difficult to conceive the intensity of Communist conviction in the 1930s. In the 1940s the critic Robert Warshow would write in *Commentary* magazine:

> For most American intellectuals, the Communist movement of the 1930s was a
> crucial experience. In Europe, where the movement was at once more serious
> and more popular, it was still only one current in intellectual life; the Communists
> could never completely set the tone of thinking. . . . But in this country there was
> a time when virtually all intellectual vitality was derived in one way or another
> from the Communist party. If you were not somewhere within the party's wide
> orbit, then you were likely to be in the opposition, which meant that much of your
> thought and energy had to be devoted to maintaining yourself in opposition.[103]

But with the defeat of Nazi Germany, it became easier to accept the reality of Soviet totalitarianism. The worldwide economic crisis of the 1930s passed. An increasing number of American Communists openly broke with the Party—as, for example, Louis Francis Budenz, managing editor of the *Daily Worker*. In 1946, Budenz broke with the Communist Party and commenced to publicly identify Party members—much as Chambers, Bentley, and others would do in Congressional testimony beginning in 1948. None of this took place without controversy, but the charges held up well enough; in the main they would seem to have been true.

Enter the Federal Bureau of Investigation. By the Second World War it had begun to deal with espionage, in that case of the Axis powers. In November 1945 Elizabeth Bentley informed the FBI of her activities as a Soviet courier, which in turn led to renewed interest in Chambers. In late August or early September 1947, the FBI was informed that the Army Security Agency had begun to break into Soviet espionage messages. The FBI proceeded to identify the cover names used in the Soviet dispatches. Thus, Theodore A. Hall, a 19-year old Harvard physicist at Los Alamos in 1944, was code named "MLAD," Russian for "youngster." By 1950, the FBI, working with the Army, knew Hall to be the "MLAD" identified in the VENONA messages.

In 1936 the FBI began infiltrating the Communist Party itself, typically using disillusioned Party members as agents.[104] In short order, the Party itself was useless as a source of Soviet recruits. Very likely the Soviets came to realize this early on and began looking elsewhere for spies. The period of organized effort—more or less based in an American political party—to infiltrate the American Government in the interests of a foreign nation ended almost as abruptly as it had begun.

This "Brief Account" has attempted to search out uniformities in America's encounter with foreign espionage and domestic treason that began early in the 20th century. One pattern is that of learning. We have remarked that NATO arose from the United States' understanding that it was no longer possible to stay out of a major European conflict. Might once have been; was no more. That realization was central to the avoidance of the "world wars" of the first two phases of the Hundred Years' War.

Now we encounter further examples of what could legitimately be called learning. Faced with the facts of espionage and treason, this time the American Government did not lose its head. The Communist Party of the United States of America *was there*. Its leaders and many of its members were guilty of all manner of misfeasance and violence. The incitement to hysteria was considerable indeed. Palmer Raids, internment camps, deportations, ethnic demonizing (anti-Semitism not least), a general shredding of civil rights—all those were possible during the Cold War. Each had forebears. Virtually none actually happened.

This may appear a provocative judgment. By the late 1940s there was a great agitation in the land about Communists and "comsymps." As early as January 1947 the U.S. Chamber of Commerce warned of infiltration in a publication *Communists Within the Government: The Facts and the Program* (not all the facts within which were wrong). Next came Congressional investigations, notably those associated with Senator Joseph R. McCarthy. Careers were damaged, of this there is no doubt. But compared to the earlier outrages, the society, notably the Government, responded with comparative restraint. Again, there were casualties, but compared to the provocation. . .?

In 1948 former Vice President Henry A. Wallace, now a presidential candidate, announced that he would name Harry Dexter White as his Secretary of the Treasury. (White died of a heart attack before the election and one week after denying any espionage activities before the House Un-American Activities Committee.) Wallace lost the election; President Truman did not send him to prison.

The more singular fact of the fairly rapid discovery of Communist espionage and Soviet agents in the United States is the relatively muted response of the United States Government. For every spy, every traitor tried for espionage, there would be another left untroubled and untried. In March 1949, Judith Coplon, a 27-year old official of the Justice Department, was arrested and charged with theft and distribution of secret Department documents and with conspiracy. Her convictions in two separate prosecutions were overturned on procedural grounds, but the effort had been made. (And one could assume that Coplon was of no further use, and her trial put others on notice.)

Then the following year, it was discovered that William Weisband, cipher clerk and translator, had informed the Soviets of the existence of the VENONA project. The Soviets now knew that we were "reading their mail." We knew that they knew. They could not know just how many messages, or which messages had been decoded, but we could not know how much they did know. And so into the house of mirrors. *But, as noted, Weisband was not prosecuted for espionage.* (He was sentenced to a year in jail for failing to respond to a subpoena, but the Government's knowledge of his treason apparently was not revealed until its publication in a 1990 book co-authored by a high-level KGB defector).[105]

A more striking contrast can be seen in the treatment of atomic spies. As noted, in January 1950, in the United Kingdom, Klaus Fuchs confessed to espionage while part of the British team at Los Alamos; his activities had turned up in the VENONA files. He implicated Harry Gold as his courier. Gold in turn implicated David Greenglass, who implicated his brother-in-law Julius Rosenberg, formerly of the Army Security Agency. The Rosenberg prosecution, including that of Julius' wife Ethel, now commenced.

But at this time our attention again is drawn to 19-year old Theodore A. Hall. As noted earlier, by 1950 both the Army and the FBI knew that Hall was the "MLAD" referenced in several VENONA messages. It is hard to know with certainty exactly what happened next; most of the FBI files remain classified. It appears that Hall denied any illegal activity during questioning by the FBI. In any event, even assuming that a court case could have been built against Hall, the Government was evidently unwilling to pursue one if it would have meant revealing the existence of the VENONA project.

Espionage can present profound dilemmas as regards prosecution. In this period, anything told to a jury would be learned by the KGB, at a time when large issues turned on preventing the KGB from knowing what we knew. This dilemma was doubly so when dealing with an Allied government. In October 1949, the British spy Kim Philby arrived in Washington as British intelligence liaison to the U.S. intelligence community. Part of his responsibilities involved receiving VENONA material which the U.S. was providing to the U.K. In April 1951, a decoded VENONA message showed that Donald MacLean, who had served as Second Secretary at the British Embassy in Washington in 1944 and 1945 (and returned in 1947 to work on atomic energy issues), was "HOMER," a Soviet spy. Surveillance of MacLean commenced in order to obtain evidence independent of VENONA, as the U.S. and U.K. did not want to reveal publicly the existence of the project, but MacLean defected to Moscow with Guy Burgess in May 1951. Albeit the U.S. Government knew that Weisband had passed on this information more than two years earlier!

What we observe here is "tradecraft" of a high order, but also a fairly routine example of organizational behavior. Secrets are assets to an organization. It is rare for secrets to be shared with another organization, save as exchange. It is difficult at this distance to establish just how widely the VENONA project, for example, was known within the American Government. Sharing with British intelligence was one thing; we may assume the British gave something in return. But could the White House? Not necessarily. The State Department? Almost assuredly not.

Very well, what about the newly created Central Intelligence Agency? New, yes, but, again, by common understanding successor to the Office of Strategic Services.[106] How many associates might Duncan Chaplin Lee have had? Of these how many might have made the transition to the successor organization? Was it worth the risk? Evidently not. As best as these events can be reconstructed, it would appear that the Army took a good long look before it decided it could trust the Central Intelligence Agency with secrets about Soviet espionage.

The Army may be assumed to have another problem in sharing its secrets. It is entirely reasonable to conjecture that at this time in the United States a good many persons just would not have believed them anyway. Part of this was plain innocence. As remarked, most Americans had no encounter with Communists or Communism. Further, this was manifestly the case with many of the more prominent anti-Communists of the time. There was a cultural conflict: anti-Communists were perceived by some as elitists protecting bastions of corrupt privilege, and by others as vulgarians hurling groundless accusations. It is well also to keep in mind that the United States Army itself was under attack. Most notably, as when Senator McCarthy accused George C. Marshall of treason.[107]

Just as the period of a serious Communist "attack" ended precipitously in the late 1940s, so did the period of domestic agitation and alarm. The Rosenbergs were executed in Sing Sing Prison on June 19, 1953. There was a harsh injustice here. Ethel Rosenberg was an accomplice, not a principal. Still, the Government had not asked for a death sentence; a Federal judge took it on his own to impose it.

By now, Dwight D. Eisenhower had been elected President; somewhat in parallel with the succession of Harding, a kind of normalcy returned to government. In December 1954, Senator McCarthy was censured by the Senate and matters settled down.

Looking back, however, we see more clearly the dilemma of secrecy in Government. By 1950, when it was learned that Weisband had revealed the existence of the VENONA project to the Soviets, the United States Government possessed information which the American public desperately needed to know: proof that there had been a serious attack on American security by the Soviet Union, with considerable assistance from what was, indeed, an "enemy within." The fact that we knew this was now known to, or sufficiently surmised by, the Soviet authorities. Only the American public was denied this information.

The circumstances were surely extenuating. The Government knew some parts of the story: what did it not know? If innocent persons were being harassed and worse by a political mob— and many were—so might equally innocent persons be devastated by the release of government information that incriminated a good many persons, not all of whom were guilty, and for certain not found guilty by a jury?

Anyone knowledgeable of the Communist *apparat* could have predicted that the Government "secrets" would be attacked as spurious and contrived. The dilemma was awful, save that none of the principals involved seems ever to have doubted the wisdom of withholding the secrets. Much remains classified to this day. The Soviet Union has ceased to exist, but some of the divisions in the American polity from that encounter remain, and the new revelations brought a measure of recognition still very much needed.

8. <u>A Culture of Secrecy</u>

The Cold War settled in: a winter of many discontents. American society in peacetime began to experience wartime regulation. A good example would be the "fallout shelters," located and identified in urban settings across the nation, preparing the civilian population for the explosion of a nuclear weapon of the sort that had by then become quite obsolete in nuclear arsenals. Cabinet officers routinely went through evacuation exercises to shelters some miles distant from Washington. Schoolchildren learned to duck under desks. If this seems hapless, it may be asked what else civilian authorities were supposed to do? The facts of nuclear weapons and the probabilities of nuclear war were official secrets altogether withheld from the public.

As for the enemy within, by 1950 or thereabouts, the Communist Party was completely neutralized. In outward appearance it still existed, but, as much as anything, merely as a device maintained by the U.S. Government to trap the unwary. Lest they fall to the enemy.

This was the awful dilemma of the Cold War. To preserve an open society it was deemed necessary to take measures that in significant ways closed it down. A culture of secrecy evolved. There were two components, by now familiar ones: the enemy abroad, the enemy within. In both cases the United States Government over-responded; in neither can it be overly blamed. The Soviet Union was by now developing nuclear and missile capacity very much on its own, allowing for contributions from former German scientists. (A resource both sides shared.) It is not clear that espionage yielded any significant gains after Los Alamos. The Soviets continued a large-scale espionage offensive, but there were no major successes. A fairly steady yield of random information; nothing of coherent consequence.

Indeed, the terms of trade, if that image may be used concerning the "product," had quite reversed since the 1940s. It was the Soviets who were now forced to deal with an "enemy within." Marxism was a belief system which could evoke intense attachment. Of a sudden it failed. Judgments vary, but it is probably the case that Mikhail A. Suslov, who served as a member of the Politburo, almost continuously, from 1952 until he died in 1982,[108] was the last member of the Politburo to have studied Marx and Lenin and adhered to their world view.

Now came bureaucracy, disillusion, dissent, defectors. Most conspicuously, in 1967, Joseph Stalin's daughter Svetlana fled the U.S.S.R. This reached the highest levels. In 1975, as an example, Arkady N. Shevchenko, Under Secretary-General for Political and Security Council Affairs of the United Nations, a Soviet diplomat on the short list of possible successors to Foreign Minister Andrei A. Gromyko, defected to the United States and remained under cover for some years before Moscow sensed that something was wrong, evidently narrowing the suspects to Shevchenko, Oleg Troyanovsky, Ambassador to the United Nations, or Anatoly Dobrynin, the Soviet Ambassador in Washington. By now no one was beyond suspicion.[109]

But first, the United States had to live through the aftermath of the Soviet espionage that had crested at Los Alamos. Several laws were enacted, the most important of which was the Atomic Energy Act of 1946. In August 1945, the U.S. Government had released a history of the Manhattan Project, entitled *A General Account of the Development of Methods of Using Atomic Energy for Military Purposes Under the Auspices of the United States Government, 1940-1945*, commonly known as the Smyth Report (for the Princeton University physics professor who had been asked by General Leslie R. Groves, head of the Manhattan Project, to write the report). The Smyth Report said that most of the information on the development of the atomic bomb could be obtained from unclassified sources, but nothing would do. The Atomic Energy Act introduced the principle that certain information was "born classified," meaning no action need be taken in order for that information to be deemed secret.

This was by now a pattern of governance, and indeed, remains so. Government regulation expanded greatly in scope with the New Deal, as the Roosevelt administration responded to the crisis of the economic depression. During the 1930s, opponents of Roosevelt's New Deal programs grew increasingly concerned about the scope of Executive Branch discretion. For example, in 1938 Roscoe Pound, Chairman of the American Bar Association's Special Committee on Administrative Law and former Dean of Harvard Law School, denounced the trend of turning "the administration of justice over to administrative absolutism . . . a Marxian idea." In response to the growing criticism, as well as to calls for greater openness in government as a means for assuring fairness in proceedings,[110] President Roosevelt in 1939 asked Attorney General Homer Cummings to organize a committee to study existing administrative procedures and make recommendations for reform.

The Attorney General's Committee on Administrative Procedure, chaired by Dean Acheson, submitted a final report in 1941. Following the War, its efforts, coupled with extensive hearings in the Senate Judiciary Committee, resulted in enactment of the Administrative Procedure Act (APA) of 1946, which is premised on the idea that agencies should be required to keep the public informed of their organization, procedures, and rules; the public should be able to participate in the rulemaking process; there should be uniform standards for formal rulemaking and adjudicatory proceedings; and judicial review should be available in appropriate circumstances. Taken together with the Freedom of Information Act (FOIA)—an amendment to the Administrative Procedure Act which was enacted in 1966 and strengthened in 1974, 1986, and again last year—its ultimate intent was to foster more open government through various procedural requirements and by doing so to promote greater accountability in decisionmaking.

As enacted, the APA recognized few exceptions to the standard of crafting a more open government, but an important one was set out in Section 3 of the 1946 statute: "(1) any function of the United States requiring secrecy in the public interest." (This provision later was to be modified as part of the FOIA.) Then Attorney General Tom Clark interpreted this exception to the APA's public information provision in his 1947 "Manual on the Administrative Procedure Act," as follows:

> This would include the confidential operations of any agency, such as the
> confidential operations of the Federal Bureau of Investigation and the Secret
> Service and, in general, those aspects of any agency's law enforcement procedures
> the disclosure of which would reduce the utility of such procedures. . . . It should
> be noted that the exception is made only to the extent that the function requires
> secrecy in the public interest. Such a determination must be made by the agency
> concerned. To the extent that the function does not require such secrecy, the
> publication requirements apply. Thus, the War Department obviously is not required
> to publish confidential matters of military organization and operation, but it would
> be required to publish the organization and procedure applicable to the ordinary
> civil functions of the Corps of Engineers.

By its terms, the APA's procedural requirements for both rulemaking and adjudication do not apply "to the extent that there is involved a military or foreign affairs function of the United States." This very broad "walling off" in 1946 of the military and foreign affairs areas was consistent with the language of the U.S. Supreme Court ten years before in the seminal case of *United States v. Curtiss-Wright Export Corp.*, where the Court supported a sweeping range of Executive Branch discretion in the conduct of foreign affairs:

> In this vast external realm, with its important, complicated, delicate and manifold problems, the President alone has the power to speak or listen as the representa-tive of the nation. . . . The nature of transactions with foreign nations, moreover, requires caution and unity of design, and their success frequently depends on secrecy and dispatch . . . . He has his agents in the form of diplomats, consular and other officials. Secrecy in respect of information gathered by them may be highly necessary, and the premature disclosure of it productive of harmful results. . . ."[111]

As one scholar has noted, the dichotomy between domestic regulation and foreign affairs func-tions could not have been clearer. "Even in 1936, during the only era in which delegation of authority in the domestic area was being found unconstitutional, the Court was prepared, in most generous terms, to grant the Executive great latitude in foreign affairs."[112]

The encounter with espionage, some of it involving U.S. Government employees, even military personnel, led inevitably to the matter of loyalty. Years of civil service reform had been designed to remove party affiliation, as the term was, from considerations of government employment. In 1939, however, the Hatch Act prohibited Federal employees from "membership in any political party or organization which advocates the overthrow of our constitutional form of government in the United States."[113]

In March 1948, the celebrated Attorney General's List was first promulgated. Some 71 organiza-tions and eleven schools which were viewed as "adjuncts of the Communist Party" were listed as in some way "subversive," although no effort was made to define just what that might be. The regulation, duly published in the *Federal Register*, was at pains to state that "it is entirely possible that many persons belonging to such organizations may be loyal to the United States. . . ." As will be seen below, the striking aspect of the listing is the prominence of Japanese and German organizations, some years now after the end of the Second World War. Some of the listings seem doubtful. Sakura Kai—veterans of the Russo-Japanese War? The Dante Alighieri Society? For that matter, the Ku Klux Klan. But also, well-established Communist-front organizations.

From proscribing organizations as subversive, it was a short step to querying government employ-ees as to membership. In 1947, President Truman, by executive order, directed that Federal employment be denied where "there is a reasonable doubt as to the loyalty of the person involved."

President Truman's Executive Order, and President Eisenhower's Order that followed three years later and remains the cornerstone of today's personnel security system, can only be understood in their historical context. Although, as described above, Woodrow Wilson's Executive Order of April 7, 1917 had introduced the concept of "loyalty" as a condition of government service for the first time, the Hatch Act had marked the first statutory initiative in this regard. (Previously, under the Pendleton Act of 1883 and the Lloyd-LaFollette Act of 1912, civil service investigations had

FEDERAL REGISTER

VOLUME 13 — 1934 — NUMBER 56

THE NATIONAL ARCHIVES OF THE UNITED STATES

LITTERA SCRIPTA MANET

Washington, Saturday, March 20, 1948

TITLE 3—THE PRESIDENT

EXECUTIVE ORDER 9936

CREATING AN EMERGENCY BOARD TO INVESTIGATE A DISPUTE BETWEEN THE TERMINAL RAILROAD ASSOCIATION OF ST. LOUIS AND CERTAIN OF ITS EMPLOYEES

WHEREAS a dispute exists between the Terminal Railroad Association of St. Louis, a carrier, and certain of its employees represented by the Brotherhood of Locomotive Engineers, the Brotherhood of Locomotive Firemen and Enginemen and the Brotherhood of Railroad Trainmen, labor organizations; and

WHEREAS this dispute has not heretofore been adjusted under the provisions of the Railway Labor Act, as amended; and

WHEREAS this dispute, in the judgment of the National Mediation Board, threatens substantially to interrupt interstate commerce to a degree such as to deprive a large portion of the country of essential transportation service:

NOW, THEREFORE, by virtue of the authority vested in me by section 10 of the Railway Labor Act, as amended (45 U. S. C. 160), I hereby create a board of three members, to be appointed by me, to investigate said dispute. No member of the said board shall be pecuniarily or otherwise interested in any organization of railway employees or any carrier.

The board shall report its findings to the President with respect to the said dispute within thirty days from the date of this order.

As provided by section 10 of the Railway Labor Act, as amended, from this date and for thirty days after the board has made its report to the President, no change, except by agreement, shall be made by the Terminal Railroad Association of St. Louis or its employees in the conditions out of which the said dispute arose.

HARRY S. TRUMAN

THE WHITE HOUSE,

March 18, 1948.

[F. R. Doc. 48–2573; Filed, Mar. 19, 1948; 10:07 a. m.]

TITLE 5—ADMINISTRATIVE PERSONNEL

Chapter II—The Loyalty Review Board

PART 210—THE OPERATIONS OF THE LOYALTY REVIEW BOARD

PART 220—DIRECTIVES TO THE DEPARTMENTS AND AGENCIES; CASES OF INCUMBENT AND EXCEPTED EMPLOYEES

PART 230—DIRECTIVES TO THE REGIONAL LOYALTY BOARDS; CASES OF APPLICANTS AND APPOINTEES IN THE COMPETITIVE SERVICE

MISCELLANEOUS AMENDMENTS

1. Section 210.11 (b) (6) is amended by the addition of the following sentence at the end of the first undesignated paragraph therein: "The organizations so designated by the Attorney General are listed in Appendix A to this part."

2. Appendix A to Part 210 is hereby issued as follows:

APPENDIX A—LIST OF ORGANIZATIONS DESIGNATED BY THE ATTORNEY GENERAL PURSUANT TO EXECUTIVE ORDER No. 9835

After the issuance of Executive Order No. 9835 by the President, the Department of Justice compiled all available data with respect to the type of organization to be dealt with under that order. The investigative reports of the Federal Bureau of Investigation concerning such organizations were correlated. Memoranda on each such organization were prepared by attorneys of the Department. The list of organizations contained herein has been certified to the Board by the Attorney General on the basis of recommendations of attorneys of the Department as reviewed by the Solicitor General, the Assistant Attorneys General, and the Assistant Solicitor General, and subsequent careful study of all by the Attorney General.

In connection with the designation of these organizations, the Attorney General has pointed out, as the President had done previously, that it is entirely possible that many persons belonging to such organizations may be loyal to the United States; that membership in, affiliation with, or sympathetic association with, any organization designated is simply one piece of evidence which may or may not be helpful in arriving at a conclusion as to the action which is to be taken in a particular case. "Guilt by association" has never been one of the principles of our American jurisprudence. We must be satisfied that reasonable grounds exist for con-

(Continued on p. 1473)

CONTENTS

THE PRESIDENT

cluding that an individual is disloyal. That must be the guide.

The organizations named herein do not represent a complete or final compilation. For example, a number of small and local organizations are not listed. As to many organizations not named, the presently available information is insufficient to warrant a final determination as to their character. Others, presently innocuous, may become the victims of dangerous infiltrating forces and, as a consequence, become proper subjects for designation. New organizations may come into existence whose purposes and activities are in conflict with loyalty to the United States. From time to time, therefore, as contemplated and directed by the Executive order, there will be furnished to the Board the names of organizations and groups as to which the information received by the Department of Justice, resulting from continued investigation, indicates similar designations are required.

The names of the organizations listed below were transmitted by the Attorney General to the Loyalty Review Board on November 24, 1947, and the Loyalty Review Board disseminated such information to all departments and agencies on December 4, 1947. The first group is reported as having been previously named as subversive by the Department of Justice and as having been previously disseminated among the Government agencies for use in connection with consideration of employee loyalty under Executive Order No. 9300, issued February 5, 1943, entitled "Establishing the Interdepartmental Committee to Consider Cases of Subversive Activity on the Part of Federal Employees," and under other relevant authority. Such list included the following organizations:

American League Against War and Fascism.
American Patriots, Inc.
American Peace Mobilization.
American Youth Congress.
Association of German Nationals (Reichsdeutsche Vereinigung).
Black Dragon Society.
Central Japanese Association (Beikoku Chuo Nipponjin Kai).
Central Japanese Association of Southern California.
The Central Organization of the German-American National Alliance (Deutsche-Amerikanische Einheitsfront).
Communist Party of U. S. A.
Congress of American Revolutionary Writers.
Dai Nippon Butoku Kai (Military Virtue Society of Japan or Military Art Society of Japan).
Dante Alighieri Society.
Federation of Italian War Veterans in the U. S. A., Inc. (Associazione Nazionale Combattenti Italiani, Federazione degli Stati Uniti d' America).
Friends of the New Germany (Freunde des Neuen Deutschlands).
German-American Bund (Amerikadeutscher Volksbund).
German-American Vocational League (Deutsche - Amerikanische Berufsgemeinschaft).
Heimuska Kai, also known as Nokubei Heiki Gimusha Kai, Zaibei Nihonjin, Heiyaku Gimusha Kai, and Zaibei Heimusha Kai (Japanese Residing in America Military Conscripts Association).
Hinode Kai (Imperial Japanese Reservists).
Hinomaru Kai (Rising Sun Flag Society—a group of Japanese War Veterans).
Hokubei Zaigo Shoke Dan (North American Reserve Officers Association).
Japanese Association of America.
Japanese Overseas Central Society (Kaigai Dobo Chuo Kai).
Japanese Overseas Convention, Tokyo, Japan, 1940.
Japanese Protective Association (Recruiting Organization).
Jikyoku Iin Kai (Current Affairs Association).
Kibei Seinen Kai (Association of U. S. Citizens of Japanese Ancestry who have returned to America after studying in Japan).
Kyffhaeuser, also known as Kyffhaeuser League (Kyffhaeuser Bund), Kyffhaeuser Fellowship (Kyffhaeuser Kameradschaft).
Kyffhaeuser War Relief (Kyffhaeuser Kriegshilfswerk).
Lictor Society (Italian Black Shirts).
Mario Morgantini Circle.
Michigan Federation for Constitutional Liberties.
Nanka Teikoku Gunyudan (Imperial Military Friends Group or Southern California War Veterans).
National Committee for the Defense of Political Prisoners.
National Federation for Constitutional Liberties.
National Negro Congress.
Nichibei Kogyo Kaisha (The Great Fujii Theatre).
Northwest Japanese Association.
Protestant War Veterans of the U. S., Inc.
Sakura Kai (Patriotic Society, or Cherry Association—composed of veterans of Russo-Japanese War).
Shinto Temples.
Silver Shirt Legion of America.
Sokoku Kai (Fatherland Society).
Suiko Sha (Reserve Officers Association, Los Angeles).
Washington Book Shop Association.
Washington Committee for Democratic Action.
Workers Alliance.

Under Part III, section 3, of Executive Order No. 9835, the following additional organizations are designated:

American Polish Labor Council.
American Youth for Democracy.
Armenian Progressive League of America.
Civil Rights Congress and its affiliated organizations, including: Civil Rights Congress for Texas. Veterans Against Discrimination of Civil Rights Congress of New York.
The Columbians.
Communist Party, U. S. A., formerly Communist Political Association, and its affiliates and committees, including: Citizens Committee of the Upper West Side (New York City). Committee to Aid the Fighting South. Dennis Defense Committee. Labor Research Association, Inc. Southern Negro Youth Congress. United May Day Committee. United Negro and Allied Veterans of America.
Connecticut State Youth Conference.
Council on African Affairs.
Hollywood Writers Mobilization for Defense.
Hungarian-American Council for Democracy.
International Workers' Order, including People's Radio Foundation, Inc.
Joint Anti-Fascist Refugee Committee.
Ku Klux Klan.
Macedonian-American People's League.
National Committee to Win the Peace.
National Council of American-Soviet Friendship.
Nature Friends of America (since 1935).
New Committee for Publications.
Photo League (New York City).
Proletarian Party of America.
Revolutionary Workers League.
Socialist Workers Party, including American Committee for European Workers' Relief.
Veterans of the Abraham Lincoln Brigade.
Workers Party, including socialist Youth League.

Attention is also directed to certain organizations which are operated as schools. While the Attorney General is not of the view that any institution of learning, devoted to the advancement of knowledge, is subversive, it appears that these organizations are adjuncts of the Communist Party. They are as follows:

Abraham Lincoln School, Chicago, Ill.
George Washington Carver School, New York City.
Jefferson School of Social Science, New York City.
Ohio School of Social Sciences.
Philadelphia School of Social Science and Art.
Samuel Adams School, Boston, Mass.
School of Jewish Studies, New York City.
Seattle Labor School, Seattle, Wash.
Tom Paine School of Social Science, Philadelphia, Pa.
Tom Paine School of Westchester, New York.
Walt Whitman School of Social Science, Newark, N. J.

3. Section 220.2 (a) is amended by the addition of the following sentence at the end of the paragraph: "Activities and associations which may be considered in connection with the determination of disloyalty are listed in § 210.11 (b) of this chapter."

4. Section 230.2 (a) is amended by the addition of the following sentence at the end of the paragraph: "Activities and associations which may be considered in connection with the determination of disloyalty are listed in § 210.11 (b) of this chapter."

(E. O. 9835, March 21, 1947, 12 F. R. 1935)

THE LOYALTY REVIEW BOARD,
UNITED STATES CIVIL SERVICE COMMISSION.
SETH W. RICHARDSON,
Chairman.

[F. R. Doc. 48–2427; Filed, Mar. 19, 1948; 8:54 a. m.]

focused on issues of general character for government employment.[114] The Federal Government's employment policies centered on the need to maintain a trustworthy and efficient civil service—based on the core principle of "suitability" for Federal employment, defined in the 1883 statute as "a requirement or requirements for government employment having reference to a person's character, reputation, trustworthiness, and fitness as related to the efficiency of the service."[115] Today, all government employees still must meet a standard of "suitability" that tracks the original 1883 definition; those requiring access to national security information must also be found to be "security eligible" as defined in the Eisenhower Order 10450—an additional requirement that has led to a fair amount of duplication and delay.)

The Hatch Act in turn was implemented through Civil Service Commission regulations in 1940 that were modified in 1942 to read: "Do you advocate or have you ever advocated, or are you now or have you ever been a member of any organization that advocates the overthrow of the Government of the United States by force or violence?"[116] In 1942, President Roosevelt also issued War Service Regulation II, which denied a civil service examination or appointment to anyone whose loyalty was in "reasonable doubt." This was used by the Civil Service Commission to deny Federal employment to a wide variety of individuals, ranging from members of the Communist Party to those associated with the German Bund and other alleged Fascist causes. Other wartime regulations gave the Secretaries of War and the Navy the authority to summarily remove employees considered risks to national security; after the War, this authority was extended to the Department of State and other departments. And in 1944, the Civil Service Commission established a Loyalty Rating Board to handle cases referred by regional Commission offices involving "derogatory information" concerning loyalty issues.

Even so, during World War II the standards and procedures in conducting a loyalty program still were not uniform across the Government; the development of such a program throughout the Executive Branch was left to the Truman administration following the War.[117] In March 1947 President Truman issued Executive Order 9835, establishing the Federal Employee Loyalty Program, providing uniform investigation standards and procedures, and authorizing the creation of Loyalty Review Boards across the Government. Despite the wartime regulations, "personnel security" still largely was a new discipline. The Atomic Energy Act of 1946 had mandated a security program for the newly-established Atomic Energy Commission and had directed the FBI to investigate and report on an individual's "character, associations, and loyalty," and in 1950 Congress had empowered certain agency heads to suspend employees summarily as security risks. Nevertheless, most Federal agencies still did not subject their employees to any formal system of security screening. Lt. Gen. Leslie R. Groves, who had served in the U.S. Army for 32 years and had directed the Los Alamos Project, put it succinctly when he testified in the spring of 1954 before the AEC board reviewing the suspension of Robert Oppenheimer's security clearance: "The Army as a whole didn't deal with matters of security until after the atomic bomb burst on the world because it was the first time that the Army really knew there was such a thing." A combination of the Bomb's impact and the growing fears about Communist and related threats to internal security led to a new "demi-jurisprudence" of security clearance procedures.[118]

The Truman Order—based on the findings of an interdepartmental committee established in 1946—made "loyalty" a concern across the Federal Government. The approach generally proved popular, though a cross-section of legal scholars and other academics did criticize the lack of procedural safeguards and the lack of clear standards for making decisions concerning prospective and current government employees. (For example, several Harvard law professors, including Zechariah Chafee, Jr., who had spoken out against Attorney General Palmer nearly three decades before, and Erwin Griswold published a critique of the Order in April 1947 under the heading "The Loyalty Order—Procedure Termed Inadequate and Defects Pointed Out.")[119]

The Truman Order in turn was superseded by President Eisenhower's issuance of Executive Order 10450 in April, 1953, which provided that "[t]he appointment of each civilian officer or employee in any department or agency of the Government shall be made subject to an investigation," and made each agency head responsible for ensuring that "the employment and retention in employment of any civilian officer or employee within the department or agency is clearly consistent with the interests of the national security."[120] While abolishing the loyalty program of the Truman Order (including the Loyalty Review Boards within the Civil Service Commission), which had been criticized as both ineffective and inefficient,[121] the new Order also made clear that "the interests of national security require that all persons privileged to be employed in the departments and agencies of the Government, shall be reliable, trustworthy, of good conduct and character, *and of complete and unswerving loyalty* to the United States."[122] (Emphasis added.)

In this manner, a broader "security" program—subsuming loyalty as one key criterion—was established across the Government. The political pressure to establish a broader program had increased with the passage of legislation in 1950 "[t]o protect the national security of the United States by permitting the summary suspension of employment of civilian officers and employees of various departments and agencies. . . ."[123] In addition, beginning in March 1948, the Attorney General's List was published on a regular basis—with members of organizations included on such a list to be denied employment in the Federal government or defense industries as well as the right to a U.S. passport. During the 1952 presidential campaign, Dwight Eisenhower promised to root out Communists and other security risks from government and defense industry employment—suggesting that their presence had been tolerated too easily by the Truman administration despite the existence of rules to address "loyalty" concerns. Then, on February 2, 1953, in his first State of the Union address, President Eisenhower promised a new system "for keeping out the disloyal and the dangerous." Executive Order 10450 followed within three months. Senator Joseph McCarthy (who attended the signing ceremony at the invitation of the administration) praised the new Order: "Altogether, it represents a pretty darn good program. I like it."[124] The *New York Times* reported the following day: "The new [personnel security] program will require a new investigation of many thousands of employees previously investigated, as well as many more thousands who have had no security check."[125]

Concerns about personnel security heightened further in the months that followed issuance of the Order. In early November 1953, Attorney General Herbert Brownell would allege in a speech that President Truman had nominated a Soviet spy—senior Treasury Department official Harry Dexter White—to serve as the U.S. Executive Director of the International Monetary Fund, despite what Brownell said was the President's awareness of White's involvement in Soviet espionage. And on December 3, 1953, President Eisenhower directed that a "blank wall be placed between Dr. [J. Robert] Oppenheimer and secret data"—marking the beginning of the process that led to the Atomic Energy Commission's suspension of Oppenheimer's security clearance later in December and its 4-to-1 decision on June 28, 1954, against restoring the clearance.

Thus, the personnel security system that remains in place to this day (notwithstanding a fair amount of tinkering to ensure greater due process protections and the like) developed against the background of these deep concerns about loyalty and ideological associations. In 1956, Edward Shils captured the essence of the system:

The present system is centered around the assumption that spies are recruited from among those who feel an ideological kinship with the Soviet Union and from those who can be blackmailed or personally influenced or who by loose or careless talk disclose the secrets which have been entrusted to them.[126]

Below, we return to the issue of whether a system founded on such an assumption still is a sensible structure as we approach a new millennium.

The concept of loyalty necessarily involved the notion of secrecy. Disloyal employees revealed secrets; loyal employees would not. In such a setting apprehension rose, and so did the dimension of secrecy. More and more matters became classified. In about the timeframe that concern was raised by public regulations involving, in the main, domestic activities, there now appeared a concern about this newest form of regulation, classified secrets concerning foreign affairs.

There is, indeed, a considerable symmetry. Roscoe Pound and Erwin Griswold of Harvard took to the law review journals around 1935. Twenty years later, two equally distinguished constitutionalists, Senators John C. Stennis of Mississippi and Hubert H. Humphrey of Minnesota, on January 18, 1955, introduced S. J. Res. 21, an Act to establish the Commission on Government Security (which became Public Law 304, 84th Congress). In a floor statement, Senator Humphrey described the intent of the measure:

> Our present total Government mechanism for assuring security does not inspire confidence. Not since 1917, when the Espionage Act was under consideration by the Congress, has there been full-dress consideration by the Congress of the problems of protecting national secrets, and national defense generally, against subversive penetration.
>
> Nor is there any indication that the Executive branch has ever devoted itself to consideration of the total security problem. In the past, such action as has been taken in the name of security has been more a random, sporadic response to peril, rather than a carefully considered plan for defense against peril.[127]

After discussing particular problems in the administration of the personnel security system, the Senator continued:

> We have done many things in the name of security during the past decade; indeed, as a practical matter, our present security system is a phenomenon of only the past decade. We have enacted espionage laws and tightened existing laws; we have required investigation and clearance of millions of our citizens; we have classified information and locked it in safes behind locked doors, in locked and guarded buildings, within fenced and heavily guarded reservations. But each of these actions has been taken sporadically and independently and not as part of a rational overall master plan for security.

****

> President Truman's Executive Order [Executive Order 10290], and the more recent one by President Eisenhower [Executive Order 10501], bring considerable

coordination and order out of the preexisting confusion, but there remains much that must be done before we can be sure our system makes sense and is truly effective. We still have multiple standards, some purely administrative and some statutory. I think a heavy burden of proof must rest upon those who would tell us that a single, uniform standard would not better serve the cause of security.

I wish to emphasize that the variable standards which are now applicable in the several agencies and departments of the Government defy the mind of man when it comes to bringing about any conformity, any uniformity, or any reasonable degree of fair application in a particular security case as it may go from one department to another.

****

We have not paused in our necessary, though frantic, quest for security to ask ourselves:

> What are we trying to protect, and against what?

> What can we effectively protect?

> What specific measures will give us the degree of protection we want or need?

> What price are we willing to pay for security?[128]

Having cited the duplication and contradiction among the "complex of Government security statutes, regulations, and procedures," the Senator then noted how limited Congressional involvement had been:

> To the extent Congress has legislated at all in this area, it has been primarily concerned with the problems of espionage and unauthorized disclosure of national defense secrets. The basic statute is the Espionage Act of 1917. We have amended this statute a number of times to tighten it in the light of current needs, but we have never really studied it to make sure that a statute written in 1917 to reflect the political, military, and technological problems of that era is adequate in the era of hydrogen bombs, radar, and guided missiles, and the world's most infamous conspiracy, the international Communist conspiracy, which surely is not comparable in its ramifications, its subtleties, and its treachery, to some of the old tyrannies of years gone by.[129]

We encounter here (even in the Congress!) the bureaucratic desire for uniformity and predictability—"each of these actions has been taken sporadically and independently and not as part of a rational overall master plan"—but also and equally a concern for civil liberties, a fear of too much government with too few restraints. Loyd Wright, former President of the American Bar Association, was named Chairman of the Commission, with Senator Stennis as Vice Chairman, and they were in equally distinguished company. The spirit of the time may be seen from President Eisenhower's appointments, which included luminaries such as Franklin D. Murphy, then Chancellor of the University of Kansas, and James P. McGranery, who had served as Attorney General under President Truman. In one of the first passages of the 807-page *Report of the Commission on Government Security*, which appeared in June 1957, the situation and the assignment were set forth with succinct clarity:

> Between 1947 and 1955, there grew up a vast, intricate, confusing and costly complex of temporary, inadequate, uncoordinated programs and measures designed to protect secrets and installations vital to the defense of the Nation against agents of Soviet imperialism. The ceaseless campaign of the Soviet Union and international communism to infiltrate our Government, industry, and other vital areas and to subvert our citizenry for purposes of espionage and sabotage not only was threatening our military and industrial strength but was intended to impair our national economy.

> As a result of congressional subcommittee hearings, which thoroughly reviewed and studied all phases of our security and loyalty programs, the Congress unanimously provided in Public Law 304, 84th Congress, as follows:

>> Section I. It is vital to the welfare and safety of the United States that there be adequate protection of the national security, including the safeguarding of all national defense secrets and public and private defense installations, against loss or compromise arising from espionage, sabotage, disloyalty, subversive activities, or unauthorized disclosures.

>> It is therefore, the policy of the Congress that there shall exist a sound Government program—

>> (a) establishing procedures for security investigation, evaluation, and, where necessary, adjudication of Government employees, and also appropriate security requirements, with respect to persons privately employed or occupied on work requiring access to national defense secrets or work affording significant opportunity for injury to national security;

>> (b) for vigorous enforcement of effective and realistic security laws and regulations, and

>> (c) for a careful, consistent, and efficient administration of this policy in a manner which will protect the national security and preserve basic American rights.[130]

The Commission accepted without demur "the broad Presidential supervisory and regulatory authority over the internal operations of the executive branch." In a word, no statute was required to maintain secrecy. "The Attorney General's list of proscribed organizations, or something similar to it, is essential. . . ." But the Commission "recommends a number of major changes to minimize possible abuses." This passage is taken from the Commission's Summary of Recommendations, as highlighted below:

Summary of Recommendations

The Commission's recommendations, if put into effect, would enhance the protection afforded national security while substantially increasing the protection of the individual.

The Commission recommends retention, with fundamental revisions, of the programs affecting Federal civilian and military personnel, industrial security, port security, employees of international organizations, the classification of documents, passport regulations, and the control of aliens. In addition, the Commission recommends an entirely new program to safeguard national security in the vital operations of our civil air transport system.

At the core of the Commission's plan for a uniform, comprehensive, and practical security mechanism is its recommendation for a Central Security Office to provide a continuous study of security needs and measures, conduct loyalty and security hearings, and furnish advisory decisions to heads of government departments and agencies.

And at the very basis of the Commission's thinking lies the separation of the loyalty problem from that of suitability and security. All loyalty cases are security cases, but the converse is not true. A man who talks too freely when in his cups, or a pervert who is vulnerable to blackmail, may both be security risks although both may be loyal Americans. The Commission recommends that as far as possible such cases be considered on a basis of suitability to safeguard the individual from an unjust stigma of disloyalty.

****

CENTRAL SECURITY OFFICE—The Commission recommends an independent Central Security Office in the executive branch of the Government. One of the principal deficiencies of past loyalty and security programs has been a shortage of trained, qualified personnel to administer them. Hence, the first duty of the director of the proposed central office would be to select eminently qualified personnel, including hearing examiners to conduct loyalty hearings under the Federal civilian employee program and security hearings under the industrial, atomic energy, port and civil air transport programs.

****

The various loyalty and security programs of the Government would be reviewed and inspected to insure uniformity of rules, regulations and procedures; however, the Central Security Office would not have authority to review secret or other files of any agency.

ATTORNEY GENERAL'S LIST—The Commission believes that the Attorney General's list of proscribed organizations, or something similar to it, is essential to the administration of the Federal loyalty and security programs. While it therefore recommends continuance of the list, the Commission also recommends a number of major changes to minimize possible abuses. The Commission recommends a statutory basis for the list and that future listings be authorized only after FBI investigation and an opportunity for the organization to be heard by examiners of the Central Security Office, with the right of appeal to the Central Review Board. Decisions of the examiners and the Central Review Board would be advisory to the Attorney General.

****

CONFRONTATION—The Commission recommends that confrontation and cross examination be extended to persons subject to loyalty investigations whenever it can be done without endangering the national security. Those whose livelihood and reputation may be affected by such loyalty investigations are entitled to fair hearings and to decisions which are neither capricious nor arbitrary. It is the prime duty of Government to preserve itself, and in the carrying out of this duty it has the indisputable obligation to avail itself of all information obtainable, including information from confidential sources. Full confrontation, therefore, would be obviously impossible without exposing the Government's counterintelligence operations and personnel with resulting paralysis of the Government's efforts to protect the national security.

****

FEDERAL CIVILIAN EMPLOYEES—The program recommended for civilian Government employees consists of a loyalty program applicable to all positions and a suitability program within the framework of civil service regulations. In the executive branch, the Commission would exclude the Central Intelligence Agency and the National Security Agency from the program.

****

MILITARY PERSONNEL—The Commission recommends that the standard and criteria for separation, for denial of enlistment, induction, appointment or recall to active duty in the Armed Forces, including the Coast Guard, should be that on all the available information there is a reasonable doubt as to loyalty.

****

DOCUMENT CLASSIFICATION—The changes recommended by the Commission in the present program for classification of documents and other material are of major importance. The most important change is that the Confidential classification be abolished. The Commission is convinced that retention of this classification serves no useful purpose which could not be covered by the Top Secret or Secret classification. Since the recommendation is not retroactive, it eliminates the immediate task of declassifying material now classified Confidential. The Commission also recommends abolition of the requirement for a personnel security check for access to documents or material classified Confidential. The danger inherent in such access is not significant and the present clearance requirements afford no real security-clearance check.

The report of the Commission stresses the dangers to national security that arise out of overclassification of information which retards scientific and technological progress, and thus tend to deprive the country of the lead time that results from the free exchange of ideas and information.

ATOMIC ENERGY—The Atomic Energy Commission is an employer of Federal civilian workers and also operates an industrial security program. In general, the Commission's recommendations are designed to bring both AEC's Federal civilian employee and its industrial security programs in line with the comprehensive programs planned for general application throughout the Government.

INDUSTRIAL SECURITY—Uniformity of regulations, of procedures and their application, and of administration appeared as the needed goal of any reform of the present industrial security program. Therefore, the Commission recommends the establishment of a Central Security Office in the executive branch of the Government, as previously noted. With this arrangement, the hazards of consolidation of all industrial security programs into a single agency are avoided, but the benefits of a unified program will be available by means of a monitoring system exercised through such a central office.

To insure uniformity within the armed services with respect to the Department of Defense Industrial Security Programs, the Commission recommends establishment of an Office of Security within the Office of the Secretary of Defense. This office would integrate, control, and supervise the industrial security programs of the three services, thus eliminating duplicate clearances, investigations, fingerprinting and repetitious execution of clearance applicant and related forms, and accomplishing a streamlined administrative pattern eliminating delay resulting from use of chain-of-command communications regarding security matters. Classification guides would be issued by such office, and close scrutiny maintained on the classification of materials contracted for by the services. Downgrading and declassification programs would be monitored from this office, as well as disposition of classified material upon completion of contracts.

****

Replacement of the present security standard by a more practical and positively worded one is recommended, namely, that clearance for access to classified material should be denied or revoked if it is determined on the basis of all available information that "access to classified information and materials will endanger the common defense and security." Also, ambiguous criteria relative to associations are omitted in the Commission's recommendation, and the test of refusal to testify at an authorized inquiry has been added.

****

PORT SECURITY—**** One of the problems which has arisen in the administration of the security program by the Coast Guard has been the failure to give an applicant for clearance adequate notice of the reasons for a denial of clearance. The Commission recommends that in the future the applicant be given specific and detailed notice to the extent that the interests of national security permit. The Commission recommends that standards and criteria for clearance in the Coast Guard be uniform with the standards in other major security programs. The Commission also recommends that hearings heretofore conducted by the Coast Guard be the responsibility in the future, of the Central Security Office. Compliance with this recommendation will promote uniformity in standards and procedure throughout the Government.

AIR TRANSPORT SECURITY—The Commission recommendations for a security program in civil air transport recognizes the need for initial Federal action at the industrywide level in this important field. At present, only the employees of CAA, CAB, or other Federal agencies involved in air transport are subject to the formal program, required under Executive Order 10450. The Commission has recommended, however, that only those employees actually in a position to do substantial damage should be included in the program.

****

INTERNATIONAL ORGANIZATIONS—The existing loyalty program for United States nationals employed by international organizations should be continued, but the standard should be broadened to include those who are security risks for reasons other than doubtful loyalty. The standard would be whether or not, on all the information, there is reasonable doubt as to the loyalty of the person to the Government of the United States or reasonable ground for believing the person might engage in subversive activities against the United States.

****

PASSPORT SECURITY—In the passport field, Congress should enact legislation defining the standards and criteria for a permanent passport security program. The procedures would continue to be defined by regulation.

****

IMMIGRATION AND NATIONALITY—The Commission recommends in the field of immigration and nationality that the functions of visa control, except for diplomatic and official visas, be transferred from the Department of State to the Department of Justice and that the Attorney General be authorized by law to maintain personnel abroad to carry out these functions.

****

NEW LEGISLATION—Two new substantive laws are recommended.

The first would penalize unlawful disclosures of classified information with knowledge of their classified character by persons outside as well as within the Government. In the past, only disclosures by Government employees have been punishable.

The second recommended legislation would make admissible in a court of law evidence of subversion obtained by wiretapping by authorized Government investigative agencies. Wiretapping would be permissible only by specific authorization of the Attorney General, and only in investigations of particular crimes affecting the security of the Nation.

Little came of the Commission's thoughtful, exhaustive work. The proposal to outlaw by statute "disclosures of classified information . . . by persons outside as well as within the Government" was quickly perceived, although not necessarily intended, as prior restraint on the press. The response was swift and predictable. The recommendation was criticized strongly in articles and editorials in a variety of newspapers, notably by James Reston. On June 25, 1957, four days after issuance of the Commission Report, Reston wrote an article in the *New York Times* entitled "Security vs. Freedom: An Analysis of the Controversy Stirred By Recommendation to Curb Information." Reston's article is notable for the specificity with which he described the arrangements that were then pretty much in place and which continue so:

> The history of recent years is full of illustrations of the dangers of such broad legislative proposals.
>
> Franklin D. Roosevelt's deal with Joseph Stalin at Yalta to bring the Ukraine and Bylo-Russia into the United Nations was classified "top secret." Elaborate efforts were made to conceal the arrangement. The late Bert Andrews, Washington correspondent of The New York Herald Tribune, found out about it.
>
> He "willfully," even gleefully reported it, knowing full well that it was classified "top secret." Under the proposals of the Commission on Government Security, if law at the time, he would have been subject to a fine of $10,000 and five years in jail.
>
> ****
>
> This newspaper also published the original plans of the United States, Britain, France and the Soviet Union on the formation of the United Nations. Again, they were marked "top secret" and the Federal Bureau of Investigation was called in to make an official investigation of the disclosure.
>
> In this case, though the Government maintained that publication would block information of the United Nations, the main result was a long debate on the Big Five veto power and the assumption that the five major powers could agree on a post-war settlement. This, in turn, helped clarify the issue and contributed to some modifications of the Charter, but under the legislation now proposed by the Commission on Government Security, it would have been a clear case for criminal action.[131]

(In this latter case, we would note the potential felon would have been Reston himself, who had a friend in the Chinese delegation!)

A certain innocence appears in a separate Statement by Chairman Wright, which is appended to the Commission Report. He asserts:

The final responsibility for the difficult decisions of what shall be secret must be confided in those loyal and devoted public servants who are qualified to make the judgment. No citizen is entitled to take the law, and the safety of the Nation, into his own hands. With near unanimity, the American journalism profession has conscientiously observed these limits. But there are a few exceptional cases, which for some reason have escaped prosecution. The purveyor of information vital to national security, purloined by devious means, gives aid to our enemies as effectively as the foreign agent.[132]

"The purveyor of information vital to national security, purloined by devious means. . . ." Purloined for good or ill, but predictably, classified information was by now routinely provided to journalists by officials, sometimes to enhance prestige with the press, sometimes to gain advantage in an internal dispute, sometimes to let the public know something the purveyor thought the public had a right to know.

The matter has never been quantified, but it is reasonable to assert that most "leaking" was coming from the higher reaches of the system. We have President John F. Kennedy's testament to the Ship of State as the only ship that leaks from the top! Sparingly, of course. As Max Frankel of the *New York Times* has observed, Presidents soon came to realize that "even harmless secrets were coins of power to be hoarded."[133]

It is beyond the range of an official report to speculate over much on the allure of secrecy, but this must never be discounted. The official with a secret *feels* powerful. And is. Some years after the report of the Commission on Government Security, the Committee on Government Operations of the House of Representatives would declare:

> Secrecy—the first refuge of incompetents—must be at a bare minimum in a democratic society, for a fully informed public is the basis of self-government. Those elected or appointed to positions of executive authority must recognize that government, in a democracy, cannot be wiser than the people.[134]

Which is very likely true, but not of necessity widely believed by those in authority, howsoever briefly.

.

****

The Commission on Government Security was clear-headed enough about the first attempts at press censorship and the hopelessness of it all—given the American press! Thus:

> While document classification as a form of combined censorship and information restriction has been a part of our national policy from the War of the Revolution, formal and pervasive procedures for document classification in the current sense are a comparatively recent development. Prior to World War II, in peacetime there were few formal restrictions on information availability; the major exceptions were the traditional restraints in the diplomatic and military fields. In other areas, information restrictions were based for the most part upon individual judgment, as situations arose.

The advent of World War I brought the first organized approach to document classification as a means of general restriction on public access to information. Censorship policies for control of published information commenced on March 24, 1917, with the promulgation of regulations by the State, War, and Navy Departments. Newspapers were asked to adhere voluntarily. One of the regulations requested that "no information, reports, or rumors, attributing a policy to the government in any international situation, not authorized by the President or a member of the cabinet, be published without first consulting the Department of State."

On April 13, 1917, by Executive Order 2594, President Wilson created the Committee on Public Information, named George Creel as chairman, and World War I censorship formally got under way. Creel thought that censorship as practiced at that time was unworkable. He described the whole effort as of a piece with "the hysterical 'shush-shushing' that warned against unguarded speech, just as though every citizen possessed some important military secret." He said, at the end of the War, that "virtually everything we asked the press not to print was seen or known by thousands." Creel believed the answer to be "secrecy at the source" through action by the military departments without depending upon press judgment.[135]

Even so, the Commission wandered into the inevitable ambiguity. If secrets matter, they must be kept. To keep secrets is to put in question principles more sacred than secrets.

The Commission's principal legislative proposal, a Central Security Office, might at first have appeared more promising. It fit well with public administration doctrine at this time, a time when the profession of public administration was looked to in such matters. It could well have been proposed by one of the several Hoover Commissions of the post-war period. A parallel to the Civil Service Commission that would establish uniform rules with "trained, qualified personnel to administer them."

But this, too, ran athwart the changed political culture of Washington. *It was turning out that secrets were hard to keep secret.* Organizations with the morale, incentives, and structure to hold things closely were increasingly disinclined to share, especially with organizations that were not. This is perhaps too generous. Secrets had become assets; organizations hoarded them, ¬ revealed them sparingly and in return for some consideration, and wanted no part of some Central Office busying itself with their internal affairs. This, of course, is conjecture, but for certain no Central Office emerged.[136]

To the contrary, far from centralizing, the dispersal of secrecy centers within the Government accelerated. The Federal Bureau of Investigation now began operations abroad, a necessary extension of its internal task of keeping abreast of domestic espionage and, from an organizational perspective, an opportunity of considerable import. Hence, "Operation SOLO."

Moishe Chilovsky was born in the Ukraine in 1902 of Jewish parents. His father was engaged in anti-Czarist activities and had been exiled to Siberia. He fled to the United States in 1910, and his family came the following year. As Morris Childs, the son became a charter member of the Communist Party of the United States of America. Following the expulsion of Jay Lovestone (born Jacob Liebstein in 1898 in Lithuania to Russian-Jewish parents), Childs became a Party official under Earl Browder; in 1929 he was sent to Moscow for further training. In 1934, he became a member of the Central Committee, and in 1945 he succeeded Budenz as managing editor of the *Daily Worker*. In 1947, he returned to Moscow, where he learned of Stalin's persecution of Jews and more generally of the repression there. In the early 1950s, he was "turned" by the FBI. In 1957, he became deputy head of the CPUSA and the primary contact with Soviet, Chinese, and other parties abroad, traveling regularly to Moscow and Peking. He led the U.S. delegation to the 21st Party Congress in Moscow in 1959. Reportedly a source of considerable information about Kremlin politics, and especially of Sino-Soviet tensions, his role as an American spy was kept entirely within the FBI until President Gerald R. Ford was informed in 1974. In 1987, Childs was awarded the National Security Medal by FBI Director Sessions, in a ceremony held *in camera* at FBI headquarters.

****

The Wright Commission was not the only evidence of a general stirring during the Eisenhower years over this new question of peacetime secrecy. The Truman administration had begun during the Second World War; had endured the shock of Soviet espionage and nuclear armament, the face of battle in Korea. The new President ended the war in Asia, and the nation settled into a normalcy, not without parallel in the 1950s to the Harding administration thirty years earlier. The new President was not in the least inclined to over much government, much less to intrusive government. Sectors of the citizenry, however, were even less so. The Commission on Government Security noted this:

> Despite the declared purpose of Executive Order 10501, to recognize that ". . . It is essential that the citizens of the United States be informed concerning the activities of their government . . ." and the need that certain ". . . official information affecting the national defense be protected uniformly against unauthorized disclosure . . ." the Order has been subject to continuous and sharp attack. These attacks have been led for the most part by leaders in the press and other information media as well as by numerous individuals in the legal field, and the world of science and scientific research.

> In recognition of these attacks during the 84th Congress, the Special Subcommittee on Government Information of the House Committee on Government Operations held lengthy hearings under Congressman Moss to answer these complaints. These hearings and studies were the first major congressional effort to examine the document classification program.[137]

Nor was the Wright Commission the only entity examining government secrecy and the means of classifying information in the mid-1950s. The Eisenhower administration organized its own inquiry when, in August 1956, Secretary of Defense Charles E. Wilson established a five-member Committee on Classified Information, chaired by Charles A. Coolidge, a well-known attorney and a former Assistant Secretary of Defense. (The other four members were retired high-ranking military officers.) In his letter establishing the Committee, Secretary Wilson stated that he was "seriously concerned over the unauthorized disclosure of classified military information"; he called on the Committee to examine the adequacy of all laws and regulations on classification and the safeguarding of classified information, as well as the procedures utilized at the Defense Department in this area and the Department's ability to "fix responsibility" for unauthorized disclosure of classified information.

Three months after being established, the Coolidge Committee issued a report on November 8, 1956, containing 28 recommendations—ten covering overclassification, eleven covering different issues relating to unauthorized disclosures of information; and the remaining seven matters relating to Department policies vis-a-vis Congress, industry, and the press. The first recommendation— based on a finding that Defense Department officials had a tendency to "play it safe" and classify too much—called for "a determined attack" on overclassification, "spearheaded by the responsible heads within the Department of Defense, from the Secretary of Defense down" and another called on senior officials to "throw back over-classified matter received from subordinates." The Committee also urged the Department to make clear that the classification system "is not to be used to protect information not affecting the national security, and specifically prohibits its use for administrative matters." However, the Committee did not propose any penalties or disciplinary action in cases of abuse of classification procedures, and when in July 1957 Secretary Wilson issued a new directive consolidating the rules governing the Department's classification proce- dures, it did not impose any procedures to address problems in this regard.

In addition to the commissions that were organized to examine the security classification system, in 1955 the House of Representatives created a Special Government Information Subcommittee of its Government Operations Committee. The backdrop to establishment of this Subcommittee was increasing concern on the part of some Members about the growth of postwar secrecy, including the Eisenhower administration's establishment in November 1954 of an Office of Strategic Information in the Commerce Department responsible for formulating policies concerning the production and distribution of "unclassified scientific, technical, industrial, and economic informa- tion, the indiscriminate release of which may be inimical to the defense interests of the United States."[138]

In 1953, Representative John E. Moss, a freshman Democrat on the House Post Office and Civil Service Committee, had raised the issue of public access to government information. Representa- tive Moss had sought information from the Eisenhower administration's Civil Service Commission to verify its claim that 2,800 Federal employees had been fired for "security reasons;" he wanted to know whether these "security" reasons were based on allegations of disloyalty or espionage or instead matters that could also be grounds for discharge—such as a misstatement, even uninten- tionally, on a job application. The Commission refused to release the information and Representa- tive Moss found that he had no other means to compel its release. Two years later, he urged the creation—and subsequently was made Chairman—of the Special Government Information Subcommittee, tasked with monitoring Executive Branch secrecy.

The Moss Subcommittee quickly undertook a lengthy inquiry (spanning the duration of the Coolidge Committee and Wright Commission) concerning the classification system's administration and operation and, more generally, the availability of information from agencies and departments. Among its chief concerns was the lack of any action against overclassification of information:

> In a conflict between the right to know and the need to protect true military
> secrets from a potential enemy, there can be no valid argument against secrecy.
> The right to know has suffered, however, in the confusion over the demarcation
> between secrecy for true security reasons and secrecy for "policy" reasons.
> The proper imposition of secrecy in some situations is a matter of judgment.
> Although an official faces disciplinary action for the failure to classify information
> which should be secret, no instance has been found of an official being disciplined

for classifying material which should have been made public. The tendency to "play it safe" and use the secrecy stamp has, therefore, been virtually inevitable.[139]

Aside from some attention to declassification of historical documents, however, the Subcommittee's recommendations—including those intended to provide disincentives for overclassification and to establish a security classification system based in statute—were "largely ignored" by the Executive Branch.[140]

The Moss Subcommittee did, however, remain at the forefront of legislative efforts to enhance public access to government information. It assumed the lead role, beginning in the mid-1950s, in focusing increased attention on how the security classification system related to the rights of Congress and the public to obtain information from the Executive Branch. This would lead, after eleven long years, to enactment in 1966 of the FOIA, establishing a statutory right of access by any person to Federal Government records unless the information falls into one of nine listed categories permitting it to be exempted from release.

Representative Moss first succeeded in 1958 in narrowing use of the 1789 "housekeeping" statute to withhold government information. In 1962, he helped persuade President Kennedy to narrow the use of "executive privilege" to deny the release of records. Finally, in 1965 Moss and Representative Donald Rumsfeld introduced legislation to establish a presumption that Executive Branch documents should be available to the public with only narrow exceptions and that judicial review should be available as a check on agency decisions to withhold information. By 1966, bipartisan support for the effort had grown, and it appeared that the issue of public access to information might even arise in the fall Congressional elections. The legislation passed the Senate first, and then the House in June. On July 4, 1966, President Johnson signed the FOIA into law (to go into effect exactly one year later, in order to give the Executive Branch sufficient time to prepare for its implementation).

Notable as that achievement was and remains, it did not much change the practices of the bureaucracy. In 1972, the House Foreign Operations and Government Information Subcommittee, now chaired by Representative William Moorhead of Pennsylvania, concluded after fourteen days of oversight hearings that "[t]he efficient operation of the Freedom of Information Act has been hindered by five years of foot dragging by the Federal bureaucracy." Agency procedures were deficient and employees untrained, large fees were charged to deter requests, responses were long delayed, and the exemption categories were being applied broadly to deny the release of information. So Congress responded again. With Representative Moorhead's leadership, the FOIA was amended substantially in 1974 (passing both chambers overwhelmingly following a Presidential veto) to fix some of these loopholes that the bureaucrats charged with implementing the law had discovered, and to strengthen several provisions of the statute.

Notwithstanding the accomplishments of Representatives Moss and Moorhead and their colleagues, an inevitable tension remains between the right of access prescribed in the FOIA and the authority of the Executive Branch to preserve certain secrets. Thus, the very first exception to the general FOIA principle of public access reads as follows:

> (b) This section does not apply to matters that are—
>
> > (1)(A) specifically authorized under criteria established by an
> > Executive order to be kept secret in the interest of national

> defense or foreign policy and (B) are in fact properly classified
> pursuant to such Executive order . . .[141]

This is not surprising; as noted, such matters had been treated differently in the original Administrative Procedure Act. The difference now was the availability of procedures, including use of the courts, to review bureaucrats' decisions to deny the release of information.[142]

****

From the onset of the atomic age there had been a tension between the defense establishment, as generally defined, and the science community over the nature of secrecy in science. From the time of the Smyth Report, and the arguments of Bethe and others as to the inevitability of the Soviets acquiring an H-Bomb, the level of irritation was not inconsiderable. The scientists said you could not hide nature from the Russians.

Now an argument arose about the disutility of trying to hide things from Americans. As noted earlier, the Wright Commission was on to this:

> The report of the Commission stresses the dangers to national security that arise
> out of overclassification of information which retards scientific and technological
> progress, and thus tend to deprive the country of the lead time that results from
> the free exchange of ideas and information.[143]

This aspect of the Wright Commission's report was echoed in a resounding fashion some thirteen years later by another group of eminent persons. In July 1970, a special Task Force on Secrecy, convened by the Defense Science Board and chaired by Dr. Frederick Seitz of Rockefeller University, issued its final report on the steps needed to address problems with the system for classifying scientific and technical information.[144] Responding to questions from the Director of Defense Research and Engineering, the Task Force found first that it was unlikely that classified scientific and technical information would remain secure for as long as five years; more likely it would become known to others in as little as one year through both "independent discovery" and clandestine disclosure.[145] The report went on to focus on the costs of classification, concluding that its effect in inhibiting the flow of information should be considered—and balanced against the benefits—in making classification decisions. After also finding that classifiers' attention should focus mainly on design and production-related matters (such as information on specific manufacturing techniques that might reveal operational plans), as opposed to basic research and "early exploratory" development, the Task Force concluded that, overall, the amount of scientific and technical information classified could be reduced by as much as 90 percent through the exercise of greater care concerning both the scope and duration of classification.

Finally, in its most telling passage, the Seitz Task Force wrote that "more might be gained than lost" if the United States adopted "unilaterally, if necessary—a policy of complete openness in all areas of information." (Recognizing, however, that this proposal was not practical in light of prevailing views on classification, it instead recommended adopting a "rigid schedule" for automatic declassification, with a general period of one to five years, subject to exemptions for specified categories.) That nothing subsequently came of this final recommendation speaks more to the "culture" being confronted by the Seitz Task Force and other such entities than the wisdom of the finding—one endorsed by a cross-section of the nation's leading thinkers on scientific and technology issues.

****

The apogee of absurdity as regards secrecy came in 1971 when the Nixon administration undertook to enjoin the publication by the *New York Times* and, subsequently, the *Washington Post*, of
a history of the Vietnam War compiled in the Department of Defense, and soon known as the
Pentagon Papers. In June 1996, on the occasion of the 25th anniversary of that seminal event,
Max Frankel of the *Times* recalled what had transpired:

> Twenty-five years ago today, reporters, editors and owners of The Times stood
> accused in Federal court of treasonous defiance of the United States. We had
> begun to publish a 10-part series about the Pentagon Papers, a 7,000-page study
> of how four Administrations became entrapped in Vietnam—progressively more
> committed and more frustrated than they dared at every stage to admit to the
> public. Although the documents were historical and lacking any operational value,
> they were stamped "Top Secret" and therefore withheld, like trillions of other
> Government papers, from public, press, Congress and even Executive officials
> not duly "cleared" into the priesthood of "national security."[146]

As Harold Edgar and Benno C. Schmidt, Jr. state the matter in their comprehensive analysis of
the espionage laws in the *Columbia Law Review* (written against the backdrop of the Pentagon
Papers litigation), the Government found that there was literally "no law" to prevent publication.
The problem, as Edgar and Schmidt make clear in their masterful survey, can be traced to the time
of creation—1917—when Woodrow Wilson failed in his efforts to achieve a sweeping ban on
publication of defense information. The U.S. espionage laws are, in their words, "in many respects incomprehensible," with the result being that "[w]e have lived since World War I in a state
of benign indeterminacy about the rules of law governing defense secrets."[147]

The uncertainties surrounding the legislative intent of the 1917 Act (as well as of its most significant amendment, in 1950)[148] were to have significant consequences more than half a century
later. Edgar and Schmidt note that "[n]o prosecution premised on publication has ever been
brought under the espionage laws," and that the abandoned prosecution of Daniel Ellsberg and his
colleague Anthony Russo for unlawful retention of defense information "was the first effort to
apply the espionage statutes to conduct preparatory to publication."[149] As noted, in October 1984,
Samuel Loring Morison, a civilian analyst with the office of Naval Intelligence, was arrested for
supplying a classified photograph of a Soviet nuclear-powered carrier under construction to *Jane's
Defence Weekly*—which subsequently published the photo. In October 1985, Morison became
the first person convicted under the 1917 Espionage Act for an unauthorized disclosure of classified defense information to the press. His conviction was upheld in 1988 and the Supreme Court
declined to hear the case.

The Morison prosecution remains unique; no other individual has been prosecuted since on such
grounds. While the core provisions of the espionage laws have been used with some degree of
frequency to prosecute government and defense contractor employees for actual or attempted
communication of national defense information to a foreign agent, as well as conspiracies toward
that end (thus reaching the conduct of notorious spies such as Aldrich Ames),[150] the laws have
proven virtually useless in addressing the more mundane problem of "leaks." And when a body,
such as the Wright Commission, has proposed "rectifying" this by broadening the laws' reach
beyond the classic case where defense information is provided to foreign spies to also cover
unauthorized communications between a government official and the press, it has provoked hostile

reaction based on concerns about the impact on free speech and efforts to publicize government misconduct or mismanagement.

Thus, a system persists in which the series of executive orders—beginning with Truman's—on security classification carefully instruct government employees not to transfer classified information to any outsiders not authorized to receive it (the U.S. media obviously included), but the system of criminal sanctions designed to back that instruction up proves to be a "paper tiger." Indeed, most of the executive orders on national security information issued in succession since 1951 do not even refer to the espionage laws. And, as in the case of the Commission on Government Security's proposal, Congress is not willing to make unauthorized disclosure of classified information an action subject to criminal sanctions without consideration of the *intent* of the communicator. Thus, as a former Assistant General Counsel of the CIA concluded (in an unpublished paper cited by Edgar and Schmidt):

> An individual who simply reveals to the public at large classified data is for all practical purposes immune from prosecution since his defense, of course, would be that he thought the American public had a right to know and the Government would not be able to prove intent to aid a foreign government or to harm the United States. The fact that any reasonable man would know that revelation to the general public ipso facto reveals to foreign governments is immaterial. Even if the one making the exposure is a government employee well versed in the rules governing classified information, there can be no presumption of intent which would bring him within the terms of present espionage laws.[151]

Of course, this was not the only legacy of the Pentagon Papers case. The effort to prosecute journalists for publishing the materials also revealed the deep-seated differences in perspectives concerning the breadth of appropriate classification. Erwin N. Griswold, who had been President Nixon's Solicitor General at the time of the Pentagon Papers case and therefore had the thankless task of preparing and arguing the Government's case before the Supreme Court, summed it up well nearly two decades later:

> I have never seen any trace of a threat to the national security from the publication. Indeed, I have never seen it even suggested that there was such an actual threat. Sen. Gravel's edition is now almost completely forgotten, and I doubt if there is more than a handful of persons who have ever undertaken to examine the Pentagon Papers in any detail—either with respect to national security or with respect to the policies of the country relating to Vietnam.
>
> It quickly becomes apparent to any person who has considerable experience with classified material that there is massive over-classification and that the principal concern of the classifiers is not with national security, but rather with governmental embarrassment of one sort or another. There may be some basis for short-term classification while plans are being made, or negotiations are going on, but apart from details of weapons systems, there is very rarely any real risk to current national security from the publication of facts relating to transactions in the past, even the fairly recent past. This is the lesson of the Pentagon Papers experience, and it may be relevant now.[152]

9. **After the Fall**

It is just four decades since the Report of the Commission on Government Security, the first and, until now, the only other statutory body to inquire into secrecy and security. The Commission Report was thoughtful and in no sense alarmist. Even so, it would have institutionalized the loyalty system through a Central Security Office, and would have greatly expanded the reach of government by making it a crime under the Espionage Act for persons outside of government—read "journalists"—to disclose classified information. Neither measure was adopted. (A third proposal to "make admissible in a court of law evidence of subversion obtained by wiretapping" was never formally adopted, but gradually and partially became accepted practice.) There have been numerous executive orders of differing degrees of consequence, but all fall within the overall statutory and administrative framework of the arrangements put in place during World War I. This system was designed to deal with conflict between nation states, in which the United States had to deal with internal as well as external conflict.

To say that the system has not changed appreciably is not to say that it has not degraded. Most of this degradation can be accounted for by recognizable bureaucratic behavior. First one agency; then another agency; then a third agency. First an activity exclusively directed from within the Executive Branch; next the emergence of equally forceful direction from the Legislative Branch. First a considerable degree of public concern at unfamiliar arrangements and activities, followed by familiarity and gradual acceptance.

In the years immediately following the Second World War, there was a considerable competition among the Defense Department (and its predecessor) and the State Department and the Justice Department (in the form of the Federal Bureau of Investigation) for primacy in directing what would be called "the intelligence community." In this competition the defense community won out, although the FBI remained a significant participant. Again, in the bureaucratic mode, no significant interest was entirely cut out; redundancy became the norm, especially as the extent of redundancy remained more or less undisclosed. Only the State Department lost relative influence and resources.

The secrecy system degraded most significantly in the form of "leaks," that is to say, "unlawful disclosures of classified information," as the *Report of the Commission on Government Security* put it. These occur routinely, typically in the course of contests within the Executive Branch, or between the Executive and the Legislative. It has become routine for high government officials to lament the dissonance brought on by the momentary inability to remember whether some important fact was learned in a highly classified briefing or from evening television. There is, effectively, no sanction for giving "classified information" to the press, as the term is generally understood. To the contrary, there are perceived rewards accruing to those who do so. (Not to mention the memoirs of presidents and cabinet members!)

This "Brief Account" has not attempted to judge either the gains achieved or the losses incurred by the secrecy system that developed over the course of the 20th century. Clearly, there were both. Indisputably, a vast range of contacts with other governments require secrecy while they are relevant. Clearly, covert actions require secrecy while they are relevant. Keeping in mind, however, that by definition others know of these secrets, and not always those we would wish. In a celebrated Cold War gaffe, an American official disclosed the existence, on the territory of a

Figure 1: The Intelligence Community

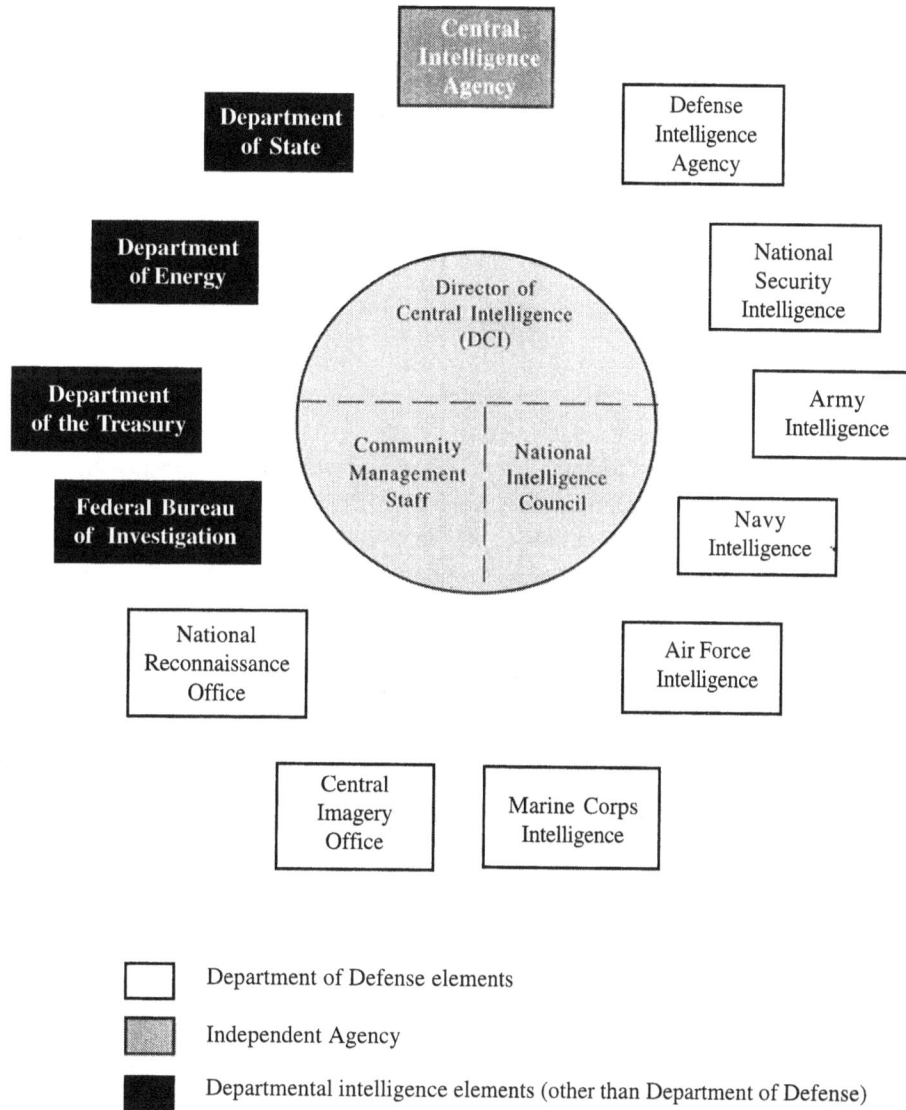

Source: Council on Foreign Relations Independent Task Force, *Making Intelligence Smarter: The Future of U.S. Intelligence*, 1996, 39.

NATO ally, of a not-inconsiderable "listening post" directed at the Soviet Union. The Soviets knew of this; they could see it. The allied government knew of it; only its citizenry did not.

Clearly, a great deal of information concerning weapons systems also needs to be secret so long as the systems are operational. Finally, and most obviously, military operations need to be kept secret from enemy forces, although by definition they do not remain secret for long. Once Allied forces had landed in Normandy, the opposing German forces knew what was up. In the course of the Cold War, however, the United States increasingly resorted to "covert" actions which, if only partially understood by adversaries, were more or less completely concealed from the American public. Even formal military operations began to be concealed. During the war in Vietnam, North Vietnamese forces in Cambodia were recurrently bombed in 1969 and 1970. Cambodians knew; Vietnamese knew; but the American public was not told until 1973. During this period domestic opposition to American foreign policy attained an intensity never previously known. The incumbent president asked himself whether constitutional government would survive.

****

For all the distraction of covert action and military engagement on the periphery of Eurasia and in parts of what would come to be known as the Third World, the central, all-consuming task of statecraft during the Cold War was to establish an effective system of deterrence by which the Soviet Union would be dissuaded from nuclear war. The BIG SECRET of the American Government during the early and middle years of the Cold War was that Soviet economic and military power was advancing at a rate which made deterrence problematic at best. By 1957, a Top Secret Report entitled "Deterrence & Survival in the Nuclear Age," warned of "spectacular progress" on the part of the Soviets in achieving substantial parity in the essentials of military strength, and forecast a "crossover," as the term would be, when the Soviets would have achieved superiority.

The document, known as "The Gaither Report," for H. Rowen Gaither, Jr., then head of the Ford Foundation, was a product of the Security Resources Panel of the President's Science Advisory Committee, this latter body having been created by President Eisenhower to provide independent advice about the state of such matters. The National Security Council requested it, and in the manner of the time, the job was done in six months. Not without cause: the Report was forwarded to the President just weeks after the October 4, 1957, launching of the Soviet Sputnik (for "Fellow Traveler"!). The first artificial Earth satellite. The conclusions were stark to the point of startling:

II. NATURE OF THE THREAT

A. Economic

> The Gross National Product (GNP) of the USSR is now more than one-third that of the United States and is increasing half again as fast. Even if the Russian rate of growth should decline, because of increasing difficulties in management and shortage of raw materials, and should drop by 1980 to half its present rate, its GNP would be more than half of ours as of that date. This growing Russian economic strength is concentrated on the armed forces and on investment in heavy industry, which this year account for the equivalent of roughly $40 billion and $17 billion,

respectively, in 1955 dollars. Adding these two figures, we get an allocation of $57 billion per annum, which is roughly equal to the combined figure for these two items in our country's current effort. If the USSR continues to expand its military expenditures throughout the next decade, as it has during the 1950's, and ours remains constant, its annual military expenditures may be double ours, even allowing for a gradual improvement of the low living standards of the Russian peoples.

This extraordinary concentration of the Soviet economy on military power and heavy industry, which is permitted, or perhaps forced, by their peculiar political structure, makes available economic resources sufficient to finance both the rapid expansion of their impressive military capability and their politico-economic offensive by which, through diplomacy, propaganda and subversion, they seek to extend the Soviet orbit.

The figures that followed the above analysis (and which are reproduced below) were uncompromising. The first showed the Soviets reaching up towards United States production of coal and steel, and already producing *twice* the number of machine tools. The while the United States frittered away resources on consumer goods such as automobiles, washing machines, and refrigerators. The second showed the Soviet military effort just about to surpass that of the United States.

The assertion that Soviet Gross National Product was growing "half again as fast" as that of the United States was traumatic. In 1956, nominal growth in the United States was 5.5 percent, which would give the Soviets a nominal rate of 8.25 percent. The former rate was in line with the forecasts of the Council of Economic Advisers, which had been estimating long-run real growth of 3.5 percent, with inflation at about 2 percent. And so, the President's Science Advisory Committee informed the President that the "crossover" date would be 1998. By the end of the century, the Soviet Union would have a larger economy than ours, and presumedly vastly greater military strength.[153]

The intelligence community accepted and "improved" the assessment of the Gaither Commission. In May 1958, Allen W. Dulles, Director of Central Intelligence, spoke to the annual meeting of the Chamber of Commerce of the United States on "Dimensions of the International Peril Facing Us." These were seen to be formidable:

Comparison of the economies of the US and the USSR in terms of total production of goods and services indicates the USSR's rapid progress.

Whereas Soviet gross national product was about 33 percent that of the US in 1950, by 1956 it had increased to about 40 percent, and by 1962 it may be about 50 percent of our own. This means that the Soviet economy has been growing, and is expected to continue to grow through 1962, at a rate roughly twice that of the economy of the United States. Annual growth over-all has been running between six and seven percent, annual growth of industry between 10 and 12 percent.

Figure 2

PRODUCTION OF SELECTED CAPITAL & CONSUMER GOODS: 1956

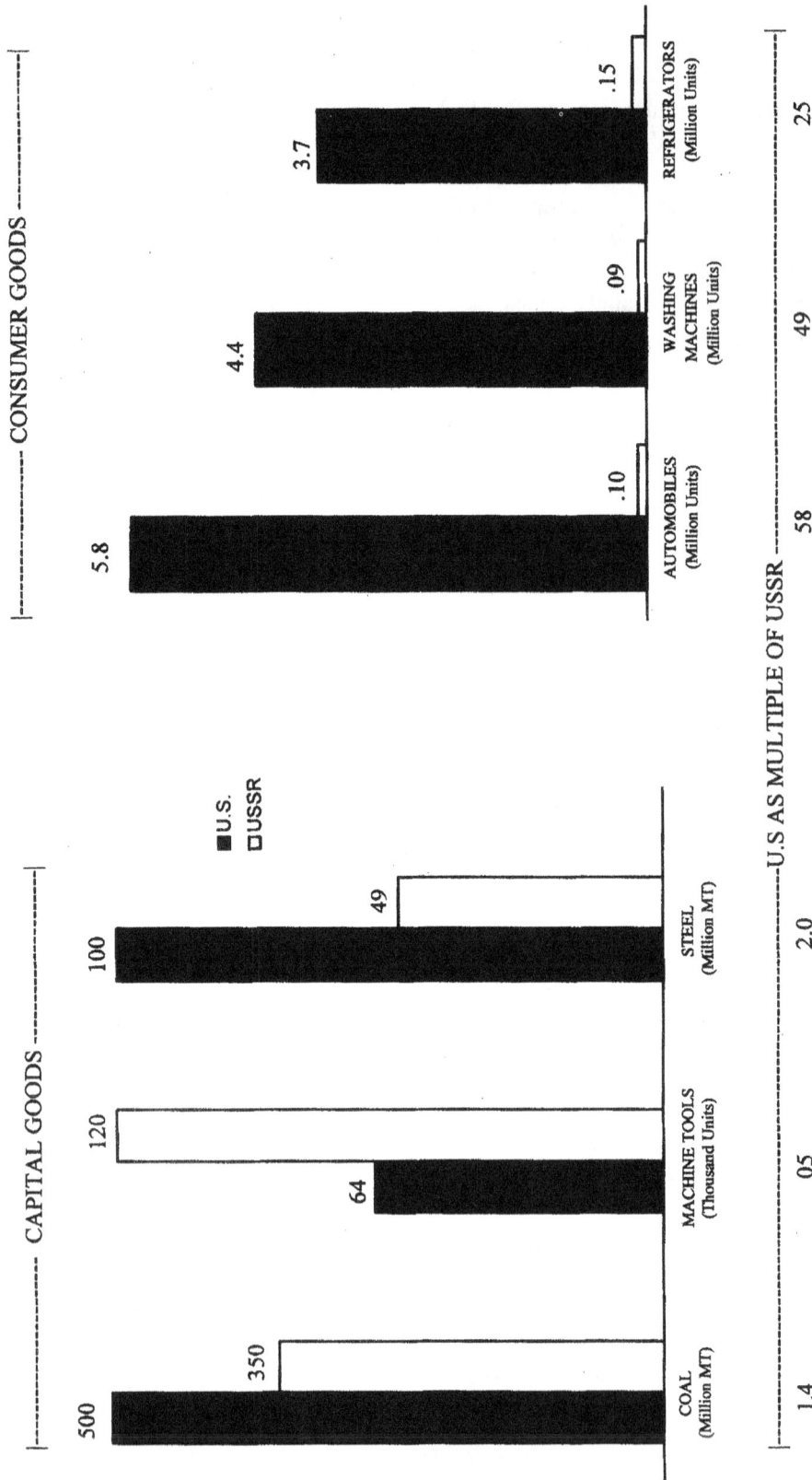

Source: Joint Committee on Defense Production, *Deterrence and Survival in the Nuclear Age (The "Gaither Report" of 1957)*, 94th Cong., 2d sess., 1957. (Reprint by the Government Printing Office, Washington, D.C., 1976), 13.

Figure 3

**PAST AND PROJECTED RELATIONSHIP
BETWEEN U.S. AND U.S.S.R. MILITARY EFFORT**

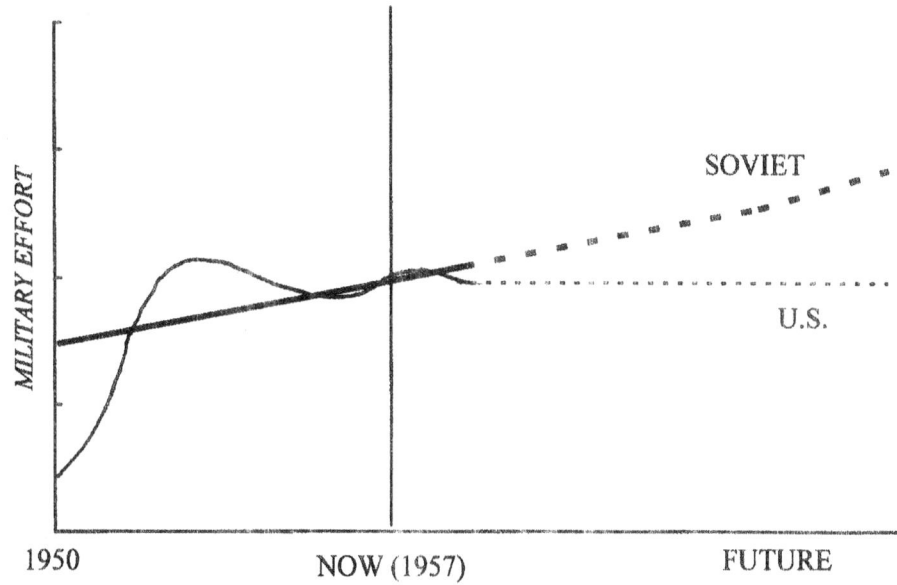

Source: Joint Committee on Defense Production, *Deterrence and Survival in the Nuclear Age (The "Gaither Report" of 1957)*, 94th Cong., 2d sess., 1957 (Reprint by the Government Printing Office, Washington, D.C., 1976), 14.

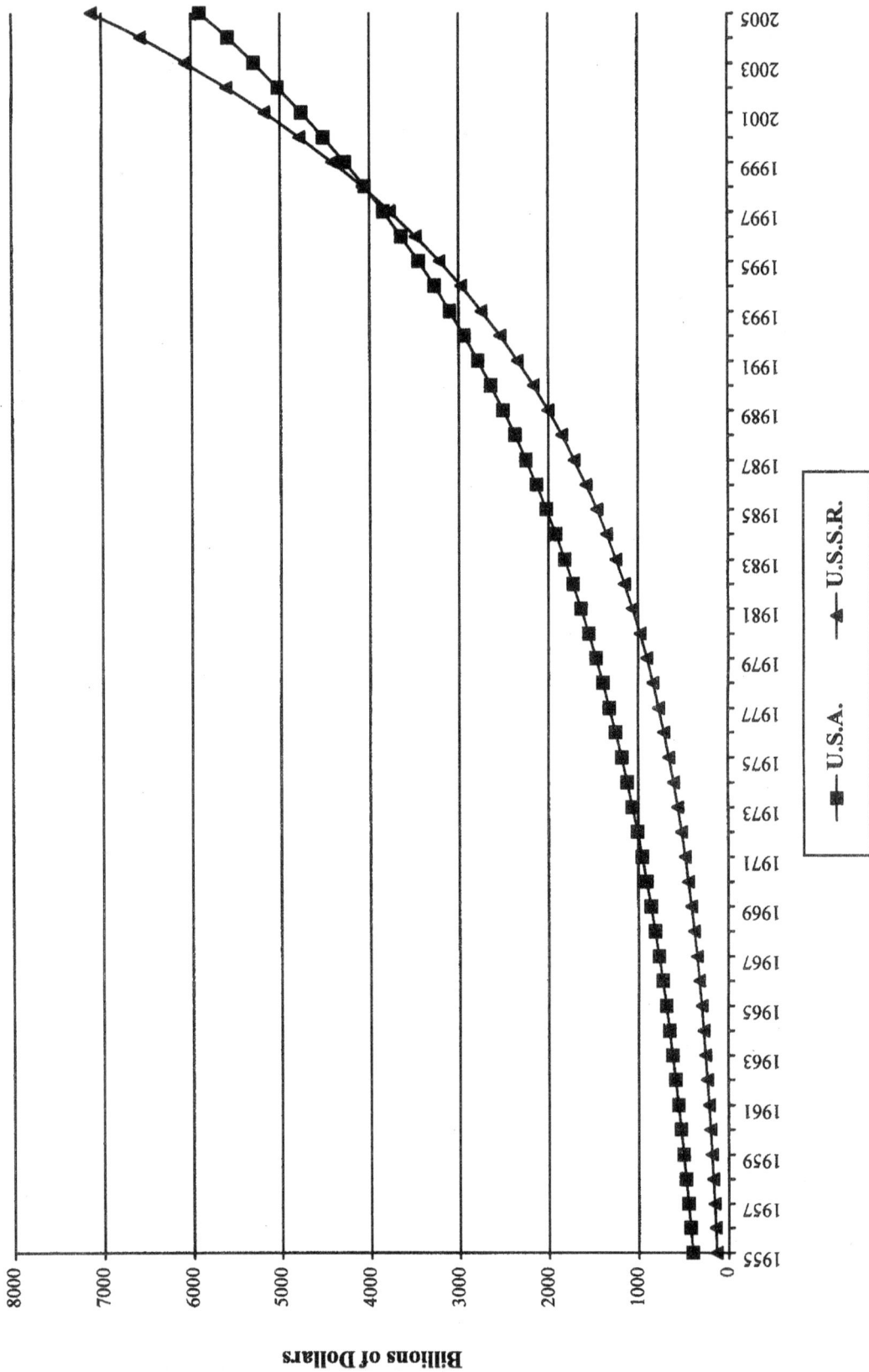

Figure 4: Gaither Commission Projections
Nominal GNP Growth Projections 1955-2005

Billions of Dollars

U.S.A.   U.S.S.R.

These rates of growth are exceedingly high. They have rarely been matched in other states except during limited periods of postwar rebuilding.

A dollar comparison of USSR and US gross national product in 1956 reveals that consumption—or what the Soviet consumer received—was less than half of total production. It was over two-thirds of the total in the U.S. Investment, on the other hand, as a proportion of GNP in the USSR, was significantly higher than in the US. Furthermore, investment funds in the USSR were plowed back primarily into expansion of electric power, the metallurgical base, and into the producer goods industries. In these fields, it was over 80 percent of actual US investment in 1956, and in 1958, will probably exceed our own. Defense expenditures, as a proportion of GNP in the USSR, were significantly higher than in the US; in fact about double.

Soviet industrial production in 1956 was about 40 percent as large as that of the US. However, Soviet heavy industry was proportionately larger than this over-all average, and in some instances the output of specific industries already approached that of the US. Output of coal in the USSR was about 70 percent of that of the US, output of machine tools about double our own and steel output about half.

Since 1956, Soviet output has continued its rapid expansion. In the first quarter of 1958, Soviet industrial production was 11 percent higher than a year ago. In comparison, the Federal Reserve Board index shows a decline of 11 percent in the United States.

According to available statistics, in the first quarter of 1958, the Sino-Soviet Bloc has for the first time surpassed the United States in steel production. The three months figures show that the USSR alone turned out over 75 percent of the steel tonnage of the US.[154]

Note that at a 6 percent growth rate for the U.S.S.R., the "crossover" date would be 1992. At 7 percent, 1983. As best this now distant history can be reconstructed, the Department of State was almost alone in questioning such fantasy. In 1962, the head of the Policy Planning Staff privately demurred that he was not one of those "6 percent forever" persons.[155] Note, also, that the CIA estimate was as public as can be. The statistical and economic bases for the estimate remained secret, and secrecy carried conviction. Presidents believed it.

The Gaither Report remained "Top Secret" until 1973. But, of course, it had leaked well before then. As John Prados records, on November 5, 1957, two days before it was forwarded to the President, the *New York Times* reported that a secret study of the entire scope of national defense was about to be sent to the NSC. Then, on December 20, Chalmers Roberts of the *Washington Post* published a very detailed article in that paper.[156] The "missile gap" now appeared. The Report had been explicit in this matter:

By 1959, the USSR may be able to launch an attack with ICBMs carrying megaton warheads, against which SAC will be almost completely vulnerable under present programs. By 1961-1962, at our present pace, or considerably earlier if we accelerate, the United States could have a reliable early-warning capability against a missile attack, and SAC forces should be on a 7 to 22 minute operational "alert." The next two years seem to us critical. If we fail to act at once, the risk, in our opinion, will be unacceptable.[157]

It is not clear, and probably never will be, whether the panel had access to the U-2 photographs then available, which evidently showed no sign of a massive ICBM build-up. In any event, President Eisenhower did know this, and was disinclined to see a crisis. Probably Senator John F. Kennedy did not know this, and so the "missile gap" entered the vocabulary of the 1960 Presidential election. For certain, the journalists Joseph and Stuart Alsop knew all manner of leading figures within the intelligence community. On August 1, 1958, they wrote:

> At the Pentagon they shudder when they speak of the "gap," which means the years 1960, 1961, 1962, and 1963. They shudder because in these years, the American government will flaccidly permit the Kremlin to gain an almost unchallenged superiority in the nuclear striking power that was once our specialty.[158]

Senator William Proxmire would later record that "Few documents have had as great an influence on American strategic thinking in the modern era. . . ."[159] The missile gap turned out not to exist, but nearly four decades later the United States is still contemplating modes of missile defense. *Civil* defense has pretty much disappeared from policy debates, but the aftermath of a massive scare echoes on and on.

The question must be asked: what was gained by secrecy? Had the Report been made public, as Senator Lyndon B. Johnson requested at the time, might not the economics profession have become more engaged with the subject in an open public debate?

For fifty years, as Bryan Hehir has recently observed, the United States confronted a direct, unambiguous issue: "how to deter a conscious, rational choice to use nuclear weapons against American territory."[160] Given the nature of the issue—a rational choice—a case surely can be made that our deliberations ought to have been much more public, much less "secret." Save for the Smyth Report of 1946, this case was never made. The Bomb created a mystique of secrecy that resisted any disposition to openness.

There was, to be sure, a vigorous public debate about nuclear strategy, principally based in universities and various "think-tanks" that now appeared. But within the Government, decisionmaking proceeded on the basis of tightly held—unless deliberately leaked—classified information and analysis. Of the roughly 100 persons associated with the Gaither Report there were few economists. None of the principals had any particular knowledge of the Soviet system, certainly not enough to add "investment in heavy industry" to outlays on the armed forces to produce an index of Soviet geopolitical strength defined as nuclear strike power. These passages from the Report are a close brush with the demented. What is merely painful is for all those physicists to measure the overall strength of an economy in terms of coal and steel production thirteen years after one of the first computers, the Mark 1 built by Howard Aiken, began operating at Harvard.

Great efforts were made within the Federal Government to get a grasp on the size and direction of the Soviet economy. In the main, the results followed the disposition put in place in the Eisenhower years to see the Soviets as a modern industrial economy growing more so. Here is testimony from Nicholas Eberstadt, presently of the American Enterprise Institute, before the

Senate Committee on Foreign Relations in July 1990, a year before the formal collapse of the Soviet regime:

> MR. EBERSTADT. As I believe you know, I do not specialize exclusively in Soviet economic affairs. I try to follow the economic and social affairs of a broad number of countries, including some with central planning systems, and others in what is sometimes called the Third World. As such, I am an interested user of estimates on trends and levels of Soviet economic output. The most comprehensive and authoritative of these estimates are produced by the U.S. Government, principally under the auspices of the Central Intelligence Agency.
>
> This is a longstanding effort involving many researchers, considerable talent, and enormous financial resources. In fact, I believe it may be safe to say that the U.S. Government's effort to describe the Soviet economy may be the largest single project in the social science research ever undertaken.

****

> How does one evaluate the results of this effort?
>
> There have been many achievements in this effort, some of them extremely interesting and important. We should neither ignore these nor belittle them. What I will focus on this morning, however, are some of the shortcomings of this effort. For, Mr. Chairman, shortcomings and contradictions are evident, even in a fairly cursory assessment of the published research.
>
> I shall outline three broad categories of problems that characterize some of these estimates.
>
> First, there are problems attendant upon using Soviet statistics. Naturally, Soviet statistics form the basic data for the U.S. analysis. But the limitations of these official statistics are well known. Very often the U.S. analysis took these figures at face value, with only minor adjustments. The problems with such credulousness are evident in the latest CIA handbook of economic statistics.
>
> That handbook, for example, suggests that per capita output of milk is today higher in the U.S.S.R. than in the United States, making the Soviet Union not only a nuclear power, but a dairy superpower.

****

> Similarly, these estimates suggest Soviet meat output in the late 1980's to be about the same as in the United States in 1960, during the Eisenhower years. Such an estimate, of course, is totally out of keeping with impressions of Western tourists and of many Soviet citizens.
>
> Now it is widely believed that the Soviet Government routinely hides many of its efforts from outside view. But where, one wonders, are the hidden stockpiles and reserves of Soviet meat?[161]

At the same hearing of the Senate Committee on Foreign Relations, Michael J. Boskin, then-Chairman of the Council of Economic Advisers, estimated that the Soviet economy was "about one-third" the size of the United States.[162] At this time, the official Handbook of Economic Statistics, produced by the intelligence community, put the ratio at 52 percent.[163] Obviously, the lunacy of the earlier projection was no more, but the disposition to exaggerate—not to take the chance of underestimating—was still much in evidence. The United States GDP for 1990 was $4.8 trillion. The intelligence community put Soviet GDP at $2.5 trillion. The President's chief economist made it more like $1.6 trillion. The difference is $900 billion. Which would buy a lot of missiles.

Government secrecy is not to be overblamed here. The CIA's estimates of Soviet GDP had been made public as early as 1959. The essential fact is that economists in general failed to grasp the stagnation that settled on the Soviet economy after a brief post-Second World War spurt in industries beloved of Heroes of Soviet Labor. Dale W. Jorgenson writes that "this has to be one of the great failures of economics—right up there with the inability of economists (along with anyone else) to find a remedy for the Great Depression of the 1930's."[164]

Henry S. Rowen of Stanford, whose distinguished government service included his chairmanship of the National Intelligence Council from 1981-83, has echoed this sentiment; "Sovietologists" both within the intelligence community and in academia, trained to rely on the same general assumptions and data, had engaged in a form of "group-think" that resulted in a monumental failure of analysis. By 1985, he circulated a paper to senior Reagan administration officials outlining his conclusion that actual Soviet economic growth was close to zero; in April 1986, he expressed his views directly to the President and Vice President.[165] Even so, the system failed and the United States paid a price.

By Fall 1991, only a few weeks before the Red Flag would be taken down at the Kremlin (on Christmas Day 1991) for the last time, Stansfield Turner, former Director of Central Intelligence, summed up:

> We should not gloss over the enormity of this failure to forecast the magnitude of the Soviet crisis. We know now that there were many Soviet academics, econo-mists and political thinkers, other than those officially presented to us by the Soviet government, who understood long before 1980 that the Soviet economic system was broken and that it was only a matter of time before someone had to try to repair it, as had Khrushchev. Yet I never heard a suggestion from the CIA, or the intelligence arms of the departments of defense or state, that numerous Soviets recognized a growing, systemic economic problem.

> Today we hear some revisionist rumblings that the CIA did in fact see the Soviet collapse emerging after all. If some individual CIA analysts were more prescient than the corporate view, their ideas were filtered out in the bureaucratic process; and it is the corporate view that counts because that is what reaches the president and his advisers. On this one, the corporate view missed by a mile.

> Why were so many of us so insensitive to the inevitable?[166]

The answer has to be, at least in part, that too much of the information was secret, not sufficiently open to the critique of the likes of Eberstadt, or the Swedish economist Anders Åslund, who for a long while described the Soviet Union as "a reasonably well developed Third World country, calling to mind Argentina, Mexico, or Portugal. . . ."[167] Too little attention was paid to ethnic issues. The Soviet Union, after all, broke up along ethnic lines. Finally, *much* too little attention was paid to the decline of Marxist-Leninist belief. It was as if the 1917 Revolution were carried out by the RAND Corporation, intent on more efficient and abundant weapon production.

****

One legacy of a century of real and imagined conspiracy, most of it cloaked in secrecy, is that the American public has acquired a distrust of government almost in proportion to the effort of government to attempt to be worthy of trust. After all, in this "long twilight struggle," men and women of singular qualities devoted much or most or all of their working lives to defending American society against manifest hostility and danger. As time went on, this effort—so much of it secret—seemed less and less rewarded with an appropriate respect. To the contrary.

While, as Richard Hofstadter and others have documented, conspiracy theories have been part of the American experience for two centuries, they would appear to have grown in dimension in recent decades. The best-known and most notorious is, of course, the unwillingness on the part of the vast majority of the American public to accept that President Kennedy was killed by Lee Harvey Oswald (or by another lone gunman). A poll taken in 1966, two years after release of the Warren Commission report concluding that Oswald had acted alone, found that 36 percent of respondents accepted this finding, while 50 percent believed others had been involved in a conspiracy to kill the President (14 percent had no opinion). By 1978, however, only 18 percent responded that they believed the assassination had been the act of one man; fully 75 percent believed there had been a broader plot. The numbers have remained relatively steady since; a 1993 poll also found that three-quarters of those surveyed believed (consistent with a popular film released that year) that there had been a conspiracy.[168]

The public concern with conspiracy has a counterpart in the "understanding," if that is the term, by Washington elites as to the extent to which the CIA and the FBI have established a *dossier* system which routinely intimidated persons in power or aspiring to it. The law that organizations in conflict become like one another may be noted: this was a KGB specialty, as regards Soviet citizens, but with Americans also targeted as opportunities arose. Writing in 1995 of the early years of the CIA, a respected journalist, citing two earlier histories, gave a fair example:

> Allen Dulles had been one of John F. Kennedy's first two appointments after the election. The other was J. Edgar Hoover of the FBI. Both men were "legends," explained Kennedy, better left undisturbed. His deference may have been encouraged by the knowledge that the CIA and FBI had thick files on the president-elect's past, including his brief affair with a German spy during World War II. The family patriarch, Joseph Kennedy, had urged his son to play it safe by reappointing Hoover and Dulles.[169]

****

Which brings us to the present. The central fact is that we live today in an Information Age. Open sources give us the vast majority of what we need to know in order to make intelligent decisions. Sound *analysis*, far more than secrecy, is the key to our security. Meaning decisions made by people after debate and argument, in which both assumptions and conclusions are scrutinized with great care. Decisions made by those who understand how to exploit the wealth and diversity of publicly available information, who no longer simply assume that clandestine collection, *i.e.,* "stealing secrets," equates with greater intelligence.

Joseph S. Nye, Jr., Dean of the Kennedy School of Government at Harvard and former Chairman of the National Intelligence Council, and Admiral William A. Owens, former Vice Chairman of the Joint Chiefs of Staff, make the point nicely in a 1996 article in *Foreign Affairs*. Knowledge is the "power resource of the future," and the key comparative advantage of the United States today and in the future will be in its "ability to collect, process, act upon, and disseminate information. . . ."[170] Even so, they note, "outmoded thinking clouds the appreciation of information as power"; senior policymakers and others apparently prefer to continue to focus on the "traditional measures" of power even though "these measures failed to anticipate the demise of the Soviet Union, and they are an equally poor means of forecasting for the exercise of American leadership into the next century."[171]

The critical point recognized by Nye and Owens, but too often ignored elsewhere, is that U.S. "information dominance" and in turn global leadership will be maintained not through the imposition of measures that preserve maximum secrecy, but instead by "selectively sharing" our dominant knowledge. The technologies that drive the Information Revolution are already available around the world; they are not secrets that adversaries are attempting to steal in order to gain an advantage. Openness, not secrecy, thus offers the better means of "winning hearts and minds" and, by so doing, of expanding American influence.[172]

The danger, simply put, is that the secrecy system will remain in place regardless. In 1996, an Independent Task Force of the Council on Foreign Relations issued a report entitled, *Making Intelligence Smarter*. The word "secrecy" does not appear anywhere in the report, save in one Additional View. That the American public surely has a right to know and a need to know much or most of what is still reflexively labeled "Secret" simply does not rise to the issue of a policy choice. But it is surely that. The Cold War is over. Yet this most pervasive of Cold War-era regulation persists without change.

There is just now a vigorous debate taking place concerning intelligence estimates of Soviet strength during the 1970s and 1980s. In particular, it can be shown that any number of papers by CIA analysts depicted a troubled, even declining economy. But it cannot be shown that any president believed this. It is to be doubted that any such proposition ever made its way through to a president. One National Security Council staffer has observed that "Intelligence estimates typically are written so they can never be wrong. The consequence, of course, is that they never are right." And, indeed, by the late 1980s the president was receiving so many daily intelligence digests from the assorted intelligence agencies that it is doubtful any were actually ever read by the person for whom they were nominally intended.

We ought not to fault American presidents for not understanding a situation any better than their Soviet counterparts. Still, there is a formidable case to be made that by the 1970s and 1980s an enormous institutional interest had developed in "threat analysis in worst possible case conditions." It is, for example, a matter of record that the American diplomats who negotiated the Strategic Arms Treaty (START) with the Soviet Union over the better part of a decade, beginning in 1982, had no intimation until the early 1990s that in the end the Treaty would be signed not with the U.S.S.R. but with four entirely "new" governments: Russia, Ukraine, Belarus, and Kazakhstan.[173] Again, we may assume that the Soviet negotiators had no inkling that their empire was about to implode, but there is a sense in which that would have been kept a secret in the U.S.S.R. when it could have easily been an open possibility within and without the American Government. Indeed, from the time Murray Feshbach, in 1976, published his findings of the decline of life expectancy in Soviet males, it *was* open in the United States.[174] Perhaps the problem was that Feshbach, then in the Bureau of the Census, had simply studied data from the Soviet census. No secrets there; accordingly, little interest.

Even so, this clearly ought to be the mode in which our Government tries to make sense of the world around us. Secrecy is natural to an information-*poor* society. Accordingly, information is hoarded, exchanged cautiously, with large transaction costs. All this is past. We live, as James S. Coleman observed some years ago, in an "information-rich society." This extends to information about getting information. Everything can be gotten. Open sources give you everything; and for practical purposes there are no closed sources.

The Soviet Union failed to realize this and, accordingly, failed to survive the 20th century. When the nuclear reactor at Chernobyl blew apart in 1986, the United States knew instantly. In those days, we photographed the U.S.S.R. once a day. American officials urged General Secretary Gorbachev to tell the world what had happened. Gorbachev, however, thought it could be kept a secret. As the radioactive fall-out drifted beyond the Soviet borders, sensors, first in one, then another Warsaw Pact country, picked it up, and in time there would be no more Warsaw Pact. It is not necessary to assert a direct connection to make the general point.

The Soviet Union is gone. But the secrecy system that grew in the United States in the long travail of the 20th century challenge to the Western democracies, culminating in the Cold War, is still in place as if nothing has changed. The system is massive, pervasive, evasive. Bureaucracies perpetuate themselves; regulations accumulate and become even more invasive.

This would be expensive and a bit absurd in any situation, but in time for the United States, it is very likely dangerous as well. The future is not likely to be any more peaceful than the past. Conflict rages in many parts of the world, but the basis of conflict is very different from that of the immediate past. The universalist ideology of Communism is past. The assumption that it will now be succeeded by a universal acceptance of legality and democracy, sustained by free and open markets, is surely open to question. It was no accident that the conflict of the 20th century which began with the assassination of the heir to the Austro-Hungarian throne in Sarajevo, had no more finally come to an end when a new ethnic/religious war broke out in . . . Sarajevo, and the Balkans generally. Harkening back to the borders of the Eastern and Western Roman empires, the medieval Christian divide, almost at the limit of Muslim conquest in the age of Suleiman.

It is reasonable to assume, at the very least prudent to assume, that such conflict will be endemic to the next century. It is characterized by acts of nontraditional warfare, which we call terrorism. It is meant to be frightening and it is. Our concern should be that we not give way to fear. To that end, we must surely strive to be as open about such matters as is ever possible. To learn from our past. Secrecy responds first of all to the fear of conspiracy, regularly and consistently associated with one or another ethnic or religious group *within* American society. (Again, it should be obvious that our Muslim citizens are now especially vulnerable.)

It should be equally obvious that in this new period, the United States will be best served by the largest possible degree of openness as to the nature of the threats we face. To do otherwise is to invite preoccupation with passing conspiracy, after all that we have sacrificed in this century to destroy sustained conspiracies that might very well have destroyed us.

DPM

---

[1]Albert Bushnell Hart, ed., *Theodore Roosevelt Cyclopedia* (New York: Roosevelt Memorial Association, 1941). "Roosevelt in the Kansas City Star," 1 October 1917, 8.

[2]Edward A. Shils, *The Torment of Secrecy,* with an introduction by Daniel Patrick Moynihan (Glencoe: The Free Press, 1956; reprint, Chicago: Ivan R. Dee, Inc., 1996), 26.

[3]The term "VENONA" is an arbitrary codeword which describes more than 2,900 Soviet diplomatic telegrams sent between 1940 and 1948 and the efforts by the United States Government to decode the messages and to identify Soviet agents mentioned therein. Robert Louis Benson and Michael Warner, eds., *VENONA: Soviet Espionage and the American Response, 1939-1957* (Washington, D.C.: National Security Agency, Central Intelligence Agency, 1996), vii-viii.

[4]Harvey Klehr, John Earl Haynes, and Fridrikh Igorevich Firsov, *The Secret World of American Communism* (New Haven: Yale University Press, 1995), xxvi.

[5]Harold Edgar and Benno C. Schmidt, Jr., "The Espionage Statutes and Publication of Defense Information," *Columbia Law Review* 73, no. 5 (May 1973), 930.

[6]U.S. Department of Defense Security Institute, *Recent Espionage Cases: Summaries and Sources* (Richmond: 1996), 12.

[7]Evan Thomas, "A Singular Opportunity: Gaining Access to CIA's Records," *Studies in Intelligence* 39, no. 5 (1996): 23.

[8]Harold C. Relyea, "National Security and Information," *Government Information Quarterly* 4, no. 1 (1987): 16.

[9]Donald L. Robinson, "The Routinization of Crisis Government," *Yale Review* 63 (Winter 1974): 161.

[10]Relyea, "National Security and Information," 17, quoting Senate Committee on Naval Affairs, *Unification of the War and Navy Departments and Postwar Organization for National Security*, 79th Congress, 1st Session, Washington, D.C.: Government Printing Office, 1945), 578-79.

[11]Relyea, "National Security and Information," 18.

[12]Ibid., 17.

[13]President, Executive Order 10290, "Regulations Establishing Minimum Standards for the Classification, Transmission, and Handling, by Departments and Agencies of the Executive Branch, of Official Information Which Requires Safeguarding in the Interest of the Security of the United States," *Federal Register* 16, no. 188 (27 September 1951): 9797.

[14]President, Executive Order 10501, "Safeguarding Official Information in the Interests of the Defense of the United States," *Federal Register* 18, no. 220 (10 November 1953): 7049.

[15]President, Executive Order 11652, "Classification and Declassification of National Security Information and Material," *Federal Register* 37, no. 48 (10 March 1972): 5209.

[16]President, Executive Order 12958, "Classified National Security Information," *Federal Register* 60, no. 76 (20 April 1995): 19825.

[17]These estimated figures were supplied by the Information Security Oversight Office, which issues an annual report on classification decisions. See Information Security Oversight Office, *1995 Report to the President* (Washington, D.C.: Information Security Oversight Office, 1996). "Derivative" classifiers are responsible for 94 percent of all classification decisions.

[18]Joseph Story, *Commentaries on the Constitution of the United States* (Boston: Little, Brown, 1891; reprint, William S. Hein, 1994), 609-10.

[19]Secrecy was present at the creation. The Constitutional Convention of 1787 met in closed session. Before final adjournment, in answer to an inquiry by George Washington, the presiding officer, the Convention resolved "that he retain the Journal and other papers subject to the order of Congress, if ever formed under the Constitution." Max Farrand, ed., *The Records of the Federal Convention of 1787*, vol. 1 (New Haven: Yale Univ. Press, 1934), xi.

[20]Harold C. Relyea, *The Evolution of Government Information Security Classification Policy: A Brief Overview (1775-1973)* (Washington, D.C.: Congressional Research Service, 11 September 1973), 1.

[21]Benson and Warner, *VENONA*, xxiv.

[22]Ibid., xxix.

[23]*Statutes at Large* 40 (1917): 451.

[24]Jerald A. Combs, "Alien and Sedition Acts," in *The World Book Encyclopedia* (Chicago: World Book, Inc., 1996), 368.

[25]*Statutes at Large* 12 (1861) 326.

[26]As Madison wrote to Jefferson on 13 May 1798, "Perhaps it is a universal truth that the loss of liberty at home is to be charged to provisions against danger, real or pretended, from abroad." James Morton Smith, ed., *The Republic of Letters, The Correspondence between Thomas Jefferson and James Madison 1776-1826* (New York: W. W. Norton & Co., 1995), 2:1048.

[27]Lansing to Wilson, 20 November 1915. Arthur Link, ed., *The Papers of Woodrow Wilson* (Princeton: Princeton University Press, 1980), 35:230.

[28]Ibid., "An Address in Philadelphia to Newly Naturalized Citizens" (10 May 1915), 33: 147-50.

[29]Ibid., "Annual Message on the State of the Union" (7 December 1915), 35: 306-07.

[30]U.S. Department of Justice, *Annual Report of the Attorney General, 1916* (Washington, D.C.: Government Printing Office, 1916), 12-20.

[31]"A Memorandum by Robert Lansing" (20 March 1917), Link, *The Papers of Woodrow Wilson*, 41:442.

[32]Ibid., "Address to a Joint Session of Congress" (2 April 1917), 41:421.

[33]Jules Witcover, *Sabotage at Black Tom: Imperial Germany's Secret War in America, 1914-1917* (Chapel Hill: Algonquin, 1989), 42; Captain Henry Landau, *The Enemy Within: The Inside Story of German Sabotage in America* (New York: G.P. Putnam's Sons, 1937), 7-8.

[34]The *New York Times* recorded in retrospect:

> SEVENTY-FIVE years ago this month, New York Harbor exploded. This is not a figure of speech; it was not an explosion of fear or an explosion of cheers. What took place was a colossal, ear-splitting, ground-shaking, glass-breaking explosion.
>
> The blast came at 2:08 A.M. on July 30, 1916, at Black Tom, a depot jutting out from Jersey City into the Hudson River opposite Manhattan. A New York newspaper said, "A million people, maybe five millions, were awakened by the explosion that shook the houses along the marshy New Jersey shores, rattled the skyscrapers on the rock foundation of Manhattan, threw people from their beds miles away and sent terror broadcast."
> The noise of the explosion was heard as far away as Maryland and Connecticut. Fire alarms and burglar alarms went off; phone lines between New York and New Jersey were severed. On both sides of the Hudson, people in their pajamas rushed out of buildings. Thousands milled around, watching the sky turn red from flames as more explosions thundered from the harbor.
>
> In Jersey City, residents swarmed into churches. On Ellis Island, terrified immigrants were evacuated by ferry to the Battery. Shrapnel from the explosion pierced the Statue of Liberty. The Black Tom terminal was completely destroyed. (Marc Mappen, "Jerseyana," *New York Times,* 14 July 1991, sec. 12, 15.)

[35]"Ram Chandra in Toils with Four Hindoo Plotters," *San Francisco Chronicle*, 8 April 1917, 1.

[36]Joan M. Jensen, "The 'Hindu Conspiracy': A Reassessment," *Pacific Historical Review*, 48 (February, 1979): 65.

[37]Ibid.

[38]John L. Heaton, *Cobb of "The World"* (New York: Dutton, 1924), 270.

[39]Samuel Eliot Morison, Henry Steele Commager, and William E. Leuchtenburg, *The Growth of the American Republic*, 6th ed. (New York: Oxford University Press, 1969), 2:383.

[40]Ibid., 2:386.

[41]*The Encyclopedia of the United States Congress*, vol. 2 (New York: Simon & Schuster, 1995), 774.

[42]Morrison et al., *Growth of the American Republic*, 2:384.

[43]Louis W. Koenig, *Bryan: A Political Biography of William Jennings Bryan* (New York: G.P. Putnam's Sons, 1971), 502-03.

[44]Arthur S. Link, *Wilson: The Struggle for Neutrality, 1914-1915* (Princeton: Princeton University Press, 1960), 420.

[45]"Josephus Daniels Dies at Age of 85," *New York Times*, 16 January 1948, 17.

[46]*New York Times,* 7 March 1916, 1.

[47]*Schenck v. United States*, 249 U.S. 47 (1919).

[48]*Debs v. United States*, 249 U.S. 211 (1919).

[49]Paul P. Van Riper, *History of the United States Civil Service* (Evanston: Row, Peterson and Company, 1958), 266.

[50]Ibid., 265-67.

[51]Max Weber, *Essays in Sociology,* trans. and ed. H.H. Gerth and C. Wright Mills (New York: Oxford University Press, 1946), 233-34; *Wirtschaft und Gesellschaft* (*Economy and Society*), 1922.

[52]William Ebenstein, "Anarchism," in *The World Book Encyclopedia* (Chicago: World Book, Inc., 1986) 424.

[53]Harold C. Relyea, *The Evolution of Government Information Security Classification Policy,* 22.

[54]"Memorandum on the Cabinet Meeting," (20 March 1917), Link, *The Papers of Woodrow Wilson*, 41:438.

[55]Ibid., 41:440.

[56]There was a quality of openness in 19th and early 20th century civil society that is all but forgotten today. Weber, a reserve Army officer called back to duty during the War, sensing the outcome, wrote a friend in 1917:

> As soon as the war has come to an end, I shall insult the Kaiser until he sues me,
> and then the responsible statesmen, Bulow, Tirpitz, and Bethmann-Hollweg, will
> be compelled to make statements under oath. (Weber, *Essays,* 22.)

[57]Robert A. Rosenstone, *Romantic Revolutionary: A Biography of John Reed* (Cambridge: Harvard University Press, 1990), 330.

[58]Klehr et al., *Secret World*, 22.

[59]Draper reproduces an estimate of the membership of the CPUSA:

English	1,900*
Non-federation Language members	1,100
Estonian	280
German	850
Hungarian	1,000
Jewish	1,000
Lettish	1,200
Lithuanian	4,400
Polish	1,750
Russian	7,000
South Slavic	2,200
Ukrainian	4,000
Total	26,680

*Including 800 of the Michigan organization which soon dropped out.

Theodore Draper, *The Roots of American Communism* (Chicago: Ivan R. Dee, Inc. 1957), 189.

[60]Ibid., 191.

[61]Ibid.

[62]Klehr et al., *Secret World,* 323.

[63]Nathan Glazer, *The Social Basis of American Communism* (New York: Harcourt, Brace & World, 1961), 3. Maurice Isserman estimates that, in the years before World War II, there were 50,000 to 75,000 CPUSA members in the United States. Maurice Isserman, *Which Side Were You On? The American Communist Party During the Second World War* (Middletown: Wesleyan University Press, 1982), 18.

[64]Stanley Coben, *A. Mitchell Palmer: Politician* (New York: Da Capo Press, 1972), 203-04.

[65]Robert K. Murray, *Red Scare: A Study in National Hysteria, 1919-1920* (Minneapolis: University of Minnesota Press, 1955; reprint, Westport: Greenwood Press, 1980), 213.

[66]Roberta Strauss Feuerlicht, *America's Reign of Terror: World War I, the Red Scare, and the Palmer Raids* (New York: Random House, 1971), 108.

[67]Draper, *Roots*, 207.

[68]Klehr et al., *Secret World*, 21-24.

[69]These subsidies continued into the 1980s, by which time the CPUSA scarcely existed. Evidently, Moscow did not realize this, assuming perhaps the greater portion of the Party had gone underground. It is ever difficult for clandestine operators to check their facts!

[70]Richard Crossman, ed., *The God that Failed: Six Studies in Communism* (London: Hamish Hamilton, 1950), introduction, 16.

[71]Klehr et al., *Secret World*, 25.

[72]Sidney Hook, *Out of Step: An Unquiet Life in the 20th Century* (New York: Harper & Row, 1987), 241.

[73]NKVD is the abbreviation for narodnyi komissariat vnutrennikh del (People's commissariat of internal affairs), predecessor to the KGB, the name formally used beginning in 1954. Often, however, early Soviet intelligence operations also are described by historians as those of the KGB for the sake of clarity. (See, for example, Klehr et al., *Secret World*, xxvii; Benson and Warner, *VENONA*, ix.)

[74]National Security Agency, Fourth VENONA release, 17 July 1996, vol. 3, nos. 174-176 (29 December 1943).

[75]Hook, *Out of Step*, 281.

[76]Ibid. In 1946, Lionel Trilling of Columbia University published his novel, *The Middle of the Journey*. It recounts the ordeal of an American Communist—clearly Chambers—who had broken with the Party and, as a means of escaping death, was now desperate to establish that he was still alive. This involved his relationship with another conspirator—just as clearly Alger Hiss. Trilling knew Chambers. He did not know Hiss existed. Yet he *did* know.

[77]Ibid., 285.

[78]David Riesman, *Abundance for What?* (Garden City: Doubleday, 1964; reprint, New Brunswick: Transaction Publishers, 1993), 80.

[79]Art Ronnie, *Counterfeit Hero: Fritz Duquesne, Adventurer and Spy* (Annapolis: Naval Institute Press, 1995), 208-09.

[80]Ibid., 214.

[81]Ibid., 2.

[82]Kathleen Neils Conzen, "Germans," in *Harvard Encyclopedia of American Ethnic Groups*, ed. Stephan Thernstrom (Cambridge: Harvard University Press, 1980), 423.

[83]Ibid.

[84]Robert Edwin Herzstein, *Roosevelt & Hitler: Prelude to War* (New York: Paragon House, 1989), 189.

[85]Ibid., 190.

[86]Don Whitehead, *The FBI Story* (New York: Random House, 1956), 212.

[87]By 16 February 1942, these numbers had expanded to a total of 2,192 Japanese, 1,393 Germans, and 264 Italians. Commission on Wartime Relocation and Internment of Civilians, *Personal Justice Denied, Report of the Commission on Wartime Relocation and Internment of Civilians* (Washington, D.C.: Government Printing Office, 1992), 55.

[88]Ibid., 73.

[89]Ibid., 81.

[90]President, Executive Order 9066, *Federal Register* 7, no. 38 (25 February 1942):1407.

[91]*Personal Justice Denied*, 308.

[92]Ibid., 287.

[93]Stephen Fox, *The Unknown Internment: An Oral History of the Relocation of Italian Americans during World War II* (Boston: Twayne, 1990), 136.

[94]*Civil Liberties Act of 1988,* 102 Stat. 94 (1988). U.S. citizens of Aleutian descent also were relocated. The Act said of them, "The United States failed to provide reasonable care for the Aleuts, and this resulted in widespread illness, disease, and death among the residents of the camps."

[95]J. L. DeWitt, "Final Report: Japanese Evacuation from the West Coast, 1942," in *Personal Justice Denied,* 83.

[96]Maurice M. Shapiro, "Echoes of the Big Bang," *New York Times,* 15 July 1995, 21.

[97]Richard Rhodes, *The Making of the Atomic Bomb* (New York: Simon & Schuster, 1986), 676.

[98]Robert K. Murray, *Red Scare: A Study in National Hysteria, 1919-1920* (Westport: Greenwood Press, 1955; reprint, Westport: Greenwood Press, 1980), 25; Edwin P. Hoyt, *The Palmer Raids 1919-1920* (New York: The Seabury Press, 1969), 115-17.

[99]Robert Lamphere and Tom Shachtman, *The FBI-KGB War* (New York: Random House, 1986), 78-98. Six years earlier, in his book *Wilderness of Mirrors*, David Martin had described the efforts of American cryptanalysts to break the Soviet code. However, he did not cite the VENONA project by name.

[100]The three others from the State Department in the U.S. delegation were Edward R. Stettinius, Jr., Secretary of State; H. Freeman Matthews, Director of the Office of European Affairs; and Wilder Foote, Assistant to the Secretary of State. See Edward R. Stettinius, Jr., *Roosevelt and the Russians: The Yalta Conference* (Garden City: Doubleday, 1949), 30.

[101]Benson and Warner, *VENONA,* xxiv.

[102]*U.S. Statutes at Large* 60 (1947): 495. *National Security Act of 1947.*

[103]Robert Warshow, "The Legacy of the 30's: Middle-Class Mass Culture and the Intellectuals' Problem," *Commentary* (December 1947): 538.

[104]Whitehead, *FBI,* 158-61.

[105]Christopher Andrew and Oleg Gordievsky, *KGB: The Inside Story* (New York: HarperCollins, 1990), 373-74.

[106]The successor to the OSS was the Central Intelligence Group (CIG), a "clearinghouse" body headed by the Director of Central Intelligence. Subsequently, the CIA was established in 1947.

[107]Senator Joseph R. McCarthy, *America's Retreat from Victory: The Story of George Catlett Marshall* (New York: Devin-Adair, 1951).

[108]Suslov joined the Politburo (then called the Presidium) in October 1952, but left in 1953 after Stalin's death. He rejoined it in 1955 and remained a member until his death on 25 January 1982.

[109]Daniel Patrick Moynihan, *A Dangerous Place* (Boston: Little, Brown and Company, 1978), ix-x.

[110]Erwin Griswold, "Government in Ignorance of the Law — A Plea for Better Publication of Executive Legislation," *Harvard Law Review* 48 (1934): 198. Griswold argued that administrative regulations "equivalent to law" had become important in the ordering of everyday life and criticized the fact that such rules were not published and thus not available to the public. The next year, Congress enacted the Federal Register Act of 1935, *Statutes at Large* 49 (1935): 500.

[111]*United States v. Curtiss-Wright Export Corp.,* 299 U.S. 304, 319 (1936).

[112]Richard Frank, "Enforcing the Public's Right to Openness in the Foreign Affairs Decision-Making Process," *Secrecy and Foreign Policy,* eds. Thomas Franck and Edward Weisband (New York: Oxford Univ. Press, 1974), 272-73.

[113]*Statutes at Large* 53 (1953): 1148.

[114]The 1912 Act provided that a government employee could not be removed except for such cause as would promote the efficiency of the civil service. It also established specific procedures for notification of any charges against an employee and responses to such charges.

[115]*Statutes at Large* 22 (1883): 403.

[116]Commission on Government Security, *Report of the Commission on Government Security* (Washington, D.C.: Government Printing Office, 1957), 3-6; Eleanor Bontecou, *The Federal Loyalty-Security Program* (Westport: Greenwood Press, 1953), 14.

[117]*Report of the Commission on Government Security,* 6.

[118]Harold Green, "The Oppenheimer Case: A Study in the Abuse of Law," *Bulletin of the Atomic Scientists* (September 1977): 12, 61.

[119]The critique was published in the *New York Times,* 13 April 1947; see Bontecou, *Federal Loyalty-Security Program,* 30-31.

[120]President, Executive Order 10450, "Security Requirements for Government Employees," *Federal Register* 18, no. 82 (29 April 1953): 2489.

[121]Attempting to respond to the criticism, President Truman had amended his Executive Order in July 1951, lowering the standard of proof for disloyalty: "The standard for the refusal of employment or the removal from employment in an Executive department or agency on grounds relating to loyalty shall be that on all the evidence, *there is reasonable doubt* as to the loyalty of the person involved." (Emphasis added.) Executive Order 10241, *Federal Register* 16, no. 84 (1 May 1951): 3690. Then, in 1952, the President convened a committee with the objective of merging the "loyalty, security, and suitability programs, thus eliminating the overlap, duplication, and confusion which apparently now exist." (Harry S Truman, letter to the Chairman of the Civil Service Commission, 8 August 1952.) But the often-partisan attacks on his loyalty program persisted, and a single, unified program for reviewing applicants for government positions and existing employees never was established — even after the Wright Commission in 1957 criticized the Eisenhower structure as an "unnatural blend" and a "hybrid product . . . neither fish nor fowl, resulting in inconclusive adjudications, bewildered security personnel, employee fear and unrest, and general public criticism." *Report of the Commission on Government Security,* 44.

[122]Under Executive Order 10450, the *scope* of the investigation varies based on the degree of adverse impact (if any) on national security that the individual could cause by virtue of his or her position.

[123]*Statutes at Large* 64 (1950): 476.

[124]Anthony Leviero, "New Security Plan Issued; Thousands Face Re-Inquiry," *New York Times,* 28 April 1953, 1.

[125]Ibid., 20.

[126]Shils, *Torment,* 213-14. Shils went on to offer a strong critique of the system:

> This seems a narrow and doctrinaire conception of the motives of treasonable conduct. It is this narrow doctrinairism which makes the present system so inefficient, even though it may well be fairly effective. Although it might catch a few potential spies, it hurts many innocent persons. The resources marshaled against the potential spy are usually almost equally dangerous to the innocent....

[127]*Congressional Record,* 84th Cong, 1st sess., 18 January 1955, 463-64.

[128]Ibid.

[129]Ibid.

[130]*Report of the Commission on Government Security,* xiii-xiv.

[131]James Reston, "Security vs. Freedom: An Analysis of the Controversy Stirred By Recommendation to Curb Information," *New York Times,* 25 June 1957, 17.

[132]*Report of the Commission on Government Security,* 688.

[133]Max Frankel, "Top Secret," *New York Times Magazine* (16 June 1996): 20.

[134]House Committee on Government Operations, *Availability of Information From Federal Departments and Agencies,* 86th Cong., 2d sess., 1960, House Rept. 86-2084, 36.

[135]*Report of the Commission on Government Security,* 153.

[136]In an even-tempered, respectful dissent to the proposal for a new, centralized security structure, former Attorney General McGranery wrote:

> It is perhaps unnecessary at this time to dwell upon the inherent evil of the pyramiding of administrative devices, the superimposing of agency upon agency and the empire-building proclivities which frequently go hand in hand with the creation of overseers. Yet it should be pointed out that no problem is solved by shifting primary executive responsibility from agencies and officials having that primary responsibility to superimposed administrative creations, even where the latter are described as advisory. The power to suggest too easily becomes the power to demand.
>
> There is no substitute for sound administrative procedures and the exercise of commonsense. The time has come for emphasis to be placed on the spirit of the law.
>
> It would have been refreshing, indeed, if the Commission had seen fit to submit a final report correcting existing procedures and practices without finding it necessary to enlarge

and complicate the Government structure while adding no guarantee of increased effectiveness. What is needed is a correction in those existing procedures which fail to
achieve Government security with minimum delay and maximum protection of the civil
rights of the loyal employee. What is needed is the will to make corrected procedures
work. There is no assurance that a new agency would be perfect. It is necessary to hold
mistakes of judgment to a minimum and, once having occurred, then fix responsibility and
seek to avoid their recurrence. This can best be done by holding accountable those
officials and agencies having the primary responsibility.

There can be no doubt that there is a need for uniformity in security procedures but there
is also a need to preserve the responsibility of the departments and agencies for the
proper administration of the security program. (Ibid., 799.)

[137]*Report of the Commission on Government Security,* 156.

[138]Relyea, *Evolution of Government Information Security Classification Policy,* 50; Robert O. Blanchard,
"Present at the Creation: The Media and the Moss Committee," *Journalism Quarterly* 49 (Summer 1972):
272.

[139]House Committee on Government Operations, *Availability of Information From Federal Departments
and Agencies (Department of Defense),* 85th Cong., 2d sess., 1958, House Rept. 85-1554, 152.

[140]House Committee on Government Operations, *Executive Classification of Information — Security
Classification Problems Involving Exemption (b)(1) of the Freedom of Information Act,* 93d Cong., 1st
sess., 1973, House Rept. 93-221, 21.

[141]*Freedom of Information Act,* 5 U.S.C. 552 (1966).

[142]Even so, significant concerns remain about the both the effectiveness and the efficiency of the procedures used under the FOIA. For example, at its Public Access Roundtable program on 16 May 1996, the
Commission heard testimony from journalist Terry Anderson concerning his efforts to use the FOIA to
reconstruct the history of his seven years of captivity in Lebanon. What he encountered from his own
Government—a mixture of outright denials of requested information, regrets for long delays, documents
blacked out completely, and piles of foreign newspaper clippings on Middle Eastern terrorism that somehow
had come to be classified once they entered agency files—led him to tell the Commission: "It's not the law
that has to be changed, but the culture of non-cooperation among the bureaucrats."

[143]*Report of the Commission on Government Security,* xx.

[144]Defense Science Board, *Final Report of the Defense Science Board Task Force on Secrecy* (1 July 1970).
Somewhat ironically, given its tone and recommendations, the Task Force Report was marked "For Official
Use Only," in an apparent effort to control its distribution.

[145]The Task Force noted that "never in the past has it been possible to keep secret the truly important
discoveries, such as the discovery that an atomic bomb can be made to work. . . ." Ibid., 3-4.

[146]Frankel, "Top Secret," 20.

[147]Edgar and Schmidt, "The Espionage Statutes and Publication of Defense Information," 934, 936.

[148]With respect to the 1950 amendments, Edgar and Schmidt term the Senate legislative history "inexplicit"
on the key issues, the House report "inexplicable." Ibid., 1023.

[149]Ibid., 937.

[150]According to data gathered by the Department of Justice, there were 67 indictments under the espionage
laws between 1975 and August 1996. Figures compiled by the Department of Defense Security Institute
show 86 new espionage cases *reported* between 1975 and 1995. (Both sets of materials are on file at the
Commission offices.) Aldrich Ames was indicted under 18 U.S.C. 794(c) of the Espionage Act for a conspiracy "to directly or indirectly communicate, deliver or transmit . . . documents and information related to
the national defense . . . to a foreign government or a representative or officer thereof . . . with the intent or
reason to believe such information could be used to the injury of the United States or to the advantage of a
foreign government." His wife, Rosario, was also indicted for conspiracy under a separate provision of the
Act, 18 U.S.C. 793(g), for "a willful combination or agreement" with her husband "to communicate, deliver or
transmit . . . documents relating to the national defense . . . to persons not authorized to receive them." Both
also were indicted on tax fraud charges. Both subsequently pled guilty, with Aldrich Ames sentenced to life
imprisonment without parole and Rosario Ames to a five-year term.

[151]Edgar and Schmidt, citing Morrison, *The Protection of Intelligence Data* (unpublished paper on file in the Columbia Law School Library). "The Espionage Statutes and Publication of Defense Information," 1055.

[152]Erwin N. Griswold, "Secrets Not Worth Keeping," *Washington Post*, 15 February 1989, A25.

[153]If real, as against nominal, growth rates are used, the "crossover" does not occur until the year 2021, but the Soviets would have, by any such calculation, long since established a potential military superiority.

[154]Allen W. Dulles, "Dimensions of the International Peril Facing Us," Address to the U.S. Chamber of Commerce, Washington D.C., April 28, 1958. *Vital Speeches of the Day*, vol. xxiv, no. 15, 15 May 1958, 453.

[155]W. W. Rostow, conversation with Daniel Patrick Moynihan, 1962.

[156]John Prados, *The Soviet Estimate: U.S. Intelligence Analysis & Soviet Strategic Forces* (Princeton: Princeton University Press, 1982), 74.

[157]Joint Committee on Defense Production, *Deterrence and Survival in the Nuclear Age (The "Gaither Report" of 1957)*, 94th Cong., 2d sess., 1976, 25.

[158]Prados, *The Soviet Estimate*, 80, quoting Joseph and Stewart Alsop, *New York Herald-Tribune*, 1 August 1958.

[159]*"Gaither Report,"* introduction, iii.

[160]Bryan Hehir, *The Uses of Force in the Post-Cold War World* (Washington, D.C.: Woodrow Wilson Center for Scholars, August 1996), 3.

[161]Senate Committee on Foreign Relations, *Estimating the Size and Growth of the Soviet Economy: Hearing Before the Committee on Foreign Relations,* 101st Cong., 2d sess., 1990, 49.

[162]Ibid., 33.

[163]Central Intelligence Agency, National Foreign Assessment Center, *Handbook of Economic Statistics, 1990*, 38.

[164]Dale W. Jorgenson, letter to Senator Daniel Patrick Moynihan, 18 March 1991.

[165]While concluding that this failure of analysis was not unique to the intelligence community, Dr. Rowen also has noted at least four major areas in which the "CIA economic assessments differed markedly from those of observers outside the community," including the overall size of the Soviet economy; the economy's performance; the military burden/share of Soviet GDP; and what he terms the "costs of empire." Henry Rowen and Charles Wolf, Jr., "The CIA's Credibility," *The National Interest* (Winter 1995/96): 111-12 (letter to the editor responding to an article in the previous issue vindicating the CIA's analysis).

[166]Stansfield Turner, "Intelligence for a New World Order," *Foreign Affairs* (Fall 1991): 162.

[167]Anders Åslund, "The CIA vs. Soviet Reality," *Washington Post*, 19 May 1988, 25.

[168]National polling data (from the Gallup Organization; Louis Harris and Associates; ABC News/Washington Post; Time/CNN/Yankelovich; CBS News/New York Times; and Gallup/CNN/USA Today surveys) provided by the Assassination Records Review Board and on file at the Commission offices. Congress in 1992 established the Assassination Records Review Board to review all records related to the Kennedy assassination and make them available to the public (subject to narrow exemptions) as soon as possible. The efforts of the Board are likely to do a great deal to clarify the historical record concerning the assassination and the activities of Oswald and others; it is far less likely that they will have much impact on future polls concerning the matter.

[169]Evan Thomas, *The Very Best Men, Four Who Dared: The Early Years of the CIA* (New York: Simon & Schuster, 1995), 239, citing Thomas C. Reeves, *A Question of Character: A Life of John F. Kennedy* (New York: Free Press, 1991), 217-18; Michael Beschloss, *The Crisis Years: Kennedy and Khrushchev, 1960-1963* (New York: Harper Collins, 1991), 103.

[170]Joseph S. Nye, Jr. and William A. Owens, "America's Information Edge," *Foreign Affairs* (March/April 1996): 20.

[171]Ibid., 22.

[172]Ibid., 27-28, 34.

[173]When the Foreign Relations Committee held a hearing on the Treaty in 1992, I had the following exchange with Ambassador Ronald F. Lehman, then Director of the U.S. Arms Control and Disarmament Agency, and Ambassador Linton F. Brooks, Chief START Negotiator and Acting Head of the U.S. Delegation to the Nuclear and Space Talks:

> Senator Moynihan: When did you, as negotiators, first contemplate the possibility that you would be signing a treaty with four countries and not one?

Ambassador Lehman: Well, if you mean informal speculation it probably began about 2 years ago [i.e., June 1990]. In terms of would this actually have come to pass, I think at the time of the Moscow coup [August 1991] people began to realize that some of the themes we were gearing around the Soviet Union might begin moving very quickly.

Senator Moynihan: Two years ago you began to think it might be possible; one year ago it became real?

Ambassador Lehman: I think it became quite obvious that we had to step up to the issue with the dissolution of the Soviet Union in December of last year.

Senator Moynihan: About December of last year, you had to begin to deal with the proposition of the dissolution of the Soviet Union. **** Could I ask Ambassador Brooks . . . [w]as there any collective memory of anybody on the Senate observers group suggesting to you that by 1992 you would indeed be negotiating with four governments and not one?

Ambassador Brooks: Senator, I certainly do not remember that. . . . I think very few of us on our end of the street predicted that. . . .

> Senate Committee on Foreign Relations, *The START Treaty: Hearings Before the Committee on Foreign Relations,* 102d Cong., 2d sess., 1992, 67-68.

[174]Murray Feshbach and Stephen Rapawy, "Soviet Population and Manpower Trends and Policies," in Joint Economic Committee, *Soviet Economy in a New Perspective*, 94th Cong., 2d sess., 14 October 1976, 113.

Appendix B:
Commission's Authorizing Statute

PUBLIC LAW 103-236 ; April 30, 1994

FOREIGN RELATIONS AUTHORIZATION ACT,
FISCAL YEARS 1994 AND 1995

TITLE IX-COMMISSION ON PROTECTING AND REDUCING GOVERNMENT SECRECY

SEC. 901. SHORT TITLE.

This title may be cited as the "Protection and Reduction of Government Secrecy Act."

Protection and Reduction of Government Secrecy Act. Classified information. 50 USC 401 note.

SEC. 902. FINDINGS.

The Congress makes the following findings:

(1) During the Cold War an extensive secrecy system developed which limited public access to information and reduced the ability of the public to participate with full knowledge in the process of governmental decisionmaking.

(2) In 1992 alone 6,349,532 documents were classified and approximately three million persons held some form of security clearance.

(3) The burden of managing more than 6 million newly classified documents every year has led to tremendous administrative expense, reduced communication within the government and within the scientific community, reduced communication between the government and the people of the United States, and the selective and unauthorized public disclosure of classified information.

(4) It has been estimated that private businesses spend more than $14 billion each year implementing government mandated regulations for protecting classified information.

(5) If a smaller amount of truly sensitive information were classified the information could be held more securely

(6) In 1970 a Task Force organized by the Defense Science Board and headed by Dr. Frederick Seitz concluded that "more might be gained than lost if our Nation were to adopt—unilaterally, if necessary—a policy of complete openness in all areas of information."

(7) The procedures for granting security clearances have themselves become an expensive and inefficient part of the secrecy system and should be closely examined.

(8) A bipartisan study commission specially constituted for the purpose of examining the consequences of the secrecy system will be able to offer comprehensive proposals for reform.

SEC. 903. PURPOSE.

It is the purpose of this title to establish for a two-year period a Commission on Protecting and Reducing Government Secrecy—

(1) to examine the implications of the extensive classification of information and to make recommendations to reduce the volume of information classified and thereby to strengthen the protection of legitimately classified information; and

(2) to examine and make recommendations concerning current procedures relating to the granting of security clearances.

SEC. 904. COMPOSITION OF THE COMMISSION.

(a) ESTABLISHMENT.—To carry out the purpose of this title, there is established a Commission on Protecting and Reducing Government Secrecy (in this title referred to as the "Commission").

(b) COMPOSITION.—The Commission shall be composed of twelve members, as follows:

President.
(1) Four members appointed by the President, of whom two shall be appointed from the executive branch of the Government and two shall be appointed from private life.

(2) Two members appointed by the Majority Leader of the Senate, of whom one shall be a Member of the Senate and one shall be appointed from private life.

(3) Two members appointed by the Minority Leader of the Senate, of whom one shall be a Member of the Senate and one shall be appointed from private life.

(4) Two members appointed by the Speaker of the House of Representatives, of whom one shall be a Member of the House and one shall be appointed from private life.

(5) Two members appointed by the Minority Leader of the House of Representatives, of whom one shall be a Member of the House and one shall be appointed from private life.

(c) CHAIRMAN.—The Commission shall elect a Chairman from among its members.

(d) QUORUM; VACANCIES.—After its initial meeting, the Commission shall meet upon the call of the Chairman or a majority of its members. Seven members of the Commission shall constitute a quorum. Any vacancy in the Commission shall not affect its powers but shall be filled in the same manner in which the original appointment was made.

(e) APPOINTMENT OF MEMBERS; INITIAL MEETING.—(1) It is the sense of the Congress that members of the Commission should be appointed not later than 60 days after the date of enactment of this title.

(2) If after 60 days from the date of enactment of this Act seven or more members of the Commission have been appointed, those members who have been appointed may meet and select a Chairman who thereafter shall have authority to begin the operations of the Commission, including the hiring of staff.

SEC. 905. FUNCTIONS OF THE COMMISSION.

The functions of the Commission shall be—

(1) to conduct, for a period of 2 years from the date of its first meeting, an investigation into all matters in any way related to any legislation, executive order, regulation, practice, or procedure relating to classified information or granting security clearances; and

Reports.
(2) to submit to the Congress a final report containing such recommendations concerning the classification of national security information and the granting of security clearances as the Commission shall determine, including proposing new procedures, rules, regulations, or legislation.

SEC. 906. POWERS OF THE COMMISSION.

(a) IN GENERAL.—(1) The Commission or, on the authorization of the Commission, any subcommittee or member thereof, may, for the purpose of carrying out the provisions of this title—

(A) hold such hearings and sit and act at such times and places, take such testimony, receive such evidence, administer such oaths, and

(B) require, by subpoena or otherwise, the attendance and testimony of such witnesses and the production of such books, records, correspondence, memoranda, papers, and documents, as the Commission or such designated subcommittee or designated member may deem advisable.

(2) Subpoenas issued under paragraph (1)(B) may be issued under the signature of the Chairman of the Commission, the chairman of any designated subcommittee, or any designated member, and may be served by any person designated by such Chairman, subcommittee chairman, or member. The provisions of sections 102 through 104 of the Revised Statutes of the United States (2 U.S.C. 192—194) shall apply in the case of any failure of any witness to comply with any subpoena or to testify when summoned under authority of this section.

(b) CONTRACTING.—The Commission may, to such extent and in such amounts as are provided in appropriation Acts, enter into contracts to enable the Commission to discharge its duties under this title.

(c) INFORMATION FROM FEDERAL AGENCIES.—The Commission is authorized to secure directly from any executive department, bureau, agency, board, commission, office, independent establishment, or instrumentality of the Government information, suggestions, estimates, and statistics for the purposes of this title. Each such department, bureau, agency, board, commission, office, establishment, or instrumentality shall, to the extent authorized by law, furnish such information, suggestions, estimates, and statistics directly to the Commission, upon request made by the Chairman.

(d) ASSISTANCE FROM FEDERAL AGENCIES.—(1) The Secretary of State is authorized on a reimbursable or non-reimbursable basis to provide the Commission with administrative services, funds, facilities, staff, and other support services for the performance of the Commission's functions.

(2) The Administrator of General Services shall provide to the Commission on a reimbursable basis such administrative support services as the Commission may request.

(3) In addition to the assistance set forth in paragraphs (1) and (2), departments and agencies of the United States are authorized to provide to the Commission such services, funds, facilities, staff, and other support services as they may deem advisable and as may be authorized by law.

(e) GIFTS.—The Commission may accept, use, and dispose of gifts or donations of services or property.

(f) POSTAL SERVICES.—The Commission may use the United States mails in the same manner and under the same conditions as departments and agencies of the United States.

SEC. 907. STAFF OF THE COMMISSION.

(a) IN GENERAL.—The Chairman, in accordance with rules agreed upon by the Commission, may appoint and fix the compensation of a staff director and such other personnel as may be necessary to enable the Commission to carry out its functions, without regard to the provisions of title 5, United States Code, governing appointments in the competitive service, and without regard to the provisions of chapter 51 and subchapter III of chapter 53 of such title relating to classification and General Schedule pay rates, except that no rate of pay fixed under this subsection may exceed the equivalent of that payable to a person occupying a position at level V of the Executive

Schedule under section 5316 of title 5, United States Code. Any Federal Government employee may be detailed to the Commission without reimbursement from the Commission, and such detailee shall retain the rights, status, and privileges of his or her regular employment without interruption.

(b) CONSULTANT SERVICES.—The Commission is authorized to procure the services of experts and consultants in accordance with section 3109 of title 5, United States Code, but at rates not to exceed the daily rate paid a person occupying a position at level IV of the Executive Schedule under section 5315 of title 5, United States Code.

SEC. 908. COMPENSATION AND TRAVEL EXPENSES.

(a) COMPENSATION.—(1) Except as provided in paragraph (2), each member of the Commission may be compensated at not to exceed the daily equivalent of the annual rate of basic pay in effect for a position at level IV of the Executive Schedule under section 5315 of title 5, United States Code, for each day during which that member is engaged in the actual performance of the duties of the Commission.

(2) Members of the Commission who are officers or employees of the United States or Members of Congress shall receive no additional pay on account of their service on the Commission.

(b) TRAVEL EXPENSES.—While away from their homes or regular places of business in the performance of services for the Commission, members of the Commission shall be allowed travel expenses, including per diem in lieu of subsistence, in the same manner as persons employed intermittently in the Government service are allowed expenses under section 5703(b) of title 5, United States Code.

SEC. 909. SECURITY CLEARANCES FOR COMMISSION MEMBERS AND STAFF.

The appropriate executive departments and agencies shall cooperate with the Commission in expeditiously providing to the Commission members and staff appropriate security clearances in a manner consistent with existing procedures and requirements, except that no person shall be provided with access to classified information pursuant to this section who would not otherwise qualify for such security clearance.

SEC. 910. FINAL REPORT OF COMMISSION; TERMINATION.

(a) FINAL REPORT.—Not later than two years after the date of the first meeting of the Commission, the Commission shall submit to the Congress its final report, as described in section 905(2).

(b) TERMINATION.—(1) The Commission, and all the authorities of this title, shall terminate on the date which is 60 days after the date on which a final report is required to be transmitted under subsection (a).

(2) The Commission may use the 60-day period referred to in paragraph (1) for the purpose of concluding its activities, including providing testimony to committees of Congress concerning its final report and disseminating that report.

Approved April 30, 1994.

LEGISLATIVE HISTORY-H.R. 2333 (S. 1281):
HOUSE REPORTS: Nos. 103-126 (Comm. on Foreign Affairs) and 103-482 (Comm. of Conference).
SENATE REPORTS: No. 103-107 accompanying S. 1281 (Comm. on Foreign Relations).
CONGRESSIONAL RECORD:
      Vol. 139 (1993): June 15, 16, 22, considered and passed House
      Vol. 140 (1994): Jan. 25-28, 31, Feb. 1, 2, S. 1281 considered Senate;
          H.R. 2333, amended, passed in lieu.
        Apr. 28, House agreed to conference report.
        Apr. 29, Senate agreed to conference report.
WEEKLY COMPILATION OF PRESIDENTIAL DOCUMENTS, Vol. 30 (1994):
      Apr. 30, Presidential statement.

Appendix C:
Summary of Recommendations

1. The Commission recommends enactment of a statute establishing the principles on which Federal classification and declassification programs are to be based. (p. 13)

2. The Commission recommends that the Security Policy Board (SPB) implement within one year the Joint Security Commission recommendation on establishing a single set of security standards for special access programs (SAPs). The SPB, in conjunction with the Department of Defense, should examine whether the National Industrial Security Program Operating Manual Supplement should continue to allow individual SAP program managers to select the security measures for their program rather than conform to a single standard. Industrial contractors should be included in this review and in the development of a single set of standards. (p. 28)

3. The Commission recommends that agencies take several steps to enhance the proficiency of classifiers and improve their accountability by requiring additional information on the rationale for classification, by improving classification guidance, and by strengthening training and evaluation programs.

Elements of this approach should include:
- Original classifiers shall provide a detailed justification for each original classification decision;
- Derivative classifiers shall be required to identify themselves on the documents they classify;
- Classification guides shall be better developed, more definitive, and updated regularly, and industry shall participate in the preparation of guides affecting industrial programs;
- Training shall be expanded to include derivative classifiers and shall conform to minimum Executive Branch standards; and
- Proper classification of information shall be included as a critical element in the performance evaluations of *all* employees authorized to classify. (p. 34)

4. The Commission recommends that classification decisions, including the establishment of special access programs, no longer be based solely on damage to the national security. Additional factors, such as the cost of protection, vulnerability, threat, risk, value of the information, and public benefit from release, could also be considered when making classification decisions. (p. 38)

5. The Commission recommends that responsibility for classification and declassification policy development and oversight be assigned to a single Executive Branch body, designated by the President and independent of the agencies that classify. This entity should have sufficient resources and be empowered to carry out oversight of agency practices and to develop policy. Based on its oversight findings, this body would then make recommendations for policy and implementation of classification and declassification issues directly to the National Security Council. The Security Policy Board would have an opportunity to comment on these policy recommendations through the NSC process. (p. 44)

6. The Commission recommends the creation by statute of a central office—a National Declassification Center—at an existing Federal agency such as the National Archives and Records Administration to coordinate national declassification policy and activities. This Center would have the responsibility, authority, and funds sufficient to coordinate, oversee, and implement government declassification activities. The Center would monitor agency declassification programs and provide annual reports on their status to the Congress and the President. (p. 68)

7. The Commission recommends that the use of sources and methods as a basis for the continuing classification of intelligence information be clarified through issuance of an Intelligence Community directive by the Director of Central Intelligence, explaining the appropriate scope of that protection. (p. 70)

8. The Commission recommends that agencies better structure their records management and systematic declassification programs to maximize access to records that are likely to be the subject of significant public interest.

Elements of this proposal should include:
  •Complying with the dates or events for declassification, including through the use of new technologies;
  •Consolidating and regularly updating declassification guidance that is easily accessible to those authorized to declassify within the agency;
  •Prioritizing declassification according to entire record groups selected through active consultation with the public and outside scholars, and regularly informing the public of systematic review results;
  •Requiring all offices with any declassification-related activities to demonstrate that they are operating in partnership with others in the agency involved in related activities; and
  •Establishing ombudsman offices in each agency that has original classification authority or engages in declassifying records: these offices would intervene in and resolve classification and declassification issues upon request, act as a conduit for public concerns about access to records, and, where appropriate, refer issues to the agency's Inspector General. (p. 71)

9. The Commission recommends five guiding principles as the essential elements of an effective personnel security system. Most already are part of the current system (including under Executive Order 12968), but too often they are not actually practiced throughout the Federal Government. The Commission recommends that these standards be incorporated into a new statute or regulation that would supersede Executive Order 10450.

The five guiding principles are:
  •Openness and clarity of standards;
  •Balanced, "whole-person" standards;
  •Reciprocity for classified access;
  •Nondiscrimination principles; and
  •Assurances of due process. (p. 80)

10. The Commission recommends that individuals in both Government and industry holding valid clearances be able to move from one agency or special program to another without further

investigation or adjudication. The single exception to this true reciprocity of security clearances shall be that agencies may continue to require the polygraph before granting access. (p. 82)

11. The Commission recommends that current requirements for neighborhood interviews and for interviewing educational references in every investigation be eliminated. (p. 86)

12. The Commission recommends that greater balance be achieved between the initial clearance process and programs for continuing evaluation of cleared employees. (p. 87)

13. The Commission recommends that both the Congress and the Executive Branch reevaluate the requirement to utilize a new financial disclosure form and consider staying its implementation until there is further evaluation concerning how it would be used and whether its benefits exceed its costs. The Congress and the Executive Branch should review alternative approaches to improving data collection, including utilization of the expanded access to certain financial and travel records provided for under Executive Order 12968. (p. 89)

14. The Commission recommends that: (1) the director of scientific research at the Department of Defense Polygraph Institute establish a committee that includes cleared, outside scientific experts to develop a coherent research agenda on the polygraph; initiate and participate in a small grant program to stimulate independent research outside the Government; and review and comment on scientific progress and the quality of government-sponsored research in this field; and (2) independent, objective, and peer-reviewed scientific research be encouraged as the best means to assess the credibility of the polygraph as a personnel security tool and identify potential technological advances that could make the polygraph more effective in the future. (p. 91)

15. The Commission recommends revising the Computer Security Act of 1987 to reflect the realities of information systems security in the Information Age.

Some of the changes to the Act might include:
> •Moving the Computer Systems Laboratory from the National Institute of Standards and Technology to a higher visibility position within the Commerce Department, thereby increasing the likelihood of funding and personnel to support the civilian side of Government;
> •Directing agencies to set aside specific funds, perhaps as a budget line item, for information systems security training; and
> •Requiring the Office of Personnel Management to create a career path for information systems security professionals that includes network administration and computer crime investigation. (p. 104)

16. The Commission recommends developing an information systems security career path across the Government. (p. 111)

Appendix D: Biographical Information

Daniel Patrick Moynihan, Chairman. Senator Moynihan served in the cabinet or sub-cabinet of Presidents Kennedy, Johnson, Nixon, and Ford. He was Ambassador to India and Permanent Representative of the United States at the United Nations. From 1977 to 1985 he was a member of the Senate Select Committee on Intelligence, serving as Vice Chairman from 1981 to 1985. In 1986, he was awarded the Seal Medallion of the Central Intelligence Agency "In recognition of his outstanding accomplishments as . . . a leader in establishing the oversight of intelligence which was and is today in the finest spirit of bipartisan government."

Larry Combest, Vice Chairman. Congressman Combest of Lubbock, Texas served from 1988 through 1996 as a member of the U.S. House Permanent Select Committee on Intelligence. Serving as Chairman from 1994 to 1996, he was responsible for the study, "IC 21: The Intelligence Community in the 21st Century." In 1996, Mr. Combest was awarded the National Intelligence Distinguished Service Medal and the Seal Medallion of the Central Intelligence Agency. Mr. Combest holds an honorary Doctorate of Strategic Intelligence from the Joint Military College. He currently is Vice Chairman of the House Agriculture Committee and the House Small Business Committee. Mr. Combest was first elected to the U.S. House of Representatives in 1984. He also served as Legislative Assistant to the late U.S. Senator John Tower from 1971 to 1978.

John M. Deutch. Dr. Deutch is a member of the faculty of the Massachusetts Institute of Technology (M.I.T.). He served as the Director of Central Intelligence from May 1995 to December 1996 and as the Deputy Secretary of Defense from March 1994 to May 1995. He became a member of the M.I.T. faculty in 1970 and served as Chairman of the Department of Chemistry, Dean of Science, Provost, and Institute Professor. His government assignments have included Under Secretary of Defense for Acquisition and Technology and service in the Department of Energy as a Director of Energy Research, Acting Assistant of Energy Technology, and Under Secretary. He has been a member of the White House Science Council, Defense Science Board, President's Commission on Strategic Forces, the President's Foreign Intelligence Advisory Board, and the President's Nuclear Safety Oversight Committee.

Martin C. Faga. Mr. Faga is a former Director of the National Reconnaissance Office and Assistant Secretary of the Air Force for Space. Currently, he is a Senior Vice President and General Manager at the MITRE Corporation. His career includes service as a professional staff member for the Select Committee on Intelligence of the House of Representatives and later as head of its program and budget staff. He also served as an engineer at the Central Intelligence Agency for several years and as a research and development officer in the U.S. Air Force.

Alison B. Fortier. Mrs. Fortier is Director of Missile Defense Programs in the Washington Operations Office of the Space and Strategic Missiles Sector of Lockheed Martin Corporation. She is a former Special Assistant to the President and Senior Director, National Security Council Staff. She began her career in Washington as a staff member for the House Foreign

Affairs Committee. She is a member of the Board of Advisors to the Superintendent of the Naval Postgraduate School and a member of the Board of the International Republican Institute.

Richard K. Fox, Jr. Ambassador Fox was a career foreign service officer in the Department of State, serving in a variety of positions in Washington and overseas. He was Ambassador to Trinidad and Tobago from 1977 to 1979, and Senior Deputy Inspector General of the Foreign Service. He is currently Senior Vice President of Meridian International Center, and serves on the board of several foreign affairs organizations.

Lee H. Hamilton. Congressman Hamilton was first elected to the House in 1965. He is the Ranking Democratic Member of the House International Relations Committee. He is the former chairman of the International Relations Committee, the Permanent Select Committee on Intelligence, the Joint Economic Committee, the House Iran-Contra Committee, and the October Surprise Task Force. Congressman Hamilton also co-chaired the Joint Committee on the Organization of Congress.

Jesse Helms. Senator Helms has served as Chairman of the Senate Committee on Foreign Relations since 1994. He also served as Chairman of the Senate Committee on Agriculture, Nutrition and Forestry from 1985 to 1987. In addition to the Foreign Relations Committee, he currently serves on the Senate Committee on Agriculture, Nutrition and Forestry and the Committee on Rules and Administration. Senator Helms was first elected to the Senate in 1972, and previously was the Vice Chairman of the Board and Assistant Chief Executive Officer of Capital Broadcasting Company in Raleigh, North Carolina.

Ellen Hume. Ms. Hume is the Executive Director of PBS's Democracy Project. She previously served as a fellow at Northwestern University's Annenberg Washington Program and as Executive Director and Senior Fellow at Harvard University's Joan Shorenstein Barone Center on the Press, Politics and Public Policy. She was a White House and political correspondent for *The Wall Street Journal* from 1983 to 1988 and a Washington-based national reporter for *The Los Angeles Times* from 1977 to 1983. Hume appears weekly as a media critic on CNN's "Reliable Sources."

Samuel P. Huntington. Professor Huntington is Albert J. Weatherhead III University Professor at Harvard University, where he is also the Director of the John M. Olin Institute for Strategic Studies and Chairman of the Harvard Academy for International and Area Studies. He served as Coordinator of Security Planning for the National Security Council from 1977 to 1978 and was co-founder and editor of *Foreign Policy* and president of the American Political Science Association. He is the author of many books and articles on national security, military policy, and international affairs.

John D. Podesta. Mr. Podesta recently returned to the Clinton Administration as a White House Deputy Chief of Staff, after teaching as a Visiting Professor at Georgetown University Law Center. He previously served in the White House as an Assistant to the President and Staff Secretary. Before joining the Administration, he was President and General Counsel of

Podesta Associates, a government relations and public affairs firm. His Capitol Hill experience includes Chief Counsel of the Senate Agriculture Committee and Chief Minority Counsel of the Senate Subcommittee on Security and Terrorism.

Maurice Sonnenberg. Mr. Sonnenberg is a member of the President's Foreign Intelligence Advisory Board. In 1995 and 1996 he also served as the Senior Advisor to the U.S. Commission on the Roles and Capabilities of the U.S. Intelligence Community. During past Administrations he served on other commissions and boards in the field of foreign policy, international trade, and foreign investment. Currently, he is a partner and Vice-Chairman of the Advisory Board of the investment banking firm of Voily, Byorum and Partners.

Appendix E: Acknowledgments

Ours has been only the second enquiry into government secrecy ever commissioned by statute. Our one predecessor finished its work 40 years ago; another era. The Commission was accordingly much on its own; there were but a few intrepid souls who, as the old navigators might say, had been down this way before. The more, then, did we depend on the extraordinary staff that volunteered for the venture.

Eric R. Biel served as Staff Director, bringing to his interminably complex and sensitive task the finest of legal skills, combined with the legislative experience acquired on the staff of the Senate Finance Committee which the finest law schools and even the finest Washington law firms simply cannot provide. The Commission could not have produced a unanimous report without his tireless attention to detail and indefatigable pursuit of consensus.

Jacques A. Rondeau, Deputy Staff Director, brought to his complementary duties the rigor and discipline of past service as Colonel in the United States Air Force, a career pilot, with exceptional experience in international affairs, including a tour as Military Assistant to the Assistant Secretary of Defense for International Security Affairs. A distinctive feature of military affairs in the present age is the unprecedented importance of cooperation: between pilot and crew, squadron and wing, ally with ally, and not least, in a nuclear age, cooperation with adversaries. Colonel Rondeau brought these mature skills to work on the Commission's behalf, and the result is evident.

Sheryl L. Walter, General Counsel to the Commission, brought to our work the unique experience of General Counsel to the Assassination Records Review Board, the first systematic effort by the United States Government to declassify documents of great sensitivity to which, even so, the public urgently required access. She brought to the Commission a rare sense of the need to balance legitimately competing and, at times, conflicting interests—all this informed by her earlier experience within the Federal Judiciary.

Joan Vail Grimson, Counsel for Security Policy, brought to the Commission singular insights acquired in the course of her service on the Staff of the National Security Council, and later with the Office of National Drug Control Policy. She was at the heart of the policymaking process in the Executive Office of the President, with the most intimate understanding of the need for protecting as well as reducing secrecy in government.

Thomas L. Becherer brought great skill and experience gained in both the Executive and Legislative Branches to his responsibilities as the Commission staff's Research and Policy Director. In addition, in his important role as the staff's legislative liaison, he ensured close communication with key congressional staff.

The Commission's efforts were hugely strengthened by the willingness of the Departments of State and Defense, the Central Intelligence Agency, and the National Security Agency to detail senior career officials to work on the staff of the Commission. The eight individuals from these agencies and departments—Cathy A. Bowers, Carole J. Faulk, John R. Hancock, Gary H. Gower, Michael J. White, Michael D. Smith, Paul A. Stratton, and Sally H. Wallace—who served so ably as senior members of the Commission staff brought substantial experience in classification, personnel security, and related security matters and a wealth of expertise to their varied staff responsibilities. In her capacity as Administrative Officer, Carole Faulk handled all of the critical tasks necessary to keep the Commission functioning; without her efforts, it simply would not have been possible to produce this report.

In a similar vein, the success of this report was greatly dependent upon the superb work of the Commission staff's three outstanding Research Associates: Maureen Lenihan, Terence P. Szuplat, and Pauline M. Treviso. In addition to mastering the substance of numerous complex issues, the three were integral to the process of researching, writing, and producing this report. The Commission also benefited from the fine work of two staff interns: Jesse C. Watson, who worked with the Commission from June-August 1996; and Caleb H. Elfenbein, who worked with the Commission from October-December 1996. Michael G. Vogel and Cameron Burks also provided valuable help during shorter internships. Gerald Mann and Judith Thorn provided excellent editorial and proofreading assistance during preparation of the final report.

Robert A. Katzmann of the Brookings Institution and the Georgetown University Law Center aided the Commission by acting "of counsel" on a pro bono basis. He contributed immeasurably to our understanding of the American experience of regulation and of the Administrative Procedure Act, subjects at the heart of our theoretical analysis. His quiet wisdom, indeed his general calm, more than once kept our proceedings from mayhem.

Genie M. Norris, Deputy Assistant Secretary of State for Operations, promptly took the Commission in from the cold, providing offices in a wing of the State Department complex on Navy Hill, possibly the most beautiful public square in Washington. This, of course, is a secret of sorts, for the public is not allowed in. A further secret, here revealed for the first time, is that the Commission occupied space where the Central Intelligence Agency had begun its work in the late 1940s. Students of organizational behavior will note that relations with the Department of State were never quite the same once the Agency crossed the river and acquired a building, now buildings, of its own. Students of this Commission, if there should be any, will record that the work could never have been finished save for the indomitable good cheer and great help of Ms. Norris and her colleagues at the Department of State, several of whom are cited below.

The Commissioners and Commission staff benefited greatly over the past two years from exceptional assistance provided by numerous individuals with expertise covering a wide range of areas. In addition to those who took the time to meet with us and are listed in Appendix F, the Commission wishes to recognize the individuals listed below. This report would not have been possible without their generous willingness to devote considerable time and energy to a variety of important tasks on our behalf.

The Commission acknowledges with gratitude the help of those who reviewed and evaluated portions of earlier drafts of the report: Maynard C. Anderson, James J. Bagley, Roger P. Denk, Steven L. Katz, Ronald Knecht, F. Lynn McNulty, Peter R. Nelson, John D. Tippit, N. McDonnell Ulsch, David E. Whitman, Ira S. Winkler, and others who requested anonymity. The Commission is also deeply grateful to Idris Rhea Traylor of Texas Tech University, who read and commented on an earlier draft. Their assistance was extremely helpful; at the same time, we emphasize that they should bear no responsibility for the content of this report.

The Commission worked closely throughout its tenure with the following individuals, who served as the primary points of contact with individual Commissioners: Michael J. Lostumbo, Joshua A. Brook, and Eleanor Ann Suntum of Senator Moynihan's staff, who aided greatly in the preparation of the Chairman's Foreword and the history, *Secrecy: A Brief Account of the American*

Experience; Louis H. Dupart, Senior Counsel to the House Permanent Select Committee on Intelligence, and Lynn E. Cowart of Vice Chairman Combest's office; Admiral James W. Nance, Patricia A. McNerney, Christopher J. Walker, and Thomas J. Callahan of the Senate Foreign Relations Committee staff; David A. Weiner of the House International Relations Committee staff; Richard L. Haver and Ronald D. Lee of the Central Intelligence Agency; Gloria J. Carrier of MITRE Corporation; Mary E. Abdellah of PBS Corporation; Carol J. Edwards of The Olin Institute at Harvard University; and Monica Francesco and Hannah H. Lee of Commissioner Sonnenberg's office. We also wish to thank Thomas G. Moore for assisting in the preparation of the Vice Chairman's Foreword.

As noted above, from the inception of its operations the Commission maintained a close working relationship with the Department of State. Under arrangements developed during consideration of the Commission's authorizing legislation in 1994, the Department provided the Commission with office space and supplied it with equipment. During the first several months of the Commission's operations, the Department of State provided several excellent professionals who assisted with secretarial and other administrative duties: Althea Castellano, Karen D. Smith, Deborah Seals, and Mary L. Lark. In addition to Deputy Assistant Secretary Norris, the Commission also benefited from the interest and support of senior Department officials and their staffs, including: Acting Under Secretary for Management and former Assistant Secretary for Administration Patrick K. Kennedy, and former Under Secretary for Management Richard M. Moose; Assistant Secretary for Diplomatic Security Eric J. Boswell, and his predecessor, Anthony C.E. Quainton, currently Director General of the Foreign Service; and Department Historian William Z. Slany.

We also thank Mark M. Stafford and Sarah C. Brennan in the Department's Publishing Services for their work in designing the cover of this report. The Commission also was aided by numerous officials in the following State Department organizations: the Publishing Services Group, the Bureau of Public Affairs, Office of the Legal Adviser, Bureau of Intelligence and Research, Bureau of Finance and Management Policy, and the Department's Library staff. In particular, James L. Millette of the Bureau of Finance and Management Policy provided invaluable assistance on budgetary matters. Finally, Thomas J. Low, Fred W. Albertson, Jr., John J. O'Brien, and Casimir L. Garczynski of the Contingency Group, who worked adjacent to the Commission offices, regularly provided much-needed help with the office computers and other equipment; their emergency assistance frequently was vital to keeping the Commission's day-to-day operations functioning, and the Commission staff is very grateful. In addition, the staff of the Agency Liaison Division of the General Services Administration, under the direction of Calvin R. Snowden, also assisted the Commission throughout its operations, including on budget and personnel matters. We wish to thank Fred Porter and Edna Span in particular for their help.

The Commission benefited greatly from the input received from the industry representatives with whom the Commission staff met on an individual company basis, as well as those who attended the Commission's Industry Roundtables in March 1996 at E-Systems, Inc. in Garland, Texas and April 1996 at Loral Federal Systems in Gaithersburg, Maryland. We would especially like to thank John E. Puckett and his colleagues at E-Systems and Chris Murray, Peter Grau, and their colleagues at Loral for hosting the two Roundtable programs, and Gregory A. Gwash and Joseph R. DeGregorio of the Defense Investigative Service for their assistance with the industry meetings. The Commission is also grateful for the active participation of the historians, scientists, journalists, present and former agency officials, and others who attended its May 1996 Public Access Roundtable at the National Archives and Records Administration in Washington. Elizabeth A. Pugh, Miriam M. Nisbet, Pat El-Ashry, and Thomas Nastick of the Archives provided valuable assistance in planning that program. Howard Gaidsieck, Phyllis Smith, Joseph Flood, and Delores Colbert of the State Department's Customer Service Division provided technical support for the Commission Roundtables, as well as in connection with earlier drafts of this report.

The Commission also thanks all of the individuals in other agencies and departments, Congress, industry, public interest organizations, journalism, and academia who arranged and participated in the numerous Commission meetings listed in Appendix F and also responded to our frequent requests for information. We would like to single out James R. Oliver, Robert J. Hallman, Claudia C. Collins, Alison E. Bolt, and Jeffrey A. Rank for their exceptional support. We also appreciate the willingness of Steven Garfinkel, Laura L.S. Kimberly, and the staff of the Information Security Oversight Office and Peter D. Saderholm, Dan L. Jacobson, and the staff of the Security Policy Board to keep the Commission staff closely informed of a broad range of information management and security policy matters. Harold C. Relyea of the Congressional Research Service, a leading scholar on government secrecy, was a great source of information on security classification and related issues. David G. Major regularly shared his extensive understanding of the history of counterintelligence and other security matters. John Earl Haynes from the Library of Congress' Manuscript Division, Robert Louis Benson of the National Security Agency, and Michael Warner of the Central Intelligence Agency each provided extremely helpful historical information on several occasions. Christopher D. Glyn-Jones and Stephanie Daman from the British Embassy in Washington regularly informed the Commission staff of pertinent developments. Finally, members of the staffs of the Joint Committee on Printing, Committee on Rules and Administration of the Senate, and Committee on House Oversight of the House of Representatives worked to ensure that funds would be available for the printing of this report.

To all of the individuals listed above, and any others whose important contributions we may have failed to mention, the Commission is profoundly grateful.

Appendix F: List of Commission Meetings and Programs

I. Formal Meetings and Programs of the Commission

January 10, 1995
    First Meeting of the Commission, U.S. Capitol, Room S-116
    Election of Chairman and Vice Chairman and Commissioner introductions

March 30, 1995
    Second Meeting of the Commission, U.S. Capitol, Room S-116
    Commissioners are sworn in by Mr. Calvin R. Snowden, U.S. General
    Services Administration; Speakers: Mr. Steven Garfinkel, Director,
    Information Security Oversight Office; and Mr. Jeffrey H. Smith, Partner,
    Arnold and Porter, and Chairman of the Joint Security Commission

May 17, 1995
    Third Meeting of the Commission, U.S. Capitol, Room S-116
    Speakers: Ms. Regina Genton, Director of Intelligence Programs,
    National Security Council; Mr. Steven Garfinkel, Director, Information
    Security Oversight Office; Dr. John Earl Haynes, Library of Congress;
    and Dr. Harvey Klehr, Emory University

June 20, 1995
    Fourth Meeting of the Commission, U.S. Capitol, Room S-116
    Speakers: The Honorable John W. Carlin, Archivist of the United States,
    National Archives and Records Administration, accompanied by other
    senior Archives officials; and Dr. Harold C. Relyea, Specialist, American
    National Government, Congressional Research Service, Library of
    Congress

July 27, 1995
    Fifth Meeting of the Commission, Dirksen Senate Office Building, Room
    SD-215
    Speakers: Mr. Edward J. Appel, National Security Council; Mr. Gerald A.
    Schroeder, Department of Justice; Mr. Eric Biel, Commission Staff
    Director; and Mr. Jacques Rondeau, Commission Deputy Staff Director

October 19, 1995
    Sixth Meeting of the Commission, U.S. Capitol, Room HC-4
    Presentation by Commission Staff

December 6, 1995
    Seventh Meeting of the Commission, U.S. Capitol, Room S-116
    Speaker: Mr. Peter D. Saderholm, Staff Director, U.S. Security Policy
    Board

March 15, 1996
    Industry Roundtable at E-Systems, Inc., Garland, TX
    Chairman Moynihan and Commissioners Faga, Podesta, and Sonnenberg
    in attendance
    Discussion Facilitators: Mr. John Hancock, Commission Senior
    Professional Staff Member; Mr. James Van Houten, Vice President for
    Security, Rockwell International Corporation; Mr. Kerry Redlin,
    Information Systems Security Specialist, Lockheed Martin Tactical

	Aircraft Systems; and Mr. David Kendrick, Manager of Defense Industrial Security Programs, E-Systems, Inc.
April 18, 1996	Industry Roundtable at Loral Federal Systems, Gaithersburg, MD Commissioners Podesta and Sonnenberg in attendance Discussion Facilitators: Ms. Shirley J. Krieger, Director of Support Services, Honeywell Space Systems Group; Mr. Daniel J. Ryan, Vice President, Science Applications International Corporation; and Mr. Marshall C. Sanders, Security Manager, TASC Systems Division
May 16, 1996	Public Access Roundtable, National Archives and Records Administration, Washington, DC Chairman Moynihan and Commissioners Deutch, Faga, Fortier, Fox, Hamilton, Hume, Huntington, Podesta, and Sonnenberg in attendance Panelists: Mr. Terry Anderson, journalist and former hostage in Lebanon; Dr. Alexander DiVolpi, Argonne National Laboratory; Mr. David G. Major, Aegis Research Corporation; Mr. Paul McMasters, The Freedom Forum; Mr. Morton Halperin, Council on Foreign Relations; Dr. Anna Kasten Nelson, Assassination Records Review Board; Mr. Tom Blanton, The National Security Archive; and Mr. David Bearman, Archives and Museum Informatics
July 12, 1996	Eighth Meeting of the Commission, Library of Congress, Members Room Discussion of draft staff findings and recommendations
November 19, 1996	Ninth Meeting of the Commission, U.S. Capitol, Room S-116 Discussion of Draft Report
December 12, 1996	Tenth Meeting of the Commission, U.S. Capitol, Room S-116 Discussion of Revised Draft Report

II. Commissioner Activities and Presentations

July 11, 1995	Chairman Moynihan delivers remarks at ceremony commemorating "VENONA: Soviet Espionage Against the U.S. Atomic Energy Program," Central Intelligence Agency
August 9, 1995	Commissioner Podesta and Commission staff visit the National Security Agency
August 29, 1995	Commissioner Sonnenberg and Commission staff visit the Federal Bureau of Investigation
October 12, 1995	Commissioners Hume and Fortier and Commission staff visit the U.S. Atlantic Command, Norfolk, VA
October 13, 1995	Commissioner Fortier and Commission staff visit the Department of Defense Security Institute, Richmond, VA

November 7, 1995   Vice Chairman Combest addresses the Open Source Solutions Conference, Washington, DC

November 28, 1995   Commissioner Faga addresses the National Security Industrial Association, Crystal City, VA

November 29, 1995   Commissioner Fortier and Commission staff meet with representatives of six major industrial associations: National Security Industrial Association, American Society for Industrial Security, National Classification Management Society, Aerospace Industries Association, Contractor SAP/SAR Working Group, and Industrial Security Working Group, Rockwell, Arlington, VA

December 13-14, 1995   Commissioner Hume and Commission staff visit the Lewisburg Federal Penitentiary, Lewisburg, PA, for interview with convicted spy Ronald Pelton, and the Allenwood Federal Correctional Facility, Allenwood, PA, for interview with convicted spy Michael Walker

January 26, 1996   Commissioner Hamilton interviewed by Lesley Stahl, *60 Minutes*, concerning secrecy issues

February 15, 1996   Commissioner Faga addresses the American Bar Association Standing Committee on Law and National Security breakfast, Washington, DC

February 15, 1996   Chairman Moynihan and Commissioners Faga, Hume, and Sonnenberg meet with Central Intelligence Agency officials and National Reconnaissance Office officials at the Department of State

March 4, 1996   Chairman Moynihan addresses the Department of State's Open Forum on "Protecting and Reducing Government Secrecy in the Information Age"

March 14, 1996   Chairman Moynihan, Commissioners Faga and Sonnenberg, and Commission staff visit Texas Instruments, Dallas, TX

March 15, 1996   Commissioners Faga and Podesta and Commission staff visit EDS (Electronic Data Systems), Plano, TX

April 10, 1996   Commissioners Hume and Sonnenberg and Commission staff visit the National Security Agency and meet with Director Lt. Gen. Kenneth Minihan (USAF) and Deputy Director William Crowell

April 12, 1996   Chairman Moynihan and Commission staff visit the National Security Agency, meet with Director Lt. Gen. Minihan (USAF) and Deputy Director Crowell, and tour the National Cryptologic Museum

April 18, 1996   Vice Chairman Combest addresses the Seventh Annual National Operations Security Conference, McLean, VA

May 28, 1996   Commissioners Fortier, Hume, and Podesta and Commission staff visit the National Security Agency and meet with Deputy Director William Crowell

July 9, 1996   Commissioner Podesta addresses the National Classification Management Society Annual Training Seminar, Baltimore, MD

August 19, 1996   Commissioner Fortier and Commission staff meet with Ambassador James Collins, Department of State

September 9, 1996   Commissioner Faga addresses the American Society of Industrial Security (ASIS) Annual Seminar, Atlanta, GA

September 10, 1996   Commissioner Fortier addresses the Seventh Annual Department of Defense Security Conference, Rockville, MD

September 13, 1996   Commissioner Podesta addresses the Center for the Study of Intelligence Conference, "The State of the Intelligence Community's Historical Declassification Program," National War College, Ft. McNair, Washington, DC

September 13, 1996   Chairman Moynihan addresses the American Society of Newspaper Editors luncheon, Arlington, VA

October 3-4, 1996   Chairman Moynihan delivers opening and closing remarks at the VENONA Conference, National War College, Ft. McNair, Washington, DC

November 20, 1996   Commissioner Fortier addresses the Contractor SAP/SAR Working Group at Lockheed Martin, Sunnyvale, CA

December 12, 1996   Commissioner Podesta addresses the American Society of Access Professionals' Conference on the 30th Anniversary of the Freedom of Information Act, Rockville, MD

III. Commission Staff Activities/Presentations

September 12, 1995   U.S. Central Command, Tampa, FL

September 13, 1995   U.S. Special Operations Command, Tampa, FL

September 14, 1995   American Society of Access Professionals Freedom of Information Act Symposium, Rockville, MD

October 25, 1995   National Policy Forum, "American Competitiveness in the Information Age," Washington, DC

October 31– November 2, 1995	Presentation by John Hancock to the Contractor SAP/SAR and Industrial Security Working Group Conference, Sunnyvale, CA
November 6, 1995	National Military Intelligence Association Seminar, Washington, DC
November 7-9, 1995	Open Source Solutions Conference, Washington, DC
November 8, 1995	Presentation to the Information Warfare course at the National Defense University, Ft. McNair, Washington, DC
December 14, 1995	"Implications of Information Technology for U.S. National Security and Foreign Economic Policy," Conference at Ft. McNair, Washington, DC
December 15, 1995	John F. Kennedy Presidential Library, Boston, MA
January 4, 1996	Carter Presidential Library, Atlanta, GA
January 5, 1996	American Historical Association Conference, Atlanta, GA
January 17, 1996	National Archives and Records Administration and the Department of Energy meeting with historians and public interest representatives on declassification of DoE records, National Archives and Records Administration, Washington, DC
February 5-6, 1996	Personnel Security Research and Education Center (PERSEREC), Monterey, CA
February 23, 1996	Department of Defense Historical Records Declassification Advisory Panel Meeting, National Archives and Records Administration, Washington, DC
March 7, 1996	Presentation by Sheryl Walter to the American Society of Access Professionals Regional FOIA Symposium, Denver, CO
March 13, 1996	Presentation by Eric Biel and John Hancock to the Industrial Security Working Group conference, Fairfax, VA
March 19, 1996	Presentation by Eric Biel to the Library of Congress/Congressional Research Service conference, Washington, DC
April 1, 1996	Presentation by Eric Biel to the National Security Institute Conference, Reston, VA
April 18, 1996	Seventh Annual Operations Security Conference, McLean, VA
May 10, 1996	Department of Defense Historical Records Declassification Advisory Panel Meeting, National Archives and Records Administration, Washington, DC

May 21-23, 1996	Second Annual Intelligence Community Information and Classification Management Conference, McLean, VA
May 22, 1996	Presentation by Sheryl Walter to the Second Annual Intelligence Community Information and Classification Management Conference, McLean, VA
May 23, 1996	Presentation by Michael Smith to the Second Annual Intelligence Community Information and Classification Management Conference, McLean, VA
May 23, 1996	Presentation by Eric Biel and John Hancock to the Non-NFIB Security Officers Conference, Tysons Corner, VA
June 6, 1996	Presentation by Eric Biel and Sheryl Walter to the Department of State's Advisory Committee on Historical Diplomatic Documentation
June 25, 1996	Presentation by Eric Biel to Personnel Security Research and Education Center (PERSEREC) conference, "Vision 2021," McLean, VA
June 25-26, 1996	Personnel Security Research and Education Center (PERSEREC) conference, "Vision 2021," McLean, VA
July 2, 1996	U.S. Army Center for Lessons Learned, Fort Leavenworth, KS
July 17, 1996	Presentation by Jacques Rondeau to the Computer Security Program Managers' Forum, National Institute of Standards and Technology, Potomac, MD
July 23-25, 1996	Controlled Access Program Oversight Committee (CAPOC) conference on the Future of SCI Control Systems, Williamsburg, VA
July 24, 1996	Department of Energy's Openness Advisory Panel, Washington, DC
August 9, 1996	Department of Defense Historical Records Declassification Advisory Panel Meeting, National Archives and Records Administration, Washington, DC
August 31, 1996	Paper by Sheryl Walter presented to the American Society of American Archivists Annual Meeting, San Diego, CA
September 13, 1996	Center for the Study of Intelligence Conference, "The State of the Intelligence Community's Historical Declassification Program," Ft. McNair, Washington, DC
September 16-18, 1996	Open Source Solutions Conference, Reston, VA
September 18, 1996	Presentation by Eric Biel to the Open Source Solutions conference, Reston, VA

October 9, 1996	Presentation by Eric Biel and Sheryl Walter to the Center for International Policy Seminar on Intelligence Reform, Washington, DC
October 14-16, 1996	"An Overview of Critical Counterintelligence Issues for CIA Managers," training conference sponsored by the Counterintelligence Center
October 22-25, 1996	Information Security Conference, Baltimore, MD
November 13, 1996	Presentation by Eric Biel to the American Society of Industrial Security DC Chapter Security Seminar, Ft. McNair, Washington, DC
November 15, 1996	Department of Defense Historical Review Declassification Advisory Panel Meeting, Defense Advanced Research Projects Agency, Washington, DC
November 20, 1996	Presentation by Eric Biel to the Foreign Service Institute Political Training Seminar, Arlington, VA
December 3, 1996	Department of Energy's Openness Advisory Panel Meeting, Washington, DC
December 5, 1996	Presentation by Sheryl Walter to the United States Information Agency Declassification Conference, Washington, DC
December 13, 1996	American Society of Access Professionals Conference on the 30th Anniversary of the Freedom of Information Act, Rockville, MD
January 3, 1997	Presentation by Sheryl Walter to the American Historical Association Annual Meeting (joint panel with the Society of Historians of American Foreign Relations), New York, NY

IV. Commission Staff Meetings

Listed below are the individuals with whom the Commission staff met during the course of its investigation (beginning in June 1995). Where the staff met with several officials from an agency or other organization (in some cases, on more than one occasion), only that agency/organization name is provided; the individuals who participated in the meeting are not listed separately. In some cases, components of a particular department or agency are listed separately (for example, the National Photographic Interpretation Center is listed separately from the Central Intelligence Agency). Finally, several individuals with whom the staff met requested that their names not be listed here. The Commission appreciates their assistance and honors their requests to remain anonymous for purposes of this report.

Agencies/Organizations
Aegis Corporation
Aerospace Industries Association
Air National Guard
American Historical Association

Assassination Records Review Board
BDM International
British Security Service
BTG, Inc.
Carter Center, Jimmy Carter Library
Center for Cryptologic History
Center for Democracy and Technology
Center for International Policy
Center for National Security Studies
Central Imagery Office
Central Intelligence Agency
Coca-Cola Company
Community Management Staff
Computer Sciences Corporation
Congressional Research Service
Customs Service
Declassification Productivity Research Center
Defense Information Systems Agency
Defense Intelligence Agency
Defense Investigative Service
Department of Defense
Department of Defense Gulf War Declassification Project
Department of Defense Historical Records Declassification Advisory Panel
Department of Defense Joint Staff
Department of Defense Personnel Security Research Center
Department of Defense POW/MIA Office
Department of Defense Security Institute
Department of Energy
Department of Justice
Department of State
Department of State Historical Advisory Committee
Department of the Air Force
Department of the Army
Department of the Navy
Department of the Treasury
Drug Enforcement Administration
E-Systems, Inc.
Embassy of Australia
Embassy of Canada
Embassy of the United Kingdom
Federal Aviation Administration
Federal Bureau of Investigation
Federal Communications Commission
Federation of American Scientists
Foreign Broadcast Information Service
Freedom Forum
General Research Corporation
House Government Reform and Oversight Committee Staff
House National Security, International Affairs, and Criminal Justice Subcommittee Staff

House Permanent Select Committee on Intelligence Staff
Information Minister of Canada
Information Security Oversight Office
Internal Revenue Service
Jaycor
John F. Kennedy Presidential Library
Kroll Associates
Lockheed Martin Corporation
Loral Federal Systems
MITRE Corporation
National Archives and Records Administration
National Computer Security Center
National Coordinating Committee for the Promotion of History
National Counterintelligence Center
National Cryptologic Museum
National Defense University
National Institute of Standards and Technology
National Intelligence Council
National Photographic Interpretation Center
National Reconnaissance Office
National Security Agency
National Security Archive
National Security Council Staff
National Treasury Employees' Union
Natural Resources Defense Council
Office of Management and Budget
Office of National Drug Control Policy
Planning Research Corporation
PRB Associates
President's Foreign Intelligence Advisory Board Staff
Rockwell International
Science Applications International Corporation
Security Division, U.K. Cabinet Office
Senate Committee on the Judiciary Staff
Senate Select Committee on Intelligence Staff
Society of American Archivists
The Analytic Sciences Corporation (TASC)
Treasury Board Secretariat, Government of Canada
U.S. Army Center for Lessons Learned
U.S. Bureau of Prisons
U.S. Security Policy Board Staff
Washington National Records Center
Wang Corporation

Individuals

Aftergood, Steven
Alger, John
Anderson, Maynard
Anderson, Terry
Andrew, Christopher
Ansley, Norm
Appel, Edward
Armstrong, Scott
Bagley, James
Baker, James
Banks, Brenda
Barnes, Judith
Barron, James
Battaglia, Charles
Bearman, David
Becker, Irv
Beers, Randy
Bellinger, Jon
Berman, Jerry
Blanton, Tom
Bok, Sissela
Bolt, Alison
Bond, James
Boorstin, Robert
Boswell, Eric
Broad, Earnest
Brown, Eileen
Bruce, Jim
Capps, Michael
Caputo, Andrew
Castillo, Joseph
Cavanaugh, James
Chambers, Marian
Chance, Velecia
Choate, Sandra
Christy, James
Cohen, Edmund
Cohen, Sheldon
Collins, Claudia
Collins, Amb. James
Cook, Blanche Wiesen
Cooney, Manus
Crawford, Kent
Crowell, William
Dalinsky, Barry
Daman, Stephanie
Davenport, Dewayne
David, James

Davidson, William
Davis, Fletcher
Davis-Harding, Rene
Deer, Tim
DeGraffenreid, Kenneth
Deitering, Randy
Dempsey, James
Dempsey, Joan
Denk, Roger
Dietrich, Lt. Col. Steve
Disher, Susan
DiVolpi, Alexander
Donahue, Arnold
Donlan, Matt
Dougherty, Martin
Doyle, Kate
Dreyfuss, Robert
Eberstadt, Nicholas
Eldridge, Joseph
Elliff, John
Engel, Lee
Epstein, Richard
Ermarth, Fritz
Falcon, Lee
Fawcett, Stephanie
Ferroggiarro, Will
Ferrone, John
Fogarty, Thomas
Forbes, Marjorie
Forbes, Suzanne
Fradel, Jim
Freeman, Bennett
Frields, John
Fuqua, Don
Gaddis, John Lewis
Garfinkel, Steven
Gasiewicz, Philip
Geiger, William
Gelbar, Daniel
Gelbard, Amb. Robert
Genton, Regina
Glyn-Jones, Christopher
Goldberg, Don
Goldberg, Stanley
Goldman, Janlori
Goodman, Mel
Grafeld, Peggy
Green, Harold
Gries, David

Gualtieri, Roberto
Guttman, Daniel
Haag, David
Hadley, Steven
Hallman, Robert
Halperin, Morton
Hammit, Harry
Hanlon, Kathy
Harris, Gary
Harris, Jeffrey
Hastings, James
Haugh, LeRoy
Haynes, John Earl
Hayward, Robert
Hershberg, James
Heusser, Roger
Hibler, Neil
Hickman, Stan
Hickock, Gene
Hill, Jimmie
Hitz, Frederick
Honts, Charles
Howe, Larry
Howell, Beryl
Huff, Dick
Huffstetler, Robert
Huffman, Linda
Irving, Peggy
Jacobson, Dan
Jelen, George
Johnson, Deborah
Kaiser, Frederick
Kanin, David
Kastenmeier, Robert
Katz, Steven
Katzke, Stuart
Katzmann, Robert
Keene, David
Kimball, Warren
Kimberly, Laura
King, Bob
Kingsley, Don
Kloss, Cynthia
Knauf, Daniel
Knecht, Ronald
Koh, Harold
Kohn, Richard
Kornbluh, Peter
Kostelnik, Maj. Gen. Michael (USAF)

Kotapish, William
Krofteck, Joseph
Kurtz, Michael
Kvetkas, Jr., William
Lafferty, John
Lamoureux, Bernard
Langbart, David
Lapham, Anthony
Lattanza, Richard
Leadbeater, J. Alan
Lee, William
Leonard, Michael
Levin, Michael
Levine, Ed
Light, Paul
Lilly, Jacqui
Lipscomb, Thomas
Locher, Jim
Machak, Frank
Major, David
Mark, Edward
Marshall, Mary
Martin, Kate
Matano, Albert
May, Ernest
Mazer, Roslyn
McDonald, Kenneth
McFadden, Maj. Gen. George (USA, ret.)
McMasters, Paul
McMenamin, Robert
McMillan, Priscilla
McNulty, F. Lynn
Mead, Walter Russell
Mellon, Christopher
Metcalfe, Dan
Michaelson, Avra
Miller, Page Putnam
Moore, Brig. Gen. William (USAF)
Moore, John Norton
Moose, Richard
Morrell, Jim
Mountcastle, Brig. Gen. John (USA)
Mulvey, Mark
Munson, Margaret
Murray, Pat
Myer, Daniel
Narath, Al
Nelson, Anna Kasten
Nelson, Peter

Neu, Richard

Newberger, Stuart

Nisbet, Miriam

Norris, Genie

Nye, Joseph

Odom, Lt. Gen. William (USA, ret.)

Oettinger, Anthony

Oleson, Peter

Oliver, James

Otey, Glen

Page, Cary

Parra, Joseph

Passarelli, James

Pastor, Robert

Pendlebury, David

Pescatore, John

Pitcher, Sadie

Pitts, William

Plesser, Ronald

Porteg, Steve

Quist, Arvin

Rademaker, Stephen

Rank, Jeffrey

Ray, Gerda

Rees, Richard

Reicher, Dan

Relyea, Harold

Rhenish, Barbara

Riccardi, Col. Frederick (USAF)

Richelson, Jeffrey

Rigamer, Elmore

Rogalski, Robert

Ronan, Mary

Rosen, Col. Rick (USAF)

Rosenau, Bill

Rossman, Kenneth

Rowen, Henry

Ryan, Daniel

Saderholm, Peter

Sanford, Bruce

Scalingi, Paula

Schauble, Jeanne

Schecter, Jerry

Schecter, Leona

Schewe, Donald

Schmidt, Raymond

Schroeder, Gerald

Schwartau, Winn

Scott, R. Adm. Hugh (USN, ret.)

Sessoms, Gayla

Sheehy, Michael

Siebert, Bryan

Simonton, Andrea

Skaggs, Congressman David

Slany, William

Smith, Jeffrey

Smith, Col. Linda (USAF)

Snider, Britt

Spaulding, Mark

Spaulding, Suzanne

Springer, Edward

Steele, Robert

Steinauer, Dennis

Stern, Gary

Stern, Todd

Stewart, Nina

Stovel, Ferris

Straub, Christopher

Studeman, Adm. William (USN, ret.)

Swietlik, Craig

Thomas, Maj. Gen. Jack (USAF, ret.)

Timm, Howard

Tippit, John

Tompkins, Frederick

Torous, Becky

Treverton, Gregory

Truchon, Pamela

Trulock, Notra

Turley, Jonathan

Turner, Robert

Ulsch, N. McDonnell

Uncapher, Mark

Van Camp, Anne

Varey, James

Waguespack, Michael

Walker, Frederick

Walsh, John

Wampler, Robert

Warshaw, Richard

Watson, Peter

Webster, Mark

Weinberg, Gerhard

Weiner, Tim

Wells, Linton

Wendt, James

White, Amb. Robert

Whitman, David

Williams, Richard

Wilson, Charles
Winer, Jonathan
Winkler, Ira
Winston, Joan
Wood, Lt. Gen. C. Norman (USAF, ret.)
Woolsey, R. James
Zubok, Vladislav
Zuckerman, Michael

Appendix G:
Major Reviews of the U.S. Secrecy System

The following provides a summary of key studies on classification, declassification, and personnel security. This summary does not include numerous other studies that have indirectly addressed these issues in the course of more broad-based examinations of Federal information policies, or studies, such as those of the General Accounting Office, that have been more limited in their scope. Nor does it include the annual reports of the Information Security Oversight Office, which have, on occasion, put forth detailed recommendations for reform to classification practices.

Coolidge Committee - 1956

Created by Secretary of Defense Charles Wilson to investigate how to prevent future leaks of classified information, the Defense Department Committee on Classified Information undertook a three-month review of DoD classification practices and policies. The Committee, composed of representatives from the military services and chaired by former Assistant Secretary of Defense Charles Coolidge, declared the classification system "sound in concept," but also found that vague classification standards and the failure to punish overclassification had caused overclassification to reach "serious proportions" and had resulted in diminishing public confidence in the classification system. Among the recommendations included in its November 8, 1956 report were: addressing overclassification from the top down, beginning with the Secretary of Defense; creating a Director for Declassification within the Office of the Secretary of Defense; and reducing the number of "Top Secret" original classifiers.

Wright Commission - 1957

The bipartisan Commission on Government Security, chaired by former American Bar Association President Loyd Wright, was the only previous Congressionally mandated review of the security system. The Commission held no public hearings, produced no press releases, and made no public statements during its eighteen-month study. In its June 23, 1957 report, the Commission stressed "the danger to national security that arises out of overclassification." Its recommendations included: abolition of the "Confidential" level and corresponding security checks; restricting original classification authority to agencies already possessing it and limiting that authority to the agency heads; improvement of classification training for those with such authority; creation of a Central Security Office to review the management of the security system and to make recommendations for change when necessary; and legislation criminalizing the unauthorized disclosure of classified information, including by the press.

Moss Subcommittee - 1958

Although the efforts of the Special Government Information Subcommittee of the House Government Operations Committee spanned two decades, its early work under Chairman John Moss (including scores of hearings and over two dozen interim reports) was especially significant. Created in 1955, the Subcommittee began its efforts with a two-year examination of Federal classification policies, focusing in particular on the Defense Department. In its first report, issued on June 16, 1958, the Subcommittee attributed overclassification at DoD in large part to the lack of punishment for *over*classification but not for *under*classification. Citing the "loss of public confidence" when information is withheld "for any other reason than true military security," it recommended: procedures for independent review of complaints about overclassification; mandatory marking of each classified document with the future date or event after which it is to be reviewed or automatically downgraded or declassified; establishment of a date by which the DoD would declassify classified material accumulating in agency files, with a "minimum of exceptions;" and disciplinary action against those who overclassify.

Seitz Task Force - 1970

The Department of Defense Science Board's Task Force on Secrecy was prompted by DoD concerns over the effectiveness of its security measures. The Task Force, chaired by Dr. Frederick Seitz, found that DoD's classification system required "major surgery" and noted negative aspects of classification such as its cost, "uncertainty in the public mind on policy issues," and impediments to the free flow of information. Chief among its conclusions was that "perhaps 90 percent" of all classification of technical and scientific information could be eliminated. The July 1, 1970 report of the Task Force included the following recommendations: a maximum duration of five years for classification of scientific and technological information, with few exceptions; overhauling classification guides by considering the benefits to technological development that would result from greater public access to information; and review and declassification of classified DoD materials within two years.

Stilwell Commission - 1985

Established by Secretary of Defense Caspar Weinberger to identify "systemic vulnerabilities," the Commission to Review DoD Security Policies and Practices found that "little scrutiny" was given decisions to classify. The Commission, chaired by Gen. Richard Stilwell (Ret.), concluded that shortcomings in the classification management arena were "primarily a matter of inadequate implementation of existing policy, rather than a matter of deficient policy." Among the recommendations included in its report, issued on November 19, 1985, were the following: banning the retention of classified documents for more than five years unless the documents are "permanently valuable;" further reduction in the number of original classifiers; a one-time review and revalidation of all DoD Special Access Programs; minimum security standards for all DoD Special Access Programs; and placement of security responsibilities within a single staff element of DoD.

Joint Security Commission - 1994

Tasked by Secretary of Defense William Perry and Director of Central Intelligence R. James Woolsey with developing a new approach to security, the Joint Security Commission engaged in a nine-month review. Finding that the system had reached "unacceptable levels of inefficiency, inequity, and cost," the Commission's February 1994 report, *Redefining Security*, included the following recommendations: a "one-level classification system with two degrees of [physical] protection;" establishing a Joint Security Executive Committee to oversee the development of policies in its new system; use of a "risk management" philosophy when developing new security policies; and a single, consolidated policy and set of security standards for special access programs and sensitive compartmented information.

Appendix H: Acronyms and Abbreviations

AEA	Atomic Energy Act
AIA	Aerospace Industries Association
CAPOC	Controlled Access Program Oversight Committee
CIA	Central Intelligence Agency
DARPA	Defense Advanced Research Projects Agency
DCI	Director of Central Intelligence
DES	Data Encryption Standard
DIA	Defense Intelligence Agency
DIS	Defense Investigative Service
DoD	Department of Defense
DoDPI	Department of Defense Polygraph Institute
DoE	Department of Energy
EAP	Employee Assistance Program
EFOIA	Electronic Freedom of Information Act
FBI	Federal Bureau of Investigation
FOIA	Freedom of Information Act
FRD	Formerly Restricted Data
GAO	General Accounting Office
GII	Global Information Infrastructure
HUMINT	Human Intelligence
IMINT	Imagery Intelligence
ISOO	Information Security Oversight Office
ISPAC	Interagency Security Policy Advisory Council
JCS	Joint Chiefs of Staff
JSC	Joint Security Commission
MASINT	Measurement and Signature Intelligence
MASS	Military Applicant Screening System
NAC	National Agency Check
NACI	National Agency Check with Inquiries
NII	National Information Infrastructure
NISP	National Industrial Security Program
NISPOM	National Industrial Security Program Operating Manual
NIST	National Institute of Standards and Technology
NPR	National Performance Review
NRO	National Reconnaissance Office
NSA	National Security Agency
NSC	National Security Council
NSD	National Security Directive
OADR	Originating Agency's Determination Required
OCA	Original Classification Authority
OMB	Office of Management and Budget
OPM	Office of Personnel Management
OSD	Office of the Secretary of Defense
OSS	Office of Strategic Services
PFIAB	President's Foreign Intelligence Advisory Board

PDD	Presidential Decision Directive
PERSEREC	Personnel Security Research Center
PN	Public Network
POW/MIA	Prisoner of War/Missing In Action
RD	Restricted Data
SAP	Special Access Program
SAPOC	Special Access Program Oversight Committee
SCI	Sensitive Compartmented Information
SIGINT	Signals Intelligence
SPB	Security Policy Board
SSBI	Single Scope Background Investigation